D0842740

General Science

by

Robert H. Marshall

Donald H. Jacobs

Allen Rosskopf

Charles J. LaRue

AGS®

American Guidance Service, Inc.
Circle Pines, Minnesota 55014-1796
1-800-328-2560

About the Authors

Robert Marshall, M. Ed., teaches high school physics and algebra for the Baltimore City Public Schools. Mr. Marshall is the co-author of *Earth Science* and *Physical Science*, both published by AGS.

Donald H. Jacobs, M.Ed., teaches high school mathematics for the Baltimore City public Schools. Mr. Jacobs is the co-author of *Basic Math Skills* and *Life Skills Math*, both published by AGS.

Allen Rosskopf, M.L.A., has taught English, journalism, and computer applications for over two decades in the Baltimore City Public Schools. Mr. Rosskopf is the co-author of *Earth Science*, published by AGS.

Charles J. LaRue, Ph.D. The late Charles LaRue held a Ph.D. in science education, zoology, and botany from the University of Maryland, and an M.A. in zoology and botany from the University of Texas. He taught biology, zoology, and botany

Consultants

Daniel A. McFarland
Science Department Chair
Durant High School
Plant city, FL

Dr. Helen Parke
Director, Center for Science,
 Mathematics, and Technology
East Carolina University
Greenville, NC

Photo Credits: pp. xviii-1, 4, 24, 46, 62, 76, 92, 110, 124—Peter Wong/Wong Photography; pp. 20, 25, 26—First Image West; p. 27—Mark E. Gibson/Visuals Unlimited; p. 28—James Randklev/Tony Stone Images; p. 53—Fisher Scientific; p. 61—Stephen Frisch; p. 115—Don Bensey/Tony Stone Images; p. 142—Peter Pearson/Tony Stone Images; pp. 150-151, 154, 172, 186, 202, 220, 232, 244, 258, 274—Peter Wong/Wong Photography; p. 153—Dan McCoy/Rainbow; pp. 173, 174—right)—Ken Lucas/Visuals Unlimited; pp. 174 (left), 250 (top left), 223 (top right), 231—A.J.Copley/Visuals Unlimited; p. 180 (top)—Ron Dengler/Visuals Unlimited; p. 180 (bottom)—Gregg Hadel/Tony Stone Images; p. 181—Glenn M. Oliver/Visuals Unlimited; p. 187 (top)—Norman Piluke/Tony Stone Images; p. 187 (bottom)—Dell R.Fouts/Visuals Unlimited; p. 188 (main)—John Lemker/Earth Scenes; pp. 188 (inset), 190—John D. Cunningham/Visuals Unlimited; p. 189—Richard Thom/Visuals Unlimited; p. 192 (right)—Frank T. Awbrey/Visuals Unlimited; p. 192 (left) Tim Hauf/Visuals Unlimited; p. 194—John Sohlden/Visuals Unlimited; p. 195—Steve McCutcheon/Visuals Unlimited; pp. 198, 208 (top left), p. 208 (bottom)—Tony Stone Images; p. 208 (top right) —UPI/Corbis-Bettmann; p. 215—Reuters/Corbis-Bettmann; p. 221—Thia Konig/Tony Stone Images; p. 222—Phil Degginger/Tony Stone Images; p. 208—Photori Inc; p. 223 (top left)—A. Kerstitch/Visuals Unlimited; p. 223 (bottom)—Howard Grey/Tony Stone Images; p. 227—David Peters/David Peters Studio; p. 248—Bill Ross/Tony Stone Images; p. 250 (right)—David Matherly/Visuals Unlimited; p. 250 (bottom left) —William Weber/ Visuals Unlimited; p. 260 —Jeff Greenberg/Unicorn Stock Photos; p. 261—Tom Edwards/Visual Unlimited; p. 262 —Charles E. Schmidt/Unicorn Stock Photos; pp. 265, 278, 279, 280, 281, 282, 283, 284, 285; —Photri; p. 269 (top)—Gay Baumgarner/Tony Stone Images; p. 269 (bottom)—Kjell B. Sandved/Visuals Unlimited; p. 286—NASA/Tom Stack & Associates; p. 290 (top)—Francois Gohier/ Photo Researchers, Inc.; p. 290 (bottom)—Richard G. Kron/Yerkes Observatory;—Terence Harding/Tony Stone Images; pp. 298-299, 302, 366, 390—Mike Krivit/Krivit Photography; p. 301—Jon Riley/Tony Stone Images; p.301—Michael Nichols/National Geographic Image Collection; p. 307—Rosemary Weller/Tony Stone Images; p. 309—Ron Kimball/Ron Kimball Studios; pp. 311, 328—Will Troyer/Visuals Unlimited; p. 313 (top)—Ray Elliot/Tony Stone Images; p. 314—J. M. Labat Jacana/Photo Researchers Inc.; p. 328—Andrew Martinez/Photo Researchers, Inc.; p. 329—Bob Cranston/Animals Animals; p. 334—Breck P. Kent/Animals Animals; p. 341—Kjell B. Sandved/Visuals Unlimited; p. 346—Alan & Linda Detrick/Photo Researchers, Inc.; pp. 347, 348—Saxon Holt/Saxon Holt Photography; p. 351—Michael P. Gadomski/Photo Researchers, Inc.; p. 352—Stephen J. Krasemann/Photo Researchers, Inc.; p. 353—JeromeWexler/Photo Researchers, Inc.; p. 355—Dr. Kari Lounatmaa/Science Photo Library/Photo Researchers, Inc.; p. 358—John D. Cunningham/Visuals Unlimited; p. 360—Ken M. Highfill/Photo Researchers, Inc.; p. 370—Michael Townsend/Tony Stone Images; p. 378—James Darell/Tony Stone Images; p. 419—Meckes/Ottowa/Science Photo Library /Photo Researchers, Inc.; p. 422—Jeff Greenberg/Science Photo Library/Photo Researchers, Inc.; p. 426—National Cancer Institute/Science Photo Library/Photo Researchers, Inc.; **Illustration Credits:** pp. 417, 429, 431, 432, 433, 434, 435, 436, 445, 446, 447, 451, 458,—David Mottet; pp. 236, 400, 408-409, 413, 414, 424, 425, 433, 440, 443, 449—John Edwards/John Edwards and Associates.

ISBN 0-7854-2182-3
Product Number 93200
A 0 9 8 7

Contents

How to Use This Book xiii

Unit 1   Physical Science 1

What Is Physical Science? 2

Chapter 1   The Metric System 4

Lesson 1   Why Do Scientists Measure? 5
Lesson 2   How Can You Use Metric Units to Measure Length? 7
Lesson 3   How Can You Use Metric Units to Measure Area? 10
     ■ *Science in Your Life: Do you have enough paint?* 11
     ■ *Investigation: Counting Squares and Calculating Area* . . 12
Lesson 4   How Can You Use Metric Units to Measure Volume? 14
Lesson 5   How Can You Use Metric Units to Measure Mass? 18
■ Chapter Summary 21
■ Chapter Review 22
■ Test Taking Tip 23

Chapter 2   The Structure of Matter 24

Lesson 1   What Are Some Properties of Objects? 25
Lesson 2   What Are Molecules? 27
Lesson 3   How Do Scientists Know What Atoms Are Like? 30
Lesson 4   What Are Elements? 33
     ■ *Science in Your Life:*
        How are elements important to health? 35
     ■ Periodic Table of Elements 36
     ■ *Investigation: Making Models of Molecules* 38
Lesson 5   What Are Symbols? 39
Lesson 6   What Are Compounds? 41
■ Chapter Summary 43
■ Chapter Review 44
■ Test Taking Tip 45

Chapter 3	**Chemical Reactions** **46**
Lesson 1	What Are Some Characteristics of Compounds? 47
	■ *Investigation: Observing a Chemical Change.* 49
Lesson 2	What Are Chemical Formulas? 51
Lesson 3	What Is a Reaction? 53
Lesson 4	How Can You Show Reactions? 55
	■ *Science in Your Life: How does film work?* 58
■ Chapter Summary. 59
■ Chapter Review 60
■ Test Taking Tip 61

Chapter 4	**Motion and Energy** **62**
Lesson 1	What Is Energy? 63
	■ *Science in Your Life: Have you ever ridden a roller coaster?* 66
Lesson 2	What Are Motion and Speed? 67
	■ *Investigation: Calculating Average Speed* 70
Lesson 3	What Is Gravity?. 71
■ Chapter Summary. 73
■ Chapter Review 74
■ Test Taking Tip 75

Chapter 5	**Work and Machines** **76**
Lesson 1	What Is Work? 77
Lesson 2	How Are Levers Used? 79
Lesson 3	What Are Some Other Kinds of Simple Machines? 83
	■ *Science in Your Life:*
	Which simple machines do you have at home? 87
	■ *Investigation: Using an Inclined Plane* 88
■ Chapter Summary. 89
■ Chapter Review 90
■ Test Taking Tip 91

Chapter 6		Heat **92**
	Lesson 1	What Is Heat?. 93
	Lesson 2	How Does Heat Affect Matter? 95
	Lesson 3	What Is Temperature? 97
		■ *Investigation: Measuring Temperature*. 102
	Lesson 4	How Does Heat Travel? 103
		■ *Science in Your Life:*
		How do different heating systems work?. 106
	■ Chapter Summary. 107
	■ Chapter Review. 108
	■ Test Taking Tip 109

Chapter 7		Sound and Light **110**
	Lesson 1	What Is Sound? 111
		■ *Investigation: Modeling Sound Waves* 113
	Lesson 2	What Is Light? 114
		■ *Science in Your Life: How are lasers used?* 117
	Lesson 3	How is Light Reflected and Bent? 118
	■ Chapter Summary. 121
	■ Chapter Review. 122
	■ Test Taking Tip 123

Chapter 8		Electricity and Magnetism. **124**
	Lesson 1	How Does Electricity Flow Through a Circuit?. 125
	Lesson 2	What Is a Series Circuit? 129
	Lesson 3	What Is a Parallel Circuit? 133
	Lesson 4	What Are Magnets? 136
	Lesson 5	What Is a Magnetic Field? 138
		■ *Investigation: Observing Magnetic Lines of Force* 140
		■ *Science in Your Life: How does an electromagnet work?*. 142
	■ Chapter Summary. 143
	■ Chapter Review. 144
	■ Test Taking Tip 145

	Unit Investigation. 146
	Unit Summary 147
	Unit Review 148

Unit 2	**Earth Science** **150**	
	What Is Earth Science? 152	

Chapter 9	**Describing Earth** **154**	
Lesson 1	What Shape and Features Does Earth Have? 155	
Lesson 2	How Is Earth's Motion Connected to Time? 158	
	■ *Science in Your Life: What Is Daylight Savings Time?* . . 160	
	■ *Investigation: Modeling Day and Night* 161	
Lesson 3	How Does Earth Move in Space? 162	
Lesson 4	What Are Latitude and Longitude? 164	
	■ Chapter Summary 169	
	■ Chapter Review 170	
	■ Test Taking Tip 171	

Chapter 10	**Minerals and Rocks** **172**	
Lesson 1	What Are Minerals? 173	
	■ *Science in Your Life:*	
	What are some common uses of minerals? 177	
	■ *Investigation: Observing Color, Streak, and Hardness* . . 178	
Lesson 2	What Are Rocks? 180	
	■ Chapter Summary 183	
	■ Chapter Review 184	
	■ Test Taking Tip 185	

Chapter 11	**Weathering and Erosion** **186**	
Lesson 1	What Is Weathering? 187	
	■ *Investigation: Chemical Weathering* 191	
Lesson 2	How Does Water Shape the Land? 192	
	■ *Science in Your Life:*	
	How do people cause too much erosion? 194	
Lesson 3	How Does Ice Shape the Land? 195	
Lesson 4	How Do Wind and Gravity Shape the Land? 197	
	■ Chapter Summary 199	
	■ Chapter Review 200	
	■ Test Taking Tip 201	

Chapter 12		Forces Inside Earth **202**
	Lesson 1	How Does Earth's Crust Move? 203
	Lesson 2	What Are Volcanoes? 207
	Lesson 3	How Do Mountains Form? 209
		■ *Investigation: Models of Folding and Faults* 211
	Lesson 4	What Are Earthquakes? 212
		■ *Science in Your Life: Play the earthquake game.* 216
	■ Chapter Summary 217	
	■ Chapter Review 218	
	■ Test Taking Tip 219	

Chapter 13		Earth's History **220**
	Lesson 1	How Do Scientists Learn About Earth's History? 221
		■ *Investigation: Making a Model of a Fossil* 224
	Lesson 2	What Events Occurred in Earth's Past? 225
		■ *Science in Your Life:*
		How do fossils help us find resources? 228
	■ Chapter Summary 229	
	■ Chapter Review 230	
	■ Test Taking Tip 231	

Chapter 14		Earth's Water **232**
	Lesson 1	Where Is Earth's Fresh Water? 233
		■ *Science in Your Life: What is your water budget?* 235
		■ *Investigation: Modeling a Water Table* 236
	Lesson 2	What Is in the Oceans? 237
	■ Chapter Summary 241	
	■ Chapter Review 242	
	■ Test Taking Tip 243	

Chapter 15   **Earth's Atmosphere** **244**

    Lesson 1   What Is the Atmosphere? 245
        ■ *Science in Your Life: Ozone—protector and pollutant* . . 248
    Lesson 2   How Do Clouds and Precipitation Form? 249
        ■ *Investigation: Making a Model of Rain* 251
    Lesson 3   How Does the Atmosphere Move? 253
    ■ Chapter Summary 255
    ■ Chapter Review 256
    ■ Test Taking Tip 257

Chapter 16   **Weather and Climate** **258**

    Lesson 1   How Is Weather Measured? 259
    Lesson 2   How Can You Predict the Weather? 263
        ■ *Investigation: Using a Weather Map* 266
    Lesson 3   What Are the Climates of the World? 268
        ■ *Science in Your Life: How do people affect climate?* 270
    ■ Chapter Summary 271
    ■ Chapter Review 272
    ■ Test Taking Tip 273

Chapter 17   **The Solar System** **274**

    Lesson 1   What Is the Solar System? 275
    Lesson 2   What Are the Inner Planets Like? 278
    Lesson 3   What Are the Outer Planets Like? 282
        ■ *Science in Your Life: How fast is that CD?* 287
        ■ *Investigation: Distances in the Solar System.* 288
    Lesson 4   What Other Objects Make Up the Solar System? 289
    ■ Chapter Summary 291
    ■ Chapter Review 292
    ■ Test Taking Tip 293

    Unit Investigation 294
    Unit Summary 295
    Unit Review 296

Unit 3	Life Science	. . . .	**298**
	What Is Life Science?	. . . .	300

Chapter 18	How Living Things Are Alike	. . . .	**302**
Lesson 1	What Is the Basic Unit of Life?	. . . .	303
	■ *Investigation: Comparing Cells*	. . . .	305
Lesson 2	What Chemicals Are Important for Life?	. . . .	306
Lesson 3	What Are Some Basic Life Activities?	. . . .	309
Lesson 4	How Are Organisms Classified?	. . . .	311
	■ *Science in Your Life: Bacteria: Helpful and harmful*	. . .	314
	■ Chapter Summary	. . . .	315
	■ Chapter Review	. . . .	316
	■ Test Taking Tip	. . . .	317

Chapter 19	Animals	. . . .	**318**
Lesson 1	How Are Animals Classified?	. . . .	319
	■ *Science in Your Life: Has everything been classified?*	. . .	322
	■ *Investigation: Classifying Objects*	. . . .	323
Lesson 2	What Are Vertebrates?	. . . .	324
Lesson 3	What Are Invertebrates?	. . . .	328
Lesson 4	How Do Animals Get and Digest Food?	. . . .	332
Lesson 5	How Do Animals Exchange and Transport Gases?	. . . . .	334
Lesson 6	How Do Animals Reproduce?	. . . .	337
	■ Chapter Summary	. . . .	339
	■ Chapter Review	. . . .	340
	■ Test Taking Tip	. . . .	341

Chapter 20		**Plants** **342**
Lesson 1	How Are Plants Classified? 343
Lesson 2	What Are Seed Plants? 346
Lesson 3	What Are Seedless Plants? 349
	■ *Science in Your Life: Energy from ferns and mosses* 350
Lesson 4	What Is the Vascular System in Plants? 351
Lesson 5	How Do Plants Make Food? 354
Lesson 6	How Do Plants Reproduce? 359
	■ *Investigation: Growing an African Violet From a Leaf* . . 361
	■ Chapter Summary 363
	■ Chapter Review 364
	■ Test Taking Tip 365

Chapter 21		**Ecology** **366**
Lesson 1	How Do Living Things and Nonliving Things Interact? . 367
	■ *Investigation: Testing the pH of Rain* 372
Lesson 2	What Are Food Chains and Food Webs? 374
	■ *Science in Your Life: What kind of consumer are you?* . . 377
Lesson 3	How Does Energy Flow Through Ecosystems? 378
Lesson 4	How Do Materials Cycle Through Ecosystems? 382
	■ Chapter Summary 387
	■ Chapter Review 388
	■ Test Taking Tip 389

Chapter 22		**Heredity and Evolution** **390**
Lesson 1	What Is Heredity? 391
	■ *Science in Your Life: What is genetic engineering?* 395
Lesson 2	What Is Evolution? 396
	■ *Investigation: Observing a Plant Adaptation* 400
	■ Chapter Summary 401
	■ Chapter Review 402
	■ Test Taking Tip 403

Unit Investigation 404
Unit Summary 405
Unit Review 406

Unit 4	**The Human Body** **408**

Chapter 23	**Meeting the Body's Basic Needs** **410**

Lesson 1   How Does the Body Move? 411
Lesson 2   How Do Body Cells Get Energy From Food? 417
■ *Investigation: Reading Food Labels* 420
Lesson 3   How Do Materials Move to and From Cells? 422
Lesson 4   How Does the Body Exchange Oxygen and
Carbon Dioxide? 428
■ *Science in Your Life:*
Cardiopulmonary resuscitation (CPR) 430
Lesson 5   How Does the Body Get Rid of Wastes? 431
Lesson 6   How Do Humans Reproduce? 433
■ Chapter Summary 437
■ Chapter Review 438
■ Test Taking Tip 439

Chapter 24	**The Body's Control Systems.** **440**

Lesson 1   How Does the Nervous System Control the Body? 441
■ *Investigation: Modeling the Human Eye* 448
■ *Science in Your Life: How do eyeglasses work?* 450
Lesson 2   How Does the Endocrine System Control the Body? . . . 451
■ Chapter Summary 453
■ Chapter Review 454
■ Test Taking Tip 455

Unit Investigation 456
Unit Summary 457
Unit Review 458

Glossary **460**

Index **472**

How to Use This Book: A Study Guide

What is general science? It is a combination of physical science, earth science, and life science. Physical science is the study of matter and energy. If you have used a machine or listened to music, you have used physical science. Earth science is the study of Earth's land, water, and air. If you have listened to a weather report or had a ride in a car or bus, you have used earth science. Life science is the study of living things. It is also called biology. It includes the study of animals, plants, and humans.

As you read the chapters and lessons of this book, you will learn many ways in which these three sciences affect your life.

How to Study

■ Plan a regular time to study.

■ Choose a quiet desk or table where you will not be distracted. Find a spot that has good lighting.

■ Gather all the books, pencils, and paper you need to complete your assignments.

■ Decide on a goal. For example: "I will finish reading and taking notes on Chapter 1, Lesson 1, by 8:00."

■ Take a five- to ten-minute break every hour to keep alert.

■ If you start to feel sleepy, take a short break and get some fresh air.

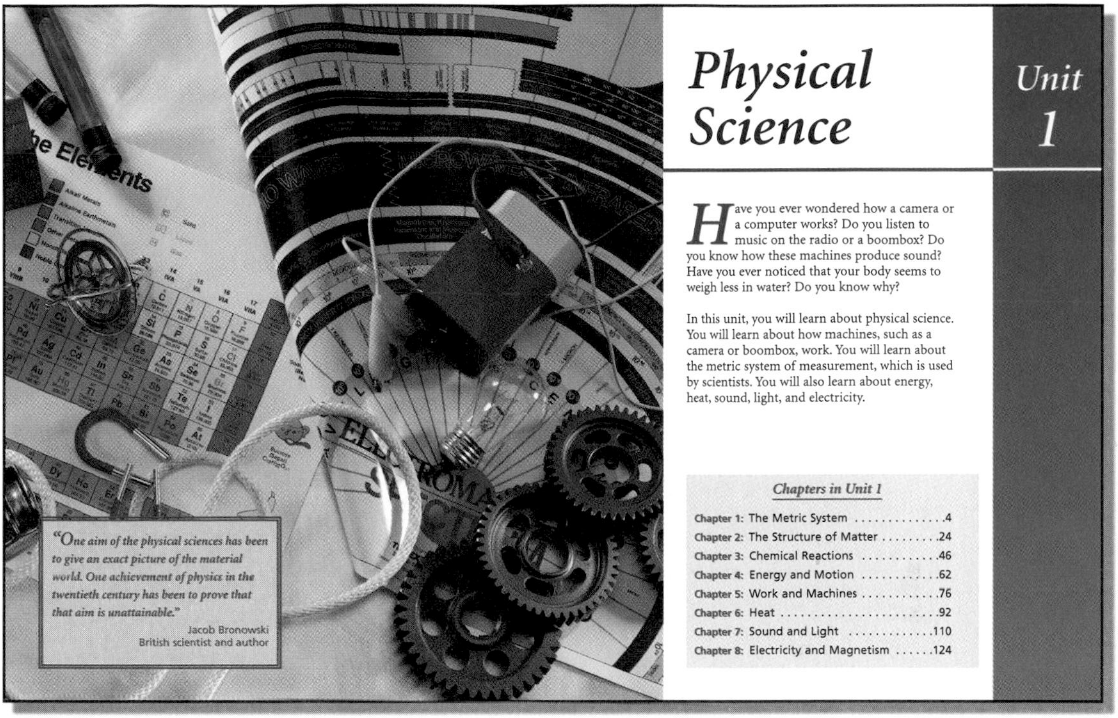

Physical Science

Unit 1

Have you ever wondered how a camera or a computer works? Do you listen to music on the radio or a boombox? Do you know how these machines produce sound? Have you ever noticed that your body seems to weigh less in water? Do you know why?

In this unit, you will learn about physical science. You will learn about how machines, such as a camera or boombox, work. You will learn about the metric system of measurement, which is used by scientists. You will also learn about energy, heat, sound, light, and electricity.

"One aim of the physical sciences has been to give an exact picture of the material world. One achievement of physics in the twentieth century has been to prove that that aim is unattainable."

Jacob Bronowski
British scientist and author

Chapters in Unit 1

Chapter 1: The Metric System 4
Chapter 2: The Structure of Matter 24
Chapter 3: Chemical Reactions 46
Chapter 4: Energy and Motion 62
Chapter 5: Work and Machines 76
Chapter 6: Heat 92
Chapter 7: Sound and Light 110
Chapter 8: Electricity and Magnetism 124

Each unit covers a different science.

Before Beginning Each Unit

- Read the title and the opening paragraph.
- Study the photograph. What does the photo tell you about the unit?
- What does the quotation say to you?
- Read the titles of the chapters in the unit.
- Look at the headings of the lessons and paragraphs to help you locate main ideas.
- Read the chapter and unit summaries to help you identify key issues.

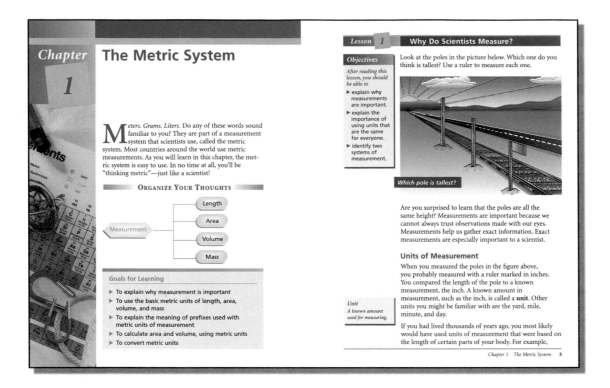

Before Beginning Each Chapter

▨ Read the chapter title.

▨ Study the Goals for Learning. The chapter review and tests will ask questions related to these goals.

▨ Look at "Organize Your Thoughts." The diagram is another way to see information that is in the chapter.

▨ Look at the chapter reivew. The questions cover the most important points from the reading.

Note these features:

▨ *Did You Know?*—Interesting facts related to the topic being studied.

▨ *Investigations*—Hands-on activities to try in class

▨ *Science in Your Life*—Relates science to your everyday life

▨ *Science Words*—A handy list of science-related words that acts as a vocabulary study aid

Before Beginning Each Lesson

Read the lesson title. It is in the form of a question that the lesson will answer. For example:

Lesson	1	Why Do Scientists Measure?

Look over the entire lesson, noting . . .

- lesson objectives
- pictures
- tables
- charts

- illustrations
- bold words
- text organization

- vocabulary definitions in the margins
- self-check questions

As You Read the Lesson

■ Read the major headings. The paragraphs that follow are about each heading.

■ Answering the self-check questions in the lesson will help you determine if you know the lesson's key ideas. If you do not, reread the lesson.

Using the Bold Words

Bold Type

Words seen for the first time will appear in bold type.

Glossary

Words listed in this column are also found in the glossary.

Knowing the meaning of all the boxed words in the left column will help you understand what you read.

These words appear in **bold type** the first time they appear in the text and are defined in the paragraph.

This central part of an atom is called a **nucleus.**

All of the words in the left column are also defined in the **glossary**.

Nucleus—The central part of an atom (p. 31)

Taking Notes in Class

Some students prefer taking notes on index cards.

Others jot down key ideas in a spiral notebook.

As you read, you will be learning many new facts and ideas. Your notes will be useful and will help you remember when preparing for class discussions and studying for tests.

- Always write the main ideas and supporting details.

- Use an outline format to help save time.

- Keep your notes brief. You may want to set up some abbreviations to speed up your note-taking. For example: *with = w/ and = + dollars = $*

- Use the same method all the time. Then when you study for a test, you will know where to find the information you need to review.

Here are some tips for taking notes during class discussion:

- Use your own words.

- Do not try to write everything the teacher says.

- Write down important information only.

- Don't be concerned about writing in complete sentences. Use phrases.

- Be brief.

- Rewrite your notes to fill in possible gaps as soon as you can after class.

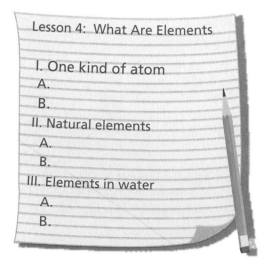

Lesson 4: What Are Elements

I. One kind of atom
   A.
   B.
II. Natural elements
   A.
   B.
III. Elements in water
   A.
   B.

Using an Outline

You may want to outline the section using the subheads as your main points. An outline will help you remember the major points of the section. An example of an outline is shown at left. Your teacher may have you use the Self Study Guide for this book.

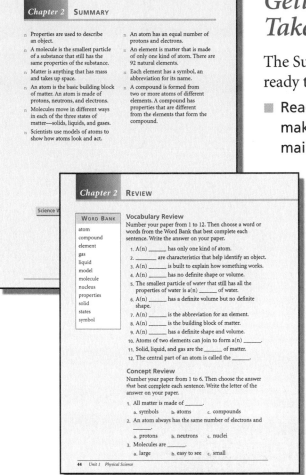

Chapter 2 SUMMARY

- Properties are used to describe an object.
- A molecule is the smallest particle of a substance that still has the same properties of the substance.
- Matter is anything that has mass and takes up space.
- An atom is the basic building block of matter. An atom is made of protons, neutrons, and electrons.
- Molecules move in different ways in each of the three states of matter—solids, liquids, and gases.
- Scientists use models of atoms to show how atoms look and act.

- An atom has an equal number of protons and electrons.
- An element is matter that is made of only one kind of atom. There are 92 natural elements.
- Each element has a symbol, an abbreviation for its name.
- A compound is formed from two or more atoms of different elements. A compound has properties that are different from the elements that form the compound.

Chapter 2 REVIEW

Science W

WORD BANK

atom
compound
element
gas
liquid
model
molecule
nucleus
properties
solid
states
symbol

Vocabulary Review

Number your paper from 1 to 12. Then choose a word or words from the Word Bank that best complete each sentence. Write the answer on your paper.

1. A(n) _____ has only one kind of atom.
2. _____ are characteristics that help identify an object.
3. A(n) _____ is built to explain how something works.
4. A(n) _____ has no definite shape or volume.
5. The smallest particle of water that still has all the properties of water is a(n) _____ of water.
6. A(n) _____ has a definite volume but no definite shape.
7. A(n) _____ is the abbreviation for an element.
8. A(n) _____ is the building block of matter.
9. A(n) _____ has a definite shape and volume.
10. Atoms of two elements can join to form a(n) _____.
11. Solid, liquid, and gas are the _____ of matter.
12. The central part of an atom is called the _____.

Concept Review

Number your paper from 1 to 6. Then choose the answer that best complete each sentence. Write the letter of the answer on your paper.

1. All matter is made of _____.
   a. symbols   b. atoms   c. compounds
2. An atom always has the same number of electrons and
   _____.
   a. protons   b. neutrons   c. nuclei
3. Molecules are _____.
   a. large   b. easy to see   c. small

44 Unit 1 Physical Science

Getting Ready to Take a Test

The Summaries and Reviews can help you get ready to take tests.

■ Read the summaries from your text to make sure you understand the chapter's main ideas.

■ Make up a sample test of items you think may be on the test. You may want to do this with a classmate and share your questions.

■ Review your notes and test yourself on words and key ideas.

■ Practice writing about some of the main ideas from the chapter.

■ Fill in the blanks under Vocabulary Review.

■ Complete the sentences under Concept Review.

■ Write what you think about the questions under Critical Thinking.

■ The questions in the reviews look like those in state and national tests you may take.

Use the Test Taking Tip

■ Read the Test Taking Tip with each Chapter Review.

Test Taking Tip   Before you choose an answer to a multiple choice question, be sure to read each answer choice carefully.

"One aim of the physical sciences has been to give an exact picture of the material world. One achievement of physics in the twentieth century has been to prove that that aim is unattainable."

Jacob Bronowski
British scientist and author

Physical Science

Have you ever wondered how a camera or a computer works? Do you listen to music on the radio or a boombox? Do you know how these machines produce sound? Have you ever noticed that your body seems to weigh less in water? Do you know why?

In this unit, you will learn about physical science. You will learn about how machines, such as a camera or boombox, work. You will learn about the metric system of measurement, which is used by scientists. You will also learn about energy, heat, sound, light, and electricity.

Chapters in Unit 1

Chapter 1: The Metric System 4

Chapter 2: The Structure of Matter 24

Chapter 3: Chemical Reactions 46

Chapter 4: Energy and Motion 62

Chapter 5: Work and Machines 76

Chapter 6: Heat 92

Chapter 7: Sound and Light 110

Chapter 8: Electricity and Magnetism 124

Unit 1

What Is Physical Science?

Physical science is the study of matter and energy.

The Study of Matter and Energy

Look around you. What do you have in common with all the objects—your desk, the floor, the air? At first, you might think you have little in common with these objects. But, in fact, all of them—including you—are made of matter. Matter is anything that takes up space. You can see other examples of matter in the picture below.

What do all of these objects have in common?

All matter has mass. Mass is the amount of material that an object has. All of the objects in the picture above have mass. The potted plant has more mass than the baseball.

Energy is different from matter. You cannot hold energy or measure it with a ruler. But you are familiar with energy. Energy is needed to make things move. You use it to move your body. A car uses energy to move, too. You will learn more about energy in Chapter 4.

Two Areas of Physical Science

Physical scientists study many different things. Physical science can be divided into two areas. One area is **chemistry**. Chemistry is the study of matter and how it changes. Chemistry can explain how a cake rises or how acid rain forms. Chemistry is also the study of how matter can be made into new materials. By studying chemistry, scientists have made new medicines, food, clothing, fragrances, and soaps. They have even made artificial skin and bones for people.

A second area of physical science is **physics**. Physics is the study of energy and how it acts with matter. Physics can explain how helium balloons rise or how lasers work. Scientists studying physics have developed television, cellular phones, stereo systems, computers, space satellites, microwave ovens, and jet airplanes.

Chemistry
The study of matter and how it changes.

Physical science
The study of matter and energy.

Physics
The study of how energy acts with matter.

Physical scientists have developed many products such as these.

The Metric System

Meters. *Grams. Liters.* Do any of these words sound familiar to you? They are part of a measurement system that scientists use, called the metric system. Most countries around the world use metric measurements. As you will learn in this chapter, the metric system is easy to use. In no time at all, you'll be "thinking metric"—just like a scientist!

ORGANIZE YOUR THOUGHTS

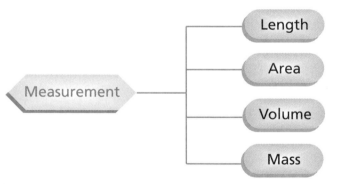

Measurement
- Length
- Area
- Volume
- Mass

Goals for Learning

▶ To explain why measurement is important
▶ To use the basic metric units of length, area, volume, and mass
▶ To explain the meaning of prefixes used with metric units of measurement
▶ To calculate area and volume, using metric units
▶ To convert metric units

Objectives

After reading this lesson, you should be able to

▶ explain why measurements are important.

▶ explain the importance of using units that are the same for everyone.

▶ identify two systems of measurement.

Look at the poles in the picture below. Which one do you think is tallest? Use a ruler to measure each one.

Which pole is tallest?

Are you surprised to learn that the poles are all the same height? Measurements are important because we cannot always trust observations made with our eyes. Measurements help us gather exact information. Exact measurements are especially important to a scientist.

Units of Measurement

When you measured the poles in the figure above, you probably measured with a ruler marked in inches. You compared the length of the pole to a known measurement, the inch. A known amount in measurement, such as the inch, is called a **unit**. Other units you might be familiar with are the yard, mile, minute, and day.

Unit
A known amount used for measuring.

If you had lived thousands of years ago, you most likely would have used units of measurement that were based on the length of certain parts of your body. For example,

Egyptians used the cubit to measure length. A cubit was the distance from the elbow to the tip of the middle finger. The Romans used the width of their thumb to measure length. This unit of measurement was called an uncia.

Compare the widths of the thumbs of each person in your classroom. Do you think they are all the same? Probably not. So you can see why using units of measurement based on body parts does not work well. The exact length of an uncia or a cubit could vary from person to person.

For a unit of measurement to be useful, it has to be the same for everybody. When one scientist tells another scientist that something is a certain length, that measurement should mean the same thing to both of them.

Systems of Measurement

English system
System of measurement that uses inches, feet, and yards.

You probably measure in units based on the **English system**. Some English units you probably are familiar with for measuring length are the inch, foot, yard, and mile. English units also can be used to measure time, weight, and other amounts.

Metric system
System of measurement used by scientists.

Scientists and most other people throughout the world use a different system of measurement. They use the **metric system**. Metric units are the most common units of measurement in the world. The metric system is simpler to use and easier to remember than the English system. You will use the metric system in this book.

Self-Check	1. Why are measurements important?
	2. How long was the Egyptian cubit?
	3. Why is it important to use units of measurement that are the same for everyone?
	4. What are some common units in the English system of measurement?
	5. What is the name of the system of measurement that scientists use?

How Can You Use Metric Units to Measure Length?

Objectives

After reading this lesson, you should be able to

▶ identify and explain some common metric units of length.

▶ explain the meaning of prefixes used with metric units of measurement.

The metric system is similar to the money system used in the United States. As the illustration below shows, there are 10 pennies in a dime, 10 dimes in a dollar, and 10 dollars in a 10-dollar bill. You can say that the money system is based on a system of tens. The metric system is also based on a system of tens.

This money system is based on tens.

Meter
The basic unit of length in the metric system (about 39 inches).

Using Meters

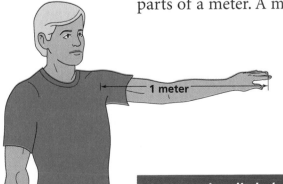

In the metric system, you measure length in **meters** or parts of a meter. A meter is a little more than 39 inches, or a bit longer than a yard. The length of an adult man's arm is about one meter. A football field is just over 90 meters long. The abbreviation for meter is *m*. A period is not used with abbreviations for metric units.

1 meter

A meter is a little longer than a man's arm.

Meterstick
A common tool for measuring length in the metric system.

The common tool for measuring length in the metric system is the **meterstick**. It is one meter long.

The illustration below shows part of a meterstick. It is divided into equal units. Each of these units is a centimeter. A centimeter is 1/100 of a meter. One meter has 100 centimeters in it. You can use centimeters when the meter is too long a unit. For example, it might be difficult to measure the width of your book in meters, but you could easily use centimeters. The abbreviation for centimeter is *cm*.

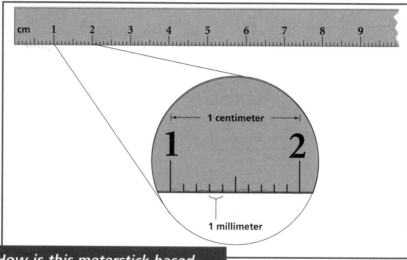

How is this meterstick based on a system of tens?

Did You Know?

The United States and Myanmar are the only countries that do not use the metric system for their principal units of measurement.

Sometimes, even the centimeter is too large a unit to measure an object. You need a smaller unit. Again look at the meter stick. Notice that each centimeter is divided into 10 smaller units. Each of these smaller units is a millimeter. A millimeter is 1/1,000 of a meter. You would measure the width of a pencil in millimeters. Use *mm* as an abbreviation for millimeter.

Using meters to measure the distance from your school to your home might be difficult. You need a unit larger than a meter. In that case, you might use the kilometer. A kilometer is 1,000 meters. The abbreviation for kilometer is *km*.

This table shows the metric units for measuring length.

Length Equivalents	
10 millimeters	1 centimeter
1,000 millimeters	1 meter
100 centimeters	1 meter
1,000 meters	1 kilometer

Using Metric Prefixes

Once you understand how the meterstick is divided, you know how to use other units of measurement in the metric system. The prefixes in front of the word *meter* have special meanings. They are used to show how many times the meter is multiplied or divided. Just as a cent is 1/100 of a dollar, a centimeter is 1/100 of a meter. The prefix *centi-* means 1/100. You will learn how to use the prefixes shown in the table with other units of measurement later in this chapter.

Prefix	Meaning	Example
kilo- (k)	1,000 ×	kilometer (km)
centi- (c)	1/100 (0.01)	centimeter (cm)
milli- (m)	1/1,000 (0.001)	millimeter (mm)

Self-Check

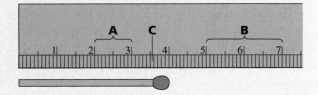

1. Which letter in the illustration above points to 1 millimeter?

2. Which letter points to 1 centimeter?

3. How many millimeters are in 1 centimeter?

4. How many millimeters are in 10 centimeters?

5. How long is the match in centimeters?

How Can You Use Metric Units to Measure Area?

Area

Amount of surface an object has on any one side.

You can use measurements of length to calculate other measurements. One example of a calculated measurement is **area**. Area is the amount of surface an object has on a side.

Notice that each side of the blue square in the figure below measures 1 cm. To find the area of the square, multiply the length by the width.

$$\text{area} = \text{length} \times \text{width}$$
$$= 1 \text{ cm} \times 1 \text{ cm}$$
$$= 1 \text{ cm}^2$$

When you calculate area, the units of length and width must be the same. Express the answer in square units. To do this, write a small 2 to the upper right of the unit. In the example above, the unit is read *square centimeter*. *Square centimeter (cm²)* means "centimeter × centimeter." The area of the square is 1 square centimeter.

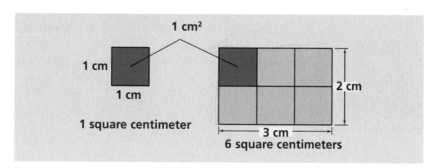

Now look at the rectangle. Its length is 3 cm. Its width is 2 cm. The figure shows that the rectangle contains 6 square centimeters. You can also find the area of the rectangle by using the same formula you used to find the area of the square.

$$\text{area} = \text{length} \times \text{width}$$
$$= 3 \text{ cm} \times 2 \text{ cm}$$
$$= 6 \text{ cm}^2$$

The area of the rectangle is 6 square centimeters.

What is the area of a rectangle with a length of 8.5 mm and a width of 3.3 mm?

$$\begin{aligned} \text{area} &= \text{length} \times \text{width} \\ &= 8.5 \text{ mm} \times 3.3 \text{ mm} \\ &= 28.05 \text{ mm}^2 \end{aligned}$$

The area is 28.05 square millimeters.

Self-Check

Find the area for each of the rectangles in the table. The first one is done for you. (*Hint*: The units being multiplied must be the same.)

Length	Width	Area (length × width)
8 cm	7.2 cm	8 cm × 7.2 cm = 57.6 cm²
8 m	8 m	
3.4 mm	5.2 mm	
2.6 m	4.7 m	
13 m	5.1 km	

SCIENCE IN YOUR LIFE

Do you have enough paint?

If you have ever gone to a store to buy paint, you know that first you have to figure out how much paint you need. It's easy to do if you use what you learned about calculating area.

8 meters

3.5 meters

Suppose you have a wall that measures 8 m long and 3.5 m high. You want to paint it. The instructions on the paint can say that the paint will cover 32 m² of surface area. Is one can of paint enough to cover the wall? Explain how you know.

1

Counting Squares and Calculating Area

Materials

✓ small sheet of paper

✓ metric ruler

✓ scissors

Purpose

To understand the relationship between area and the number of square units

Procedure

1. Copy the data table below on a sheet of paper.

	Length	Width	Area (length × width)	Total number of squares
Original Paper				
Rectangle 1				
Rectangle 2				

2. Obtain a small sheet of paper from your teacher. The sizes of paper used will not be the same for all students. Use a ruler to measure the length and the width of the paper. Record these two measurements in centimeters.

3. Calculate the area of the paper. To do so, use the following formula.

$$\text{area} = \text{length} \times \text{width}$$

Record this area. Remember that the units should be square centimeters (cm^2).

4. Use the ruler to mark off all four sides of the paper in 1-cm units. Using the ruler as a straightedge, carefully draw straight lines to connect the marks from side to side and from top to bottom. A grid of squares similar to the one on the next page should result.

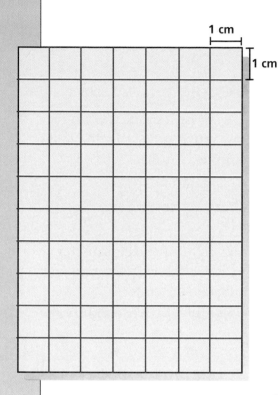

1 cm

1 cm

5. Count the squares on the paper. The area of each square is 1 square cm. That is because area = length × width = 1 cm × 1 cm = 1 cm². Since each square is 1 square cm, the area of the sheet of paper is the number of squares × 1 cm². Record that number. The answer should be in square centimeters.

6. Cut the paper into squares along the lines you drew. Be as accurate as you can in cutting.

7. Use all the individual squares to make two smaller rectangles of different lengths and widths. To do this, carefully set the squares down next to each other in rows and columns. Make sure the squares have almost no space between them and that they do not overlap.

8. Measure the length and width of each new rectangle. Find the area of each.

Questions

1. Did the area you found for the original paper in step 5 match the area you calculated in step 3? Do you think it should? Explain.

2. How did the sum of the areas of the two new rectangles compare with the total number of squares in the two rectangles? How did it compare to the calculated area of the original sheet of paper? Explain these results.

Volume
The amount of space an object takes up.

Another calculation that you can make using metric measurements is **volume**. Volume describes the amount of space an object takes up.

Volume of a Rectangular Solid

The small blue box in the figure below measures 1 cm on each edge. You can find out how much space the box takes up—its volume—by using a simple formula.

$$\text{volume} = \text{length} \times \text{width} \times \text{height}$$
$$= 1 \text{ cm} \times 1 \text{ cm} \times 1 \text{ cm}$$
$$= 1 \text{ cm}^3$$

The small 3 written to the upper right of the centimeter unit means "cubic." It is read *cubic centimeter* or *centimeter cubed*. *Cubic centimeter (cm³)* means "centimeter × centimeter × centimeter." The volume of the small box is 1 cubic centimeter.

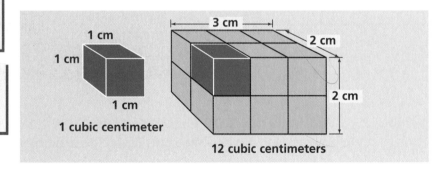

1 cubic centimeter

12 cubic centimeters

Now look at the figure of the larger box. Its length is 3 cm. Its width is 2 cm. Its height is 2 cm. You can see that 12 small boxes fit into the larger box. If each small box is 1 cm³, then the large box has a volume of 12 cm³.

You also can use the formula to find the volume of the larger box.

$$\text{volume} = \text{length} \times \text{width} \times \text{height}$$
$$= 3 \text{ cm} \times 2 \text{ cm} \times 2 \text{ cm}$$
$$= 12 \text{ cm}^3$$

Liter
*Basic unit of volume
in the metric system.*

Volume of a Liquid

You might be familiar with another unit of volume in the metric system—the **liter**. You can see liter containers at the supermarket, especially in the soft-drink section. A liter is slightly more than a quart. The abbreviation for liter is *L*. The liter is often used to measure the volume of liquids. A liter takes up the same amount of space as 1,000 cubic centimeters.

You learned earlier in this chapter that you can use the same prefixes you used with the meter to form other units of measurement. The only prefix that is commonly used to measure volume is *milli-*. Recall that *milli-* means "1/1,000." A milliliter is 1/1,000 of a liter. The abbreviation for milliliter is *mL*. There are 1,000 milliliters in a liter. Since there are also 1,000 cubic centimeters in one liter, a milliliter is the same as one cubic centimeter.

Volume Equivalents	
1 liter (L)	1,000 cubic centimeters (cm³)
1 cubic centimeter (cm³)	1/1,000 liter (0.001 L)
1 milliliter (mL)	1/1,000 liter (0.001 L)
1 milliliter (mL)	1 cubic centimeter (cm³)

Sometimes you will have to convert cubic centimeters to liters. Since one cubic centimeter is 1/1,000 of a liter, you can convert by dividing by 1,000.

Express 1,256 cm³ as liters.

$$1,256 \div 1,000 = 1.256 \text{ L}$$

You can also convert liters to cubic centimeters. Simply multiply by 1,000.

Express 4.3 L as cubic centimeters.

$$4.3 \text{ L} \times 1,000 = 4,300 \text{ cm}^3$$

Measuring With a Graduated Cylinder

To measure the volume of a liquid, you can use a **graduated cylinder**. Follow this procedure.

1. Pour the liquid into the graduated cylinder.

2. Position yourself so that your eye is level with the top of the liquid. You can see the correct position in the figure below.

3. Read the volume from the scale that is on the outside of the cylinder. The top of the liquid usually is curved. This curve is called a **meniscus**. You can see the meniscus in the figure to the left. Read the scale on the bottom of the curve as shown. The volume of this liquid is 16 mL.

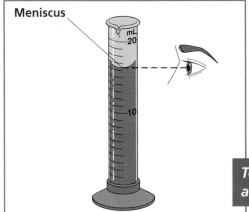

Meniscus

To read the volume of a liquid, sight across the bottom of the meniscus.

To measure the volume of a liquid in a graduated cylinder, you need to know what the spaces between the lines represent. Follow this procedure.

1. Subtract the numbers on any two long lines that are next to each other.

2. Count the spaces between the two long lines.

3. Divide the number you got in step 1 by the number you counted in step 2. In the figure below, each space equals 2 mL.

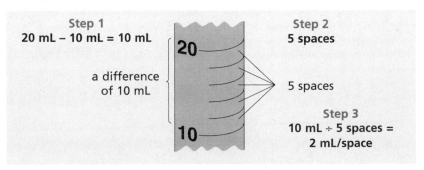

Step 1
20 mL – 10 mL = 10 mL

a difference of 10 mL

Step 2
5 spaces

5 spaces

Step 3
10 mL ÷ 5 spaces = 2 mL/space

Volume of an Irregular Solid

You have already learned the formula for finding the volume of a rectangular solid. You cannot use a formula to find the volume of a solid with an irregular shape. Instead, you can use the **displacement of water method** to find the volume of irregularly shaped objects.

If a glass is partially filled with water and you place an object in the glass, the level of the water will rise. In fact, the water level will rise by an amount equal to the volume of the object that was placed in the glass.

To measure the volume of a small solid object using the displacement of water method, follow the procedure below. Remember to cover the object completely with water when using this method.

Figure A

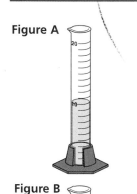

1. Pour water into a graduated cylinder. Record the volume of the water. (Figure A)

    volume = 10 cm³

Figure B

2. Place the object in the cylinder. The water level will then rise. Record this new volume. (Figure B)

    volume = 16 cm³

Object

3. Subtract the volume of the water from the volume of the water plus object. The difference will be the volume of the object.

    16 cm³ – 10 cm³ = 6 cm³

The volume of the object is 6 cm³.

Self-Check

1. A box measures 8 cm by 9 cm by 12 cm. What is its volume?

Convert each of these measurements.

2. 3 L = _____ mL
3. 5.5 L = _____ mL
4. 3,700 cm³ = _____ L
5. A stone is placed in a graduated cylinder, which has been filled to the 35-mL mark. The level rises to 42 mL. What is the volume of the stone?

You learned earlier in this unit that all matter has **mass.** Remember that mass is the amount of material an object has. But how can you measure mass?

In the metric system, the **gram** is the basic unit of mass. One gram equals the mass of one cubic centimeter of water. That's about the same mass as a large wooden match or a small paper clip. There are 454 grams in one pound. The abbreviation for gram is *g*.

Mass Equivalents

Recall that the meter sometimes is too large or too small to measure the length of certain objects. The same is true for the gram. You can use the same prefixes you use with meters to show parts of a gram or multiples of a gram. The table below shows these units of mass.

Mass Equivalents	
1 kilogram (kg)	1,000 g
1 centigram (cg)	1/100 g (0.01 g)
1 milligram (mg)	1/1,000 g (0.001 g)

To measure the mass of a person, you probably would use kilograms. One kilogram is about 2.2 pounds. The mass of a single hair from your head would be measured in smaller units called milligrams. A milligram is 1/1,000 of a gram.

Measuring Mass

To measure mass you can use an instrument called a **balance,** like the one pictured on the next page. You find the mass of an object by balancing it with objects of known masses. **Standard masses** are small objects— usually brass cylinders—with the mass stamped on each.

1 cm³ water

1 g = **1 g** = **1 g**

Measuring Liquid Mass

You can use a similar procedure to find the mass of a liquid. Measure the mass of an empty beaker. Pour the liquid into the beaker. Measure the mass of the liquid plus beaker. Subtract the mass of the empty beaker from the mass of the beaker plus liquid. The answer will be the mass of the liquid.

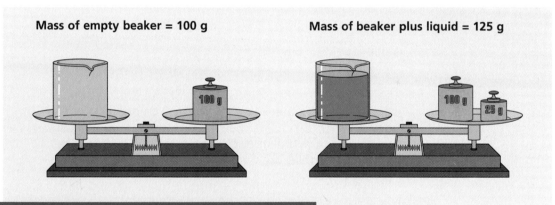

Mass of empty beaker = 100 g   Mass of beaker plus liquid = 125 g

The mass of the liquid is 125 g – 100 g = 25 g.

Mass and Weight

Mass and *weight* are often used to mean the same thing. However, scientists have different meanings for these two words. Mass is how much matter is in an object. **Weight** is a measure of how hard gravity pulls on an object. You can measure weight with a bathroom scale.

Weight
The measure of gravitational pull on an object.

This astronaut's weight is less on the moon than on Earth.

The mass of an object never changes under normal conditions. But the weight of an object can change when it is moved to some other place. For example, the pull of gravity on the moon is less than the pull of Earth's gravity. So an astronaut weighs less on the moon than on Earth. But the astronaut's mass didn't change.

Self-Check

Make these conversions.

1. 6 g = _____ mg
2. 80,000 g = _____ kg
3. 3,000 cg = _____ mg
4. 25,300 mg = _____ kg
5. The table below lists some planets of the solar system. It also tells each planet's force of gravity compared with Earth's. Copy the chart on a sheet of paper. Then calculate the weight of a 100-kg dog on each of the planets. The first two examples are done for you. Write your answers on your paper.

Planet	Force of gravity compared with Earth	Weight on Earth	Weight on this planet	Method
Earth	1.00	100 kg	100 kg	1.00 × 100
Jupiter	2.54	100 kg	254 kg	2.54 × 100
Mars	0.379	100 kg		
Saturn	1.07	100 kg		
Mercury	0.378	100 kg		
Venus	0.894	100 kg		

Chapter 1   SUMMARY

- Measurements are important because we cannot always trust observations made with our eyes.

- Measurements help scientists gather exact information.

- The gram is the basic unit of mass in the metric system.

- For a unit of measurement to be useful, it has to be the same for everyone.

- Scientists use the metric system. The metric system is based on a system of tens.

- The meter is the basic unit of length in the metric system.

- A system of prefixes in the metric system shows multiples or parts of a unit.

- Area is the amount of surface an object has on one side. The formula *length × width* is used to calculate area.

- Volume is the amount of space an object takes up. The volume of a rectangular solid can be calculated by using the formula *length × width × height*.

- The liter is the basic unit of volume in the metric system.

- You can easily convert from one unit to another in the metric system.

- Mass is the amount of material in an object.

- Weight can change when moving from one place to another, but mass stays the same.

Science Words	
area, 10	meniscus, 16
balance, 18	meter, 7
displacement of water, 17	meterstick, 8
English system, 6	metric system, 6
graduated cylinder, 16	standard mass, 18
gram, 18	unit, 5
liter, 15	volume, 14
mass, 18	weight, 19

Vocabulary Review

Number your paper from 1 to 6. Match each word in Column A with the correct definition in Column B. Write the letter of the definition on your paper.

Column A

_____ 1. gram

_____ 2. liter

_____ 3. mass

_____ 4. area

_____ 5. meter

_____ 6. volume

Column B

a. amount of surface an object has on one side

b. the amount of material an object has

c. the basic unit of length in the metric system

d. the amount of space an object takes up

e. the basic unit of volume in the metric system

f. the basic unit of mass in the metric system

Concept Review

Number your paper from 1 to 10. Then choose a word or words from the Word Bank that best complete each sentence. Write the answer on your paper.

1. The unit of length equal to 1/1,000 of a meter is the _____.

2. The unit of volume equal to 1,000 cubic centimeters is the _____.

3. One _____ is equal to 1,000 grams.

4. There are 10 millimeters in one _____.

5. One cubic centimeter of water has a mass of one _____.

6. The system of measurement that scientists use is the _____.

WORD BANK
centimeter
English system
graduated cylinder
gram
kilogram
liter
metric system
millimeter
unit
volume

7. Inches, feet, yards, and miles are all part of the _____.

8. The measure of how much space an object takes up is its _____.

9. Use a _____ to measure the volume of a liquid.

10. A known amount used to measure things is a _____.

Critical Thinking

Write the answer to each of the following questions.

1. Some ancient civilizations used units of measure based on the length of certain seeds. What kind of problems might you expect with such a system?

2. How would you measure the volume of each of the objects shown below?

3. For each of the following objects, tell which unit of measurement you would use.

    a. length of an ant

    b. mass of a postage stamp

    c. volume of a large jug of milk

    d. mass of a truck

4. Explain how the metric system is based on a system of tens.

Test Taking Tip | If you have to choose the correct ending to a sentence, combine the first part of the sentence with each ending. Then choose the one that best fits the sentence.

The Structure of Matter

How would you describe sugar? You might tell about its properties, such as its color, taste, and texture. Now think about how you might describe a single grain of sugar. You'd probably say that it is very small. But how small is the smallest piece of sugar? In this chapter, you will find out about the tiny particles that make up all substances. You will also learn about molecules, elements, and compounds.

ORGANIZE YOUR THOUGHTS

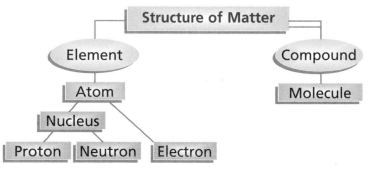

Goals for Learning

▶ To describe objects by listing their properties
▶ To explain what molecules, atoms, elements, and compounds are
▶ To explain how scientists use models
▶ To identify the parts of an atom
▶ To identify the symbols used to represent different elements

Property
A characteristic that helps identify an object.

If someone asked you to describe sugar, what would you say? You might say, "It is a solid made of small individual pieces." Each part of that description tells a **property** of sugar. A property is a characteristic that helps identify an object. The description identifies two properties of sugar.

■ It is a solid.

■ It is made of small individual pieces.

This description of sugar is correct. But it isn't enough to identify sugar for sure. As you can see in the photo, sand has the same properties. The description could be made more useful by adding other properties. For example, you might add color and taste. Your description of sugar becomes, "It is a white solid made of small individual pieces that have a sweet taste." Sand could be described as "a tan solid made of small individual pieces that have no taste."

How are the properties of these two materials alike and different?

Some Common Properties

The photo on the next page shows some common properties that might describe objects. Scientists prefer to use some properties more than others. For example, scientists often use mass, because it is easily measured. If someone asked you to describe a rock you saw, you might say it was big. But how big is big? Would someone else think the same rock was big? By using specific measurements of mass, everyone can agree on the measurement. Everyone can find the mass of the rock and agree that it is 50 kg. Another property that can easily be measured is volume (length × width × height).

Which of these properties are easily measured?

Color:
yellowish-red

Shape:
almost round

Volume:
about 20 mL

Feel:
fuzzy, soft

Size: similar
to a baseball

Mass:
about 0.4 kg

Taste:
sweet

Smell:
pleasant, sweet

Some properties, such as color, aren't measured as easily. Because of this, descriptions based on color can be misunderstood. For example, how would you describe the color of the fruit in the photo above? One person might describe the shade as "pink," while another would call it "yellowish-red." When describing properties, it is important to be as exact as you can and to use measurements whenever possible.

Self-Check

1. For each of the following statements, tell whether it is a good description. Explain your answer.
   a. It was a large, colorful box.
   b. The rock has a mass of 25 kilograms.
   c. The solid that formed was dark, shiny, and lumpy.
2. Choose an object. Write a detailed description of the object. Read your description to the class. Can classmates identify the object from your description?

Objectives

After reading this lesson, you should be able to

▶ explain what a molecule is.

▶ explain how molecules move in each of the three states of matter.

Molecule

The smallest particle of a substance that has the same properties as the substance.

Look at the water spraying out of the fountain in the photograph on this page. Imagine dividing one drop of this water into smaller and smaller drops. The smallest drop you could make that still had the properties of water would be one molecule of water.

Describing Molecules

Molecules are the smallest particles of a substance that still have the properties of that substance. Each molecule of water has exactly the same properties. How small can molecules be? Molecules of some substances are so small that billions of them could be placed side by side on a line one centimeter long.

In general, all water molecules are alike. A water molecule from the fountain is the same as a water molecule in a raindrop, in the ocean, or in the water you drink. The figure on the next page shows a molecule of water. You can see that each water molecule has three parts—one large part and two smaller parts.

If you divided a water molecule into its three parts, it would no longer be a molecule of water. The parts would no longer have the properties of water.

This fountain contains billions of molecules of water.

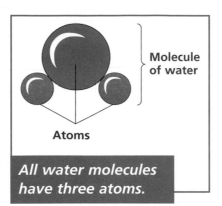

All water molecules have three atoms.

Molecule of water

Atoms

When a water molecule is divided into its separate parts, each individual part is called an **atom**. An atom is a building block of **matter**. Matter is anything that has mass and takes up space. A water molecule has three atoms. Each kind of atom has its own properties. All matter is made of atoms. **Density** is the number of atoms, or mass, in a given space.

States of Matter

You can describe matter by telling about its properties. For example, you might tell about its mass or volume. The form that matter has is another of its properties.

In the photo below you can see three forms of matter. The grass and trees are **solids**. The molecules in a solid attract, or pull toward, each other. In a solid, molecules stay close together. For this reason, a solid keeps a certain shape and volume.

How many solids, liquids, and gases can you find?

Gas
Form of matter that has no definite shape or volume.

Liquid
Form of matter that has a definite volume but no definite shape.

State of matter
The form that matter has—solid, liquid, or gas.

The water in the photo is a **liquid**. The pull between the molecules is weaker in liquids than it is in solids. The molecules can slide past each other. A liquid has a certain volume, but it can change its shape because its molecules can easily move around. For example, suppose you had a liter of water in a container. If you poured the liter of water into a larger container, the water would still take up one liter of space. But its shape would be different. It would take the shape of the new container.

Notice the shape of the helium balloons in the photo. Helium is a **gas** that fills the balloon. The molecules of a gas are much farther apart than they are in a liquid or a solid. The pull between the molecules in a gas is very weak. A gas takes the same shape as its container because its molecules move around freely. The gas molecules will always fill a container completely. A container of water can be half full, but gas in a container will be evenly distributed all through the container. The volume of a gas can change.

These forms of matter—solid, liquid, and gas—are called the **states of matter**. The drawing summarizes the spacing between molecules in each of these three states of matter.

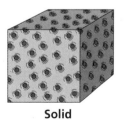 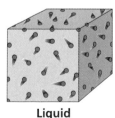 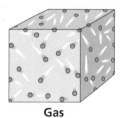

| Solid | Liquid | Gas |

Self-Check

1. Can you see a single molecule of water? Explain.
2. What parts make up a molecule of water?
3. Describe how molecules move in a solid.
4. How do molecules move in a liquid?
5. How do molecules move in a gas?

How Do Scientists Know What Atoms Are Like?

Objectives

After reading this lesson, you should be able to

▶ describe what a model is and explain how scientists use it.

▶ explain how models of the atom have changed.

▶ describe the electron cloud model.

Model
A picture, an idea, or an object that is built to explain how something else looks or works.

Since atoms are too small to be seen with the eyes alone, people have wondered for a long time what atoms look like. In fact, scientists have been studying atoms since the 1800s. But if scientists can't see an atom, how do they know what atoms look like?

Using Models

Sometimes scientists can tell what things look like by studying how they act. For example, what does wind look like? If you said wind blows things, you are describing what wind does, not what it looks like.

Scientists use the same kind of evidence to study things they can't see, such as atoms. Scientists study how atoms act and then decide what an atom must look like. Scientists make **models**. You have probably seen models of cars or airplanes or buildings. In science, a model is an idea, a picture, or an object that is built to explain how something else looks or works.

Models of Atoms

Scientists use models of atoms to show how atoms look and act without having actually to see them. Many scientists have developed models of atoms. In the early 1900s, a scientist developed a model of an atom like those shown below.

These models of atoms show that they are made of protons and electrons.

Figure A
An atom of hydrogen

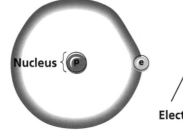

Nucleus

Figure B
An atom of helium

Proton

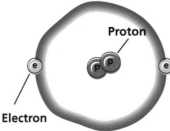

Electron

Find the center of each atom. This central part of an atom is called a **nucleus**. The nucleus of an atom contains small particles called **protons**. Protons are labeled with the letter *p*. Another symbol for a proton is a plus (+) sign. Now look in the figures for the letter *e*. This letter stands for **electrons**. Electrons are particles in an atom that move around the outside of the protons. Electrons are smaller than protons. Another symbol for an electron is a minus (–) sign. The protons and electrons of an atom stay together because they attract each other.

Notice that the numbers of protons and electrons in the models are different. Figure A shows a model of an atom of hydrogen. You can see that hydrogen has one proton and one electron. Figure B shows an atom of helium, a gas that is often used to fill balloons. How many protons and electrons does helium have?

In 1932, scientists had evidence that the nucleus of an atom had another kind of particle. This particle is called a **neutron**. Because of the new evidence, scientists changed the model of the atom. Figure C shows how the model changed. Find the neutrons, labeled with the letter *n*.

Today scientists use another model of atoms. You can see this new electron cloud model in Figure D. This new model was developed because scientists have evidence that electrons are not in separate layers around the nucleus. They could be anywhere in the cloud at a given time. As scientists learn more about atoms, perhaps the model will change again.

How are these two models of the atom different?

Figure C
An atom of boron

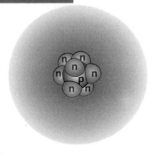

Figure D
Electron cloud model of an atom

You have looked at models showing the number of protons and electrons in different atoms. The table below lists some other atoms and tells the numbers of protons and electrons in each. Find the number of protons in carbon. How many electrons does carbon have? Compare the numbers of protons and electrons in nitrogen. How many of each does it have? Now look at the numbers of protons and electrons in each of the other atoms. What do you notice? The number of protons in an atom is equal to the number of electrons in the atom.

$$\boxed{\text{Number of protons in an atom}} \; = \; \boxed{\text{Number of electrons in an atom}}$$

Kind of atom	Number of protons	Number of electrons
hydrogen	1	1
helium	2	2
lithium	3	3
beryllium	4	4
boron	5	5
carbon	6	6
nitrogen	7	7
oxygen	8	8
fluorine	9	9
neon	10	10

Self-Check

1. If scientists cannot see atoms, how do they know what atoms look like?

2. What is a model?

3. How do scientists use models?

4. How many protons are in the atom shown in the drawing? How many electrons?

5. What is the name of the kind of atom? (*Hint:* Use the table.)

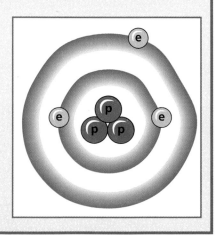

Objectives

After reading this lesson, you should be able to

▶ explain what an element is.
▶ explain what a natural element is.
▶ give examples of natural elements.

Element
Matter that has only one kind of atom.

Natural element
An element that is found in nature.

Did You Know?

Look at the tip of your pencil. It is made of a soft, black material that is a form of the element carbon. The small pencil point has billions of carbon atoms.

In Lesson 2, you learned that atoms are very tiny. In fact, they are one of the smallest particles that make up matter. Remember the balloons that were filled with helium? A balloon as small as a softball would hold many billions of atoms of helium.

One Kind of Atom

Most of the matter you see around you is made up of many different kinds of atoms. However, some matter has only one kind of atom. Matter that is made of only one kind of atom is called an **element.** All atoms of the same element are alike in their number of protons and electrons. The atoms of oxygen are different from the atoms of all other elements.

Natural Elements

Scientists know of about 109 different elements. Of these elements, 92 are called **natural elements**. Natural elements are those that are found in nature. The table on this page lists some natural elements.

Some Natural Elements	
Name	**Used for or found in**
copper	coins, frying pans, electrical wire
silver	jewelry, photography
carbon	"lead" pencils, charcoal, diamonds
helium	balloons, airships
nitrogen	air that we breathe, fertilizers
chlorine	bleach, table salt
aluminum	airplanes, cookware, soft-drink cans
neon	"neon" signs
gold	jewelry, seawater, dentistry
mercury	thermometers, drugs, pesticides
iron	steel, eating utensils

Not all elements are natural elements. Scientists are able to produce a few elements in specialized laboratories. Some of the elements that scientists produce last only a short time—a fraction of a second—before they change into other elements.

Elements in Water

In Lesson 2, you learned that a molecule of water is made of three parts like those in the figure below. These parts are elements. The large part of the molecule, shown in blue, is an atom of the element oxygen. The two small parts, shown in red, are atoms of the element hydrogen. The atoms of the element oxygen are different from the atoms of the element hydrogen.

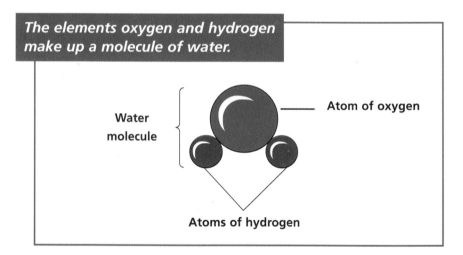

The elements oxygen and hydrogen make up a molecule of water.

Water molecule

Atom of oxygen

Atoms of hydrogen

Self-Check

1. What is an element?
2. What is a natural element?
3. Give three examples of natural elements.
4. What elements make up a water molecule?
5. Table salt is made up of one sodium atom and one chlorine atom. Is table salt an element? Explain.

SCIENCE IN YOUR LIFE

How are elements important to health?

Your body needs many natural elements to stay healthy and work properly. The table lists some of these elements and tells how they are important for your health. The table also lists some foods that contain these elements. Write a menu for a day. Include healthy foods in your menu that provide a variety of natural elements.

Element	Purpose in the body	Food where it is found
calcium	builds and maintains teeth and bones; helps blood clot; helps nerves and muscles work properly	cheese; milk; dark green vegetables; sardines; legumes
phosphorus	keeps teeth and bones healthy; helps release energy from the food you eat	meat; poultry; fish; eggs; legumes; milk products
magnesium	aids breaking down of foods; controls body fluids	green vegetables; grains; nuts; beans; yeast
sodium	controls the amount of water in body; helps nerves work properly	most foods; table salt
potassium	controls the fluids in cells; helps nerves work properly	oranges; bananas; meats; bran; potatoes; dried beans
iron	helps move oxygen in the blood and in other cells	liver; red meats; dark green vegetables; shellfish; whole-grain cereals
zinc	helps move carbon dioxide in body; helps in healing wounds	meats; shellfish; whole grains; milk; legumes

The Periodic Table

Metals

Nonmetals

Noble gases

1								
1 1 **H** Hydrogen 1.01	**2**							
2 3 **Li** Lithium 6.94	4 **Be** Beryllium 9.01							
3 11 **Na** Sodium 22.99	12 **Mg** Magnesium 24.30	**3**	**4**	**5**	**6**	**7**	**8**	**9**
4 19 **K** Potassium 39.10	20 **Ca** Calcium 40.08	21 **Sc** Scandium 44.96	22 **Ti** Titanium 47.90	23 **V** Vanadium 50.94	24 **Cr** Chromium 52.00	25 **Mn** Manganese 54.94	26 **Fe** Iron 55.85	27 **Co** Cobalt 58.93
5 37 **Rb** Rubidium 85.47	38 **Sr** Strontium 87.62	39 **Y** Yttrium 88.91	40 **Zr** Zirconium 91.22	41 **Nb** Niobium 92.91	42 **Mo** Molybdenum 95.94	43 **Tc** Technetium 98.91	44 **Ru** Ruthenium 101.07	45 **Rh** Rhodium 102.91
6 55 **Cs** Cesium 132.91	56 **Ba** Barium 137.33	71 **Lu** Lutelium 174.97	72 **Hf** Hafnium 178.49	73 **Ta** Tantalum 180.95	74 **W** Tungsten 183.85	75 **Re** Rhenium 186.21	76 **Os** Osmium 190.20	77 **Ir** Iridium 192.22
7 87 **Fr** Francium 223	88 **Ra** Radium 226.02	103 **Lr** Lawrencium 260	104 **Unq** Unnilquadium 261	105 **Unp** Unnilpentium 262	106 **Unh** Unnilhexium 263	107 **Uns** Unnilseptium 264	108 **Uno** Unniloctium 265	109 **Une** Unnilennium 266

6	57 **La** Lanthanum 138.91	58 **Ce** Cerium 140.12	59 **Pr** Praseodymium 140.91	60 **Nd** Neodymium 144.24	61 **Pm** Promethium 145	62 **Sm** Samarium 150.40	63 **Eu** Europium 151.96
7	89 **Ac** Actinium 227	90 **Th** Thorium 232.04	91 **Pa** Protoactinium 231.04	92 **U** Uranium 238.03	93 **Np** Neptunium 237.05	94 **Pu** Plutonium 244	95 **Am** Americium 243.13

# of Elements

								18
								2 **He** Helium 4.00

			13	**14**	**15**	**16**	**17**	
			5 **B** Boron 10.81	6 **C** Carbon 12.01	7 **N** Nitrogen 14.01	8 **O** Oxygen 16.00	9 **F** Fluorine 19.00	10 **Ne** Neon 20.17

10	**11**	**12**	13 **Al** Aluminum 26.98	14 **Si** Silicon 28.09	15 **P** Phosphorus 30.97	16 **S** Sulfur 32.06	17 **Cl** Chlorine 35.45	18 **Ar** Argon 39.95
28 **Ni** Nickel 58.70	29 **Cu** Copper 63.55	30 **Zn** Zinc 65.38	31 **Ga** Gallium 69.74	32 **Ge** Germanium 72.59	33 **As** Arsenic 74.92	34 **Se** Selenium 78.96	35 **Br** Bromine 79.90	36 **Kr** Krypton 83.80
46 **Pd** Palladium 106.42	47 **Ag** Silver 107.87	48 **Cd** Cadmium 112.41	49 **In** Indium 114.82	50 **Sn** Tin 118.69	51 **Sb** Antimony 121.75	52 **Te** Tellurium 127.60	53 **I** Iodine 126.90	54 **Xe** Xenon 131.30
78 **Pt** Platinum 195.09	79 **Au** Gold 196.97	80 **Hg** Mercury 200.59	81 **Tl** Thallium 204.37	82 **Pb** Lead 207.20	83 **Bi** Bismuth 208.98	84 **Po** Polonium 209	85 **At** Astatine 210	86 **Rn** Radon 222

64 **Gd** Gadolinium 157.25	65 **Tb** Terbium 158.93	66 **Dy** Dysprosium 162.50	67 **Ho** Holmium 164.93	68 **Er** Erbium 167.26	69 **Tm** Thulium 168.93	70 **Yb** Ytterbium 173.04
96 **Cm** Curium 247	97 **Bk** Berkelium 247	98 **Cf** Californium 251	99 **Es** Einsteinium 254	100 **Fm** Fermium 257	101 **Md** Mendelevium 258	102 **No** Nobelium 259

2

Making Models of Molecules

Purpose

To make models of specific molecules showing the atoms in them

Procedure

1. The table below lists some common substances and the atoms they are made of.

Substances	Atoms in one molecule
Water	2 hydrogen + 1 oxygen
Sodium chloride (table salt)	1 sodium + 1 chlorine
Iron oxide (rust)	2 iron + 3 oxygen
Carbon dioxide	1 carbon + 2 oxygen
Methane (natural gas)	1 carbon + 4 hydrogen
Calcium carbonate (seashells)	1 calcium + 1 carbon + 3 oxygen

2. Use a small clay ball to represent atoms of a water molecule. Use different colors for different kinds of atoms. The diagram on page 34 may help you. Connect the "atoms" with toothpicks.

3. Choose another molecule listed in the table below. Make a model of it. Draw a picture of your model. Label your drawing with the name of the substance and the names of the atoms in it.

Questions

1. What two kinds of atoms are in a water molecule? How many of each kind are in one water molecule?

2. Which molecule did you model in step 3? What kinds of atoms are in that molecule? How many of each kind of atom are in the molecule?

Objectives

After reading this lesson, you should be able to

► explain what a symbol is.

► explain how element symbols are alike and different.

► identify symbols for common elements.

Symbol
One or two letters that represent the name of an element.

Think about addressing an envelope for a letter you write to a friend. You probably use an abbreviation to indicate the state to which the letter should be delivered. What is the abbreviation for your state?

Element Symbols

Scientists also use abbreviations to represent each of the elements. The abbreviations for elements are called **symbols**. The tables on this page and the next page list some symbols for elements. All these symbols are alike in the following ways.

- All of the symbols have either one or two letters.

- The first letter of each symbol is a capital letter.

- If the symbol has a second letter, the second letter is a small letter.

- No period is used at the end of a symbol.

Table 1

Element name	Element symbol
hydrogen	H
boron	B
carbon	C
nitrogen	N
oxygen	O
fluorine	F
phosphorus	P
sulfur	S
iodine	I
uranium	U

Table 2

Element name	Element symbol
helium	He
lithium	Li
neon	Ne
aluminum	Al
silicon	Si
argon	Ar
calcium	Ca
cobalt	Co
bromine	Br
barium	Ba
radium	Ra

Table 3

Element name	Element symbol
magnesium	Mg
chlorine	Cl
chromium	Cr
manganese	Mn
plutonium	Pu
zinc	Zn
strontium	Sr
platinum	Pt

Table 4

Element name	Element symbol
sodium	Na
potassium	K
iron	Fe
silver	Ag
tin	Sn
tungsten	W
gold	Au
mercury	Hg
lead	Pb
antimony	Sb
copper	Cu

Notice that the symbols in Table 1 use only the first letter of the element name. Look at the symbols in Table 2. This group of symbols uses the first two letters of the element name. The symbols in Table 3 also use two letters. The first letter is the first letter of the element name. The second letter is another letter from the element name.

How do the symbols in Table 4 differ from the other symbols? Most of these symbols come from the Latin names for the elements. For example, the symbol for iron is Fe, which comes from the Latin word *ferrum*, meaning "iron."

In recent years, scientists have made new elements in the laboratory. Some of these elements have symbols with three letters. You can see the symbols for these elements in the chart on pages 36 and 37.

Self-Check

1. How are all of the element symbols alike?
2. Write the symbol for each of the following elements.
   a. helium   b. silver   c. carbon   d. chlorine   e. calcium
3. Write the element name for each of the following symbols.
   a. Hg   b. Ne   c. Mn   d. O   e. P

Objectives

After reading this lesson, you should be able to

▶ explain what a compound is.

▶ give examples of compounds.

Compound

A substance formed when atoms of two or more elements join together.

All the substances in the picture are different from the elements you learned about in Lesson 4. The substances in the picture are each made of two or more different kinds of atoms. When two or more atoms of different elements join together, the substance that forms is called a **compound.** A compound has properties that are different from the properties of the elements that form the compound.

All of these substances are compounds.

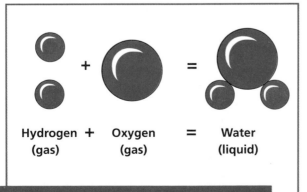

Hydrogen + Oxygen = Water
(gas)   (gas)   (liquid)

The properties of water are different from those of oxygen or hydrogen.

Think again about a molecule of water. The drawing shows that an atom of oxygen combines with two atoms of hydrogen to form a molecule of the compound water. Water is different from the elements that form it. Water is a liquid. Both oxygen and hydrogen are gases.

Another compound that probably is familiar to you is table salt. The chemical name of salt is sodium chloride. It is formed when the element sodium is combined with the element chlorine. Sodium chloride is different from each of the elements it contains. Sodium is a solid. You might be surprised to learn that chlorine is a poisonous gas. However, when chlorine is combined with sodium to form sodium chloride, chlorine no longer has its poisonous property. Remember that a compound can have completely different properties from the elements that form it.

Most kinds of matter on Earth are compounds. In fact, there are more than 10 million known compounds. The table lists some common compounds and tells the elements that make up each compound.

Some Common Compounds

Name	Elements in this compound	Used for
table salt	sodium, chlorine	cooking
water	hydrogen, oxygen	drinking
sugar	carbon, hydrogen, oxygen	cooking
baking soda	sodium, hydrogen, carbon, oxygen	baking
Epsom salts	magnesium, sulfur, oxygen	medicine

You might wonder if you can tell by looking at a substance whether it is an element or a compound. An unknown substance must be tested in a laboratory to determine whether it is an element or a compound.

Self-Check

1. Explain what a compound is.
2. Give two examples of compounds.
3. Suppose you test a gas in the laboratory. You learn that the gas is made up of carbon atoms and oxygen atoms. Is the gas a compound? Explain.

Chapter 2 SUMMARY

- Properties are used to describe an object.

- A molecule is the smallest particle of a substance that still has the same properties of the substance.

- Matter is anything that has mass and takes up space.

- An atom is the basic building block of matter. An atom is made of protons, neutrons, and electrons.

- Molecules move in different ways in each of the three states of matter—solids, liquids, and gases.

- Scientists use models of atoms to show how atoms look and act.

- An atom has an equal number of protons and electrons.

- An element is matter that is made of only one kind of atom. There are 92 natural elements.

- Each element has a symbol, an abbreviation for its name.

- A compound is formed from two or more atoms of different elements. A compound has properties that are different from the elements that form the compound.

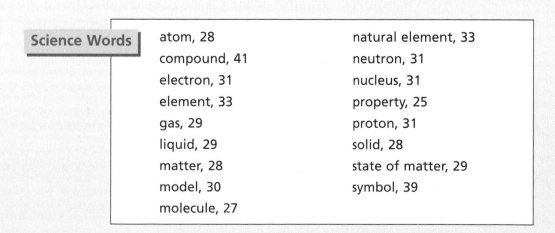

Science Words

atom, 28	natural element, 33
compound, 41	neutron, 31
electron, 31	nucleus, 31
element, 33	property, 25
gas, 29	proton, 31
liquid, 29	solid, 28
matter, 28	state of matter, 29
model, 30	symbol, 39
molecule, 27	

WORD BANK
atom
compound
element
gas
liquid
model
molecule
nucleus
properties
solid
states
symbol

Vocabulary Review

Number your paper from 1 to 12. Then choose a word or words from the Word Bank that best complete each sentence. Write the answer on your paper.

1. A(n) _____ has only one kind of atom.

2. _____ are characteristics that help identify an object.

3. A(n) _____ is built to explain how something works.

4. A(n) _____ has no definite shape or volume.

5. The smallest particle of water that still has all the properties of water is a(n) _____ of water.

6. A(n) _____ has a definite volume but no definite shape.

7. A(n) _____ is the abbreviation for an element.

8. A(n) _____ is the building block of matter.

9. A(n) _____ has a definite shape and volume.

10. Atoms of two elements can join to form a(n) _____.

11. Solid, liquid, and gas are the _____ of matter.

12. The central part of an atom is called the _____.

Concept Review

Number your paper from 1 to 6. Then choose the answer that best complete each sentence. Write the letter of the answer on your paper.

1. All matter is made of _____.

    a. symbols   b. atoms   c. compounds

2. An atom always has the same number of electrons and _____.

    a. protons   b. neutrons   c. nuclei

3. Molecules are _____.

    a. large   b. easy to see   c. small

4. An example of an element is _____.

   a. oxygen   b. water   c. sodium chloride

5. Molecules move most freely in _____.

   a. solids   b. liquids   c. gases

6. An example of a compound is _____.

   a. helium   b. hydrogen   c. carbon dioxide

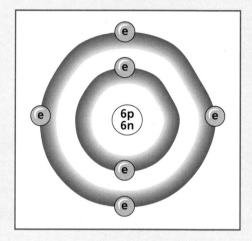

Critical Thinking

Write the answers to each of the following questions.

1. Look at the drawing to the left. Give the following information about the atom: How many protons does it have? How many neutrons? How many electrons?

2. Does the drawing below show an atom or a molecule? Explain your answer.

Test Taking Tip | Before you choose an answer to a multiple-choice question, be sure to read each answer choice carefully.

Chapter

3

Chemical Reactions

What happens to a metal tool that is left outside in the rain? The iron in the metal combines with the water to make a new substance—rust. Rusting is one example of a simple chemical reaction. When chemical reactions take place, new substances are formed. In this chapter, you will learn about chemical reactions and how you can show them.

ORGANIZE YOUR THOUGHTS

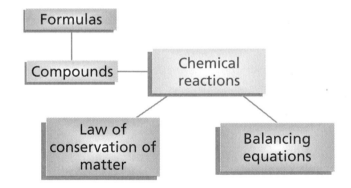

Formulas

Compounds — Chemical reactions

Law of conservation of matter

Balancing equations

Goals for Learning

▶ To describe compounds
▶ To explain what the information in a formula means
▶ To explain what a chemical reaction is
▶ To state the law of conservation of matter
▶ To interpret and write balanced chemical equations

What Are Some Characteristics of Compounds?

Look at the different elements in the periodic table. They combine in various ways to form the millions of different compounds you see around you. Do these millions of compounds have any common characteristics? How do these compounds form?

Compounds and Chemical Changes

In Chapter 2 you learned that two or more elements combine to form a compound. For example, hydrogen gas combines with oxygen gas to form the liquid compound water. Water has different properties from the elements that form it.

Chemical change
A change that produces one or more substances that differ from the original substances.

When atoms of elements combine to form a compound, a **chemical change** takes place. A chemical change produces new substances with new properties. A chemical change occurs when hydrogen and oxygen combine to form water.

The drawing illustrates another example of a chemical change. As the wood burns, it changes to gases and ash. The ash is a soft, gray powder that cannot burn. Wood and ash are different substances and have different properties.

A chemical change takes place when wood burns.

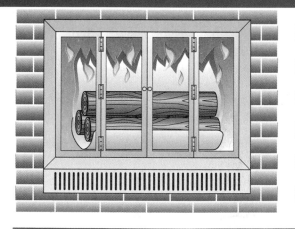
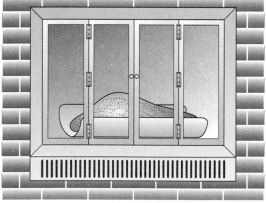

Now think about taking a similar piece of wood and chopping it into tiny pieces. Does a chemical change take place when this happens? Ask yourself if the pieces of wood have properties that are different from the original piece of wood. In this case, they do not. Each small piece is still wood. The pieces just have different sizes and shapes. Changes like this are called **physical changes**. A physical change is a change in which the appearance of a substance changes but the properties stay the same. In a physical change, no new substances are formed.

Characteristics of Compounds

Although there are millions of compounds, they all share some basic characteristics. Any particular compound always contains the same elements. For example, the elements that make up water—hydrogen and oxygen—are always the same. The water can be from a faucet, a river, or a puddle in the road.

Another characteristic of compounds is that the atoms in a particular compound always combine in the same numbers. A molecule of water always contains two hydrogen atoms and one oxygen atom. If you change the molecule by adding another oxygen atom, the compound is no longer water. It becomes hydrogen peroxide, the clear liquid that people can use to clean cuts and other wounds to the skin. Water and hydrogen peroxide are different substances with different properties.

Self-Check

Copy the table on a sheet of paper. Identify each change as a chemical change or a physical change. Tell how you know. (*Remember*: In a chemical change, the properties are different after the change.)

Change	Chemical or physical?	How do you know?
melting ice cream		
rusting a nail		
chopping onions		
baking a cake		

INVESTIGATION

Observing a Chemical Change

Purpose

To observe physical and chemical changes

Procedure

1. Copy the data table below on your paper.

	Appearance
washing soda in water	
Epsom salts in water	
washing soda and Epsom salts in water	

2. Put on your safety goggles.

3. Fill each jar about halfway with distilled water.

4. Add a spoonful of washing soda to one jar. Put the lid tightly on the jar. Shake for about 30 seconds. Record your observations.

5. Use a clean spoon to add a spoonful of Epsom salts to the second jar. Place the lid on the jar and shake it for about 30 seconds. Record your observations.

6. Carefully pour the contents of one jar into the other jar. Observe for 5 minutes. Record the results.

Questions

1. What happened when you added the washing soda to water?

Materials

✓ safety goggles
✓ 2 small jars with lids
✓ distilled water
✓ 2 plastic spoons
✓ washing soda
✓ Epsom salts
✓ clock

2. What happened when you added the Epsom salts to water?

3. What did you observe when you mixed the contents of the jars together in step 6?

4. Did a chemical change or a physical change take place in steps 4 and 5? Explain your answer.

5. Did a chemical change or a physical change take place in step 6? Explain your answer.

Explore Further

Place a small amount of vinegar in a soft-drink bottle. Add a small amount of baking soda. Immediately cover the mouth of the bottle with a balloon. What do you observe happening? Has a chemical change taken place? Explain.

Objectives

After reading this lesson, you should be able to

▶ explain how to write a chemical formula.

▶ interpret a chemical formula.

Suppose you want to describe a particular beverage such as the one in the drawing. You might tell about its recipe. Notice that the recipe lists all the ingredients. It also tells the amount of each ingredient the drink has.

Recipe

Banana-Strawberry Slush

1 cup sliced bananas
1 cup fresh sliced
    strawberries
4 mint leaves
1 cup skim milk
1/4 cup crushed ice cubes

Mix all of the ingredients in a blender until slushy. Serve immediately.

You can describe a compound by using the same kind of information you use in a recipe. You can tell what elements form the compound. You can also tell the amount of each element contained in the compound.

Formulas for Compounds

Chemical formula
A way to write the kinds and numbers of atoms in a compound.

Scientists use the symbols for the elements to write a **chemical formula** for each compound. A chemical formula tells what kinds of atoms are in a compound and how many atoms of each kind are present. You know that sodium and chlorine combine to form table salt. The symbol for sodium is Na. The symbol for chlorine is Cl. The chemical formula for table salt is NaCl. The formula shows that sodium and chlorine combine to form table salt.

Subscript

A number in a formula that tells the number of atoms of an element in a compound.

Scientists use a number called a **subscript** to indicate the number of atoms of each element in a compound. For example, the formula for water is H_2O. The number *2* tells that a water molecule contains two atoms of hydrogen. You can see that the subscript number *2* is smaller than the *H* and written slightly below the letter.

Notice that no subscript is written after the *O*. If no subscript number is given after the symbol of an element, the compound has only one atom of that element. The formula H_2O shows that one molecule of water contains three atoms—two of hydrogen and one of oxygen.

Look at the tables to learn the chemical formulas for some other compounds. Read carefully to find out what each formula shows about the compound it represents.

CH_4

Symbol	Element	Subscript	Number of atoms
C	carbon	none	1
H	hydrogen	4	+ 4
			5 Total atoms

$C_{12}H_{22}O_{11}$

Symbol	Element	Subscript	Number of atoms
C	carbon	12	12
H	hydrogen	22	22
O	oxygen	11	+11
			45 Total atoms

Self-Check

Copy the chart on a sheet of paper. Fill in the missing information. Use the periodic table on pages 36 and 37 if you need help naming the elements. The first compound is done for you.

Compound	Symbols	Elements	Subscripts	Number of atoms of each kind
$NaHCO_3$	Na H C O	sodium hydrogen carbon oxygen	none none none 3	1 1 1 3
$K_2Cr_2O_7$				
H_2SO_4				
$KClO_3$				

After reading this lesson, you should be able to

▶ explain what a reaction is.

▶ explain the difference between solutions, solutes, and solvents.

Hundreds of years ago, people known as alchemists tried to change different materials into gold. Imagine being able to change iron or lead into solid gold!

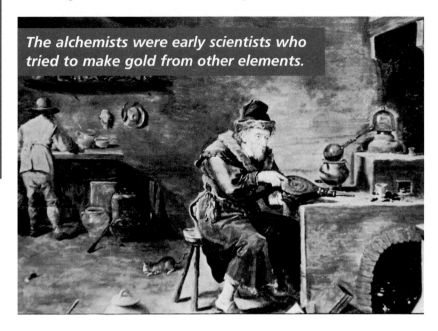

The alchemists were early scientists who tried to make gold from other elements.

Unfortunately for the alchemists, they never succeeded. Today, scientists know that chemically changing one element into another is not possible. But during a chemical change, elements can be combined to form compounds. The elements in compounds can be rearranged to form new compounds. When elements combine or rearrange, they are said to react. The process is called a **chemical reaction**. For some reactions, it is necessary to heat the substances. In other cases, the substances must be mixed with water for a chemical reaction to take place.

Substances do not always react. Many elements and compounds can be mixed together and nothing at all happens. A **mixture** is formed when substances are simply stirred together and no new substance is formed. When you stir sugar and cinnamon together, you form a mixture.

Chemical reaction
Chemical change in which elements are combined or rearranged.

Mixture
A combination of substances in which no reaction takes place.

Dissolving

Dissolve
Break apart.

Solute
The substance that is dissolved in a solution.

Solution
A mixture in which one substance is dissolved in another.

Solvent
The substance in which the dissolving occurs in a solution.

Many reactions take place only when the substances have been **dissolved** in other liquids. To dissolve means to break up substances into individual atoms or molecules. An example of dissolving occurs when sugar is placed in water. The sugar mixes with the water and seems to disappear. But the sugar is still there. The pieces of the sugar have been broken down into tiny particles—molecules.

When a substance is thoroughly dissolved in another, the result is a mixture called a **solution**. The substance that dissolves is called the **solute**. When you dissolve sugar in water, the solute is sugar. The substance in which the dissolving is done is called the **solvent**. In the sugar–water solution, water is the solvent. Can you think of other examples of solutions, solutes, and solvents?

A solution does not always have to be a solid dissolved in a liquid. Solutions can be formed by dissolving substances in solids and gases. The table gives some examples of solutions.

Types of Solutions

Substance (solute)	Dissolved in (solvent)	Examples
liquid	liquid	alcohol in water
	gas	water vapor in air
	solid	ether in rubber
gas	liquid	club soda in water (CO_2 in water)
	gas	air (nitrogen, oxygen, other gases)
	solid	hydrogen in palladium
solid	liquid	salt in water
	gas	iodine vapor in air
	solid	brass (copper and zinc)

Self-Check

1. What metal were the alchemists trying to produce? Did they succeed?
2. What are two things a scientist can do to cause some substances that are mixed together to react?
3. Suppose you dissolve salt in water. Name the solvent and the solute.

Objectives

After reading this lesson, you should be able to

▶ explain how chemical equations describe a chemical reaction.

▶ balance chemical equations.

A **chemical equation** is a statement that uses symbols, chemical formulas, and numbers to stand for a chemical reaction. You can see an example of a simple chemical equation below.

Reactants		Products
HCl + NaOH	→	NaCl + H$_2$O
hydrogen chloride plus sodium hydroxide	yields	sodium chloride plus water

Notice that the arrow symbol (→) stands for "yields" or "makes." The chemicals on the left side of the arrow are called **reactants.** They are the substances that are reacting together. The chemicals on the right side of the arrow are called **products.** They are the substances that form from the reactants. In the above example, HCl and NaOH are the reactants. The products are NaCl and H$_2$O.

Law of Conservation of Matter

The reactants present *before* a reaction can be different from the products present *after* the reaction. But the kinds and numbers of atoms do not change during the reaction. Different substances are formed, but the same atoms are there. They are just rearranged. In the reaction below, methyl chloride and fluorine react to form methyl fluoride and chlorine. Notice how the atoms are rearranged.

Chemical equation
A statement that uses symbols, formulas, and numbers to stand for a chemical reaction.

Product
A substance that is formed in a chemical reaction.

Reactant
A substance that is changed to form a product in a chemical reaction.

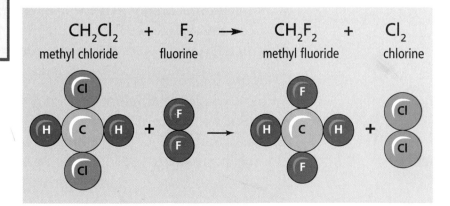

$$CH_2Cl_2 + F_2 \rightarrow CH_2F_2 + Cl_2$$

methyl chloride   fluorine   methyl fluoride   chlorine

Mass does not change during a reaction. The mass of the reactants equals the mass of the products. This fact illustrates the **law of conservation of matter**. The law states that matter cannot be created or destroyed in any chemical change.

Balancing Equations

To satisfy the law of conservation of matter, a chemical equation must show the same number of each kind of atom on both sides of the equation. Scientists say that the equation must be **balanced** to keep the number of atoms the same.

Look at the following equation. It shows that hydrogen plus oxygen makes water.

$$H_2 + O_2 \rightarrow H_2O$$

This equation is not balanced. Two oxygen atoms are shown on the left side of the equation. Only 1 oxygen atom is shown on the right. The left side of the equation has a total of 4 atoms, but the right side has only 3 atoms. These facts are summarized below.

$H_2 + O_2$	$\rightarrow$	H_2O
H 2 atoms		H 2 atoms
O 2 atoms		O 1 atom
Total of 4 atoms		Total of 3 atoms

You can see that there are 4 atoms in the reactants and only 3 in the products. The law of conservation of matter says that atoms do not disappear in chemical reactions. You cannot change the formulas for the reactants or products. How do you balance the equation?

To make the two sides come out even, you can place numbers called **coefficients** before the formulas. Coefficients multiply the numbers of molecules or other formula units. For example, $2H_2O$ would mean 2 water molecules.

By changing coefficients, the numbers of atoms can be changed. By writing $2H_2O$, you are saying that 4 atoms of hydrogen and 2 atoms of oxygen are in the products. If you write $3H_2O$, you are saying that 6 atoms of hydrogen and 3 atoms of oxygen are in the products.

By placing a *2* in front of the H_2O, you have made the number of oxygen atoms equal on both sides of the equation. But the number of hydrogen atoms is not equal.

$H_2 + O_2$	$\rightarrow$	$2H_2O$
H 2 atoms		H 4 atoms
O 2 atoms		O 2 atoms
Total of 4 atoms		Total of 6 atoms

You can see that there are 2 hydrogen atoms in the reactants. There are 4 hydrogen atoms in the product. Therefore, you need 2 more hydrogen atoms in the reactants. Again you can change the number of atoms by using a coefficient. You can balance this equation like this.

$2H_2 + O_2$	$\rightarrow$	$2H_2O$
H 4 atoms		H 4 atoms
O 2 atoms		O 2 atoms
Total of 6 atoms		Total of 6 atoms

The equation is now balanced. The coefficients show that there are 2 molecules each of hydrogen and water. Since the oxygen has no coefficient, it means that there is 1 molecule. The equation tells you that whenever hydrogen and oxygen combine to form water, 2 molecules of hydrogen will combine with 1 molecule of oxygen to produce 2 molecules of water.

Self-Check

Study the following equation. Then answer the questions on a sheet of paper. $2Na + Cl_2 \rightarrow 2NaCl$
Write the following chemical equations in words.

1. $Mg + S \rightarrow MgS$
2. $Ca + O_2 \rightarrow CaO_2$
3. What are the reactants?
4. What is the product?
5. Is the equation balanced? Explain.

SCIENCE IN YOUR LIFE

How does film work?

When you take a photo, you capture an image on film, almost as if by magic. But how does that "magic" really happen? The answer has to do with a chemical reaction.

When you take a picture with a camera, you push the button that releases the shutter. The shutter opens. Light enters the camera and reaches the film.

Film that produces black-and-white photos has a material that is sensitive to light. White silver bromide (AgBr) often is used as the coating. When light hits the film, the silver bromide breaks down easily into its elements. These elements are silver and bromine (Ag and Br). The silver bromide breaks down only on the areas of the film that light has struck.

When the film is developed, the areas where silver bromide was hit by light turn dark. The rest of the film stays light. The brightest objects photographed look darkest on the film. That is because the brightest objects sent the most light onto the film. The developed film is thus a "negative." It looks the opposite of the original scene. Look at the negative shown below.

The final photo print, also shown below, is made by sending light through the negative. The light hits a special white paper that turns dark in light. The dark parts on the negative send the least light through to the paper. In those areas, the white paper stays light. The negative makes something that is the opposite of itself. The result is an image that resembles the scene that was photographed.

Negative

Print of photograph

Chapter 3　Summary

- A compound forms when two or more elements combine. A chemical change takes place when elements combine to form a compound. In a chemical change, new substances with new properties are formed.

- A physical change causes the appearance of a substance to change, but the properties stay the same.

- Molecules of the same compound always contain the same elements. The atoms in the molecules of the same compound always combine in the same numbers.

- A chemical formula is used to show what kinds of atoms and how many atoms of each kind are in a compound.

- A chemical reaction involves a change of substances into other substances.

- Reactions can be represented by chemical equations, which should be balanced for atoms.

- The law of conservation of matter states that matter cannot be created or destroyed in any chemical change.

- A combination of materials in which no reaction takes place is called a mixture.

- Many reactions take place only when a substance has been dissolved in another substance. Dissolving one substance in another substance creates a mixture called a solution.

Science Words		
balance, 56	mixture, 53
chemical change, 47	physical change, 48
chemical equation, 55	product, 55
chemical formula, 51	reactant, 55
chemical reaction, 53	solute, 54
coefficient, 56	solution, 54
dissolve, 54	solvent, 54
law of conservation of matter, 56	subscript, 52

WORD BANK

chemical equation

chemical formula

chemical reaction

coefficient

law of
   conservation
   of matter

mixture

physical change

product

reactant

solute

solution

solvent

subscript

Vocabulary Review

Number your paper from 1 to 13. Then choose a word or words from the Word Bank that best complete each sentence. Write the answer on your paper.

1. A substance formed in a chemical reaction is called a _____.

2. The _____ for sodium chloride is NaCl.

3. A change in which the appearance of a substance changes but the properties stay the same is a _____.

4. Any change in which substances turn into other substances is called a _____.

5. A substance that dissolves another is called a _____.

6. A mixture in which one substance is dissolved in another is called a _____

7. A _____ is a number placed before a formula in a chemical equation.

8. The _____ states that material cannot be created or destroyed in any chemical change.

9. A substance that is dissolved in another is called a _____.

10. A substance that changes to produce another substance is called a _____.

11. A _____ is a number that tells how many atoms of an element are in a compound.

12. A combination of substances in which no reaction takes place is called a _____.

13. A _____ uses symbols, formulas, and numbers to stand for a chemical reaction

Concept Review

Number your paper from 1 to 5. Then choose the answer that best completes each sentence. Write the letter of the answer on your paper.

1. In the reaction $C + H_2O \longrightarrow CO + H_2$, the reactants are _____.

   a. C and CO
   b. C and H_2O
   c. CO and H_2
   d. H_2O and H_2

2. When sugar is dissolved in water, _____.

   a. water is the solute
   b. sugar is the solvent
   c. sugar is the solute
   d. there is no solvent

3. The coefficients in the expression $5Na_2HPO + 3C_6H_{10}$ are _____.

   a. 2, 6, 10
   c. 5, 2, 1, 4
   b. 3, 2
   d. 5, 3

4. A chemical _____ tells what elements and how many atoms of each element are in a compound.

   a. symbol   b. equation   c. formula

5. A molecule of water always contains two hydrogen atoms and _____ oxygen atom(s).

   a. one   b. two   c. three

Critical Thinking

Write the answer to each of the following questions.

1. Balance the following equation by adding coefficients: $Al + O_2 \longrightarrow Al_2O_3$. Then identify the reactant(s) and the product(s).

2. Look at the photograph. What is happening?

Test Taking Tip | Read test questions carefully to identify those questions that require more than one answer.

Energy and Motion

Motion—it's happening all the time. People walk and skateboard. Cars rush along the highway. Rivers flow. Leaves rustle in the wind. All these things involve motion. All motion involves energy. In this chapter, you will learn about the different forms of energy and how energy can change from one form to another.

ORGANIZE YOUR THOUGHTS

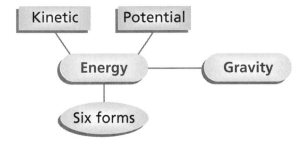

Goals for Learning

▶ To explain what energy is
▶ To name six forms of energy
▶ To calculate speed of motion
▶ To explain what gravity is
▶ To explain the law of universal gravitation

Objectives

After reading this lesson, you should be able to

- ▶ relate energy to work.
- ▶ explain the difference between kinetic and potential energy.
- ▶ explain the law of conservation of energy.

Energy
The ability to do work.

Kinetic energy
Energy of motion.

Potential energy
Stored energy.

Have you ever tried to play a radio with a "dead" battery? The radio would not play because the battery had no more **energy** stored inside. In science, *energy* is defined as "the ability to do work." Without energy, no work could be done. You will learn the scientific meaning of *work* in Chapter 5.

Kinetic and Potential Energy

A moving object has the energy of motion, called **kinetic energy.** When a car is moving, it can do work. It can overcome road friction and air resistance and keep going forward. The amount of kinetic energy a moving object has depends on the object's mass and speed. The greater the mass or speed, the greater the kinetic energy.

Some objects are not moving, but they have the potential to move because of their position. These objects have stored energy. This stored energy is called **potential energy**. A book sitting on the floor has no potential energy. It cannot do work. But if you set the book so that it hangs over the edge of a table, the book has more stored energy. It can do work by falling to the floor. Then the potential energy changes to kinetic energy. If you place the book over the edge of a higher table, the book has more potential energy because it can fall farther.

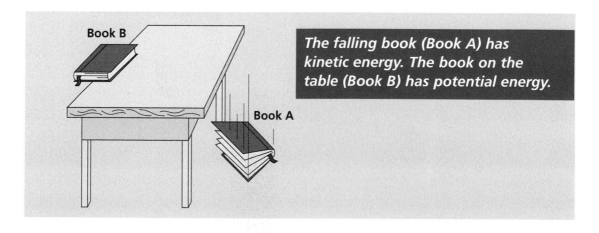

The falling book (Book A) has kinetic energy. The book on the table (Book B) has potential energy.

The Forms of Energy

The energy you use to do work exists in six main forms. These six forms of energy can be stored. They can also produce motion. That is, each form of energy can be potential or kinetic.

Chemical energy is stored in the bonds between atoms. When substances react, they can release some of the chemical energy in the substances and warm the surroundings. For example, burning coal produces heat.

Heat energy is associated with the moving particles that make up matter. The faster the particles move, the more heat energy is present. All matter has some heat energy. You will learn more about heat in Chapter 6.

Mechanical energy is the energy in moving objects. Objects such as a moving bicycle, wind, and a falling rock have mechanical energy in kinetic form. Sound is a form of mechanical energy that you will learn about in Chapter 7.

Nuclear energy is energy that is stored in the nucleus, or center, of an atom. It can be released in devices such as nuclear power plants and atomic weapons.

How many forms of energy can you find in this room?

Radiant energy is associated with light. Some energy that Earth receives from the sun is in the form of light energy. You will learn more about light in Chapter 7.

Electrical energy is the pushing and pulling of electric charges. Electrons are the negatively charged particles in atoms. Appliances such as refrigerators and vacuum cleaners use electrical energy. You will learn about electricity in Chapter 8.

Generator
Device used to convert mechanical energy to electrical energy.

Energy can be changed from one form to another. At an electric power plant, for example, chemical energy is converted to heat energy when fuel is burned. The heat energy is used to make steam. The steam turns a turbine and produces mechanical energy inside a **generator**. The generator converts mechanical energy to electrical energy. The electrical energy is sent to your home, and you can use it to do work.

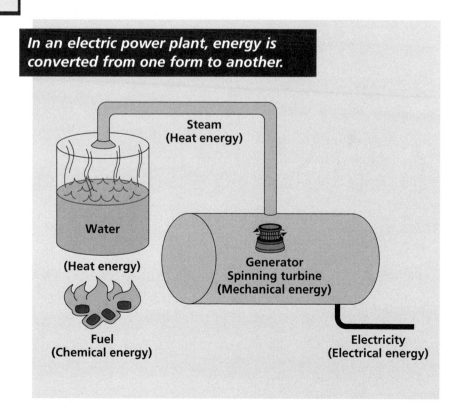

In an electric power plant, energy is converted from one form to another.

Steam
(Heat energy)

Water

(Heat energy)

Fuel
(Chemical energy)

Generator
Spinning turbine
(Mechanical energy)

Electricity
(Electrical energy)

The Law of Conservation of Energy

Energy might change its form, but it does not disappear. You can add energy to an object or take energy away from it, but the total amount of the energy does not change. The **law of conservation of energy** states that energy cannot be created or destroyed. A book falling from a table illustrates the law of conservation of energy. As the book falls, its potential energy decreases and its kinetic energy increases. The amount of energy stays the same.

Law of conservation of energy
Energy cannot be created or destroyed.

Self-Check

1. What is energy?
2. What is the difference between kinetic and potential energy?
3. The illustration shows an example of energy changing form. List the energy changes that take place when wood burns.

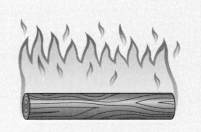

SCIENCE IN YOUR LIFE

Have you ever ridden a roller coaster?

A roller coaster is a good example of how energy can change from one form to another. When you first climb into the car at the bottom of the hill, the car has no potential energy. A chain must pull you up the first big hill. That chain changes electrical energy into potential energy. When the cars are at the top, they can fall downward. Potential energy changes to kinetic energy as the cars plunge down one hill and up the next hill. The cars slow as they reach the top of the hill. The kinetic energy that pushed them up the hill has changed back to potential energy. That stored energy converts to kinetic energy as the cars zoom down again.

Objectives

After reading this lesson, you should be able to

▶ explain what motion is.

▶ calculate elapsed time.

▶ explain what speed and average speed are.

▶ perform calculations involving speed.

Elapsed time
Length of time that passes from one event to another.

Motion
A change in position.

Earth travels through space. A car carries you from place to place. You walk to the store. An amusement park ride spins you around. What do all these actions have in common? In each case, objects are changing position in space. We say they are moving. **Motion** is simply a change of position.

All change, including change in position, takes place over time. So to help you understand motion, you will begin by learning how the passage of time is measured.

Elapsed Time

Suppose you have just taken an airplane trip from New Orleans to New York in the same time zone. Your flight began at 8:00 P.M. It ended at 11:00 P.M. How long did this trip take?

To answer this question, you calculate the **elapsed time**. Elapsed time is the amount of time that passes from one event to another. To calculate elapsed time, just subtract the time of the earlier event from the time of the later event.

In the case of the flight, subtract the departure time from the arrival time.

11:00	arrival time
− 8:00	departure time
3	hours travel time = elapsed time

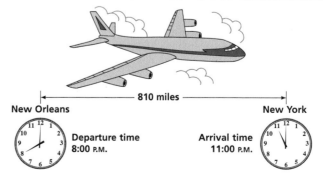

New Orleans ⊢———— 810 miles ————⊣ New York

Departure time
8:00 P.M.

Arrival time
11:00 P.M.

Speed

Speed
Rate at which the position of an object changes.

Once you know that something is moving, it's natural to wonder how fast it's going, or what its **speed** is. Speed tells how fast an object is moving. The more distance a moving object covers in a given time, the greater is its speed. For example, a cheetah can travel at a speed of 100 kilometers per hour. But an ant can cover only 36 meters in an hour. The cheetah has greater speed than the ant.

Notice that speed uses two units—distance and time. Distance is the length of the path traveled by the object in motion. You can use the following formula to find the speed of an object.

$$\text{speed} = \frac{\text{distance}}{\text{time}}$$

Suppose the airplane mentioned on the previous page traveled 810 miles between the two cities. The elapsed time for the trip was 3 hours. You can use the formula to calculate the speed of the airplane.

$$\text{speed} = \frac{810 \text{ miles}}{3 \text{ hours}}$$

$$\text{speed} = \frac{270 \text{ miles}}{1 \text{ hour}}$$

The speed of the airplane was 270 miles per hour. This means that each hour, the plane traveled 270 miles.

In the example, it is unlikely that the airplane traveled at a constant speed of 270 miles per hour during the entire flight. The plane starts and stops very slowly. Between the beginning and the end of the trip, the speed varies during the flight. The speed calculated is actually the average speed. The actual speed at any particular moment could be more or less than the average speed.

Speed does not have to be measured in miles per hour.

Think about a race at a track meet where the distance around the track is 400 meters. Suppose a runner completes the race in 40 seconds. What was the runner's speed?

$$speed = \frac{distance}{time}$$

$$speed = \frac{400\ meters}{40\ seconds}$$

$$speed = \frac{10\ meters}{1\ second}$$

The average speed of the runner is 10 meters per second. The runner covers an average distance of 10 meters each second.

Self-Check

Copy the following table. Calculate the average speed for each of these examples. The first one is completed for you.

Distance traveled	Time	Average speed
30 miles	5 hours	6 miles/hour
100 yards	13 seconds	
10 centimeters	5 seconds	
380 kilometers	2 hours	
3,825 feet	30 minutes	
15 inches	4 hours	
82 miles	10 hours	
10,000 meters	36 minutes	
23 feet	6 minutes	
120 kilometers	2 hours	

INVESTIGATION

4

Calculating Average Speed

Purpose

To calculate average speed over a given distance

Materials

✓ meterstick

✓ masking tape or powdered chalk

✓ stopwatch (or watch with second hand)

✓ calculator (optional)

Procedure

1. Copy the data table below on your paper. In the last column, *m/sec* means "meters per second."

Student's Name	Time (seconds)	Average speed
#1		m/sec
#2		m/sec
#3		m/sec

2. In a long hallway indoors or an open space outdoors, measure a straight racecourse 20 m long. Mark the starting and finish lines with tape or chalk.

3. Work with two classmates. Students #1 and #2 stand at the starting line. Student #3 holds the stopwatch at the finish line. Student #2 shouts "Go." Student #1 starts running. Student #3 starts the stopwatch. When student #1 reaches the finish line, student #3 stops the watch. Record the racer's time in the data table.

4. Allow all three students a chance to race.

Questions

1. Calculate each student's average speed. Use the formula

$$\text{speed} = \frac{\text{distance}}{\text{time}}$$

Record each average speed in the data table.

2. Did you run at your average speed for the entire race? Explain.

Objectives

After reading this lesson, you should be able to

▶ explain what gravity is.

▶ state the law of universal gravitation.

▶ explain how air resistance and gravity affect acceleration.

Gravity
Force of attraction between any two objects that have mass.

Law of universal gravitation
Gravitational force depends on the mass of the two objects involved and on the distance between them.

What Is Gravity?

One force with which you are probably familiar is the force of **gravity**. You might know that gravity keeps you from flying off Earth. If you are like many people, you might think of gravity as the pull exerted by Earth on other objects. But gravity is a force of attraction between any two objects that have mass.

The Law of Universal Gravitation

The gravitational force caused by an object depends on its mass. An object like Earth has a large mass. So it also produces a large gravitational force. Smaller objects, such as people, trees, and buildings, have much smaller gravitational forces because they have less mass. These forces are so small that they are difficult to observe.

Mass isn't the only thing that affects the pull of gravity. The distance between objects also determines how strong the force is due to gravity. The greater the distance between objects, the smaller the gravitational force is between them.

Think about an astronaut. When the astronaut is on Earth, gravity keeps him or her from flying off Earth. Earth pulls on the astronaut. But the astronaut also pulls on Earth. Earth's gravity is strongest near Earth's surface. As the astronaut travels away from Earth in a spaceship, the pull of Earth's gravity gets weaker. The astronaut may travel far from Earth, but Earth still exerts a force. In fact, Earth's gravity extends millions of kilometers into space.

Sir Isaac Newton, who stated the three laws of motion, put these ideas about gravity together in the **law of universal gravitation**. That law says two things. First, gravitational force depends on the mass of the two objects involved. Second, gravitational force depends on the distance between the objects.

Gravity and Acceleration

Have you ever jumped off a low diving board and then a high one? If so, you might have noticed that when you jumped from the higher board, you were moving faster when you struck the water. You hit the water harder. That is because the force of gravity causes an object to speed up as it falls.

After reaching a certain rate of falling, all objects have the same **acceleration** as they fall. Acceleration is a change in speed or direction. But another force—air resistance—also acts on a falling object. Air resistance is a form of friction caused by molecules of air rubbing against a moving object. Air resistance causes objects to fall at different speeds. The amount of air resistance acting on a moving object depends on the shape of the object. You can see in the picture that a sheet of paper will fall slower than a small stone. This is because the mass of the paper is spread out over a wider, thinner area than that of the stone. More molecules of air hit the surface of the paper.

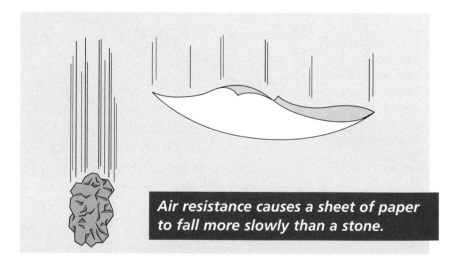

Air resistance causes a sheet of paper to fall more slowly than a stone.

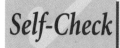

Self-Check

1. What two factors affect the pull of gravity?
2. Weight is a measure of the pull of gravity on an object. Use this information to explain why an astronaut weighs less on the moon than on Earth.
3. How are gravity and acceleration related?

Chapter 4 SUMMARY

- Energy is the ability to do work.
- Kinetic energy is energy of motion. Potential energy is stored energy.
- The six main forms of energy are chemical, heat, mechanical, nuclear, radiant, and electrical energy.
- Energy can change from one form to another.
- Energy cannot be created or destroyed.
- Motion is a change of position.
- Elapsed time is the time between events. It is calculated by subtracting the time of the earlier event from the time of the later event.

- Speed is the rate at which the position of an object changes. It is equal to distance divided by time.
- Gravity is a force of attraction between any two objects that have mass. According to the law of universal gravitation, the greater the masses are, the greater the force is. The greater the distance is, the less the force is.
- Due to gravity, all falling objects have the same acceleration. Air resistance acts on falling objects to slow them down.

Science Words		
acceleration, 72		law of conservation of energy, 66
elapsed time, 67		
energy, 63		law of universal gravitation, 71
generator, 65		motion, 67
gravity, 71		potential energy, 63
kinetic energy, 63		speed, 68

WORD BANK

distance

energy

gravity

kinetic energy

law of
    conservation
    of energy

law of universal
    gravitation

motion

nuclear energy

potential energy

speed

Vocabulary Review

Number your paper from 1 to 10. Then choose a word or words from the Word Bank that best completes each sentence. Write the answer on your paper.

1. _____ is a force of attraction between any two masses.

2. The _____ states that the force of attraction between two objects depends on their mass and their distance.

3. _____ is a change in position.

4. _____ is the ability to do work.

5. _____ is energy associated with the center of an atom.

6. The rate of an object's change in position is its _____.

7. _____ is stored energy.

8. _____ is the length of the path between two points.

9. _____ is energy of motion.

10. The _____ states that energy cannot be created or destroyed.

Concept Review

Number your paper from 1 to 8. Then choose the answer that best completes each sentence. Write the letter of the answer on your paper.

1. Light is an example of _____ energy.

   a. radiant   b. mechanical   c. nuclear

2. To calculate speed, you must _____.

   a. divide distance by time

   b. divide time by distance

   c. multiply time by distance

3. An unmoving object that could move has _____ energy.

   a. kinetic   b. potential   c. chemical

4. When energy changes from one form to another, the total amount of energy _____.

   a. decreases   b. increases   c. stays the same

5. The pull of gravity is affected by an object's _____ .

   a. weight   b. temperature   c. mass

6. A sheet of paper falls slower than a stone because of _____.

   a. air resistance   b. gravity   c. the stone's weight

7. A generator converts mechanical energy to _____ energy.

   a. heat   b. electrical   c. radiant

8. _____ energy is stored in the bonds between atoms.

   a. Chemical   b. Heat   c. Nuclear

Critical Thinking

Write the answer to each of the following questions.

1. Suppose some grease is being warmed on an electric stove and catches fire. The hot smoke causes a battery-powered fire detector to sound a siren and flash a warning light. Trace the conversions between energy forms involved.

2. The figure below shows the motion of a bicycle. Calculate the speed of the bicycle.

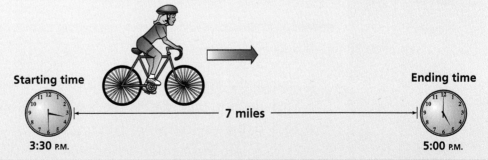

Starting time   Ending time

3:30 P.M.   7 miles   5:00 P.M.

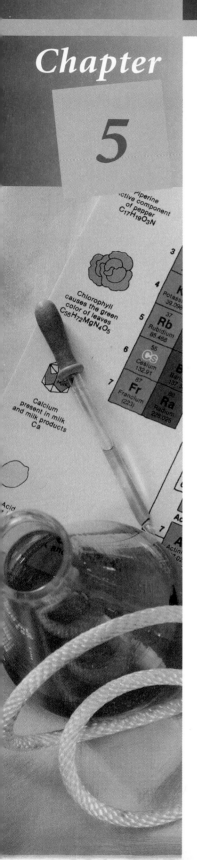

Work and Machines

Imagine what life would be like without machines. There would be no tools, no cars, no appliances. Most tasks would be much harder and take more time. Some would be impossible. In this chapter, you will explore work and simple machines. You will also learn about the role machines play in your daily life.

ORGANIZE YOUR THOUGHTS

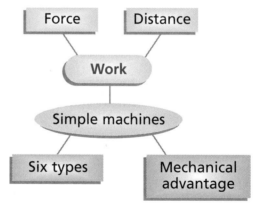

Force   Distance

Work

Simple machines

Six types   Mechanical advantage

Goals for Learning

▶ To explain what work is and to calculate work
▶ To name and describe six types of simple machines
▶ To describe the classes of levers
▶ To calculate mechanical advantage

Objectives

After reading this lesson, you should be able to

▶ explain what work is.

▶ measure and calculate work.

Joule
Metric unit of work.

Work
What happens when something changes its motion in the direction of the force being applied.

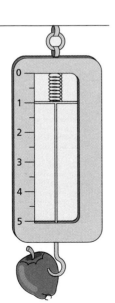

You probably do some "work" around your home. What things do you consider work? You might think of ironing clothes, washing dishes, taking out the garbage, and sweeping the floors. In everyday language, we use the word *work* as another word for *labor*.

Work

To scientists, however, **work** is what happens when a force makes something move in the direction of the force. A force is a push or a pull.

Suppose you struggled for an hour to lift a heavy box, but you could not budge it. No work was done in the scientific sense, because the box did not move. If you rolled a ball down a ramp, however, work was done because the ball changed its direction due to the force of gravity.

Measuring Work

How can you measure work? You can start by measuring how much force is used to do the work. Spring scales, like the one shown to the left, are used to measure force. In the metric system, force is measured in newtons. The spring scale shows that the apple is exerting a force of 1 newton. (In the English system, force is measured in pounds.)

To measure work, you must also measure the distance (in meters) through which the force acted. To find out how much work was done, use this formula.

> work = force × distance

Your answer will be in newton-meters. Scientists have a simpler name for a newton-meter. It is called a **joule**. So when calculating work, your answer will be in joules.

Suppose a woman is pushing a bike. She uses a force of 2 newtons and pushes the bike a distance of 10 meters. How much work did she do?

work = force × distance

work = 2 newtons × 10 meters

work = 20 newton-meters

work = 20 joules

Because force, distance, and work are always related, you can calculate any one of them if you know the other two. For example, if you know how much work was done and you know the distance, you can find out how much force was used. Simply take the amount of work done and divide it by the distance.

$$\text{force} = \frac{\text{work}}{\text{distance}}$$

If you know how much work was done and how much force was needed, you can calculate the distance. Take the amount of work done and divide it by the amount of force that was used.

$$\text{distance} = \frac{\text{work}}{\text{force}}$$

Self-Check

1. What is the metric unit of work?
2. What must you know to find the amount of work done on an object?
3. A man pushed a table, using a force of 8 newtons. He moved the table 13 meters. How much work did he do?
4. A woman lifted a box from the floor to a shelf. She used a force of 12 newtons. She did 18 newton-meters of work. How far did she lift the box?
5. One person solved 40 math problems in her head, and the other person picked up a kitten. Which one did more work, in the scientific sense?

Effort force
Force applied to a machine by the user.

Fulcrum
Fixed point around which a lever rotates.

Lever
Simple machine containing a bar that can turn around a fixed point.

Simple machine
Tool with few parts that makes it easier or possible to do work.

Have you ever tried to open a paint can using only your fingers? It is hard, if not impossible, to do so. With a screwdriver, you can easily pry the lid from the can. A screwdriver used in this way is an example of a **simple machine**. Simple machines make it easier or possible to do work. Simple machines change the size or direction of the force you apply or the distance through which the force moves.

The Lever

A **lever** is a simple machine. Levers can have many shapes. In its most basic form, the lever is a bar that is free to turn around a fixed point. The fixed point is called a **fulcrum**.

In the figure below, the woman is using a lever to move a boulder. Notice that the lever changes the direction of the force the woman applies. She pushes down, but the boulder moves up. The force the woman applies to the machine is called the **effort force** (F_E).

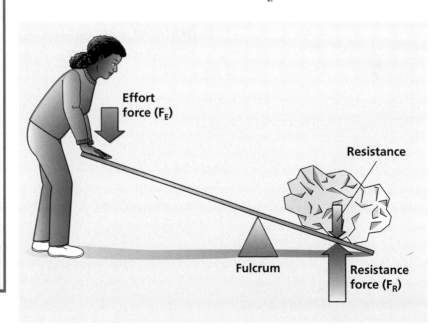

Effort force (F_E)

Resistance

Fulcrum

Resistance force (F_R)

The object to be lifted is called the resistance. In this example, the boulder is the resistance. Gravity is pulling down on the boulder, so the machine must exert a force upward to lift it. The force the machine uses to move the resistance is called the **resistance force** (F_R). The force the machine exerts is greater than the force the woman exerts. In other words, using the lever makes the woman's job easier. The lever takes the amount of force she exerts and increases that force.

Resistance force
Force applied to a machine by the object to be moved.

The Three Classes of Levers

Levers can be grouped into three classes. The classes of levers are based on the positions of the resistance force, the fulcrum, and the effort force.

The figure below illustrates a first-class lever. In a first-class lever, the fulcrum is positioned between the effort and the resistance. A first-class lever changes the direction of a force and can also increase the force.

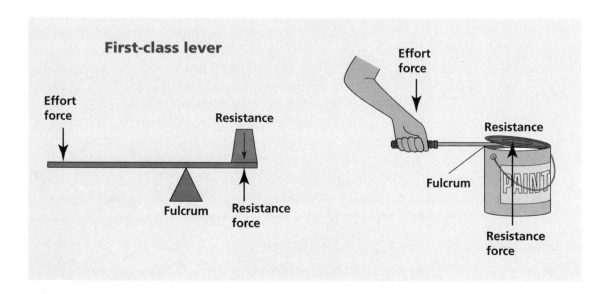

First-class lever

In a second-class lever, shown below, the resistance is positioned between the effort and the fulcrum. Second-class levers always increase the force applied to them. They do not change the direction of the force. Wheelbarrows, paper cutters, and most nutcrackers are examples of second-class levers.

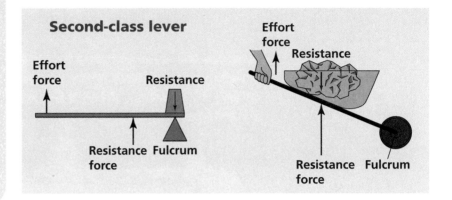

The diagram below shows a third-class lever. Notice that the effort is between the fulcrum and the resistance. Third-class levers increase the distance through which the force moves, which causes the resistance to move farther or faster. A broom is an example of a third-class lever. You use effort force on the handle between the fulcrum and the resistance force. When you move the handle of the broom a short distance, the brush end moves a greater distance.

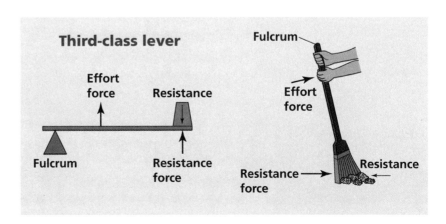

Mechanical Advantage

The number of times a simple machine multiplies your effort force is called the **mechanical advantage** of the machine. You can find a lever's mechanical advantage (MA) with this formula.

$$\text{mechanical advantage} = \frac{\text{resistance force}}{\text{effort force}}, \text{ or } MA = \frac{F_R}{F_E}$$

Suppose the lever pictured below lifts a resistance weighing 30 newtons when you apply an effort force of only 10 newtons. What is the lever's mechanical advantage?

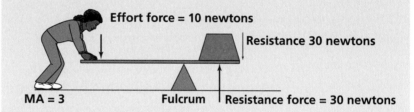

Effort force = 10 newtons

Resistance 30 newtons

MA = 3　　　　　Fulcrum　Resistance force = 30 newtons

$$MA = \frac{F_R}{F_E}$$

$$MA = \frac{30 \text{ newtons}}{10 \text{ newtons}}$$

$$MA = 3$$

The mechanical advantage is 3. The lever has multiplied your effort force by 3. This makes the object easier for you to lift.

Self-Check

1. Draw a first-class, second-class, and third-class lever. Show the fulcrum, effort force, and resistance for each.
2. What is mechanical advantage?
3. Suppose a lever lets you lift a rock weighing 60 newtons when you apply an effort force of 12 newtons. What is the lever's mechanical advantage?

What Are Other Kinds of Simple Machines?

Pulley
Simple machine made up of a rope, chain, or belt wrapped around a wheel.

There are six types of simple machines, including the lever. In this lesson, you will learn about the other five types.

The Pulley

A **pulley** is a wheel with a rope, chain, or belt around it. The figure shows a single pulley.

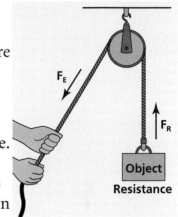

A single pulley changes the direction of the force you apply, but it does not multiply that force. The mechanical advantage is 1. You can use this type of pulley to lift a heavy object by pulling down instead of lifting up.

The pulley shown above is called a fixed pulley because it is fixed or attached at the top. The wheel is free to spin, but it cannot move up and down.

The pulley shown below is a movable pulley. As effort is applied to a movable pulley, the entire pulley and the object attached will rise. You can use this type of pulley to make a lifting job easier. Because the rope supports the pulley from two directions, you need to apply only half as much force to lift the object. Therefore, the pulley has a mechanical advantage of 2.

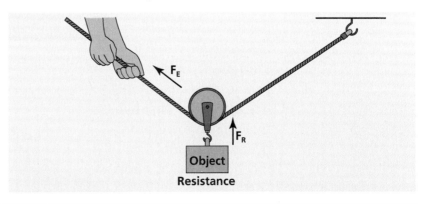

However, you must pull twice as far on the rope as the object actually moves. For example, to lift the object 1 meter, you must pull the rope 2 meters. The direction of the force is not reversed. To lift the object up, you must pull up.

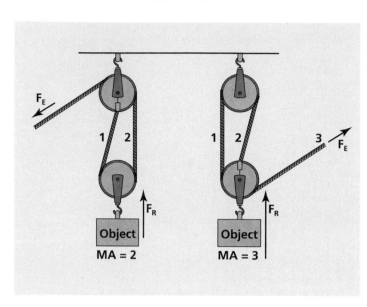

Pulleys can be combined. Look at the examples to the left. Note the number of ropes supporting the object. Note the mechanical advantage (MA) of each system. The MA is usually about equal to the number of supporting ropes. In the left pulley system, two ropes support the object. MA is 2. In the right pulley system, three ropes support the object, so MA is 3.

Inclined plane
Simple machine made up of a ramp, used to lift an object.

The Inclined Plane

The **inclined plane** has no moving parts, but it is a machine.

Inclined planes, such as the one pictured below, decrease the force you need to move an object. Once again, you pay for this decrease in effort force by an increase in the distance the object has to be moved. For example, if a delivery person needs to put a box on a truck that is 1 meter from the ground, he might use an inclined plane, or ramp,

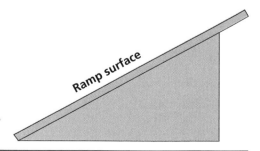

An inclined plane is a ramp on which an object can be pushed up.

Ramp surface

to make his job easier. Rather than lifting the box 1 meter straight up, he can push it up the ramp. It takes less force to push an object than to pick it up. However, he must move the object farther, as shown in the figure below.

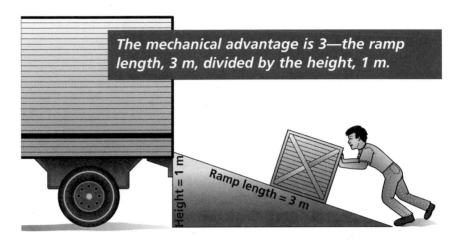

The mechanical advantage is 3—the ramp length, 3 m, divided by the height, 1 m.

Height = 1 m

Ramp length = 3 m

The mechanical advantage of an inclined plane is the length of the ramp divided by the vertical (up-and-down) height. The more gradual the slant, the greater the mechanical advantage, but the farther the object must go.

Screw
Simple machine made up of an inclined plane wrapped around a straight piece of metal.

The Screw

Another kind of simple machine, the **screw**, is a form of inclined plane. Think of a screw as a straight piece of metal with an inclined plane wrapped around it.

The mechanical advantage of a screw depends on the distance between the threads. The smaller the distance, the more times the inclined plane is wrapped around, and the greater is the mechanical advantage.

The smaller the distance between threads, the greater the mechanical advantage.

Unwrapped

Thread

Inclined plane wrapped around, forming a screw

An inclined plane

Wedge
Simple machine made up of an inclined plane or pair of inclined planes that are moved.

Wheel and axle
Simple machine made up of a wheel attached to a shaft.

The Wedge

A **wedge** is an inclined plane that moves when it is used. It is thick at one end and thinner at the other. A wedge is often made up of two inclined planes joined together. Both edges are slanted. A wedge can be used for jobs like splitting wood apart. A force applied to the thick end is multiplied and acts at the thin end, piercing the wood. The thinner and more gradual the wedge, the greater is the mechanical advantage.

This person is using a wedge tool called an adze to split a log.

Inclined planes

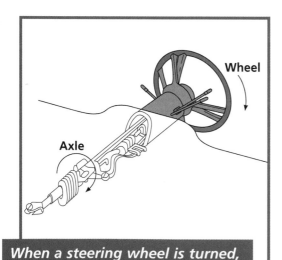

Wheel

Axle

When a steering wheel is turned, it rotates a steering shaft (an axle).

The Wheel and Axle

An automobile steering wheel and a doorknob are examples of a simple machine called a **wheel and axle**. In this machine, a wheel is attached to a shaft called an axle.

A wheel and axle increases the force you apply to the wheel. The multiplied force can then turn something else attached to the axle. The mechanical advantage of a wheel and axle depends on the size of the wheel compared to the thickness of the axle. The bigger the wheel is in comparison to the thickness of the axle, the greater is the mechanical advantage.

1. What is the difference between a fixed pulley and a movable pully?

2. In each of the pulleys shown, what is the mechanical advantage?

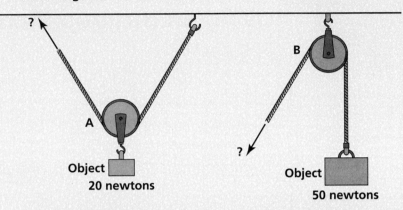

A

Object
20 newtons

B

Object
50 newtons

3. What is an inclined plane? How can you find the mechanical advantage of an inclined plane?

4. Screws and wedges are variations of what simple machine?

5. Which will have a greater mechanical advantage: a thin, gradual wedge or a thick, greatly sloping one?

SCIENCE
IN YOUR LIFE

Which simple machines do you have at home?

Many common objects that people use every day are actually simple machines. Some examples are listed below. How many examples of simple machines can you find in your home? How does each object help you do work?

Levers: wheelbarrow, broom, rake, paper cutter, crowbar, punch-type can opener, car jack, shovel

Two levers joined together: scissors, pliers, tweezers, paper punch

Wedge: ax blade, knife blade

Wheel and axle: doorknob, steering wheel, knob on a TV set or other device

Using an Inclined Plane

Purpose

To compare the force needed to lift an object straight up with the force needed to pull the object up an inclined plane

Materials

✓ heavy wooden block
✓ string
✓ spring scale
✓ wide board 75 cm long

Procedure

1. Copy the data table below on your paper.

Distance block moved	Force needed to lift block	Mechanical advantage
25 cm straight up	g	
50 cm on inclined plane	g	0

2. Tie string around the block. Hang it on the spring scale. Lift the block 25 cm straight up. How much force is needed to lift the block? Record the force in the table.

3. Use books to raise one end of the board 25 cm high. Pull the block up the board with the spring scale. How much force is needed to raise the block 25 cm using the inclined plane? Record the force in the data table.

Questions

1. Calculate the inclined plane's mechanical advantage, using the formula. Record the results in the data table.

$$MA = \frac{\text{length of inclined plane}}{\text{distance block was raised}}$$

2. Compare the force needed to lift the block straight up and the force needed to pull it up the inclined plane. Which force was greater? How many times greater?

Chapter 5   SUMMARY

- Work is what happens when a force makes something move in the direction of the force.

- To measure work, force and distance must be measured.

- Simple machines make doing work easier by changing the size or direction of a force or the distance across which the force moves.

- Effort force is the force applied to a machine by the person using it. Resistance force is the force applied by a machine against a resistance.

- A lever is a bar that turns around a fulcrum. A lever is a simple machine.

- Levers are grouped into three classes, based on the positions of the resistance force, the fulcrum, and the effort force.

- The mechanical advantage of a simple machine is the number of times by which the machine multiplies effort force.

- There are six kinds of simple machines.

- A pulley is a simple machine made up of a rope, chain, or belt wrapped around a wheel.

- An inclined plane has no moving parts but is a simple machine.

- A screw and a wedge are special forms of inclined planes.

- A wheel and axle is a simple machine with a wheel attached to a shaft.

Science Words

effort force, 79	resistance force, 80
fulcrum, 79	screw, 85
inclined plane, 84	simple machine, 79
joule, 77	wedge, 86
lever, 79	wheel and axle, 86
mechanical advantage, 82	work, 77
pulley, 83	

WORD BANK

effort force

inclined plane

joule

lever

mechanical advantage

pulley

resistance force

simple machine

spring scale

wedge

wheel and axle

work

Vocabulary Review

Number your paper from 1 to 12. Then choose a word or words from the Word Bank that best complete each sentence. Write the answer on your paper.

1. Resistance force divided by effort force equals _____.

2. A(n) _____ is a ramplike simple machine.

3. Force multiplied by distance equals _____.

4. A(n) _____ consists of a rope, chain, or belt wrapped around a wheel.

5. _____ is the force applied by a machine against the resistance.

6. A(n) _____ is a bar that turns around a fixed point.

7. A(n) _____ is a tool with few parts.

8. A(n) _____ is an inclined plane that moves when it is used.

9. _____ is the force applied to a machine by the user.

10. A newton-meter is also called a(n) _____ .

11. A(n) _____ has a wheel attached to a shaft.

12. A(n) _____ is used to measure force.

Concept Review

Number your paper from 1 to 6. Then choose the answer that best completes each sentence. Write the letter of the answer on your paper.

1. A paper cutter is an example of a _____ lever.

   a. first-class   b. second-class   c. third-class

2. A pulley that has five upward-pulling ropes has a mechanical advantage of approximately _____.

   a. 1/5   b. 5   c. 10

3. A screw contains a(n) _____.

    a. axle   **b.** wheel   **c.** inclined plane

4. A doorknob is an example of a _____.

    a. wedge   **b.** wheel and axle   **c.** pulley

5. To calculate how much work was done, you should _____.

    a. multiply force by distance

    b. divide force by distance

    c. divide resistance force by effort force

6. Force is measured in units called _____.

    a. joules   **b.** newtons   **c.** meters

Critical Thinking

Write the answer to each of the following questions.

1. What class of lever is shown in the diagram below? How can you tell?

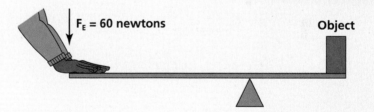

2. Which type of simple machine would you use to lift an engine out of a car? Could you lift the engine using only one of those machines? Explain your answer.

Test Taking Tip | Be sure you understand what the test question is asking. Reread it if you have to.

Chapter

6

Heat

Imagine curling up in front of a fire on a chilly night. The light from the fire would probably cast an inviting glow throughout the room. The heat from the fire might make your fingers and toes feel warm. In this chapter, you'll find out about heat. You'll learn different ways to measure heat. You will also find out how heat moves from one place to another.

ORGANIZE YOUR THOUGHTS

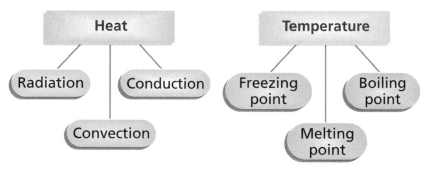

Goals for Learning

▶ To explain how heat energy can be produced
▶ To explain how heat changes matter
▶ To explain how temperature is measured
▶ To explain the difference between temperature and heat
▶ To explain how matter is heated by conduction, convection, and radiation

Objectives

After reading this lesson, you should be able to

▶ define heat.

▶ explain how heat energy can do work.

▶ explain how heat is produced.

▶ describe some sources of heat.

What happens if you hold an ice cube in your hand? The heat from your hand melts the ice cube. **Heat** is a form of energy that results from the motion of particles in matter. Heat energy flows from a warmer object, such as your hand, to a cooler object, such as the ice cube.

In Chapter 4, you learned that heat is a form of energy. Energy can do work. Therefore, heat can do work. Machines can change heat energy into useful mechanical energy. For example, a steam engine uses the heat energy contained in steam to move the parts of the engine.

Sources of Heat

The sun is Earth's most important heat source. A **heat source** is a place from which heat energy comes. The motion of the atoms and molecules in the sun gives off the heat energy that warms Earth.

Other forms of energy can be changed into heat energy. For example, hold your hands as shown in the picture below and rub them together rapidly. Notice that your hands begin to feel warm. Friction between your hands is a form of mechanical energy that produces heat.

Heat

A form of energy resulting from the motion of particles in matter; heat energy flows from a warmer object to a cooler object.

Heat source

A place from which heat energy comes.

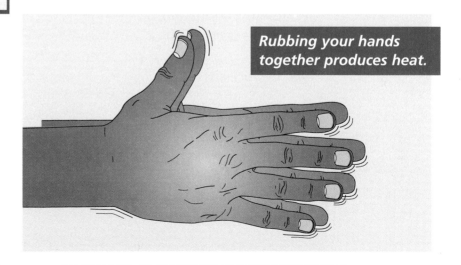

Rubbing your hands together produces heat.

Electricity is also a heat source. Look at the toaster below. When energy from an electric current passes through the wires of the toaster, the wires become hot. This energy can toast bread. What other appliances can you name that change electrical energy into heat energy?

Electricity produces heat energy that can toast bread.

Another source of heat is chemical energy. When substances react chemically with each other, they sometimes release heat. For example, when natural gas and other fuels burn, they produce heat.

Nuclear energy is another form of energy you have learned about. Nuclear energy is released when the centers of the atoms split or join together. Stars shine because their atoms release nuclear energy. Nuclear energy also produces heat.

Self-Check

1. What is heat?
2. Why does an ice cube melt when you hold it in your hand?
3. What produces heat energy in the sun?
4. Name three sources of heat energy.
5. Give an example of how another form of energy can be changed into heat energy.

Evaporate
To change from a liquid to a gas.

Matter exists in different states. In a solid, the particles are closer together than they are in a liquid or a gas. The particles move slower in the solid. Heat can cause particles to move faster and move farther apart. Heat can change matter from one state to another.

Changing From a Liquid to a Gas

You might have noticed that if you boil water for a period of time, the amount of water gradually decreases. What happens to the water? Heat makes the water molecules move faster. As the molecules move faster, they bump into each other and push each other apart more often. As a result, the water **evaporates**, or changes from a liquid to a gas.

Heat rises.

Heat causes the particles of water to move farther apart.

Changing From a Solid to a Liquid

Why does an ice cube (a solid) melt if it is left in a warm room? Heat speeds up the moving molecules in the ice cube. The molecules move apart. The solid ice cube changes to liquid water.

Expanding and Contracting Matter

Contract
To become smaller in size.

Expand
To become larger in size.

Heat causes particles in matter to push each other farther apart. Then the matter **expands**, or fills up more space. The figure shows a joint in a metal bridge. Summer heat makes the material in the bridge expand. What might happen if the bridge had no expansion joint?

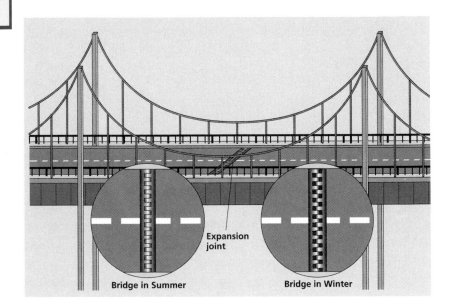

Expansion joint

Bridge in Summer   Bridge in Winter

Solids, liquids, and gases do not expand equally. In most cases, liquids expand more than solids. Gases usually expand the most.

Sometimes, matter loses heat. Particles in matter move more slowly and stay closer together as they lose heat. The matter **contracts**, or takes up less space. In the figure above, notice the joint of the bridge in winter. The material in the bridge contracts in cold weather. Water is a material that behaves differently. Cooled water contracts until it reaches 4°C. Below this temperature, water expands until it freezes at 0°C.

Self-Check

1. What happens to an ice cube when it is heated?
2. What happens when water in a puddle evaporates?
3. How does heat affect the amount of space matter fills?

Objectives

After reading this lesson, you should be able to

► explain how temperature is measured.

► compare and contrast temperature scales.

► describe freezing point, melting point, and boiling point.

► explain the difference between temperature and heat.

Temperature
A measure of how fast an object's particles are moving.

Suppose you place your hand into a bowl of cool water such as the one in the picture. Heat energy from your hand flows into the water and makes the water warmer.

Heat from your hand will increase the temperature of the cool water.

The more your hand heats the water, the faster the water particles move. **Temperature** measures how fast an object's particles are moving. The faster an object's particles move, the higher its temperature is.

Touching an object does not always give an accurate measurement of the object's temperature. For example, if you place your hand in cold water, heat energy from your hand moves to the water and your hand becomes cooler. If you move the same hand out of the cold water and into a container of lukewarm water, the water will feel hotter than it actually is because your hand is cool.

Thermometers

You often can't rely on your sense of touch to accurately tell temperature. So how can you measure temperature accurately? A **thermometer** is a measuring instrument used to measure temperature. The pictures show different kinds of thermometers.

Thermometer
A device that measures temperature.

How does this thermometer show temperature?

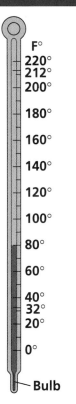

F°
220°
212°
200°
180°
160°
140°
120°
100°
80°
60°
40°
32°
20°
0°

Bulb

The thermometer shown to the left is a glass tube with a small amount of liquid inside. The liquid is usually colored alcohol. As heat causes the particles of liquid to expand, or move farther apart, the liquid moves up the tube, measuring higher temperatures. The more heat that passes to the liquid, the more the liquid will expand and the higher the liquid moves in the tube. When the liquid stops expanding, it stops beside a number on the tube. This number tells the temperature of the substance touching the bulb of the thermometer.

The picture below shows an electronic thermometer. Many doctors and medical workers use this kind of thermometer to take people's temperatures. It measures temperatures very quickly.

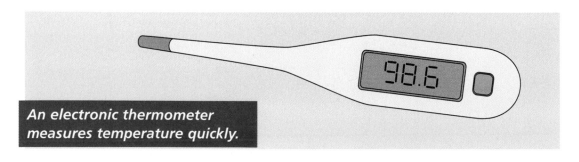

An electronic thermometer measures temperature quickly.

Temperature Scales

Two common scales are used to measure temperature. People in the United States usually use the **Fahrenheit scale**. Fahrenheit is abbreviated as F. People in most other countries use the **Celsius scale**. Scientists also use the Celsius scale. Celsius is abbreviated as C. It is the metric measure of temperature.

Look at the thermometers on this page to compare the Fahrenheit scale with the Celsius scale. Find the equally spaced units on each scale. For both temperature scales, temperature is measured in units called **degrees** (°). The temperature shown on the Fahrenheit scale is 68 degrees Fahrenheit. It is written as 68°F. The same temperature in the Celsius scale is 20 degrees Celsius. It is written as 20°C.

Any temperature below zero degrees is written with a minus (−) sign. For example, a temperature of 10 degrees below zero on the Celsius scale is written as −10°C. The table on the next page shows how temperatures on the Fahrenheit scale and the Celsius scale are written. The table also shows how to read the temperatures on each scale.

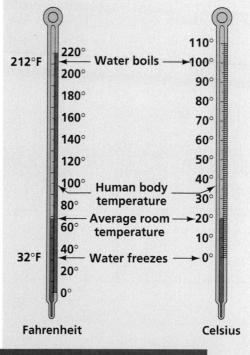

How do the temperatures on these two scales compare?

Temperature conversion table				
°C	°F		°C	°F
100	212		45	113
95	203		40	104
90	194		35	95
85	185		30	86
80	176		25	77
75	167		20	68
70	158		15	59
65	149		10	50
60	140		5	41
55	131		0	32
50	122			

If you know the temperature of a substance on one scale, you can convert to an equal temperature on the other scale. The table shows how temperatures convert from one scale to the other.

Freezing Point

What happens when you place a container of water in the freezer? The water gradually changes to ice. The temperature at which a liquid changes to a solid is called its **freezing point**. On the Celsius scale, the temperature at which water freezes is 0°. On the Fahrenheit scale, the temperature at which water freezes is 32°.

Boiling point
The temperature at which a liquid changes to a gas.

Freezing point
The temperature at which a liquid changes to a solid.

Melting point
The temperature at which a solid changes to a liquid.

Melting Point

The temperature at which a solid changes to a liquid is called its **melting point**. The melting point of a substance is the same as its freezing point. The term *melting point* is used when a substance is being heated. When ice is heated, it changes to a liquid at a temperature of 0°C. Therefore, the melting point of ice is 0°C.

Boiling Point

The **boiling point** of a substance is the temperature at which it changes from a liquid to a gas. The temperature at which water boils is 100° on the Celsius scale. On the Fahrenheit scale, the boiling point is 212°

Every substance has its own freezing and boiling points. For example, alcohol freezes at −130°C and boils at 78°C. Scientists use the freezing and boiling points of substances to help identify unknown substances.

Temperature and Heat

Temperature and heat are different. Temperature is a measure of how fast the molecules in a substance are moving. Heat depends on the temperature of a substance and the amount of matter, or mass, the substance has.

As the temperature of an object increases, the amount of heat in the object also increases. If two objects of different mass are at the same temperature, the object with the greater mass will give off more heat. The temperature of the lighted candle in the picture is the same as the temperature of the bonfire. But the bonfire has more mass, so it gives off more heat.

The bonfire gives off more heat than the candle does.

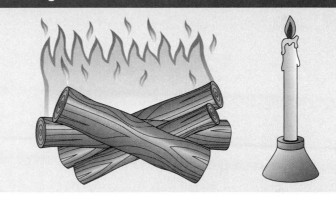

Self-Check

1. Explain how a liquid thermometer works.
2. Write the following temperatures, using words and symbols.
   a. thirty-four degrees Fahrenheit
   b. sixty-six degrees Celsius
   c. four degrees below zero on the Fahrenheit scale
   d. one hundred ten degrees on the Celsius scale
3. What is meant by the freezing point, the melting point, and the boiling point of a substance?
4. Explain the difference between heat and temperature.
5. Container A contains 10 L of water. Container B contains 2 L of water. The water in both containers is the same temperature. Which container has more heat energy? Explain.

6

Measuring Temperature

Purpose
To use thermometers to measure water temperatures in °F and °C

Materials
✓ 3 foam-plastic cups
✓ masking tape
✓ water
✓ 3 thermo-meters marked with both °F and °C
✓ 4 ice cubes

Procedure
1. Copy the data table below on your paper.

Water temperature						
	Cup 1 (in shade)		Cup 2 (in sun)		Cup 3 (with ice)	
Start	°C	°F	°C	°F	°C	°F
After 15 minutes	°C	°F	°C	°F	°C	°F

2. Use masking tape to label the cups 1, 2, and 3. Fill each cup about half full with water.

3. Put a thermometer in each cup. Read the temperature of the water in each cup in °F and °C. Record these starting temperatures in the data table.

4. Leave cups 1 and 3 in the shade. Put cup 2 where it will get sunlight. Put four ice cubes in cup 3.

5. After 15 minutes, read and record the temperatures.

Questions
1. What happened to the temperature of the water in cup 1? in cup 2? in cup 3?

2. What caused the temperature change in cup 1? in cup 2? in cup 3?

Explore Further
Repeat the investigation. Let the cups sit for 1 hour or more. Record the temperatures every 5 minutes. What happens to the temperature in cup 2? in cup 3?

Objectives

After reading this lesson, you should be able to

▶ explain how matter is heated by radiation.

▶ explain how matter is heated by conduction.

▶ explain how matter is heated by convection.

Radiation
The movement of energy through a vacuum.

Vacuum
Space that contains no matter.

Think about different ways you can travel from one place to another. You might walk or run. You might ride a bicycle. You might travel in cars, buses, trains, boats, or airplanes. Energy also has different ways of moving from warm matter to cool matter.

Radiation

The sun is a long distance from Earth—150 million kilometers. Yet the sun heats Earth. How does the sun's energy travel the long distance from its surface to Earth? The energy must travel through a **vacuum**. A vacuum is a space that has no matter. Energy from the sun reaches us by **radiation**. Radiation moves energy without traveling from particle to particle. The energy can heat matter.

Heat from sources other than the sun can also travel by radiation. You can see an example in the drawing below. Heat energy from the fire moves into the room by radiation and then heats the air.

Conduction

You probably know that if you held a strip of metal in a flame it would get hot. Why does this happen? The metal gets hot because of **conduction**. Heat travels by conduction when molecules bump into each other.

Look at the strip of copper in the drawing. Heat from the flame makes the copper particles near the flame move faster. As the particles move faster, they hit other particles. These particles then bump into the particles farther up on the strip of copper. They transfer energy. As a result, the slower particles move faster. Eventually, all the molecules in the copper are moving fast. In other words, the entire piece of copper becomes hot.

Energy moves easily through some kinds of matter. A substance that allows heat energy to flow through it easily is called a **conductor**. Most metals, such as copper, silver, gold, aluminum, and tin, are good conductors.

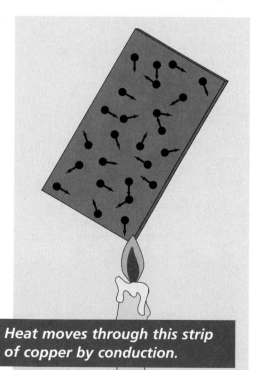

Heat moves through this strip of copper by conduction.

A material that does not conduct heat well is called an **insulator**. Insulators are used in the walls and ceilings of homes to keep heat out in summer and keep heat inside in winter. Some good insulators are glass, wood, sand, soil, Styrofoam, and air.

Convection

Convection
Flow of energy that occurs when a warm liquid or gas rises.

Convection is a method of heat movement that happens when the particles of a gas or a liquid rise. As they rise, they carry heat.

Find the heater in the drawing below. First, conduction heats the air touching the heater. Then the warm air rises. Cool air moves in to take its place. The heater warms the cool air and it rises. The warm air cools as it moves through the room. Then it flows back to the heater and is warmed again. The arrows show how heat energy flows up and around the room. Convection keeps the air moving.

Convection also happens in liquids. Suppose a pot of cold water is placed on the stove. Heat is conducted from the hot burner to the pot and then to the water at the very bottom of the pot. Then convection heats the rest of the water. The warm water rises and the cooler water sinks.

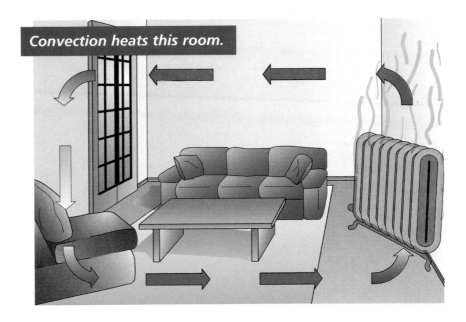

Convection heats this room.

Self-Check

1. How does the sun's heat travel to Earth?
2. How does heat move by conduction?
3. Explain how convection heats a room.

How do different heating systems work?

How can you control the temperature of your home? The chart describes some types of heating systems that people use to keep their homes at a comfortable temperature.

Heating Systems

Type of system	Description	Special features
Hot water	A furnace heats the water. A pump circulates the water through pipes to a radiator in each room.	Convection and radiation circulate heat throughout the room.
Steam	A boiler sends steam to pipes. Steam carries heat through the pipes to radiators in each room.	Radiation and convection circulate heat throughout the room.
Forced air	Air is heated by a furnace. It is then pumped into rooms through vents at the floor of each room.	Forced convection circulates heat throughout the room.
Passive solar	The sun's rays pass through a large door or window. They heat up a large tile or rock wall. Heat radiates into the room from the wall and sets up convection currents.	Radiation and convection distribute heat.
Radiant electric	Electric current heats up wires in baseboards, walls, and/or ceilings.	Heat radiates from these specific places.

1. Which heating systems heat a home by convection?

2. Which heating systems provide radiant heat?

3. Which type of heating system would be more efficient in a hot, sunny climate than in a cold climate? Why?

- Heat is a form of energy. It results from the motion of the particles in matter. Heat energy flows from a warmer object to a cooler object.

- Mechanical, solar, electrical, chemical, and nuclear energy are sources of heat.

- Heat can cause matter to change from one state to another.

- Heat causes matter to expand; loss of heat causes matter to contract.

- Temperature measures the motion of molecules.

- Thermometers with Fahrenheit and Celsius scales are used to measure temperature.

- The freezing point, the melting point, and the boiling point are important temperatures for all substances.

- Heat depends on the temperature and the mass of an object.

- Heat travels by radiation, conduction, and convection.

Science Words		
boiling point, 100		freezing point, 100
Celsius scale, 99		heat, 93
conduction, 104		heat source, 93
conductor, 104		insulator, 104
contract, 96		melting point, 100
convection, 105		radiation, 103
degree, 99		temperature, 97
evaporate, 95		thermometer, 98
expand, 96		vacuum, 103
Fahrenheit scale, 99		

WORD BANK

Celsius scale
conductors
contracts
convection
degree
expands
freezing point
heat
insulators
melting point
thermometer

Vocabulary Review

Number your paper from 1 to 11. Then choose a word or words from the Word Bank that best complete each sentence. Write the answer on your paper.

1. _____ are materials that carry heat easily.

2. A device used to measure temperature is a(n) _____.

3. The temperature at which water changes to ice is the _____ of water.

4. Scientists use thermometers with the _____ to measure temperature.

5. The _____ of a substance is the same as its freezing point.

6. The flow of energy that occurs when a warm gas rises is _____.

7. A _____ is a unit of measurement on a temperature scale.

8. Matter usually fills up more space when it _____.

9. _____ is the flow of energy from a warmer object to a cooler object.

10. When matter _____, it usually takes up less space.

11. Glass, wood, and air are examples of _____.

Concept Review

Number your paper from 1 to 7. Then choose the answer that best completes each sentence. Write the letter of the answer on your paper.

1. The flow of heat energy from one molecule to the next is _____.

   a. convection   b. conduction   c. radiation

2. Earth's most important heat source is _____.

   a. heating systems   b. heating oil   c. the sun

3. When water changes from a liquid to a gas, it _____.

   a. evaporates   b. radiates   c. conducts

4. The temperature scale commonly used in the United States is the _____.

   a. Fahrenheit scale   b. heat scale   c. Celsius scale

5. A vacuum is a space that has no _____.

   a. heat   b. radiation   c. matter

6. A material that does not carry heat well is a(n) _____.

   a. conductor   b. insulator   c. vacuum

7. The motion of particles of matter produces _____.

   a. vacuums   b. radiation   c. heat energy

Critical Thinking

Write the answer to each of the following questions.

1. The objects shown in the picture to the left are the same temperature. Do they contain the same amount of heat energy? Explain your answer.

2. Look at the picture to the right. Explain how the water in the pot is being heated.

Test Taking Tip   When you read over your written answer, imagine that you are someone reading it for the first time. Ask yourself if the information makes sense. Revise your answer to make it as clear as you can.

Chapter

7

Sound and Light

Perhaps you have heard your favorite music being played by a band. Musical instruments usually make pleasing sounds. In this chapter, you will learn how sounds are produced and how sounds travel from one place to another. You also will find out that sound and light are alike in some ways.

ORGANIZE YOUR THOUGHTS

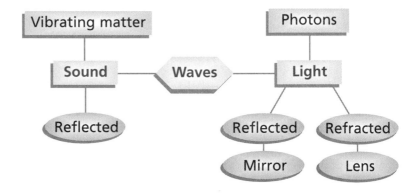

Goals for Learning

▶ To explain how sounds are produced
▶ To explain how sound travels
▶ To describe the nature of light
▶ To describe the visible spectrum
▶ To explain reflection and refraction of light
▶ To explain how mirrors and lenses affect light rays

Objectives

After reading this lesson, you should be able to

▶ explain what sound is.

▶ explain how sound is produced.

▶ explain how sound energy moves in waves.

Vibrate
To move rapidly back and forth.

You hear many kinds of sounds every minute of every day. But do you know what sound is? Sound is a form of energy. Scientists who study sound also study human hearing and the effect of sound on different objects.

How Sound Is Produced

All the sounds you hear are made when matter **vibrates**. To vibrate means to move quickly back and forth. Look at the bell on this page. When the clapper hits the bell, energy from the clapper causes the bell to vibrate. When the bell vibrates, it moves back and forth. The bell pushes the air around it. You can see in the diagram that as the bell vibrates to the right, it pushes together the air particles to the right of the bell. When it vibrates back to the left, the air particles to the right of the bell move apart. Those particles to the left of the bell are squeezed together. As the bell continues to vibrate, the air particles on each side are squeezed together and spread apart many times.

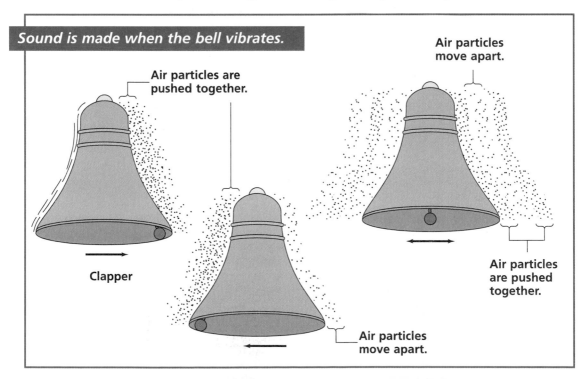

Sound is made when the bell vibrates.

Air particles are pushed together.

Air particles move apart.

Clapper

Air particles move apart.

Air particles are pushed together.

How Sound Travels

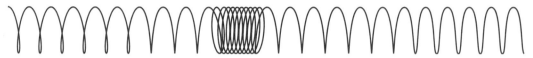

The movement of the air molecules around a vibrating object is a **sound wave**. You cannot see a sound wave. Sound waves move out from the object in all directions. As the sound waves travel farther from the object, they become weaker. The figures of the wire spring show how sound energy travels in waves.

Sound wave
A wave produced by vibrations.

Figure A
The wire is pinched together at one end.

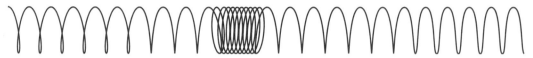

Figure B
The "wave" moves across the spring.

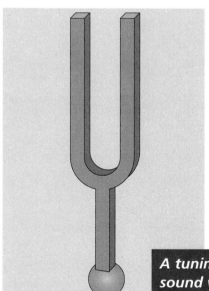

Some things make sounds even though you cannot see them vibrate. For example, if you strike a tuning fork, you will not see it vibrate. But you will hear the sound it makes. You can see evidence of sound waves by placing the end of a tuning fork that has been struck into a small container filled with water. You will notice water splashing out of the container. The vibrations of the tuning fork cause the water to move about.

A tuning fork vibrates, producing sound waves, when it is struck.

Self-Check

1. How is sound produced?
2. How does sound travel?

7

Modeling Sound Waves

Purpose

To model the vibration of molecules in a sound wave

Procedure

1. Work with two classmates. Students #1 and #2 sit about 2 m apart on the floor and stretch the Slinky™ between them. Student #3 ties the red ribbon to the Slinky near one end, the blue ribbon near the other end, and the yellow ribbon in the middle.

2. Student #1 quickly bumps his or her end of the Slinky forward one time. Watch the Slinky.

3. Wait until the Slinky stops moving. Then student #2 quickly bumps his or her end of the Slinky back and forth several times. Watch the Slinky.

4. Switch places and repeat until each student has had a turn being #1, #2, and #3.

Questions

1. What happened when the Slinky was bumped once? What happened when it was bumped several times?

2. How did the ribbons move?

3. In this model, what did the "bumps" represent?

4. What did the coils of the Slinky represent?

You see **light** everywhere. You see objects because light is reflected from them. But what is light? Light is a form of energy that you can sometimes see. Visible light is produced by objects that are at high temperatures. The sun is the major source of light on Earth.

Light as a Particle

Scientists have done experiments to gather information about light. Some scientific experiments suggest that light acts like a particle. Evidence tells scientists that light is made up of bundles of energy called **photons**. Photons are like small particles. A single photon is too small to be seen.

Look at the light coming from the flashlight. Streams of photons make up each beam of light. Each photon carries a certain amount of energy.

Light
A form of energy that sometimes can be seen.

Photons
Small bundles of energy that make up light.

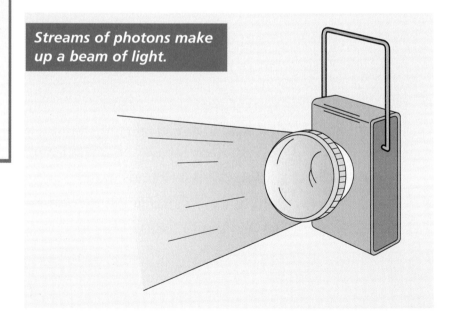

Streams of photons make up a beam of light.

Did You Know?

Light as a Wave

Other scientific evidence suggests that, like sound, light travels in waves. As a result of their findings, most scientists agree that light seems to have properties of both particles and waves. Scientists agree that light travels as waves in a straight line. Most properties of light can be explained in terms of its wave nature.

Light waves move like waves in water.

Light waves move like waves in water. However, light waves travel fastest through empty space. Light waves move more slowly as they pass through matter. In fact, light waves cannot pass through some matter at all.

Light waves travel more quickly than sound waves. Light waves travel about 300,000 km per second. This is the fastest possible speed anything is known to travel.

Colors in White Light

The light you see from the sun is white light. Did you know that white light is actually made of many colors of light? If you have ever seen a rainbow, you have actually seen the colors that make up white light. The rainbow below shows the colors that make up the white light you see.

A rainbow contains all the colors of the visible spectrum.

Prism
A clear piece of glass or plastic that is shaped like a triangle and can be used to separate white light.

Visible spectrum
The band of colors that make up white light.

The band of colors you see in a rainbow is known as the **visible spectrum**. The colors of the visible spectrum always appear in the following order: red, orange, yellow, green, blue, indigo, and violet.

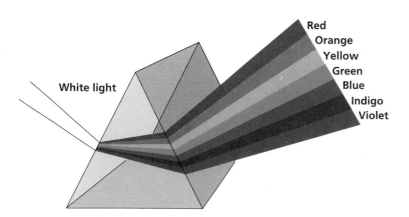

White light

Red
Orange
Yellow
Green
Blue
Indigo
Violet

You can use a **prism** like the one in the picture to see the colors in white light. A prism is a piece of glass or plastic shaped like a triangle. A prism can separate white light into the colors of the visible spectrum.

Self-Check

1. What is the major source of light on Earth?
2. What makes up a beam of light?
3. How does light travel?
4. Would light travel faster through space or through a window? Explain.
5. What colors make up white light?

SCIENCE IN YOUR LIFE

How are lasers used?

A laser is a device that produces a powerful beam of light. Ordinary light travels in all directions from its source, like the waves made when a stone is thrown into a puddle of water. Laser light travels in only one direction. As a result, laser beams can be brighter and narrower than ordinary light beams. In fact, laser beams can be so bright that they can seriously damage your eyes if you look directly into them or even into their reflection. The table shows some of the many uses for lasers.

Some uses of lasers	
Communication	■ transmission of telephone signals ■ production of compact discs ■ transmission of television signals
Business	■ bar code identification on products for inventory and sales transactions
Medicine	■ detection of medical problems, diseases, and disorders ■ surgery, such as removing cataracts from eyes, removing cancerous cells, clearing blocked arteries, removing tonsils ■ treatment of skin conditions including removal of birthmarks
Environment	■ detection of pollutants in air ■ detection of natural gas leaks
Scientific research	■ collection of data from the moon ■ studies of the atom ■ studies of chemical reactions

Objectives

After reading this lesson, you should be able to

► explain how light is reflected.

► describe how mirrors reflect light.

► explain how light is refracted.

► describe how lenses refract light.

Image
A copy or likeness.

Plane mirror
A flat, smooth mirror.

Reflection
The bouncing back of a light wave.

What happens when you look into a mirror? Why can you see yourself? These questions can be answered by understanding how light waves act.

Light Bounces

When you throw a ball to the floor, it bounces back. Light also bounces back when it hits an object. When light bounces off a surface, we say that the light is reflected. **Reflection** is the bouncing back of a light wave. Few objects give off their own light. We see most objects only because of the light they reflect.

You can see an **image**, or likeness, in a mirror because light waves are reflected. As you can see in the diagram, light from the cup hits the mirror and is reflected toward your eye. Then your eye forms an image. The cup looks as if it is behind the mirror. The image is the same size as the original cup, but it is reversed. The handle of the cup appears on the opposite side when you see it in the mirror. The angles at which the light reflects back cause this reversal. Follow the lines of light in the diagram to see how this happens.

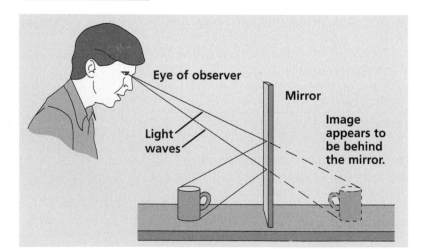

Eye of observer

Mirror

Light waves

Image appears to be behind the mirror.

Types of Mirrors

A mirror with a flat, smooth surface is called a **plane mirror**. The flatter the surface of the mirror, the clearer the image.

Many mirrors have curved surfaces rather than flat surfaces. A **concave mirror** has a reflecting surface that curves inward, like the inside of a spoon. A concave mirror creates an image that looks larger than the real object.

A convex mirror allows you to see more area

The reflecting surface of some mirrors curves outward like the outside of a spoon. This kind of mirror is called a **convex mirror**. A convex mirror creates an image that looks smaller than the real object. However, you can see much more area in a convex mirror. For this reason, side-view mirrors on cars often are convex mirrors.

Light Bends

When light moves from one kind of matter to another, the light waves bend. The bending of a light wave as it moves from one material to another is called **refraction**.

Concave mirror
A mirror that curves in at the middle.

Convex mirror
A mirror that curves outward at the middle.

Refraction
The bending of a light wave as it moves from one material to another.

Notice that the pencil in the picture appears to be bent. Light travels more slowly in water than it does in air. When light passes from the water to the air, the light waves change speed and change direction. As a result, the pencil seems to bend.

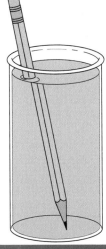

Refraction causes the pencil to look bent.

Types of Lenses

A **lens** bends light by acting like the water in the container. A lens is a curved piece of glass or other clear material that refracts light waves that pass through it. Lenses are used in eyeglasses, cameras, magnifying glasses, microscopes, and telescopes. What you see through a lens depends on the kind of lens you use.

A **concave lens** is curved inward. The lens is thin in the middle and thick at the edges. Light rays that pass through a concave lens spread apart.

A **convex lens** is curved outward. The lens is thick in the middle and thin at the edges. Light rays that pass through a convex lens are refracted inward. You can see that a convex lens focuses light.

If you hold a convex lens close to your eye, the lens will magnify an image. If you hold a convex lens far from your eye and observe an object at a distance, you see an upside-down image.

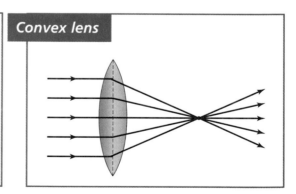

Concave lens

Convex lens

Self-Check

1. What happens to light rays when they are reflected?
2. What is a plane mirror?
3. How do a concave mirror and a convex mirror differ?
4. What happens to light waves when they are refracted?
5. How do a concave lens and a convex lens refract light in different ways?

- Sound is caused by vibrations.
- Sound travels in waves.
- People see objects because light is reflected from them.
- Light is made up of bundles of energy called photons.
- Light has properties of both particles and waves.
- White light can be separated into the colors of the visible spectrum.

- Reflection is the bouncing back of a light wave.
- A plane mirror, a concave mirror, and a convex mirror reflect light in different ways.
- Refraction is the bending of a light wave.
- Concave and convex lenses refract light.

Science Words

concave lens, 120	plane mirror, 118
concave mirror, 119	prism, 116
convex lens, 120	reflection, 118
convex mirror, 119	refraction, 119
image, 118	sound wave, 112
lens, 120	vibrate, 111
light, 114	visible spectrum, 116
photons, 114	

WORD BANK

concave lens

concave mirror

convex lens

convex mirror

light

prism

reflection

refraction

sound wave

vibrates

Vocabulary Review

Number your paper from 1 to 10. Then choose the term from the Word Bank that best completes each sentence. Write your answer on your paper.

1. A _____ separates white light into bands of colors.
2. A _____ is thick in the middle and thin at the edges.
3. Sound is produced when matter _____.
4. The bouncing back of a light wave is called _____.
5. The reflecting surface of a _____ curves inward.
6. A _____ reflects light rays so objects appear smaller than they are.
7. The bending of a light wave is called _____.
8. Light rays that pass through a _____ are spread apart.
9. The movement of air particles around a vibrating object is a _____ .
10. _____ is a form of energy that can be seen.

Concept Review

Number your paper from 1 to 8. Then choose the answer that best completes each sentence. Write the letter of the answer on your paper.

1. A vibrating object pushes against the _____ around it.

   a. sound waves   b. visible spectrum   c. air molecules

2. Light waves travel _____ than sound waves.

   a. slower   b. faster   c. shorter distances

3. The bands of colors in a rainbow are known as _____.

   a. photons   b. a prism   c. the visible spectrum

4. A lens _____ light waves.

   a. reflects   b. reverses   c. refracts

5. Sound travels in _____.

   a. waves   b. particles   c. images

6. Particles of light are called _____.

   a. protons   b. photons   c. electrons

7. A _____ mirror has a flat, smooth surface.

   a. convex   b. concave   c. plane

8. A vibrating object produces _____ .

   a. light   b. sound   c. heat

Critical Thinking

Write the answer to each of the following questions.

1. Copy the drawings of the lenses below. Draw lines to show how the light waves are refracted as they pass through each lens. Write a sentence to explain what you drew for each lens.

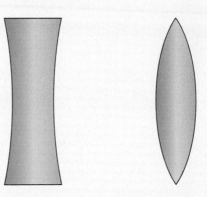

2. Suppose you wanted to use a mirror for shaving or putting on makeup. Would you use a convex mirror or a concave mirror? Explain your answer.

Test Taking Tip | Drawing pictures or diagrams is one way to help you understand and solve problems.

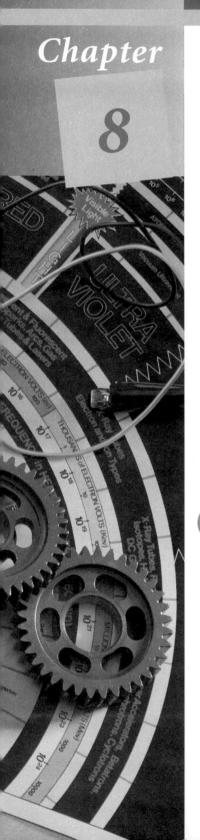

Chapter

8

Electricity and Magnetism

Electricity! It flows on demand from outlets in the wall. It flashes across the sky during summer storms. It is useful in many ways. Yet it can be dangerous. How can something so familiar also seem so mysterious? Electricity is not hard to understand, once you know a few basics. You will learn about electricity in this chapter. You will also learn how magnets work.

ORGANIZE YOUR THOUGHTS

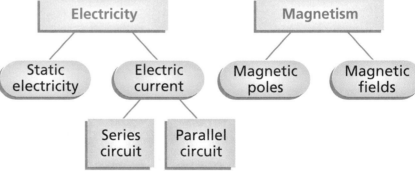

Goals for Learning

▶ To explain how electric current flows through a circuit

▶ To compare series and parallel circuits

▶ To describe various kinds of magnets

▶ To explain what a magnetic field is

Electricity
Flow of electrons.

Static electricity
Buildup of electrical charges.

In Chapter 2, you read about atoms and the particles that make them up. Electrons are negatively charged particles. Under the right conditions, electrons can escape from one atom and move to another one. The atom that loses the electron becomes positively charged. The atom that has picked up the electron becomes negatively charged. In turn, this negatively charged atom can pass the electron on again. This movement of electrons is the basis of **electricity**.

Static Electricity

Have you ever gotten a shock when you touched metal after walking across a carpet? The shock was caused by a buildup of charge, called **static electricity**. Walking across the carpet caused electrons to leave the carpet and enter your body. When you touched the metal, the extra electrons jumped from your finger to the metal.

When electrons move from one place to another, energy is transferred. Lightning is a discharge of static electricity between clouds or between a cloud and Earth.

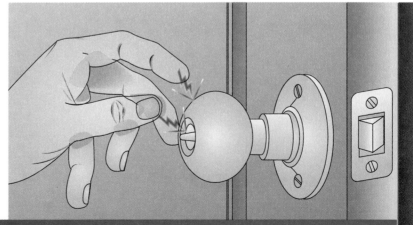

The spark you sometimes see when you touch metal is a discharge of static electricity. So is a lightning bolt.

Closed Circuits

The flow of electric charge that moves from one place to another is called **electric current**. The rate of electrical flow can vary. Electric current is measured in **amperes**. An ampere tells how much current is moving past a point in a circuit in one second. The energy that a power source gives to electric charge in a circuit is called the **voltage**. This energy is measured by units called **volts**.

Currents from static electricity are not easy to control. But an electric current produced by a power source can be controlled and is easy to use.

When electric charge travels in an electric current, it follows a path. This path is called a **circuit**. Follow the path of current in the figure below. The circuit begins at the power source. It travels through the wire to the light bulb. It lights up the bulb, and then returns to the power source.

Electric charge can follow only a complete, unbroken path. You can see that the path in this circuit is unbroken. This path is called a **closed circuit**. As long as the current continues to flow in the circuit, the light will remain lit.

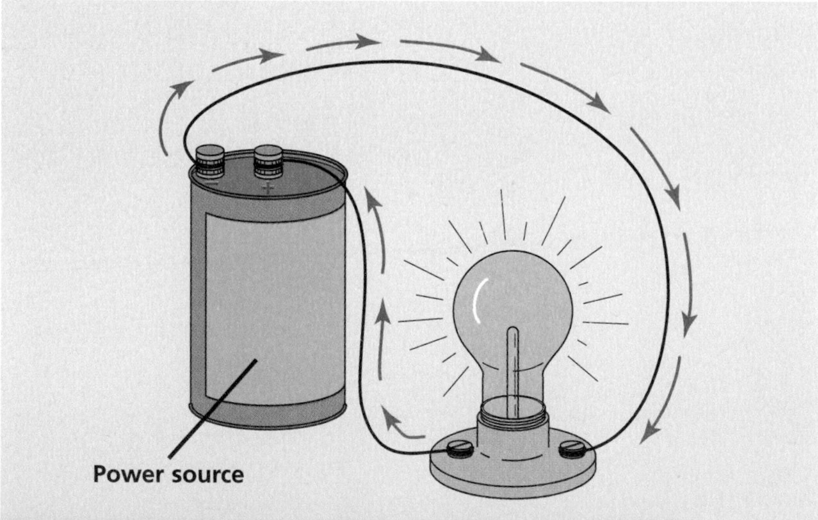

Ampere
The unit used to describe how much electric current flows through a wire.

Circuit
Path for electric current.

Closed circuit
Complete, unbroken path for electric current.

Electric current
Movement of electric charge from one place to another.

Volt
Metric unit used to measure electromotive force.

Voltage
The energy that a power source gives to electrons in a circuit.

Power source

Electricity can flow only through a closed circuit.

Open Circuits

Suppose you have a light turned on in your room. You decide you want to turn off the light. What do you do? Most likely you turn off a switch. To turn on the light again, you turn the switch on.

How does a switch work? Look at Figure A below. You can see that the wires of the circuit are connected to a switch. When the switch is closed, the current can flow in an unbroken path. The light stays lit.

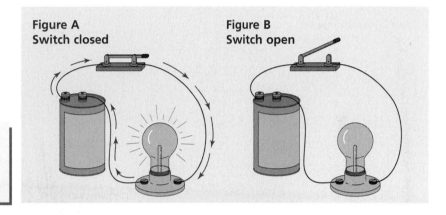

Figure A
Switch closed

Figure B
Switch open

Open circuit
Incomplete or broken path for electric current.

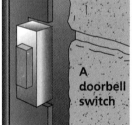

A doorbell switch

A lamp switch

In Figure B, the switch is open. The current can't pass through it. The bulb doesn't light. This is an incomplete path. It is called an **open circuit**.

The switches you see in the diagram above are called knife switches. The switches that you use in your home are different from a knife switch, but they work the same way. They break the flow of electrons when the switch is turned off. The pictures at left show some of the switches you might find in your home.

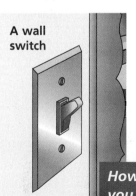

A wall switch

How many of these common switches can you find in your home?

Schematic Diagrams

Scientists often use drawings of circuits. To make this job easier, they have developed symbols to show different parts of a circuit. Wires, switches, bulbs, and power sources are each represented by a different symbol. You can see some of these symbols below.

Schematic diagram
A diagram that uses symbols to show the parts of a circuit.

A diagram of a circuit that uses such symbols is called a **schematic diagram**. The schematic diagram below shows a battery in a circuit with a closed switch, wiring, and a bulb.

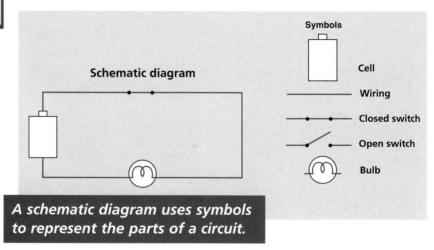

A schematic diagram uses symbols to represent the parts of a circuit.

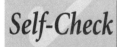

Self-Check

1. Explain what happens when you get a shock from a metal doorknob after walking across a carpet.

2. Look at the following schematic diagrams, a and b. Which of the circuits is a closed circuit? Which is an open circuit?

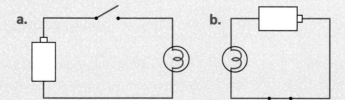

3. In which of the schematic diagrams above would current flow? Explain.

Objectives

After reading this lesson, you should be able to

▶ describe a series circuit.

▶ explain how adding electrical devices or batteries to a series circuit affects the voltage of the circuit.

▶ explain the advantage of using fuses and circuit breakers.

Have you ever had a string of decorative lights? You might know that with some strings of lights, if one light burns out, all the remaining lights stay lit. But in other strings, all the lights will go out if one burns out. Then you have to change each bulb on the string until you find the one that's burned out. Why do these strings of lights act differently? The answer is in the way the circuit is made.

Devices in Series Circuits

Look at the circuit below. It includes a source of energy, such as a battery, and wire to carry the current. It also has light bulbs attached one by one along the wire. This kind of circuit is called a **series circuit**.

Series circuit
Circuit in which all current flows through a single path.

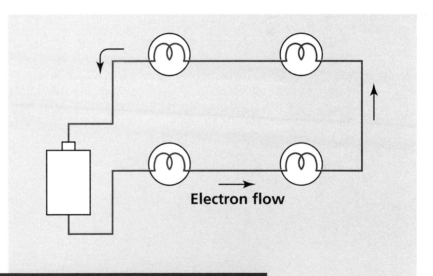

Electron flow

In a series circuit, all electrons must pass through each electrical device.

In a series circuit, electric charge can flow through only one path around the circuit. In the circuit on the previous page, you can see that all the charge must pass through each electrical device. In the example of the decorative lights, each light is a separate device. The electric charge must pass through each light bulb.

Series circuits have a disadvantage. If one light is unscrewed or burns out, all of the other lights will go out. That is because the circuit becomes open and electric charge cannot flow.

When electrical devices are connected in series, the current is the same throughout the circuit. However, adding electrical devices lowers the voltage through each device. Notice in the diagram below that if only one bulb is connected to a **dry cell battery**, the bulb may shine brightly. If another bulb is added in series, each of the bulbs will be dimmer than the single bulb was. A dry cell battery has a dry or a pastelike center.

Dry cell battery
Electric power source with a dry or pastelike center.

Adding bulbs in series causes the bulbs to glow more dimly.

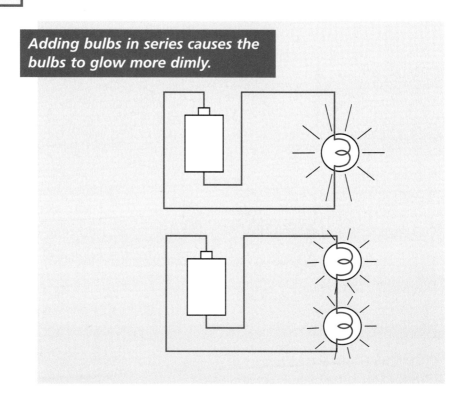

Batteries in Series Circuits

Batteries in a circuit can be connected in series too. Batteries in series increase the voltage of the circuit. To find the total voltage, add the voltages of the cells together.

In the circuit shown below, the batteries are in series. A wire connects a positive terminal to a negative terminal. A second wire connects the lamp and switch to the batteries. When batteries are connected in series, they can deliver more energy in the same amount of time. Bulbs in this kind of circuit burn brighter because the voltage is higher.

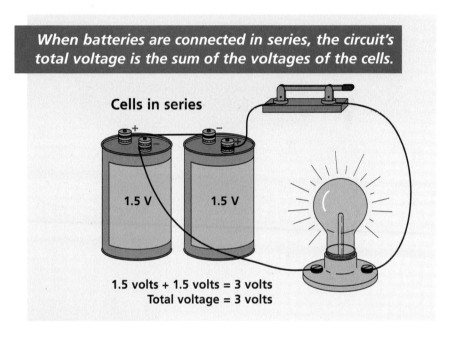

When batteries are connected in series, the circuit's total voltage is the sum of the voltages of the cells.

Cells in series

1.5 V   1.5 V

1.5 volts + 1.5 volts = 3 volts
Total voltage = 3 volts

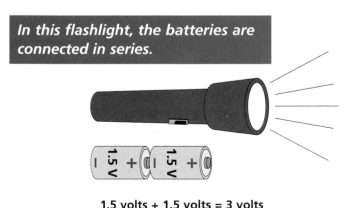

In this flashlight, the batteries are connected in series.

1.5 V + 1.5 V

1.5 volts + 1.5 volts = 3 volts

In a flashlight, dry cell batteries are usually connected in series. You can see in the drawing to the left how the positive terminal of one battery touches the negative terminal (the bottom metal plate) of the next battery.

Fuses and Circuit Breakers

Connecting electrical devices in series can be inconvenient. But there are practical uses for series circuits too. For example, your home is probably protected by fuses or circuit breakers. Fuses and circuit breakers help prevent fires.

Look at the fuse in the drawing. Notice the piece of metal on the top of the fuse. It is designed to melt at a certain temperature. When the wires get too hot, the fuse will melt and break the circuit. When a fuse melts, it must be replaced. A circuit breaker, on the other hand, is a switchlike device that can be reset after the circuit has been repaired.

Fuses and circuit breakers are designed to prevent fires.

Fuse

Circuit breaker

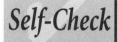

Self-Check

1. What is a series circuit?
2. What is one advantage of a series circuit?
3. What happens to the brightness of a bulb when more bulbs are added to the same series circuit?
4. When two cells with the same voltage are connected in series, what happens to the voltage?
5. Compare a fuse and a circuit breaker.

Objectives

After reading this lesson, you should be able to

▶ describe a parallel circuit.

▶ explain what happens to the brightness of bulbs in a parallel circuit when more bulbs are included.

▶ explain what happens to voltage when two batteries with the same voltage are connected in parallel.

Parallel circuit
Circuit in which there is more than one path for current.

The lights and appliances in your home are not wired in a series circuit. If they were, every time a bulb burned out, none of the other lights and appliances would work! Instead, most circuits in houses are **parallel circuits**. In a parallel circuit, there is more than one path for the current to follow.

Devices in Parallel Circuits

Look at the following diagram of two lamps connected in parallel. As you can see, there are two paths through this circuit. If one bulb burned out, the other bulb would stay lit, because current can follow more than one path.

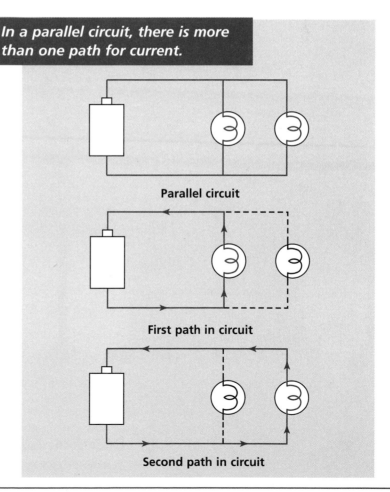

In a parallel circuit, there is more than one path for current.

Parallel circuit

First path in circuit

Second path in circuit

When several bulbs are connected in parallel, all the bulbs will remain as bright as just one bulb alone would. However, more current must be drawn from the battery to power the extra bulbs. Therefore, the battery will not last as long as in a series circuit.

When more electrical devices are added to the same circuit, more current runs through the circuit. As current in a circuit increases, wires begin to heat up. If they get too hot, the wires can start a fire. The fuses and circuit breakers you read about in Lesson 2 help prevent this problem.

Batteries in Parallel Circuits

Batteries can be connected in parallel. A parallel connection between batteries allows them to keep providing energy longer. A parallel connection does not increase the voltage.

Look at the drawings below. Figure A shows a circuit with only one 1.5-volt battery. The circuit in Figure B has two 1.5-volt batteries connected in parallel. The bulb in the circuit will stay lit longer. However, it will not burn brighter than the other bulb. The total voltage is still only 1.5 volts.

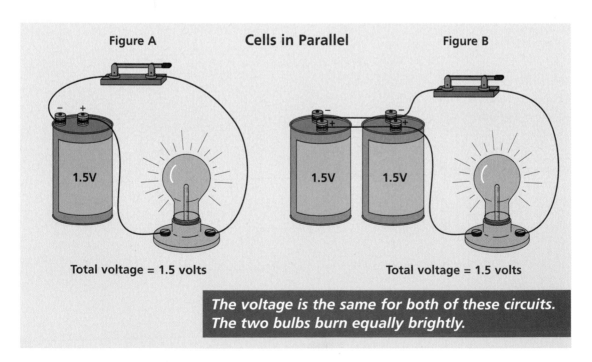

Figure A

Cells in Parallel

Figure B

1.5V

Total voltage = 1.5 volts

1.5V   1.5V

Total voltage = 1.5 volts

The voltage is the same for both of these circuits. The two bulbs burn equally brightly.

1. What happens to the bulbs in a parallel circuit when one bulb burns out?

2. Determine the number of paths in each of the following parallel circuits.

a.

b.

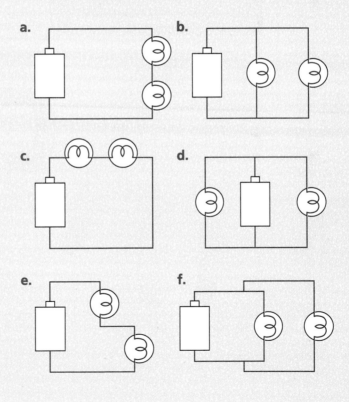

3. What happens to the brightness of bulbs in a parallel circuit when more bulbs are added?

4. When two batteries with the same voltage are connected in parallel, what happens to the voltage?

5. Identify each of the following circuits as a parallel circuit or a series circuit.

a.

b.

c.

d.

e.

f.

Objectives

After reading this lesson, you should be able to

▶ describe several kinds of magnets.

▶ explain what magnetic poles are.

▶ describe how magnetic poles behave.

You probably are familiar with **magnets**. If you have ever used them, you know that they can pick up certain objects, such as paper clips and other things made from iron. Most of the magnets you have seen are made by people. Did you know that there are naturally occurring magnets? Lodestone is one such magnetic material. It is made of iron oxide. It is found naturally in the earth and comes in many sizes and shapes.

Most magnets that are made by people come in one of several common shapes. These shapes include the horseshoe, bar, cylinder, and doughnut shapes. You can see these magnets in the figure below.

Magnet
An object that attracts certain kinds of metals, such as iron.

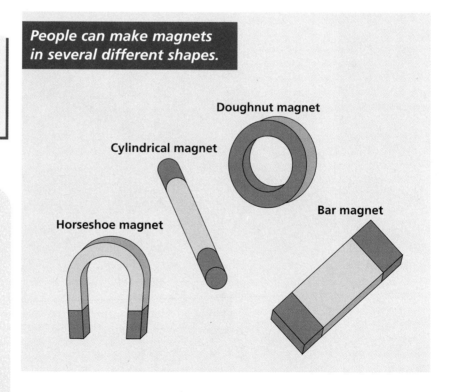

People can make magnets in several different shapes.

Doughnut magnet

Cylindrical magnet

Horseshoe magnet

Bar magnet

Did You Know?

The ancient Greeks knew about the magnetic properties of lodestone, also called magnetite. The word *magnet* comes from the name Magnesia, the Greek province where the mineral was mined.

Magnetic Poles

Look at the magnets shown on this page. The ends of the magnet are called its **magnetic poles**. Whatever the shape, all magnets have two opposite magnetic poles. The magnetic forces are greatest at the poles. You know this because the ends of the magnet will pick up more paper clips than the center of the magnet.

The poles on a magnet are called the north pole and the south pole. On a marked magnet, the north pole is shown by an *N*. The south pole is marked with an *S*.

You can't tell whether the end of an unmarked magnet is a north pole or a south pole simply by looking at it. You can however, find out by placing the magnet close to another magnet whose poles are marked. Observe whether the poles **attract** (pull together) or **repel** (push away) each other. To figure out the poles of the unmarked magnet, use the following rules.

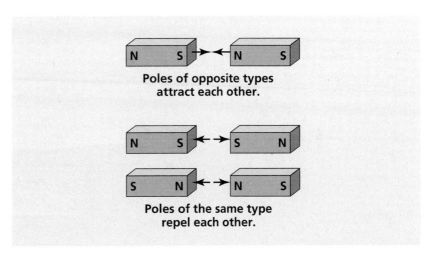

Poles of opposite types
attract each other.

Poles of the same type
repel each other.

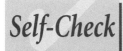
Self-Check

1. How can you determine the poles of an unmarked magnet?

2. If two south poles are placed close together, what will happen?

3. If a north and a south pole are placed close together, what will happen?

Objectives

After reading this lesson, you should be able to

► explain what a magnetic field is.

► describe Earth as a magnet.

► explain how a magnet works.

Surrounding all magnets is a **magnetic field**. A magnetic field is an area in which magnetic forces can attract or repel other magnets.

Although you cannot see magnetic fields, you can easily see their effects. All you need to do is place a bar magnet under a sheet of paper. Then sprinkle iron filings on top of the paper. The filings will line up in a pattern of curving lines like those shown in the figure. These lines are called **lines of force**. They are caused by the magnetic field. The lines of force reach around the magnet from one pole to another. The lines are closest together near the poles. That is where the field is strongest and the forces are greatest.

Lines of force
Lines that show a magnetic field.

Magnetic field
Area around a magnet in which magnetic forces can act.

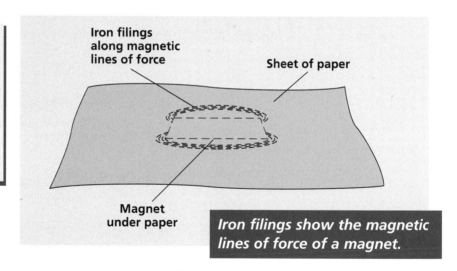

Iron filings along magnetic lines of force

Sheet of paper

Magnet under paper

Iron filings show the magnetic lines of force of a magnet.

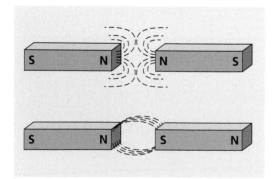

You can see in the figure to the left how the lines of force of two magnets affect each other. Notice how they cause the poles of magnets to attract or repel each other.

Earth as a Magnet

You may be surprised to learn that Earth itself is a giant bar magnet. Like other magnets, Earth has magnetic poles. These magnetic poles are located near the geographic north and south poles.

Earth's natural magnetism allows compasses to work. The needle of a compass is a magnet too. It has a north pole and a south pole. They are located at opposite ends of the needle.

Like magnetic poles repel each other. However, you can see in the figure that the north magnetic pole of Earth attracts the north pole of a compass. It is called the north magnetic pole because it is located near the geographic North Pole. The north pole of a magnet is called the north pole because it is the part of the magnet that points toward the north magnetic pole.

Earth's magnetic field attracts and lines up the compass needle. The north pole of the magnet in a compass is attracted to the Earth's magnetic pole. As a result, it points north.

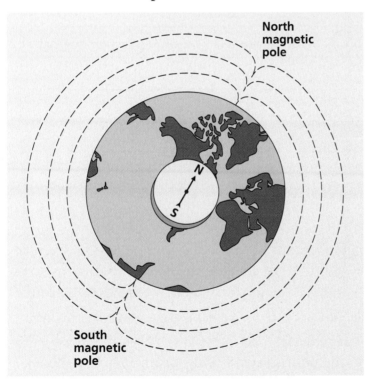

North magnetic pole

South magnetic pole

Self-Check	1.	What is a magnetic field?
	2.	What pattern is made by magnetic lines of force around a bar magnet?
	3.	How does a compass work?

INVESTIGATION

8

Observing Magnetic Lines of Force

Materials

✓ 2 horseshoe magnets

✓ 2 bar magnets

✓ 2 sheets of paper

✓ cup of iron filings

Purpose

To observe the lines of force around magnets

Procedure

Part A

1. Copy the data table below on your paper.

	Bar magnet	Horseshoe magnet
Part A		
Part B		
Part C		

2. Place one magnet of each shape on a flat surface. Cover each magnet with a sheet of paper.

3. Sprinkle some of the iron filings on each of the pieces of paper. Do not pour the filings. It is best to sprinkle them lightly from a height of about 1 foot (about 31 cm).

4. Observe the pattern of iron filings made by the lines of force. Record your observations on your data table.

5. Carefully pour the iron filings from each paper back into the cup.

Part B

6. Place the bar magnets end to end with like poles close together.

7. Place a sheet of paper over the magnets and sprinkle with iron filings.

8. Record your observations.

9. Carefully pour the iron filings from the paper back into the cup.

Part C

10. Reverse the poles of one of the bar magnets so that opposite poles are close together. Cover with a sheet of paper.

11. Sprinkle the paper with iron filings. Record your observations.

12. Repeat Part B and Part C with the horseshoe magnets. Record your observations.

Questions

1. Describe the pattern made by the lines of force of the single bar magnet.

2. In Part B, did the poles of the bar magnets attract or repel each other? How did the lines of force show this?

3. In Part C, did the poles of the bar magnets attract or repel each other? How do you know?

4. How were the patterns on the bar magnet similar to those on the horseshoe magnet?

How does an electromagnet work?

Magnets are not the only things that can produce a magnetic field. Electricity can produce a magnetic field too. Electricity can be used to make a type of magnet called an electromagnet. An electromagnet is magnetic only when an electric current is flowing through it.

An electromagnet is made by wrapping electrical wire around an iron core. When an electric current flows through the wire, the core creates a magnetic field. The magnetism produced by an electromagnet is the same as the magnetism produced by a regular magnet.

The strength of an electromagnet depends on a number of factors. Power sources with higher voltages create more powerful electromagnets. More turns of wire around the core also increases the strength of an electromagnet.

Unlike a regular magnet, an electromagnet can be switched on and off. This makes electromagnets useful. For example, the photo shows an electromagnet. When the current is turned on, the electromagnet picks up pieces of metal from piles of scrap. When the current is turned off, the electromagnet loses its magnetism, and the metal pieces are dropped.

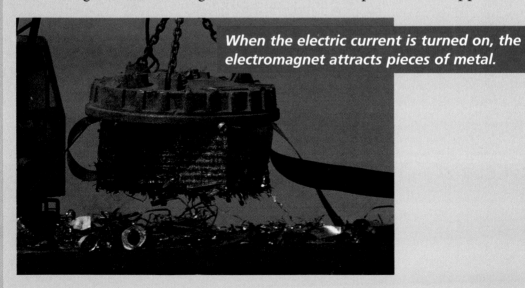

When the electric current is turned on, the electromagnet attracts pieces of metal.

- Electricity is the movement of electrons from one place to another.

- Static electricity is a buildup of electric charge.

- Current is the rate of flow of electricity. It is measured in amperes.

- Voltage is the energy that a power source gives to electrons in a circuit. The energy is measured in volts.

- A closed circuit is a complete, unbroken path for current. An open circuit is an incomplete or broken path for current.

- A schematic diagram uses symbols to show the parts of a circuit.

- Fuses and circuit breakers prevent fires when electrical wires get too hot.

- In a series circuit, all current flows through a single path. In a parallel circuit, current flows in more than one path.

- Magnets can attract materials such as iron. Magnets may be natural, such as lodestone, or may be made by people.

- A magnet has a north pole and a south pole. Unlike poles attract. Like poles repel.

- A magnetic field surrounds a magnet. Magnetic lines of force extend from pole to pole.

- Earth is a magnet. It has a north magnetic pole and a south magnetic pole.

Science Words		
ampere, 126	magnetic poles, 137
attract, 137	open circuit, 127
circuit, 126	parallel circuit, 133
closed circuit, 126	repel, 137
dry cell battery, 130	schematic diagram, 128
electric current, 126	series circuit, 129
electricity, 125	static electricity, 125
lines of force, 138	volt, 126
magnet, 136	voltage, 126
magnetic field, 138	

WORD BANK

ampere

circuit

closed circuit

magnet

magnetic field

magnetic pole

open circuit

parallel circuit

schematic
    diagram

series circuit

static electricity

voltage

Vocabulary Review

Number your paper from 1 to 12. Then choose the term from the Word Bank that best completes each sentence. Write the answer on your paper.

1. A(n) _____ is the area around a magnet in which magnetic forces can act.

2. A path for current to flow is a(n) _____.

3. The energy that a power source gives to electrons in a circuit is the _____.

4. A(n) _____ may be either north or south.

5. In a(n) _____, all current flows through a single path.

6. An electron path that is incomplete or broken is called a(n) _____.

7. In a(n) _____, current can flow through more than one path.

8. The unit used to measure electric current is the _____.

9. A complete, unbroken path for current is called a(n) _____.

10. _____ is a buildup of electrical charges.

11. Any object that can attract metals, such as iron, is called a(n) _____.

12. A(n) _____ uses symbols to show the parts of a circuit.

Concept Review

Number your paper from 1 to 5. Then choose the answer that best completes each sentence. Write the letter of the answer on your paper.

1. When a magnet is broken in half, _____ result.

a. two magnets   b. two poles   c. no magnets

2. When cells are connected in _____, the circuit's voltage is the sum of the voltages of the cells.

   a. parallel   b. series   c. an open circuit

3. A north pole of one bar magnet is _____ by the north pole of another bar magnet.

   a. not affected   b. attracted   c. repelled

4. Magnetic lines of force of a magnet are closest together _____.

   a. midway between the poles

   b. near both poles

   c. near the north pole only

5. The negatively charged particles in atoms are the _____.

   a. protons   b. neutrons   c. electrons

Critical Thinking

Write the answer to each of the following questions.

1. Explain what circuit breakers are and why they are important.

2. How could you find the poles of the magnet shown here?

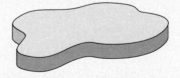

3. Suppose an electrician wants to install a doorbell and a porch light in the same circuit. Should the circuit be a series circuit or a parallel circuit? Explain your answer.

| Test Taking Tip | When studying, highlight important facts and terms in your notes. When you review, reread the highlighted areas. |

Writing a Chemical Equation

Purpose

To measure volume in metric units; to write the equation for a chemical reaction

Procedure

1. The table below lists the chemical formulas for the substances you will observe in this investigation.

Before reaction		After reaction	
Substance	Chemical formula	Substance	Chemical formula
Baking soda	$NaHCO_3$	Carbon dioxide	CO_2
Vinegar (acetic acid + water)	$HC_2H_3O_2$	Water	H_2O
		Sodium acetate	$NaC_2H_3O_2$

2. Measure 50 mL of vinegar. Pour it into the plastic cup. Rinse and dry the graduated cylinder.

3. Measure 50 cm³ of baking soda. (*Hint*: 1 cm³ = 1 mL) Pour the baking soda into the plastic cup and stir with the craft stick. Watch what happens.

Questions

1. In the chemical reaction you observed, which substances were the reactants? Which substances were the products?

2. Write the chemical equation for the reaction. Use the formulas listed in the table.

3. Is your equation balanced? How can you tell?

Materials

✓ medium-size plastic cup
✓ small graduated cylinder marked with mL scale
✓ vinegar
✓ baking soda
✓ craft stick

Unit 1   SUMMARY

- Scientists use the metric system. The metric system is based on a system of tens.

- Area is the amount of space the surface of an object takes up.

- Volume is the amount of space an object takes up.

- Mass is the amount of material in an object.

- A molecule is the smallest particle of a substance that still has the same properties of the substance.

- Matter is anything that has mass and takes up space.

- An atom is the basic building block of matter. An atom is made of protons, neutrons, and electrons.

- Molecules move in different ways in each of the three states of matter—solids, liquids, and gases.

- In a chemical change, new substances with new properties are formed. In a physical change, the appearance of a substance changes but the properties stay the same.

- The law of conservation of matter states that matter cannot be created or destroyed in any chemical change.

- Energy is the ability to do work.

- Energy can change from one form to another.

- Motion is a change of position.

- Gravity is a force of attraction between any two objects that have mass.

- Work is what happens when a force makes something move in the direction of the force.

- Simple machines make doing work easier by changing the size or direction of a force or the distance across which the force moves.

- Heat is a form of energy. It results in the increased motion of molecules in matter.

- Temperature measures the motion of molecules.

- Sound is caused by vibrations.

- People see objects because light is reflected from them.

- Electricity is the movement of electric charge from one place to another.

- A magnet has a north pole and a south pole. Unlike magnetic poles attract. Like magnetic poles repel.

WORD BANK

chemical equation

circuit

conductor

element

energy

mass

matter

molecule

vibrates

work

Vocabulary Review

Number your paper from 1 to 10. Then choose the term from the Word Bank that best completes each sentence. Write the answer on your paper.

1. Anything that has mass and takes up space is called _____.

2. A path for electrical current to flow is a(n) _____.

3. Force multiplied by distance equals _____.

4. A(n) _____ has only one kind of atom.

5. The amount of material an object has is its _____.

6. A(n) _____ uses symbols, formulas, and numbers to stand for a chemical reaction.

7. _____ is the ability to do work.

8. Sound is produced when matter _____.

9. A material that carries heat easily is a(n) _____.

10. The smallest particle of water that still has all the properties of water is a(n) _____ of water.

Concept Review

Number your paper from 1 to 8. Then choose the answer that best completes each sentence. Write the letter of the answer on your paper.

1. All matter is made of _____.

   a. symbols   b. atoms   c. compounds

2. The amount of space an object takes up is its _____.

   a. mass   b. area   c. volume

3. When sugar is dissolved in water, _____.

   a. sugar is the solute
   b. sugar is the solvent
   c. water is the solute

4. A paper cutter is an example of a _____ lever.

   a. first-class   b. second-class   c. third-class

5. The flow of heat energy from one molecule to the next is called _____.

   a. convection   b. conduction   c. radiation

6. A north pole of one bar magnet is _____ by the north pole of another bar magnet.

   a. not affected   b. attracted   c. repelled

7. The basic unit of mass in the metric system is the _____.

   a. meter   b. gram   c. liter

8. Atoms of two elements can join to form a _____.

   a. compound   b. mixture   c. solution

Critical Thinking

Write the answer to each of the following questions.

1. How would you measure the volume of each of the objects shown below?

2. A girl rides her bicycle to her friend's house 24 km away. She leaves her own house at 10:00 A.M. and gets to her friend's house at 11:30 A.M. What was the average speed of the bicycle?

"It takes an earthquake to remind us that we walk on the crust of an unfinished planet."

Charles Kuralt

Earth Science

Unit 2

Earth science is important in your life. In fact, you probably use earth science in some ways every day. Did you ride in a car or bus today? The fuel was made from oil that was located underground by geologists. Have you heard a forecast for the weather? The weather forecast was made by a meteorologist, a scientist who studies the weather.

In this unit, you will learn about earth science. You will learn about Earth, inside and out. You will learn about what goes on above your head in the sky. Finally, you will learn what makes up the solar system.

Chapters in Unit 2

Chapter 9: Describing Earth 154

Chapter 10: Minerals and Rocks 172

Chapter 11: Weathering and Erosion 186

Chapter 12: Forces Inside Earth 202

Chapter 13: Earth's History 220

Chapter 14: Earth's Water 232

Chapter 15: Earth's Atmosphere 244

Chapter 16: Weather and Climate 258

Chapter 17: The Solar System 274

Unit 2

What Is Earth Science?

The study of Earth's land, water, and air is called **earth science**. Earth science also includes the study of outer space and the objects in it.

Earth science can be divided into many fields of science. The table describes the main fields, or subject areas, that make up earth science. Which field concerns itself with the question "Why did it rain today?" Which field would include scientists who learn about dinosaurs? Compare the table with the chapters listed on page 151 to see which chapters deal with each field or fields of earth science.

Field of earth science	What is studied
Geology	Earth's land, including the surface of Earth and the inside of Earth; how Earth changes; history of Earth
Oceanography	Earth's oceans, including what they contain and how they interact with the air
Meteorology	Earth's air, including weather
Astronomy	Outer space, including planets, stars, and other objects in space
Paleontology	Fossil remains from past geological eras

Earth's land, water, and air are constantly changing and interacting with one another. For example, when rain washes mud off a hillside and into a river, the land and water interact with each other. When a puddle dries up, the water and air interact with each other. Because of these interactions, a change in one part of Earth affects other parts of Earth.

The Importance of Earth Science

Your own knowledge of earth science can help you make wise decisions. For example, knowledge about soils can help you when planting a garden. Knowing how Earth's surface changes can come in handy when deciding where to buy a house. Communities often face questions about how to use the land and other resources. An earth science background will help you make wise decisions on such issues.

The **meteorologist** in the photo below studies deadly winds called tornadoes. By making small tornadoes in his laboratory and by observing real ones, he is learning more about how and when tornadoes form. A better understanding of tornadoes could lead to predictions of these storms and save lives.

How is the work of meteorologist Dr. T. Theodore Fujita important to your life?

Describing Earth

Imagine that you are taking a voyage into space. The spacecraft blasts off and climbs higher and higher above the ground. As you gaze back at Earth, you see large sections of land and huge bodies of water. You see that Earth's surface curves. You notice that half of Earth is bathed in sunlight while the other half lies in darkness. This chapter discusses these observations and some of the ways they affect you.

ORGANIZE YOUR THOUGHTS

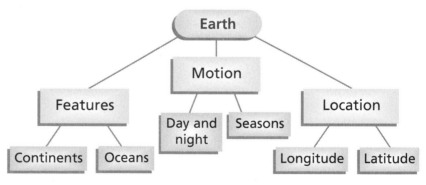

Goals for Learning

▶ To describe Earth's shape and features

▶ To explain what causes day and night

▶ To explain what causes seasons

▶ To use latitude and longitude to locate points on Earth's surface

What Shape and Features Does Earth Have?

Objectives

After reading this lesson, you should be able to

▶ describe Earth's shape.

▶ name the seven continents.

▶ name the four major oceans.

At one time many people believed that Earth was flat. They thought that if they walked past its edge, they would fall off Earth! Of course, Earth is not flat and you cannot fall off.

Earth's Shape

If you could view Earth from space, you would see that it has a shape almost like a ball. Most balls are perfectly round. If you measured the distance around a ball in any direction, you would find that all the measurements would be equal. Compare the shape of Earth and the ball below. You can see that Earth is not perfectly round. If you could measure the distance around Earth in different places, how would the measurements compare?

The shape of Earth and of a ball are slightly different.

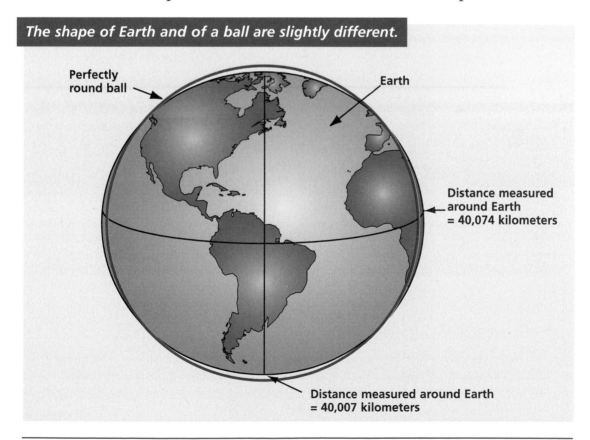

Perfectly round ball

Earth

Distance measured around Earth = 40,074 kilometers

Distance measured around Earth = 40,007 kilometers

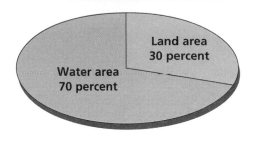

Water area
70 percent

Land area
30 percent

Earth's Land

Earth's surface includes areas of land and water. The land areas make up about 30 percent of Earth's surface. Look at the circle graph. How much of Earth's surface is water?

The land on Earth's surface is divided into seven major areas called **continents.** Find Earth's continents on the map. Which continent do you think is the largest? Which is the smallest? Check your answers against the table below.

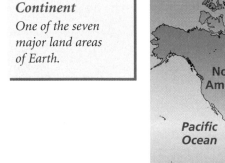

Continent
One of the seven major land areas of Earth.

The seven continents are labled in red on this map.

Information About the Continents

Continent	Area (square kilometers)	Percent of Earth's land area
Asia	43,608,000	29.2
Africa	30,355,000	20.3
North America	25,349,000	17.0
South America	17,611,000	11.9
Antarctica	13,338,500	8.9
Europe	10,498,000	7.0
Australia	8,547,000	5.7

Earth's Oceans

Look again at the map on the previous page. The major areas of water connect with one another to form one huge, continuous ocean. Earth's ocean, however, is usually divided into four major bodies of water: the Pacific Ocean, Atlantic Ocean, Indian Ocean, and Arctic Ocean. Locate each of these on the map. There are smaller bodies of water too. Among them are lakes, bays, gulfs, and seas. Oceans are much larger than any of these.

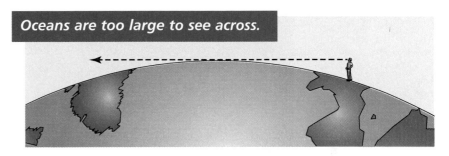

Oceans are too large to see across.

You cannot see across an ocean to land on the other side. The drawing shows why. Just like you cannot see around a ball, Earth's curve keeps you from seeing across the ocean.

Use the table below to compare the sizes of the four major oceans. Which ocean is the largest? Which is the smallest?

The Four Major Oceans		
Ocean	Area (square kilometers)	Average depth (kilometers)
Pacific	166,000,000	3.9
Atlantic	86,000,000	3.3
Indian	73,000,000	3.8
Arctic	10,000,000	1.0

Self-Check

1. Describe Earth's shape.
2. Name the seven continents.
3. Name the four major oceans.
4. What percentage of Earth's surface is covered with water?
5. Why can't you see across an ocean to land on the other side?

Axis
Imaginary line through Earth, connecting the North and South Poles.

North Pole
Point farthest north on Earth.

Rotation
Spinning of Earth.

South Pole
Point farthest south on Earth.

Earth's Rotation

If you spin a top, at first it stands upright, turning around and around. After a while, friction slows down the top. It begins to wobble and stops spinning. Like a top, Earth also spins around. But unlike a top, Earth does not stop—it keeps on spinning. The spinning of Earth is called **rotation.**

Notice in the picture that Earth spins, or rotates, from west to east around an imaginary line that passes through the center of Earth. This line is called the **axis** of Earth. The axis passes through two points called the poles. The **North Pole** is the point farthest to the north on Earth. The **South Pole** is the point farthest to the south.

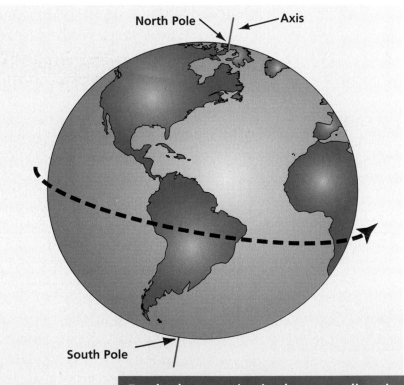

Earth always spins in the same direction.

Day and Night

Earth takes 24 hours, or one day, to rotate once on its axis. Notice in the drawing how the sun shines on Earth as Earth rotates. The sun can shine on only one side at a time. As a result, one side of Earth is lighted and has daytime. The opposite side is dark and has nighttime.

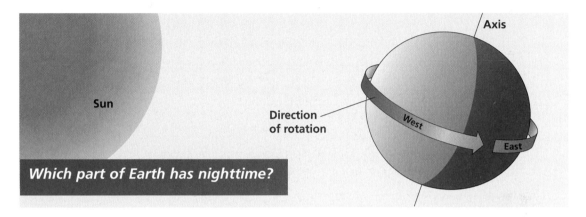

Sun

Axis

Direction of rotation

West

East

Which part of Earth has nighttime?

Because Earth continues to rotate, the places on Earth that have daytime keep changing. In other words, the time of day keeps changing everywhere on Earth. The time of day depends on where the sun appears to be in the sky. The sun does not really move across the sky, but the Earth's rotation makes the sun appear to move. As Earth turns from west to east, the sun appears to rise in the east in the morning. Then it appears to move across the sky and set in the west at night.

Standard Time Zones

When it is noon at one point on Earth, it is midnight at a point that is halfway around Earth. The remaining hours of the day are equally spread around Earth between noon and midnight.

Standard time zone
Area that has the same clock time within the zone.

All 24 hours in the day are occurring somewhere on Earth right now. Earth has been divided into 24 **standard time zones**, one for each hour of the day. A standard time zone is an area of Earth that has the same clock time everywhere in the zone.

What Is Daylight Savings Time?

Twice each year—on the first Sunday in April and the last Sunday in October—people in most parts of the United States reset their clocks. In April, clocks are set forward one hour. In October, clocks are set back one hour. Clock time from October to April is called Standard Time. Clock time from April to October is called Daylight Savings Time (DST).

Daylight Savings Time was created to provide more light in the evening hours during the seasons when people are outdoors more. Benjamin Franklin first suggested the idea of DST in the 1700s. In 1967 the U.S. government established DST throughout the country, but states are not required to use DST. Arizona, Hawaii, and part of Indiana do not observe DST, for example.

This simple saying can help you remember which way to reset your clocks in April and October: *In the spring you spring forward; in the fall, you fall back.*

Self-Check

1. What is rotation?
2. In which direction does Earth rotate?
3. What causes day and night?
4. What is a standard time zone?
5. How many standard time zones are there on Earth?

9

Modeling Day and Night

Purpose

To model day and night on Earth

Materials

✓ Earth globe on stand
✓ small piece of masking tape
✓ flashlight

Procedure

1. Copy the data table below on your paper.

Observations in step 3	Observations in step 4

2. Put a small piece of masking tape on the globe to show where you live. Have a partner hold the flashlight and stand about 1 m away from the globe. Turn the globe so the tape faces your partner. Then darken the room.

3. Have a partner shine the flashlight directly at the globe. Estimate what time it is where the tape is located. Record your observations in the data table.

4. Slowly turn the globe to model Earth's rotation. Stop when the tape is facing away from your partner. Record your observations in the data table.

Questions

1. In step 3, what time was it where you live? What time was it when you stopped turning the globe in step 4?

2. In which direction did you turn the globe in step 4?

3. When it's 3:00 P.M. where you live, what time is it halfway around Earth? one-quarter way around Earth to the *east?* one-quarter way around Earth to the *west?*

4. Which country has sunrise first, Japan or Korea?

Objectives

After reading this lesson, you should be able to

▶ describe the movement of Earth around the sun.

▶ explain how Earth's revolution and the tilt of its axis causes seasons.

Revolution
The movement of one object in its orbit around another object in space.

Why is a year about 365 days? Why do seasons change throughout the year? You can answer these questions once you know how the Earth moves in space.

Earth's Revolution

The movement of Earth in its orbit around the sun is Earth's **revolution.** A single revolution of Earth takes about 365 days, which is one year.

While Earth is revolving around the sun, it is also rotating on its axis. Earth rotates once every 24 hours, or one day. Earth's axis is tilted at an angle of 23½° as shown in the drawing below. This tilt causes the seasons.

The Seasons

As Earth revolves around the sun, Earth's axis always stays tilted at 23½°. The tilt causes sunlight to fall more directly on different parts of Earth throughout its orbit. The drawing on the next page shows how this action causes seasons. When it is summer in the northern half of Earth, that half is tilted toward the sun. When it is winter in the northern half of Earth, it is tilted away from the sun.

23½° **Axis**

Tilt a pencil to show about how much Earth tilts on its axis.

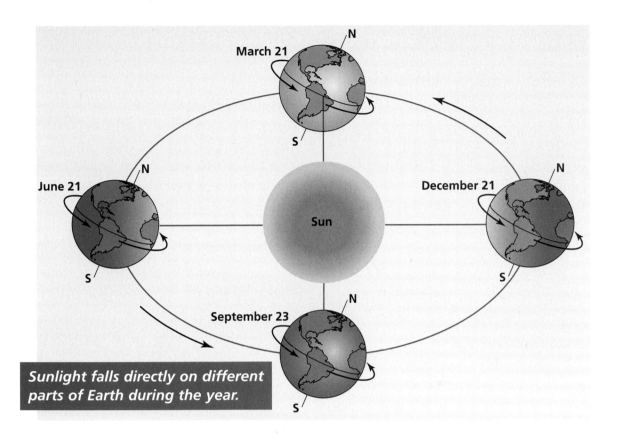

Sun

March 21

June 21

December 21

September 23

Sunlight falls directly on different parts of Earth during the year.

When it is summer in the northern part of Earth, it is winter in the southern part. Therefore, when it is summer in the United States, it is winter in Argentina. During the spring and the fall, both receive about the same amount of sunlight.

In the summer, the sun appears at its highest in the sky. During the winter, it appears at its lowest. The sun's rays strike Earth more directly in the summer than in the winter. The more direct the sunlight is, the more it heats up the ground. Thus, it is warmer in the summer than it is in the winter. Also, there are longer periods of daylight in the summer

Self-Check

1. Why is a year about 365 days long?
2. How far is Earth tilted on its axis?
3. When the northern half of Earth is tilted toward the sun, what season is it in that half?

Lines of Latitude

Lines of **latitude** are imaginary lines that run in an east–west direction around Earth. Latitude is the distance north or south of the **equator**. The equator is the line of latitude halfway between the North and South Poles. Find the lines of latitude on the globe below. Lines of latitude are also called **parallels.**

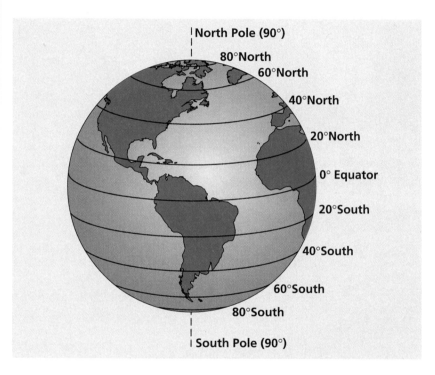

Parallels are numbered beginning at the equator and ending at each of the poles. The latitude numbers begin with 0° at the equator and increase to 90° at the North Pole. All latitude numbers north of the equator are followed by the letter *N*, for *north*. The latitude numbers also begin at 0° at the equator and increase to 90° at the South Pole. South of the equator, all latitude numbers are followed by the letter *S*, for *south*. No line of latitude is greater than 90°.

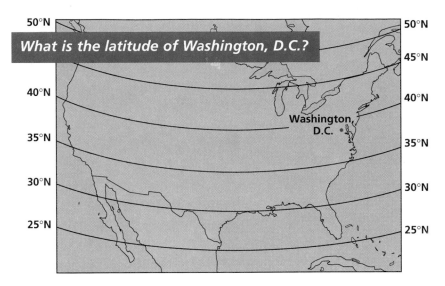

What is the latitude of Washington, D.C.?

Estimating Latitude

When a map, such as the one above, does not show all the parallels, the person using the map must estimate the parallels that are not shown. To do that, the person must divide the space that is between parallels that are shown. The divisions should be equal.

Find the city of Washington, D.C., on the map above. To find the latitude of Washington, D.C., use the following procedure.

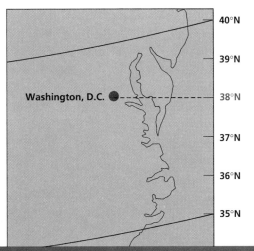

The position of the missing parallels between 35° N and 40° N can be estimated.

1. Find the two parallels on either side of Washington, D.C. (35°N and 40°N)

2. In your mind or on paper, divide up the space between the two latitude lines into equal parts that represent the parallels that are not shown on the map. See the example in the map to the left.

3. Use your divisions to estimate the latitude point to the nearest degree (38°N). The latitude of Washington, D.C., is about 38°N.

Lines of Longitude

Lines of **longitude** are imaginary lines that run in a north–south direction around Earth. Longitude lines are also called **meridians.** Longitude is the distance east or west of the **prime meridian.** The prime meridian is the line of 0° longitude.

Like parallels, meridians are numbered in degrees. Numbering begins with 0° at the prime meridian and ends at the 180° line. The 180° line is on the opposite side of the earth from the prime meridian. Numbers east of the prime meridian are followed by the letter *E.* Numbers west of the prime meridian are followed by the letter *W.*

As you can see in the drawing below, meridians run between the two poles. Meridians are not spaced equally at all points. They come together at the poles and are farthest apart at the equator.

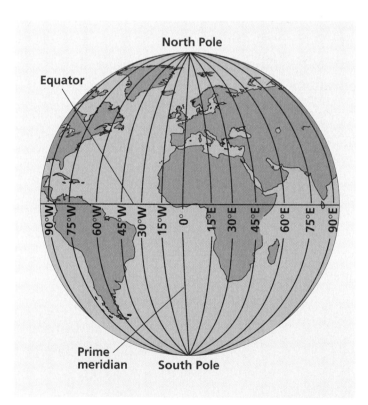

Estimating Longitude

When you use a map that does not show all the meridians, you have to estimate the meridians that are not shown. Recall the procedure for estimating parallels that you read about on page 165. Follow the same procedure to estimate meridians.

Locating Points by Latitude and Longitude

To locate any point on Earth's surface, you need to know both the latitude and longitude of that point. When stating any point's location, the latitude is written before the longitude.

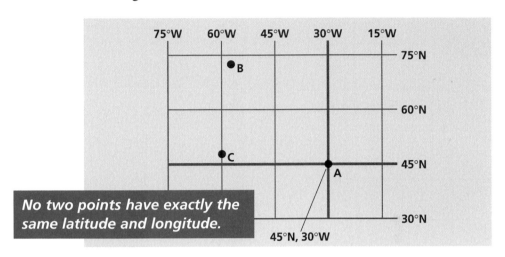

No two points have exactly the same latitude and longitude.

For example, find point A on the illustration above. Point A lies on the 45°N parallel and the 30°W meridian. Its location is written as 45°N, 30°W. In other words, point A is 45° north of the equator and 30° west of the prime meridian.

On the illustration, what is located at about 48°N, 60°W? By estimating the position of any missing grid lines, you should be able to locate point C at about 48°N, 60°W. What is the location of point B? It is about 72°N, 57°W.

The Hemispheres

The equator is the line of latitude halfway between the North and South Poles. This line divides Earth into two **hemispheres**. A hemisphere is half of Earth. The half north of the equator is called the Northern Hemisphere. The half south of the equator is the Southern Hemisphere.

Hemisphere
Section of Earth that is north or south of the equator or east or west of the prime meridian.

If Earth were cut in half through the prime meridian, it would be divided into another set of hemispheres. The two halves are called the Eastern Hemisphere and the Western Hemisphere. In which of these hemispheres is the United States?

Use the map below to answer the questions that follow.

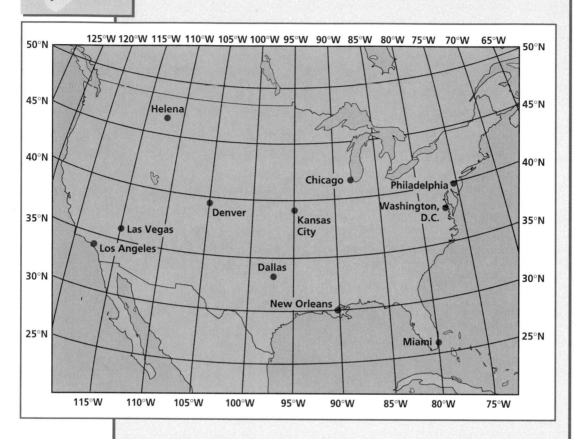

1. Which city is located at each of the following points?
   a. 30°N, 90°W
   b. 38°N, 77°W
   c. 40°N, 75°W
   d. 39°N, 105°W
   e. 36°N, 115°W

2. What is the latitude and longitude of each of these cities?
   a. Miami
   b. Chicago
   c. Dallas
   d. Helena
   e. Los Angeles
   f. Kansas City

Chapter 9   SUMMARY

- Earth has a rounded shape, but it is not perfectly round.

- About 30 percent of Earth's surface is land, which is broken up into seven continents.

- About 70 percent of Earth's surface is water, most of which is divided into four oceans.

- Rotation is the spinning of Earth on its axis. Earth rotates from west to east.

- The turning of Earth on its axis results in day and night.

- Earth is divided into standard time zones, areas within which the same clock time occurs.

- Revolution is Earth's movement in an orbit around the sun. One revolution takes about 365 days.

- Earth's axis is always tilted, which causes the seasons.

- Latitude lines are imaginary lines that run east–west around Earth. Latitude lines are called parallels.

- Latitude is the distance from the equator.

- Longitude lines are imaginary lines that run north–south around Earth. Longitude lines are called meridians.

- Longitude is the distance from the prime meridian.

- Intersecting parallels and meridians make it possible to locate a single point anywhere on Earth's surface.

- A hemisphere is half of Earth.

- The equator divides Earth into the Northern and Southern Hemispheres. The prime meridian divides Earth into the Eastern and Western Hemispheres.

Science Words		
axis, 158	North Pole, 158
continent, 156	parallel, 164
earth science, 153	prime meridian, 166
equator, 164	revolution, 162
hemisphere, 167	rotation, 158
latitude, 164	South Pole, 158
longitude, 166	standard time zone, 159
meridian, 166	
meteorologist, 153	

Vocabulary Review

Number your paper from 1 to 10. Then choose the term from the Word Bank that best completes each sentence. Write the answer on your paper.

1. The imaginary line through Earth around which it rotates is called the _____.

2. The seven major land areas of Earth are called _____.

3. The _____ is the line of latitude halfway between the North and South poles.

4. Within any _____, the same clock time occurs.

5. The prime meridian is the line of 0° _____.

6. Lines of latitude are called _____.

7. The point farthest north on Earth is called the _____.

8. Most of Earth's surface is _____.

9. Half of Earth is a(n) _____.

10. Latitude and longitude are measured in _____.

Concept Review

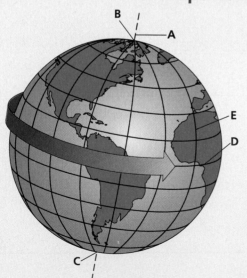

Number your paper from 1 to 8. Then answer each of the following questions. Write the answers on your paper.

1. Name each of the lettered features in the diagram.

2. What is the shape of Earth?

3. About what percentage of Earth's surface do the continents cover?

4. Which is the largest ocean?

5. When it is midnight at one point on Earth, what time is it at a point exactly halfway around the earth?

6. What is the line of 0° latitude called?

7. On which line of longitude does a point at 31°S, 92°W lie?

8. Which hemispheres lie on either side of the prime meridian?

Number your paper from 9 to 13. Choose the answer that best completes each sentence. Write the letter of the answer on your paper.

9. Earth rotates from _____.

   a. east to west   b. north to south   c. west to east

10. Earth rotates once every _____.

   a. day   b. week   c. month

11. The time in New York City is _____ the time in Los Angeles.

   a. earlier than   b. later than   c. the same as

12. A point at latitude 80°N is located near the _____.

   a. equator   b. North Pole   c. prime meridian

13. Antarctica is located in the _____ Hemisphere.

   a. Northern   b. Eastern   c. Southern

Critical Thinking

Write the answer to each of the following questions.

1. How are latitude and longitude alike? How are they different?

2. How would day and night be different than they are now if Earth did not rotate?

Test Taking Tip | Answer all questions you are sure of first, then go back and answer the others.

Chapter

10

Minerals and Rocks

Suppose you were hiking and found a gleaming chunk of rock. Would you think that you had struck gold? Or would you know that you had found pyrite, sometimes called "fool's gold"? Gold and pyrite are minerals that look alike and feel alike, but they are different. In this chapter, you will learn what minerals are and how you can tell them apart. You will also learn how rocks form, how they wear away, and how they form again.

ORGANIZE YOUR THOUGHTS

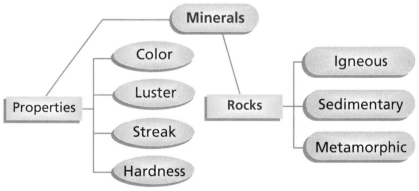

Minerals

Properties
- Color
- Luster
- Streak
- Hardness

Rocks
- Igneous
- Sedimentary
- Metamorphic

Goals for Learning

▶ To explain what a mineral is

▶ To identify basic properties of all minerals

▶ To compare minerals by their properties

▶ To explain what a rock is

▶ To describe how igneous, sedimentary, and metamorphic rocks are formed

▶ To describe the rock cycle

Objectives

After reading this lesson, you should be able to

▶ explain what a mineral is.

▶ name some common minerals.

▶ identify four properties of minerals.

▶ explain how to test the streak and hardness of a mineral.

Mineral
Element or compound found in Earth's crust.

Did You Know?

Quartz vibrates at a precise, constant speed when electricity is passed through it. Watches use tiny bits of vibrating quartz to keep time.

Earth's top layer is a mixture of useful compounds and elements. Scientists classify some of these compounds and elements as **minerals**.

Minerals

What do gold, quartz, and diamond have in common? They are all minerals. Elements or compounds are called minerals if they have these five features.

- They are solids.
- They are formed naturally.
- They have the same chemical makeup throughout.
- They are not alive or made of living things.
- They have a definite arrangement of atoms.

Common Minerals

About 3,000 different minerals are found on Earth. Only a small number of minerals make up most of Earth's surface. The most common minerals are quartz, feldspar, mica, calcite, dolomite, halite, and gypsum.

Some minerals, such as gold (Au on the periodic table) and sulfur (S), are pure elements. Most minerals, however, are made up of two or more elements. For example, quartz (SiO_2) is made up of the elements silicon (Si) and oxygen (O).

Quartz is a chemical compound of silicon and oxygen.

Properties of Minerals

Pyrite is sometimes called "fool's gold" because people can easily mistake it for gold. However, no two minerals share all the same physical properties. For example, pyrite has almost the same color as gold, but it is harder than gold. Four properties can be used to identify minerals: color, luster, streak, and hardness.

Color

Some minerals have a unique color. For example, sulfur is usually bright yellow. However, most minerals can be found in more than one color. For example, quartz might be clear, purple, pink, black, or white. Many minerals are similar in color, such as pyrite and gold. Color is one clue to a mineral's identity, but color alone is usually not enough of a clue.

Luster

Different minerals reflect light differently. Some minerals are shiny, but others look dull. The way that a mineral reflects light is called **luster.** There are two main kinds of luster—metallic and nonmetallic. Shiny minerals, such as gold and pyrite, have a metallic luster.

Minerals with a nonmetallic luster can be described further. For example, if a mineral looks like a pearl, its luster is described as "pearly." A mineral that looks like glass is said to have a "glassy" luster. The table shows some examples of minerals and their lusters.

Luster
The way a mineral reflects light.

The Luster of Some Minerals	
Mineral	**Luster**
gold	metallic
quartz	glassy
calcite	glassy
halite	glassy
talc	pearly
garnet	glassy
silver	metallic
pyrite	metallic

Talc has a pearly luster. Calcite has a glassy luster.

Streak

When you rub a soft mineral across a tile, it leaves a mark. The color of the mark is the mineral's **streak.** A streak test helps you identify a mineral. The streak of a mineral may be different from the mineral's color. For example, gold always has a gold streak, but pyrite always has a black streak. However, some minerals are so hard that they do not leave a streak.

Hardness

The **hardness** of a mineral describes how well the mineral resists being scratched. Geologists measure hardness on a scale of 1 to 10, called the Mohs scale of hardness. The higher the number a mineral has, the harder the mineral is. A mineral will scratch any other mineral that has a lower number. Look at the table. The mineral fluorite has a hardness of 4. It scratches calcite but does not scratch apatite. Feldspar will scratch calcite, fluorite, and apatite.

Mohs Scale of Hardness		
Mineral	**Hardness**	**Quick test**
talc	1	scratched easily by fingernail
gypsum	2	scratched by fingernail
calcite	3	barely scratched by copper penny
fluorite	4	scratched easily by steel
apatite	5	scratched by steel
feldspar	6	scratches glass easily
quartz	7	scratches both glass and steel easily
topaz	8	scratches quartz
corundum	9	no simple test
diamond	10	no simple test

You can use the Mohs scale to find the hardness of an unknown sample. Scratch the sample against each mineral on the scale, starting with the softest mineral. If the unknown sample scratches one mineral, test it with the next. Keep moving up the hardness scale, testing until the sample itself is scratched by one of the minerals. Its hardness is between that of the last two minerals tested. For example, a mineral that scratches feldspar but is scratched by quartz has a hardness of about 6.5.

If you do not have a set of minerals, you can use the "quick test" instead. The quick test shows how to use common materials to test hardness. For example, suppose you cannot scratch a mineral with your fingernail but you can easily scratch it with a penny. The mineral probably has a hardness between 2 and 3. Geologists working in the field usually use a quick test.

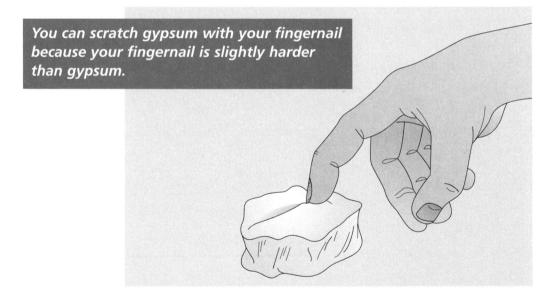

You can scratch gypsum with your fingernail because your fingernail is slightly harder than gypsum.

Self-Check

1. What is a mineral?
2. Name two common minerals.
3. Why can't color alone be used to identify minerals?
4. Why is the streak test helpful in identifying a mineral?
5. The hardness of quartz is 7. The hardness of topaz is 8. Will quartz scratch topaz? Explain.

What are some common uses of minerals?

Minerals are all around you. Most of them have been crushed, melted, or chemically changed to do a specific job. Each mineral has a property that makes it valuable for the job it does. For example, copper is used inside power cords for household appliances because it conducts electricity well.

Minerals have many uses in your daily life. The "lead" in your pencil is the soft mineral graphite. When crushed, graphite can be used as a lubricant for locks. Talc is crushed to make talcum powder. Quartz is found in sand, which is melted to make glass for windows, bottles, and drinking glasses. The mineral bauxite contains aluminum, which is used to make soda cans and cookware.

The table shows the uses of some minerals. Look around your home. How many different examples of minerals can you find?

Mineral	How it is changed	Material
talc	crushed	paint
iron	melted	nails
bauxite	melted	cookware
gypsum	crushed	plaster
corundum	crushed	sandpaper
quartz	melted	glass

INVESTIGATION

10

Observing Color, Streak, and Hardness

Materials

✓ labeled
  samples of
  halite
  galena
  pyrite
  mica
  hematite
  amphibole
✓ streak plate
✓ copper
  penny
✓ steel spoon

Purpose

To describe the color and streak and estimate the hardness of six mineral samples

Procedure

1. Copy the data table below on a sheet of paper.

Mineral sample	Color	Streak	Hardness
halite			
galena			
pyrite			
mica			
hematite			
amphibole			

2. Observe the color of each sample. Record your observations.

3. Rub each sample across the streak plate, as shown in the picture on the next page. Record the streak of each mineral in your data table.

4. Refer to the Quick Test column of the Mohs scale on page 175. Try to scratch each sample with your fingernail, the penny, and the steel spoon. Use the test results and the Mohs scale to estimate the hardness of each sample. Record your data.

Questions

1. Which property was the easiest to observe?

2. Which property was the hardest to observe?

3. How did the colors of the minerals compare with the colors of their streaks?

Explore Further

Identify an unknown sample by finding its hardness. Use the materials and minerals you already have. Ask your teacher for the sample. Explain how you tested the unknown sample. (*Hint:* The unknown sample is one of the minerals from the Mohs scale of hardness.)

Objectives

After reading this lesson, you should be able to

▶ explain what rocks are.
▶ name the three main types of rock.
▶ describe the rock cycle.

Minerals Make Up Rocks

About 3,000 minerals occur in Earth's crust. Most of them are not found in a pure form. They are mixed together in **rocks.** A rock is a solid, natural material made of one or more minerals. Only about 20 minerals make up 95 percent of Earth's rocks.

Earth scientists who study rocks are interested in which minerals make them up and how the rocks formed. This information helps scientists and engineers locate valuable resources such as oil and metals. Knowledge of rocks is necessary for undertaking construction projects and understanding the environment. Rocks also provide clues about Earth's history and how Earth changes.

Igneous rock

Rock
Natural solid material made of one or more minerals.

Sedimentary rock

Three Types of Rock

Geologists group, or classify, rocks into three main types, depending on how they form. Some rock forms when hot, melted minerals called **magma** cool and harden. This rock is **igneous rock.** Another type of rock forms when bits of other rocks and the remains of living things are pressed and cemented together. The result is **sedimentary rock.** Heat, pressure, and chemical reactions can change sedimentary or igneous rock into **metamorphic rock.** The photos on these two pages show examples of the three rock types. What features do you notice about each type of rock?

Igneous rock
Rock formed from melted minerals that have cooled and hardened.

Magma
Hot liquid rock inside Earth.

Metamorphic rock
Rock that has been changed by intense heat, pressure, and chemical reactions.

Sedimentary rock
Rock formed from pieces of other rock and organic matter that was pressed and cemented together.

Metamorphic rock

Igneous	Sedimentary	Metamorphic
basalt	chalk	amphibolite
diorite	dolomite	gneiss
granite	flint	marble
obsidian	limestone	metaquartzite
pumice	sandstone	schist
rhyolite	shale	slate

The Rock Cycle

Rocks are always changing. The series of changes through which one kind of rock becomes another kind of rock is called the **rock cycle.** Study the diagram as you consider the following pathway through the rock cycle.

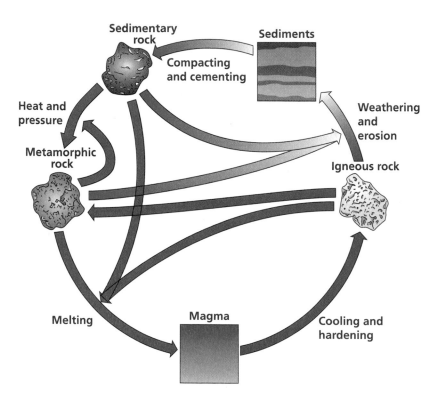

As magma rises, it cools and hardens into igneous rock. Pressure lifts the rock to Earth's surface, where it slowly begins to break apart, forming sediment. Rivers carry the sediment to the ocean. Layers of sediment build up and eventually become sedimentary rock. Heat and pressure from within Earth change the sedimentary rock into metamorphic rock. Continued heating melts the rock, which cools, hardens, and becomes igneous rock once again.

Rocks do not always cycle from igneous to sedimentary to metamorphic. What other pathways do you see?

1. What is a rock?
2. What are the three main types of rocks?
3. Which type of rock is granite?
4. How do metamorphic rocks form?
5. What is the rock cycle?

Chapter 10   SUMMARY

- A mineral is an element or a compound that occurs naturally, is a solid, is not alive or made of living things, has the same chemical makeup throughout, and has a definite arrangement of atoms.

- A mineral can be identified by its properties, including color, luster, streak, and hardness.

- Minerals have either a metallic or nonmetallic luster.

- A mineral's streak is tested by rubbing the mineral across a streak plate.

- The Mohs scale of hardness ranks minerals according to how well they resist being scratched.

- A rock is a solid, natural material made of one or more minerals.

- The three main types of rocks are igneous, sedimentary, and metamorphic.

- Igneous rocks form from magma that cools and hardens.

- Sedimentary rocks form from solid particles called sediment. The sediment accumulates in layers, which get pressed and cemented into rock.

- Metamorphic rocks form from other rocks that are changed by heat and pressure.

- Rocks change from one type to another in the rock cycle.

Science Words		
hardness, 175		mineral, 173
igneous rock, 181		rock, 180
luster, 174		rock cycle, 182
magma, 181		sedimentary rock, 181
metamorphic rock, 181		streak, 175

WORD BANK
color
hardness
igneous rock
luster
metamorphic rock
mineral
rock
rock cycle
sedimentary rock
streak

Vocabulary Review

Number your paper from 1 to 10. Then choose the term from the Word Bank that best completes each sentence. Write the answer on your paper.

1. The _____ of a mineral can be tested by scratching it.

2. The color that a mineral leaves on a tile is its _____.

3. Rocks change from one type to another as they go through the _____.

4. A(n) _____ is an element or compound found in Earth's crust.

5. A mineral's _____ may be glassy, pearly, or metallic.

6. _____ forms from rocks that have been changed by heat, pressure, and chemical reactions.

7. A(n) _____ is a natural solid made of one or more minerals.

8. Layers of sediments that are pressed together and cemented can form _____.

9. Fool's gold and real gold have almost the same _____.

10. Hot liquid rock that cools and hardens forms _____.

Concept Review

Number your paper from 1 to 6. Choose the answer that best completes each sentence. Write the letter of the answer on your paper.

1. Not all minerals are _____.

   a. solids   b. formed naturally   c. shiny

2. Mineral A is harder than mineral B if A _____.

   a. weighs more than B   c. streaks B

   b. scratches B

3. Gold and pyrite are different in _____.

   a. color   b. luster   c. streak

4. Two kinds of luster are _____.

   a. shiny and hard   c. yellow and cube-shaped

   b. metallic and nonmetallic

5. You test a mineral sample for streak by _____.

   a. rubbing it on a white tile   c. weighing it

   b. breaking it

6. On the Mohs scale of hardness, diamond has the _____.

   a. lowest number   b. darkest streak   c. highest number

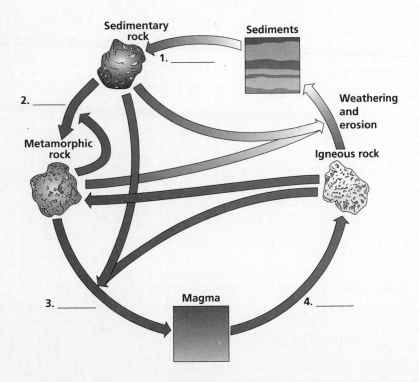

Sedimentary rock

Sediments

1. _____

2. _____

Weathering and erosion

Metamorphic rock

Igneous rock

3. _____

Magma

4. _____

Critical Thinking

The diagram at left shows the rock cycle. Some words are missing from the diagram. What words belong in each numbered blank? Write your answers on a sheet of paper.

Test Taking Tip | When answering multiple-choice questions, first identify the choices you know are untrue.

Chapter

11

Weathering and Erosion

Have you ever visited the Grand Canyon or seen a picture of it? It took millions of years for wind and running water to carve the Grand Canyon. Water and wind continue to shape the canyon today. In fact, water and wind constantly shape the land where you live too. In this chapter, you will find out how the same forces that wash dirt off a driveway create the most breathtaking scenery in the world.

ORGANIZE YOUR THOUGHTS

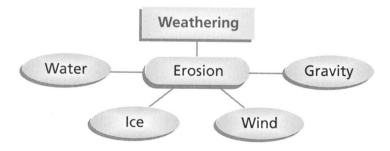

Goals for Learning

▶ To define *weathering*
▶ To identify different kinds of weathering
▶ To describe how water, wind, ice, and gravity cause erosion
▶ To describe how deposition creates landforms

Objectives

After reading this lesson, you should be able to

▶ define *weathering.*

▶ give examples of mechanical and chemical weathering.

▶ identify different soil layers.

Mechanical weathering
The breaking apart of rocks without changing their mineral composition.

Weathering
The breaking down of rocks on Earth's surface.

Rocks Break Down

Earth is constantly changing. Even a hard material like rock changes over time. How have the tombstones below changed? Over the years, these slabs of limestone have broken down so that it is difficult to read the carvings.

The breaking down of rocks on Earth's surface is **weathering.** Weathering occurs when the rock is exposed to air, water, or living things. All these factors help to break rocks apart.

Limestone breaks down more easily than other rocks, such as granite.

Mechanical Weathering

In **mechanical weathering**, rocks break into smaller pieces, but their chemical makeup stays the same. The photo below shows one way that rocks break. The tree started growing in soil that collected in a crack of the rock. As the tree grew, its roots pushed against the rock and split it. You might see this kind of mechanical weathering in a sidewalk near a tree. The growing roots often lift and crumble the sidewalk.

The growing roots of a tree act like a wedge driven into the rock.

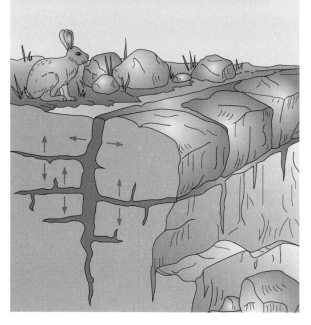

Freezing water wedges rocks apart and makes smaller pieces.

Mechanical weathering also occurs as water freezes in the cracks of rocks. When water freezes, it expands. As the freezing water expands, it pushes the rock apart, as shown in the drawing. The ice may melt, and the water may refreeze. Each time the water freezes, the cracks get bigger. Finally, the rock breaks apart.

Chemical Weathering

In **chemical weathering**, changes occur in the chemical makeup of rocks. New minerals might be added to or taken away from the rock. The minerals might be changed into new substances.

Chemical weathering
The breaking apart of rocks caused by a change in their chemical makeup.

Oxidation
Process in which minerals combine with oxygen to form new substances.

For example, in a process called **oxidation**, oxygen from the air or water combines with the iron in rocks. As a result, a new substance called iron oxide, or rust, forms. Iron oxide stains rocks various shades of yellow, orange, red, or brown. How are the rocks like the rusty old cans in the photo?

A rusting can slowly crumbles. "Rusting" rock also slowly breaks apart.

Chemical weathering also occurs when water changes minerals in the rocks. For example, water changes the mineral feldspar, which is part of many rocks. The water changes feldspar to clay and washes it away. Without the feldspar to hold the other minerals together, the rock falls apart.

Carbonic acid dissolves limestone, leaving huge caves.

The limestone cave shown here is the result of chemical weathering. Rain and groundwater combine with carbon dioxide in the air to form carbonic acid. This is the same acid found in carbonated soft drinks. As carbonic acid trickles through the ground, it dissolves calcite—the main mineral in limestone. As more and more limestone is dissolved, small holes become huge caves.

Weathering Forms Soil

Soil
Mixture of tiny pieces of weathered rock and the remains of plants and animals.

When rock has weathered for a long time, **soil** may develop. Soil is a mixture of tiny pieces of weathered rock and the remains of plants and animals. The makeup of soil depends on the types of rock particles and remains that are found in it.

As soil develops, it forms layers. Fully developed soil has three layers. Compare the drawing and photo on the next page as you read about soil layers.

Subsoil

Layer of soil directly below the topsoil.

Topsoil

Top layer of soil, rich with remains of plants and animals.

Most soil you see is **topsoil.** This layer has the greatest amount of oxygen and decayed organic matter. The organic matter helps the soil hold moisture.

Directly below the topsoil is the **subsoil.** It contains minerals that were washed down from the topsoil. Many of these minerals are iron oxides and give the subsoil a yellowish or reddish color. Plant roots grow down into the subsoil to get minerals and water.

The next layer contains chunks of partially weathered rock. Near the bottom of this layer, rock fragments sit directly on solid rock.

The three layers of soil are not clear-cut; they blend into each other.

Topsoil

Subsoil

Weathered rock

Solid rock

Self-Check

1. What is weathering?
2. How are mechanical and chemical weathering different?
3. What happens in the process of oxidation?
4. What is soil made of?
5. Name the layers in soil from top to bottom.

Chemical Weathering

Purpose
To model and observe how chemical weathering occurs

Procedure
1. Copy the data table below on your paper.

Materials

✓ safety goggles
✓ paper towels
✓ hand lens
✓ 5 limestone chips or pieces of chalk
✓ clear plastic 12-oz cup
✓ 1 cup vinegar
✓ strainer
✓ water

Appearance of Limestone Chips	
Before weathering	**After weathering**

2. Put on your safety goggles.

3. Use the hand lens to look at the limestone chips. Describe their appearance in the data table.

4. Put the chips in the cup. Add vinegar to the cup to cover the chips. Let the chips sit overnight.

5. Pour the vinegar and chips into a strainer over a sink. Rinse the chips with water.

6. Place the limestone chips on paper towels. Use the hand lens to look at the chips again. In the data table, describe any changes you see.

Questions
1. How did the surfaces of the chips change?
2. Vinegar is an acid. What did the vinegar do to change the appearance of the limestone?

Explore Further
Repeat the experiment using other kinds of rocks.

Erosion

After rock has been loosened by weathering, it is worn away and moved to another place. The wearing away and moving of weathered rock and soil is called **erosion.** The main agents, or causes, of erosion are rivers, waves, moving ice, wind, and gravity.

Erosion by Rivers

Rivers and the water that flows into them change more of the landscape than any other agent of erosion. After rain falls to Earth's surface, the water flows downhill. The water picks up soil and rock fragments as

Gullies are tiny valleys that direct water to a larger stream.

it moves. These solid particles are sediments. The water and sediments flow into small gullies, which lead to rivers.

As water flows in a river, it erodes the banks and riverbed, which is the bottom of the river. Compare the eroding power of a river to a hose. The force of water from the

Water and sediment act like sandpaper to wear these boulders smooth.

hose can easily dig up soil and move it across a lawn. A jet of water may even chip away at a sidewalk. Similarly, river water erodes the land. Sand and stones in the river scrape against the banks and riverbed, causing more erosion. The fast-moving water and sediment in the stream shown here have worn these boulders smooth.

Deposition by Rivers

Sediments that are carried by the agents of erosion are eventually dropped in a process called **deposition.** For example, when a river slows down, it may drop, or deposit, its sediment. Heavier sediments such as stones drop out first. As the river slows down further, lighter sediments such as sand and clay particles drop out.

A river slows down considerably as it empties into a lake or an ocean. The sediment settles out. Eventually, the sediment builds up above the water level and forms a fan-shaped area of land called a **delta.** A delta provides rich farmland. Much of Egypt's farmland, for example, is located on the fertile Nile River delta.

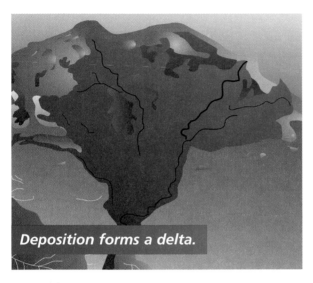

Deposition forms a delta.

Alluvial fan
Fan-shaped area of land deposited where a mountain stream moves onto flat land.

Delta
Fan-shaped area of land formed when sediment is deposited where a river empties into a lake or an ocean.

Deposition
The dropping of eroded sediment.

Notice the fan-shaped land in the drawing below. This feature is an **alluvial fan.** How do you think it formed? An alluvial fan is similar to a delta. It forms at the base of a mountain where a mountain stream meets level land.

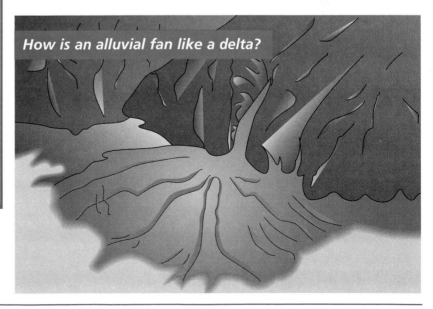

How is an alluvial fan like a delta?

Erosion and Deposition by Waves

Waves in an ocean or a large lake change the shoreline through erosion and deposition. As waves pound the shoreline, they hurl water, rocks, and sand against the coast. These materials erode the shore.

Beaches are areas where waves have deposited sand, pebbles, or shells. Some of this beach material is sediment from nearby eroded rocks. Other beach material is sediment carried to the sea by rivers. Currents carry sediment to different parts of the shoreline. As waves break on shore, the sediment is pushed onto the beach.

Self-Check

1. What is erosion?
2. How does a delta form?
3. Where does the sand on a beach come from?

SCIENCE IN YOUR LIFE

How do people cause too much erosion?

People's actions sometimes cause too much erosion, which becomes harmful to the environment. One way people increase erosion is through the use of off-road vehicles (ORVs). Dirt bikes, dune buggies, four-wheel drives, and all-terrain vehicles can be fun. But their overuse has damaged the land. The photo illustrates this problem. The hillside used to be covered with grass. The roots of grass and other plants hold soil in place. Within weeks, the use of ORVs dug up the vegetation and created ruts. Rainwater followed these ruts and formed deep gullies. The soil now erodes quickly from the hill. Areas have been set aside for ORVs, but users often venture into "closed" areas.

Glaciers Are Moving Ice

In cold climates, snow can build up into thick layers. Pressure causes the lower layers to form solid ice. Year after year, more ice builds up. Eventually, a **glacier** may form. A glacier is a huge sheet of moving ice that covers a large area. The weight of the snow and ice and the pull of gravity may cause the glacier to move slowly down hill.

An alpine glacier is a river of ice moving down a mountain valley.

Erosion by Glaciers

Because of their great size, glaciers move large amounts of sediment. As glaciers move, they pick up loose rocks and soil. These materials freeze onto the bottom and sides of the glacier. They act like grinding and cutting tools as the glacier continues to move. Rocks in the bottom of a glacier cut long grooves in the surface rock. Small rocks in the ice act like sandpaper, smoothing and shaping the bedrock.

Deposition by Glaciers

As a glacier melts, it deposits its sediment. The sediment forms ridges called **moraines.** Huge blocks of ice are also left behind when a glacier melts. The ice may be partly covered with sediment. When the ice melts, it leaves a hole in the ground. The hole fills with water and becomes a lake. Many of the lakes of Wisconsin and Minnesota formed this way.

Moraine
Ridge of sediment deposited by a glacier.

A glacial ice block can form a lake.

a. Ice block breaks off glacier.

b. Ice block gets partly buried in sediment.

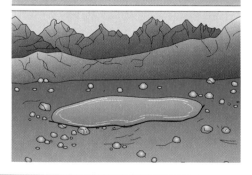

c. Ice block melts to form lake.

Some large lakes formed as glaciers moved through large valleys. The glaciers carved the valleys into wide, deep basins. The melting glacier helped fill the basins with water. Moraines dammed parts of the lakes. This process created the Great Lakes, the Finger Lakes in New York, and Lake Winnipeg in Canada.

Self-Check

1. Describe how a glacier forms.
2. How does a glacier erode the land?
3. What is a moraine?

Wind Erosion

Wind is another cause of erosion. Like water, wind picks up and carries materials from one place to another. Wind also erodes by blowing sand against rock. This action is similar to a sandblaster used to clean buildings discolored by pollution. If you have ever been stung in the face by windblown sand, you know wind can be an effective agent of erosion. Much rock in desert areas is pitted with tiny holes from windblown sand.

Wind Deposition

You are probably familiar with the wind deposit called sand dunes. These are mounds formed as the wind blows sand from one place to another. Sand dunes are most common in deserts, but they also occur around beaches.

Wind may bounce sand along the ground until it hits an obstacle, such as a small rock. A small pile forms behind the rock. The pile blocks other sand grains, and a larger mound forms. The mound continues to grow, forming a sand dune. The dune moves as wind blows sand up the gentle slope and deposits it on the steeper back slope, as shown below.

Did You Know?

Some sand dunes in the Sahara, a desert in Africa, grow to be hundreds of meters tall.

A sand dune moves as sand is blown from one side to the other.

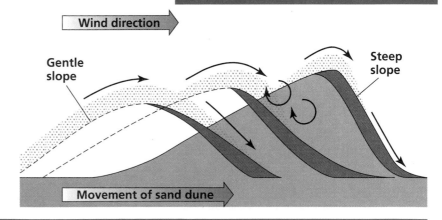

Wind direction

Gentle slope

Steep slope

Movement of sand dune

Gravity Moves the Land

Gravity plays a part in all erosion. For example, rivers and glaciers flow downhill because of gravity. Gravity can move only material that has been loosened in some way, such as by freezing and thawing or by lubrication. Sometimes gravity makes erosion happen rapidly. For example, the photo shows a common form of erosion on hillsides in California. Heavy winter rains lubricate the soil. The soil flows downhill as a mudflow. If you've ever seen a sign that reads "Caution: Falling Rock," you are aware of another way gravity makes erosion happen rapidly.

A mudflow can cause heavy damage.

Gravity works slowly too. You may have noticed old telephone poles or tombstones that tilt downhill. Loose soil and rock is moving slowly downhill, tilting objects along the way.

Self-Check

1. What are two ways that wind erodes the land?
2. How does a sand dune form?
3. What are two causes of a mudflow?

Chapter 11 Summary

- All rock exposed at the surface begins to break apart.
- Mechanical weathering is the process of breaking up rocks without changing their minerals.
- Chemical weathering is the process of breaking up rocks by changing the minerals in them.
- Soil is a mixture of weathered rock and the remains of plants and animals.
- Fully developed soil includes topsoil, subsoil, and a layer of partially weathered rock.
- The wearing away and moving of weathered rock and soil is called erosion.
- Erosion is caused by water, glaciers, wind, and gravity.
- As a river erodes the land, it carves out a valley.
- A river deposits sediment where it flows into a lake or an ocean or onto flat land. This process is called deposition.
- Waves wear away the shoreline in some places and build it up in others.
- Glaciers are moving sheets of ice on land.
- Glaciers leave ridges of sediment called moraines. Glaciers have formed many lakes.
- Wind erodes by carrying material away and by blowing it against rock.
- Gravity moves rock and soil downhill. This process can occur quickly or slowly.

Science Words		
alluvial fan, 193		mechanical weathering, 187
chemical weathering, 188		moraine, 196
delta, 193		oxidation, 188
deposition, 193		soil, 189
erosion, 192		subsoil, 190
glacier, 195		topsoil, 190
		weathering, 187

Vocabulary Review

Number your paper from 1 to 10. Then, from each pair of terms in parentheses, choose the one that best completes each sentence.

1. (Erosion, Weathering) is the wearing away and moving of rock.

2. An example of chemical weathering is (deposition, oxidation).

3. The part of the soil that includes most remains of plants and animals is the (subsoil, topsoil).

4. Sediment that settles out where a river empties into an ocean forms a (delta, fan).

5. Moving bodies of ice are (deltas, glaciers).

6. Sediment that drops from a glacier forms ridges called (alluvial fans, moraines).

7. (Weathering, erosion) breaks down rocks on Earth's surface.

8. Rivers and glaciers flow downhill because of (deposition, gravity).

9. Many lakes were formed by (glaciers, deposition).

10. Sand dunes move because of erosion and deposition by (water, wind).

Concept Review

Number your paper from 1 to 4. Then name each layer shown in the diagram.

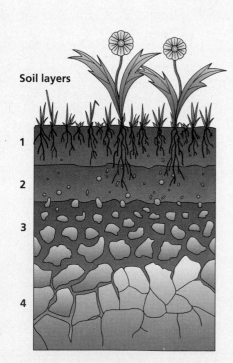

Soil layers

1
2
3
4

Number your paper from 5 to 8. Then choose the answer that best completes each sentence. Write the letter of the answer on your paper.

5. Water freezing in the cracks of rocks is an example of _____.

   a. deposition   c. mechanical weathering

   b. chemical weathering

6. During oxidation, oxygen combines with iron to form iron oxide, or _____.

   a. acid   b. rust   c. feldspar

7. _____ both cause erosion.

   a. Gravity and wind   c. Oxygen and limestone

   b. Topsoil and subsoil

8. The main process that creates a beach is _____.

   a. weathering   b. erosion   c. deposition

Critical Thinking

Write the answer to each of the following questions.

1. Why would a farmer plow across a hillside instead of plowing straight down the slope?

2. Once rock breaks into pieces, weathering occurs faster. Explain why this is true.

Test Taking Tip | Try to answer all questions as completely as possible. When asked to explain your answer, do so in complete sentences.

Chapter

12

Forces Inside Earth

What forces deep inside Earth cause a volcano to erupt? Why do volcanoes occur only in some locations? The answers to these questions begin with the ground on which you stand. It is moving. You don't notice it—usually. But a fiery volcano or a shattering earthquake reminds us that large sections of Earth's surface are moving and interacting with each other. In this chapter, you will discover how these giant slabs of rock move and what happens when they do.

ORGANIZE YOUR THOUGHTS

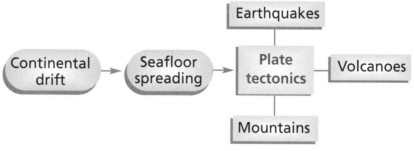

Goals for Learning

▶ To describe the structure of Earth

▶ To explain the theory of plate tectonics

▶ To relate volcanoes to plate tectonics

▶ To explain how mountains form

▶ To relate earthquakes to plate tectonics

Core
The solid and melted layer at the center of Earth.

Crust
The top layer of Earth.

Mantle
The layer of Earth that surrounds the core.

Although we cannot directly see the interior of Earth, scientists use instruments to collect data about it. These data are used to make a model of what the inside of Earth is like.

Earth is made up of three main layers. At the center is the **core**. The core is solid iron and nickel, surrounded by melted iron and nickel. The core is about 3,500 kilometers thick. Outside the core is the **mantle**. The mantle is mostly solid rock. But the top of the mantle is partly melted. The entire mantle is about 2,800 kilometers thick. The top layer of Earth is the **crust**. Compared with the other layers, the crust is very thin. It is between 8 and 70 kilometers thick. The continents and ocean floor are part of the crust. The thickest crust is below large mountain ranges.

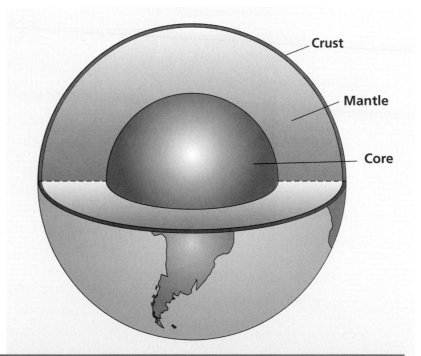

Crust

Mantle

Core

Compare the thicknesses of the crust, mantle, and core.

Continental Drift

Have you ever noticed that the edges of some continents look as if they might fit together? For example, Africa and South America could almost fit together. In 1912, a German scientist named Alfred Wegener proposed the theory of **continental drift** to explain why.

According to this theory, Earth's continents used to be joined as a single large landmass called **Pangaea**. Wegener believed Pangaea started breaking up millions of years ago. The continents slowly moved to their present positions.

Besides the puzzlelike fit of the continents, Wegener had other evidence to support his theory. For example, fossils found on one continent were similar to those found on other continents. Mountain ranges and rock layers also seemed to continue from one continent to another. In addition, glacial deposits were found at the equator where no glaciers could exist today. Could the glacial deposits have formed when the continents were in a different place? Wegener thought so.

What evidence supports the existence of Pangaea?

225 million years ago

180 million years ago

Present day

Seafloor Spreading

After World War II, new instruments allowed scientists to map the ocean floor. They discovered more about a long underwater mountain range called the **midoceanic ridge**. A **rift** valley splits the ridge in half. In the box on the next page, read some of the discoveries made about these features.

Plate
Large section of Earth's crust that moves.

Plate tectonics
Theory that Earth's crust is made up of large sections that move.

Seafloor spreading
Theory that the ocean floor spreads apart as new crust is formed at the mid-oceanic ridge.

The theory of **seafloor spreading** explains these observations. This theory states that hot magma from the mantle rises and pours out onto the ocean floor through cracks in the rift. The magma cools, hardens, and forms new crust. This new crust piles up around the rift, forming the midoceanic ridge. More rising magma pushes the new crust away on both sides of the ridge. This process widens the oceans and pushes the continents apart.

Plate Tectonics

The information from seafloor spreading and continental drift has led to one of the most important ideas in science—the theory of **plate tectonics**. This theory states that Earth's crust is made up of large sections, or **plates**. As shown on the map, most plates include ocean crust and continental crust.

Discoveries on the ocean floor

- The amount of heat coming from the midoceanic ridge is almost eight times greater than from other parts of the ocean floor.

- Magma rises from beneath the ocean floor through cracks in the rift.

- The age of the ocean crust increases with distance from the ridge.

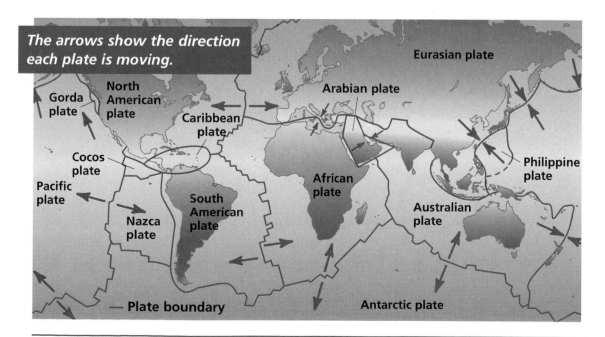

The arrows show the direction each plate is moving.

Gorda plate · North American plate · Caribbean plate · Cocos plate · Pacific plate · Nazca plate · South American plate · African plate · Arabian plate · Eurasian plate · Australian plate · Philippine plate · Antarctic plate

— Plate boundary

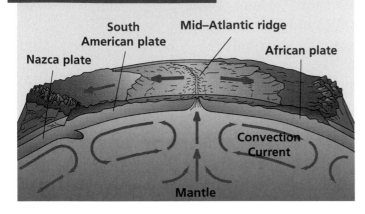

Plates spread apart, collide, or slide past each other.

South American plate

Nazca plate

Mid–Atlantic ridge

African plate

Convection Current

Mantle

Plate Movement

Plates move in three different ways. They collide, move apart, or slide past each other. How they move determines what happens where they meet.

Look at the drawing. The South American and African plates are moving apart. Where plates move apart, a rift forms. The Nazca and South American plates move toward each other. Here the Nazca plate is forced under the South American plate. A deep trench forms. The Nazca plate melts as it sinks into the mantle. Some plates slide past each other. The map on the previous page shows the Pacific plate sliding northwest past the North American plate.

The pushing, pulling, and grinding of plates cause volcanoes and earthquakes. Magma that reaches the surface produces volcanoes where plates collide or spread apart. You will learn more about volcanoes and earthquakes later in this chapter.

Convection Currents

The last piece in the plate tectonics puzzle is what causes the plates to move. In other words, why does magma rise at the midoceanic ridge in the first place? Most scientists think the answer is **convection currents**. A convection current is the circular movement of a liquid or gas as it heats. Convection currents in the partly melted upper mantle can push the plates along as if on a conveyor belt.

Did You Know?

Plates usually move slowly, an average of about 2 centimeters per year. That's about as fast as your fingernails grow.

Convection current
Circular motion of gas or liquid as it heats.

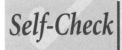

Self-Check

1. What are the layers of Earth?
2. What is the theory of continental drift?
3. What is the theory of plate tectonics?

How Volcanoes Develop

A **volcano** is a mountain that builds around a **vent**, or opening, where magma pushes up through Earth's surface. The mountain is the cone and consists of ashes and hardened lava that erupt from the volcano.

Most volcanoes form where two plates meet. For example, Mount St. Helens in Washington formed where the Gorda plate sinks beneath the North American plate. The sinking Gorda plate melts into magma, which then rises to the surface. Where plates collide beneath the oceans, the volcanoes may rise above sea level to form islands. The Aleutian Islands of Alaska and the islands of Japan formed this way.

Types of Volcanoes

Volcanoes are grouped into three types. This grouping is based on how the volcano erupts, the material that comes out, and the shape of the volcano's cone. The three types of volcanoes are shown on the next page.

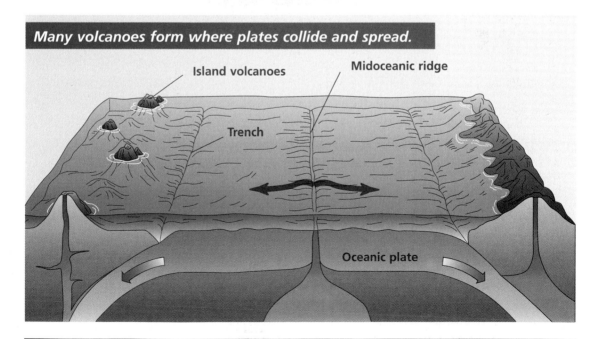

Many volcanoes form where plates collide and spread.

Island volcanoes   Midoceanic ridge

Trench

Oceanic plate

Cinder cones are small volcanoes with steep sides. Their eruptions are explosive and include mostly ash and rock. Cerro Negro in Nicaragua is a cinder cone.

Shield volcanoes are low and broad with wide craters. They are not very explosive. The thin lava from shield volcanoes spreads out in layers. The Hawaiian Islands formed from shield volcanoes.

Cinder cone
Small volcano with steep sides and explosive eruptions of ash and rocks.

Composite volcano
Tall volcano formed from eruptions of ash and rock followed by quiet lava flows.

Shield volcano
Volcano with a wide crater, developing from layers of lava.

A **composite volcano** forms when gentle eruptions of lava alternate with explosive eruptions of ash and rock. Composite volcanoes grow to be very tall. Mount Fuji in Japan is a composite volcano.

Self-Check

1. What is a volcano?
2. How do volcanoes relate to plate tectonics?
3. What are three volcano types?

Objectives

After reading this lesson, you should be able to

▶ describe three ways that mountains form.

▶ compare the different forces that cause mountains to form.

▶ identify types of movement along faults.

Folding
Bending of rock layers that are squeezed together.

You may have heard the expression "as old as the hills." In fact, mountains and hills are still being built. The process is usually so slow, however, that you don't notice it. Movements of Earth's crust cause these landforms to rise above the surrounding landscape.

Mountains and Colliding Plates

Mountains can form when plates collide. You have already read about how volcanic mountains form when one plate sinks beneath another. This usually happens when ocean crust sinks beneath continental crust. The Cascade Range in the northwestern United States and the Andes in Peru were built this way.

When continental crust collides with other continental crust, the plates usually crumple like a rug. The rock layers of the plates bend, as shown in the diagram. This process is called **folding**. The Himalayas have formed this way where two plates collide in Asia.

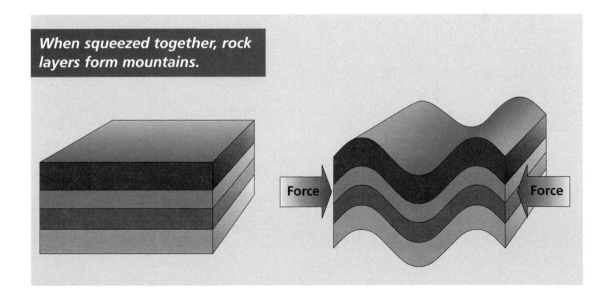

When squeezed together, rock layers form mountains.

Force   Force

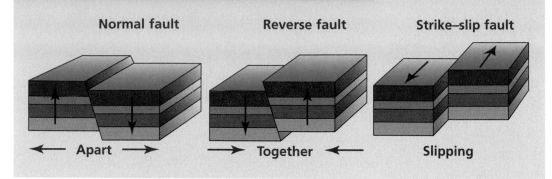

The rocks along a fault move in different directions.

Normal fault Reverse fault Strike–slip fault

← Apart → → Together ← Slipping

Mountains and Faults

Fault
Break in Earth's crust along which movement occurs.

Normal fault
Break in the crust in which the overhanging block of rock has slid down.

Reverse fault
Break in the crust in which the overhanging block of rock has been raised.

Strike–slip fault
Break in the crust in which the blocks of rock move horizontally past each other.

When pressed together, some rocks break rather than bend. A **fault** is a break in Earth's crust along which movement occurs. Some faults are visible on Earth's surface. Most faults, however, are deep underground. Rock movement along faults can cause mountains to form.

Three types of faults are shown in the diagram. In a **normal fault**, the two sides of the fault pull apart. The rocks on one side drop down lower than the other side. In a **reverse fault**, the two sides push together. Rocks on one side get pushed up over rocks on the other side. In a **strike–slip fault**, rocks on each side slide against each other horizontally. The San Andreas fault in California is a strike–slip fault.

Movement along faults can raise large blocks of rock, forming mountains. Rock movement along faults built the Grand Tetons of Wyoming and the Wasatch Range of Utah.

Self-Check

1. What is folding?
2. What is a fault?
3. What are three ways that mountains form?

Models of Folding and Faults

Purpose

To model the movement of rock layers where folding and faults occur

Procedure

1. Work with a partner to model folding rock layers. Hold one telephone book as shown in Figure A. Be sure to grasp it firmly with both hands.

2. Slowly push both hands together, squeezing the book. On a sheet of paper, sketch the folds that appear.

Materials

✓ 2 thick telephone books or catalogs

Figure A

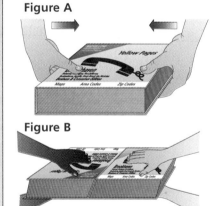

Figure B

3. Use the telephone books to model rock layers along a fault. Hold the telephone books together as shown in Figure B. Be sure to place the book spines at an angle.

4. Slowly move the phone books to model rock movement at a normal fault. If needed, refer to the diagram in the lesson.

5. Sketch what happens to the books.

6. Repeat steps 4 and 5 to model rock movement along a reverse fault.

Questions

1. What kind of plate motion might produce the change you saw in step 2?

2. Compare and contrast the motion of the rock layers you modeled for a normal and a reverse fault.

3. How do the fault models demonstrate mountain building?

Objectives

After reading this lesson, you should be able to

▶ explain what causes earthquakes.

▶ describe the motion of earthquake waves.

▶ identify what a seismograph does.

Earthquake
Shaking of Earth's crust.

What does it feel like when you sit in the bleachers at a sporting event? When someone stands up, sits down, or walks nearby, you probably feel the bleachers shake. Shaking also occurs in the rocks of Earth's crust. This shaking is called an **earthquake**.

Causes of Earthquakes

An earthquake is a shaking of Earth's crust that occurs when energy is suddenly released. An erupting volcano releases energy and causes some earthquakes. But most earthquakes occur when rocks break or move suddenly along a fault. For example, two blocks of rock that are sliding past each other may get snagged on the jagged rocky sides. Friction holds the blocks together, but they are still being pushed. Energy builds up. When the pushing forces overcome the friction, the blocks move suddenly and a lot of energy is released, which causes an earthquake.

Like volcanoes, most earthquakes occur near plate boundaries. This is where most movements along faults occur. In fact, the boundary between two plates that are sliding past each other is a large fault. Smaller faults occur near such large faults. Compare this map of major earthquake zones to the map of plates on page 205. What do you notice?

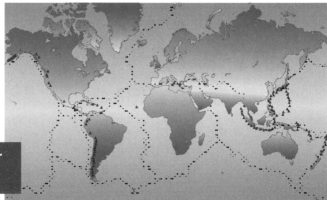

Most earthquakes occur near plate boundaries.

▲▲▲ Volcanoes ⌐⌐ Earthquakes

Did You Know?

Astronauts have placed seismographs on the moon to detect "moonquakes" from meteorite impacts and forces within the moon.

Seismograph
Instrument that detects and records earthquake waves.

Earthquake Waves

The energy from an earthquake travels through rock in waves. There are three different types of earthquake waves. Primary waves, or P-waves, cause rock particles to vibrate back and forth. Secondary waves, or S-waves, cause rocks to vibrate up and down. Both P-waves and S-waves travel inside Earth. When P-waves or S-waves reach Earth's surface, they cause long waves, or L-waves. L-waves travel along the surface of Earth. L-waves are the most destructive of earthquake waves because they cause the ground to bend and twist.

Earthquake waves are detected by an instrument called a **seismograph**. A seismograph uses a pen that does not move and a chart that does move. When the crust shakes, the paper chart also shakes. This makes the pen record a jagged line instead of a straight one. A seismograph records all three kinds of earthquake waves. P-waves are recorded first. They move the fastest and are the first to arrive at the recording station. P-waves also make the shortest lines on the chart. S-waves make longer lines. The L-waves arrive last. They make the longest lines. In the diagram below, you can see how the recordings of the different waves look.

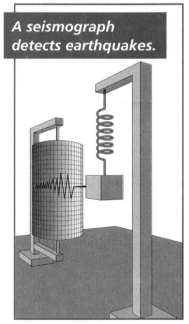

A seismograph detects earthquakes.

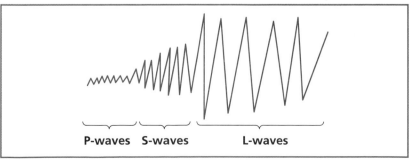

P-waves S-waves   L-waves

Locating an Earthquake

Epicenter

Point on Earth's surface directly over the focus of an earthquake.

Focus

Point inside Earth where rock first moves, starting an earthquake.

Richter scale

A scale used to measure the strength of an earthquake.

The point inside Earth where the earthquake starts is called the **focus**. The point on Earth's surface directly above the focus is called the **epicenter**. Scientists can pinpoint the epicenter of an earthquake. To do this, they compare the arrival times of the P-waves and the S-waves.

To locate the epicenter, scientists compare seismograph readings from at least three different locations. For example, suppose Station A detects earthquake waves. The P-waves and the S-waves show that the earthquake started 100 kilometers away. A circle with a 100-km radius is drawn around Station A. The reading at Station B puts the earthquake at 200 kilometers away. So, a 200-km radius circle is drawn around Station B.

A third reading at Station C shows the earthquake to be 50 kilometers away. A circle with a 50-km radius is drawn around Station C. The point where the three circles meet is the approximate location of the earthquake's epicenter.

Earthquake Strength

The strength of an earthquake is measured between 1 and 9 on the **Richter scale**. Each number on the Richter scale represents an earthquake that is about 10 times stronger than the next lowest number. The strongest earthquake ever recorded had a measurement of 8.9 on the Richter scale.

You need three different seismograph readings to locate the source of an earthquake.

An earthquake caused the San Francisco–Oakland Bay Bridge to collapse in 1989.

The Effects of Earthquakes

Earthquakes can cause great damage and loss of life. Most injuries result from the collapse of buildings, bridges, and other structures in heavily populated areas.

Even earthquakes on the ocean floor can cause much damage. They may trigger **tsunamis**, or large sea waves. A tsunami may reach heights of up to 35 meters, as tall as a 10-story building. Large tsunamis can destroy coastal towns.

Tsunami

Large sea wave caused by an earthquake on the ocean floor.

Predicting Earthquakes

Scientists hope to save lives by learning to predict where and when an earthquake will occur. They watch for several signs. For example, a sudden drop in the level of well water often precedes an earthquake. Bulges in Earth's surface near a fault could indicate the buildup of stress. Near a fault, seismic activity produces an almost constant occurrence of P-waves and S-waves. A change in the speed of the P-waves may signal a coming earthquake. Scientists use these clues to predict earthquakes. If earthquakes could be accurately predicted, many lives could be saved.

Play the earthquake game

Players	Any number
Time to play	20 minutes
Materials	Earthquake survival kit
Objective	Increase earthquake safety

Advance preparation

1. Pack an earthquake survival kit. The contents: can opener (hand-operated); flashlight; battery-operated radio; first-aid kit; canned and dried food; fresh water; batteries.

2. Look around at the room you are in. Predict what hazards an earthquake might cause. For example, hanging objects or ceiling tiles might fall. Windows might break. Objects in cupboards might tumble out.

3. Find a spot in the room that would be safe during an earthquake. You might stand under a doorway or crawl under a table. You would need to hold onto the table so it doesn't move away. Corners and solid walls, away from windows, are other good choices.

The game

One member of the group yells "earthquake." All players stop what they are doing and find a safe spot in the room. Players take turns calling out what is happening to the room. When the "shaking" has ended, the players gather and discuss the next steps to take. Players should pass around the earthquake survival kit and offer reasons why they would need it.

Self-Check

1. What is an earthquake?
2. Compare and contrast the three kinds of earthquake waves.
3. What instrument is used to measure earthquake waves?
4. What is the difference between the focus and the epicenter of an earthquake?
5. What does the Richter scale measure?

Chapter 12 SUMMARY

- Earth has three main layers: the core, the mantle, and the crust.
- The theory of continental drift states that the continents were once in a single landmass. That landmass has slowly separated into smaller continents that have moved apart over time.
- The theory of seafloor spreading states that the ocean floor spreads as new crust is formed at the midoceanic ridge.
- The theory of plate tectonics states that Earth's crust is made up of several large plates that move about over the mantle.
- Convection currents in the mantle push the crust, causing the plates to move.
- Volcanoes occur where magma pushes up through Earth's surface.
This happens most often at plate boundaries.
- Volcanoes are grouped into three types: cinder cones, shield volcanoes, and composite volcanoes.
- Mountains can form from volcanic eruptions, from folding, and from movement at faults.
- An earthquake is a shaking of Earth's crust.
- Most earthquakes occur near plate boundaries.
- Earthquake energy travels through Earth's crust as waves.
- Earthquakes can be located by using the arrival times of earthquake waves at different locations.
- The strength of an earthquake is measured on the Richter scale.

Science Words		
cinder cone, 208	Pangaea, 204	
composite volcano, 208	plate, 205	
continental drift, 204	plate tectonics, 205	
convection current, 206	reverse fault, 210	
core, 203	Richter scale, 214	
crust, 203	rift, 204	
earthquake, 212	seafloor spreading, 205	
epicenter, 214	seismograph, 213	
fault, 210	shield volcano, 208	
focus, 214	strike–slip fault, 210	
folding, 209	tsunami, 215	
mantle, 203	vent, 207	
midoceanic ridge, 204	volcano, 207	
normal fault, 210		

Vocabulary Review

Number your paper from 1 to 10. Match each term in Column A with the correct definition in Column B. Write the letter of the answer on your paper.

Column A

_____ 1. cinder cone

_____ 2. convection currents

_____ 3. earthquake

_____ 4. fault

_____ 5. folding

_____ 6. mantle

_____ 7. Pangaea

_____ 8. plate tectonics

_____ 9. seafloor spreading

_____ 10. seismograph

Column B

a. shaking of Earth's crust

b. bending of rock layers

c. instrument that detects and records earthquake waves

d. theory that new crust forms along a rift on the ocean floor

e. single landmass that slowly separated into continents

f. kind of volcano that is small and made of ash and rocks

g. circular motion of gas or liquid as it heats

h. theory that Earth's crust is made up of sections that move

i. layer of Earth between the core and the crust

j. break in Earth's crust along which movement occurs

Concept Review

Number your paper from 1 to 3. Choose the answer that best completes each sentence. Write the letter of the answer on your paper.

1. Earth's surface is part of the _____.

   a. core   b. mantle   c. crust

2. Continental drift, seafloor spreading, and plate tectonics all help explain _____.

   a. how Earth's surface changes

   b. where convection currents come from

   c. why Earth has layers

3. Where plates meet, they usually _____.

   a. explode   c. stop moving

   b. scrape or squeeze each other

Number your paper from 4 to 8. Answer each question.

4. How do volcanoes form?

5. Describe two ways that mountains form.

6. What causes earthquakes?

7. What do volcanoes and earthquakes have to do with Earth's plates?

8. Which of the figures to the left is a strike–slip fault?

A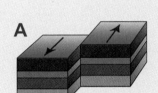

B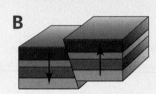

C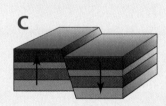

Critical Thinking

Answer each of the following questions.

1. Los Angeles, California, is in an area that has many earthquakes. Brick was once used to construct buildings there. New buildings are constructed of materials that are not as likely to break as brick is. Why do you think new buildings are built this way?

2. A string of active volcanoes rings the Pacific Ocean basin. In fact, the string is called the Ring of Fire. What conclusion might you draw about Earth's crust under this ring? Why?

Test Taking Tip | In a matching test, make sure each item should be used just once. Check your answers. If you repeated one item, then another item was left out. Find the best spot for the item you left out.

Earth's History

Imagine a quiet forest. All is still. Suddenly a blurry shape flies by close to the ground. Landing on a low branch, the shape shows itself to be a bird about the size of a crow. At least it looks like a bird. It has wings and feathers. But it also has a head like a lizard. Sharp teeth line its mouth. Its wings end in claws. Is this a creature from a movie? No, it is a real part of our past, preserved in fossils. Fossils and other evidence provide clues to what life on Earth was like long ago. In this chapter, you will find out about the kinds of evidence scientists use to reconstruct Earth's history.

ORGANIZE YOUR THOUGHTS

Fossils ——— Earth's history ——— Geologic time scale

Rocks ———

Precambrian Era

Paleozoic Era

Mesozoic Era

Cenozoic Era

Goals for Learning

▶ To define *geologic time*
▶ To explain how fossils form
▶ To describe the geologic time scale
▶ To outline major events in Earth's history

Objectives

After reading this lesson, you should be able to

▶ define *geologic time*.

▶ explain what a fossil is.

▶ describe three ways fossils form.

Geologic time
All the time that has passed since Earth formed.

Geologic Time

Does a year seem like a long time to you? Your idea of time depends on what you compare it to. Compared to events in your life, a year is probably a long time. Compared to the history of most nations, a year is not long at all. Scientists who study Earth describe a long time in terms of millions and billions of years. For example, the carving of the Grand Canyon took about 10 million years. Compared to that time, a year is not even noticeable.

Most events in earth science are compared to **geologic time**—all the time that has passed since Earth formed. Scientists estimate that Earth is about 4.6 billion years old. Compared to this amount of time, even the Grand Canyon is young.

The Colorado River has carved the Grand Canyon over millions of years.

The Rock Record

When an event such as a hurricane happens today, it is recorded. Newspaper reports, videotapes, and photographs record the event. No such records exist of most of Earth's events. Yet, much has happened in Earth's long history. Mountains have built up, continents have moved, life forms have come and gone. These events left records in the rock of Earth's crust. Scientists "read" rock layers to learn what happened in the past and the order in which events took place.

What Are Fossils?

Among the most important records of Earth's history are **fossils.** Fossils are the traces or remains of plants, animals, and other organisms preserved in Earth's crust. Fossils are evidence that certain kinds of organisms existed. Other life forms may have been present on Earth in the past. However, unless these life forms left fossils, scientists have no evidence of their existence.

How Fossils Form

It's not easy to become a fossil. When an organism dies, its soft parts usually decay. They might also be eaten by other creatures. The parts most likely to become fossils are the hard parts, such as wood, teeth, bones, and shells. Usually these parts must be buried quickly in some way to become fossils. Most organisms that become fossils are buried by sediments on the seafloor. Burial might also occur during sandstorms, volcanic eruptions, floods, or avalanches.

Most fossils preserve the shape of the organism but not the actual body tissue. For example, some fossils form when minerals replace the original parts of a buried organism. This process is called **petrification**. The photo shows petrified wood. Over thousands of years, the wood was dissolved by groundwater and replaced by the minerals in the water.

What details can you see preserved in this petrified wood?

Another kind of fossil forms when a plant or an animal leaves an imprint behind. For example, a plant or an animal may become buried in sediment that later forms rock. Eventually the organism decays or dissolves. The space left in the rock, called a **mold**, has the shape of the plant or animal. If minerals fill the mold, a **cast** forms. The cast becomes a model of the original plant or animal. Compare the mold and the cast of the trilobite, a sea animal that lived millions of years ago.

Sometimes, the actual body matter of an organism is preserved as a fossil. For example, remains of wooly mammoths, ancient ancestors of elephants, have been found preserved in ice and frozen soil. The remains of saber-toothed cats have been discovered trapped in petroleum deposits called tar pits. The insects in the picture were trapped in tree sap. The sap hardened into a material called amber, preserving the entire body of the insects.

Fossils, such as this amber, offer a glimpse into the past.

How are the mold and cast of this trilobite different?

Mold

Cast

Self-Check

1. What is geologic time?
2. What is a fossil?
3. What are three ways that fossils form?

Making a Model of a Fossil

Purpose

To make a model of a fossil mold and a fossil cast

Materials

- ✓ newspaper
- ✓ modeling clay
- ✓ seashell
- ✓ petroleum jelly
- ✓ plaster of Paris
- ✓ plastic container
- ✓ water
- ✓ spoon

Procedure

1. Cover your workspace with newspaper. Flatten the modeling clay into a slab that is about 2 centimeters thick.

2. Gently press a seashell into the clay to form an impression.

3. Remove the seashell and inspect the impression. If the details of the shell cannot be clearly seen, repeat step 2.

4. Use your finger to gently coat the impression with a thin layer of petroleum jelly. Wash your hands.

5. Mix enough plaster of Paris to fill the impression.

6. Pour the plaster of Paris into the clay impression and allow it to harden overnight.

7. Remove the hard plaster of Paris from the clay.

8. Clean your workspace and wash the equipment.

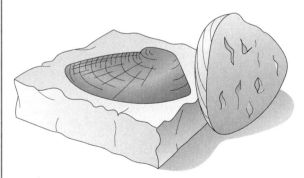

Questions

1. What part of your model represents the fossil mold?

2. What part of your model represents the fossil cast?

3. How do the mold and cast compare?

Objectives

After reading this lesson, you should be able to

▶ describe the geologic time scale.

▶ summarize events that occurred during each era of geologic time.

Geologic time scale
An outline of major events in Earth's history.

Paleozoic Era
Era of Earth's history marked by great development in sea life. It began about 570 million years ago and ended about 230 million years ago.

Precambrian Era
The oldest and longest era of Earth's history. It began about 4.6 billion years ago and ended about 570 million years ago.

Geologic Time Scale

The **geologic time scale**, shown on the next page, is an outline of major events in Earth's history. Find the four main units, or eras, of geologic time. The oldest era is at the bottom of the scale. Eras are divided into smaller units called periods. Some periods are divided into even smaller units called epochs.

The Precambrian Era

The **Precambrian Era** is the oldest and longest era. It accounts for about 85 percent of all geologic time. The Precambrian Era began with Earth's formation and ended about 570 million years ago. Precambrian rocks form the foundation of the continents. These ancient rocks are exposed in some areas where Earth's crust has lifted and eroded. Simple life forms probably first appeared early in the Precambrian Era, at least 3.5 billion years ago. The fossil record contains limited evidence of Precambrian organisms.

The Paleozoic Era

The **Paleozoic Era** began about 570 million years ago and ended about 230 million years ago. It was a time of great development of life in the oceans. Paleozoic rocks contain fossils of a variety of ocean organisms, including trilobites, sponges, and shellfish. The first land plants and animals also developed during this era.

Much of the coal, oil, and natural gas we use for energy today formed from the organisms that lived in large swamps and shallow seas during the Paleozoic Era. Many rock layers built up over the dead organic matter. Heat and pressure slowly turned the organic matter into coal, oil, and natural gas known as fossil fuels.

The Geologic Time Scale

Era	Period	Epoch	Years Before the Present (approximate) Began	Years Before the Present (approximate) Ended	Life Forms	Physical Events
Cenozoic	Quaternary	Holocene	11,000		Humans dominant	West Coast uplift continues in U.S.; Great Lakes form
		Pleistocene	2,000,000	11,000	Primitive humans appear	Ice age
	Tertiary	Pliocene	7,000,000	2,000,000	Modern horse, camel, elephant develop	North America joined to South America
		Miocene	23,000,000	7,000,000	Grasses, grazing animals thrive	North America joined to Asia; Columbia Plateau
		Oligocene	38,000,000	23,000,000	Mammals progress; elephants in Africa	Himalayas start forming, Alps continue rising
		Eocene	53,000,000	38,000,000	Ancestors of modern horse, other mammals	Coal forming in western U.S.
		Paleocene	65,000,000	53,000,000	Many new mammals appear	Uplift in western U.S. continues; Alps rising
Mesozoic	Cretaceous		136,000,000	65,000,000	Dinosaurs die out; flowering plants	Uplift of Rockies and Colorado Plateau begins
	Jurassic		195,000,000	136,000,000	First birds appear; giant dinosaurs	Rise of Sierra Nevadas and Coast Ranges
	Triassic		230,000,000	195,000,000	First dinosaurs and mammals appear	Palisades of Hudson River form
Paleozoic	Permian		280,000,000	230,000,000	Trilobites die out	Ice age in South America; deserts in western U.S.
	Pennsylvanian		310,000,000	280,000,000	First reptiles, giant insects; ferns, conifers	Coal-forming swamps in North America and Europe
	Mississippian		345,000,000	310,000,000		
	Devonian		395,000,000	345,000,000	First amphibians appear	Mountain building in New England
	Silurian		435,000,000	395,000,000	First land animals (spiders, scorpions)	Deserts in eastern U.S.
	Ordovician		500,000,000	435,000,000	First vertebrates (fish)	Half of North America submerged
	Cambrian		570,000,000	500,000,000	Trilobites, snails; seaweed	Extensive deposition of sediments in inland seas
Precambrian			4,600,000,000	570,000,000	First jellyfish, bacteria, algae	Great volcanic activity, lava flows, metamorphism of rocks. Evolution of crust, mantle, core

The Mesozoic Era

The **Mesozoic Era** began about 230 million years ago and ended about 65 million years ago. Life on land flourished during this time. Trees similar to today's palm and pine trees were common. Small mammals and birds first appeared. But this era is often called the Age of Reptiles because they were the major form of life on land. The most dominant of the reptiles were the dinosaurs.

The picture below gives you an idea of the variety of dinosaurs that lived during the Mesozoic Era. In many ways, they were like animals today. Some ate meat and some ate plants. Some were larger than an elephant, while others were as small as a chicken. Some were fierce and others were gentle. Some traveled in herds and some were loners. Even their color probably varied, though we cannot tell this from the fossil record.

The end of the Mesozoic Era is marked by the end of the dinosaurs. Why the dinosaurs died out at this time is still a mystery.

A variety of dinosaurs existed during the Mesozoic Era.

The Cenozoic Era

Cenozoic Era
Era of Earth's history described as the Age of Mammals. It began about 65 million years ago and continues today.

We are living in the **Cenozoic Era.** It began about 65 million years ago. During this era, the Alps and the Himalayas formed as Earth's plates continue to collide in this region. Late in the era, several ice ages occurred. An ice age is a period of time when ice covers large portions of the land. About 2 million years ago, ice carved out huge basins and formed the Great Lakes.

The Cenozoic Era is known as the Age of Mammals. Although the dinosaurs became extinct, mammals survived and flourished. Mammals, including humans, became the dominant life form. As time continues, the life forms and the world around us will continue to change.

Self-Check

1. What is the geologic time scale?
2. Name two life forms that first appeared during each of these eras: Paleozoic, Mesozoic, Cenozoic.
3. Identify a major change that occurred in Earth's crust during each era of geologic time.

SCIENCE IN YOUR LIFE

How do fossils help us find resources?

Scientists use fossils to find the ages of rocks and to match up rock layers from one part of the world to another. This information is useful for finding deposits of oil—an important energy source. Some fossils, called conodonts, turn certain colors when heated—from yellow to brown to black. Therefore, the color of conodonts tells scientists how hot the rock was when it formed. This is important because oil forms only at certain temperatures. The color of the conodonts, then, helps scientists locate rock layers that might include oil. Conodonts that are white or clear may indicate the presence of minerals such as copper, silver, and gold.

Chapter 13 SUMMARY

- Geologic time is all the time that has passed since Earth formed about 4.6 billion years ago.

- Rocks contain clues about events that happened in Earth's past.

- Fossils are evidence that certain organisms existed.

- Fossils form when plant or animal remains become replaced with minerals, leave an imprint, or become preserved.

- The events in Earth's history occurred over geologic time and are outlined on the geologic time scale.

- Earth's history is divided into four eras: the Precambrian, Paleozoic, Mesozoic, and Cenozoic. Each era is unique in terms of the life forms that developed and the changes that took place.

Science Words		
cast, 223	Mesozoic Era, 227	
Cenozoic Era, 228	mold, 223	
fossil, 222	Paleozoic Era, 225	
geologic time, 221	petrification, 222	
geologic time scale, 225	Precambrian Era, 225	

WORD BANK

amber

billion

cast

Cenozoic Era

dinosaurs

fossil

geologic time

mold

petrification

trilobite

Vocabulary Review

Number your paper from 1 to 10. Then choose the term from the Word Bank that best completes each sentence. Write the answer on your paper.

1. A _____ is a trace or remains of an organism preserved in Earth's crust.

2. A fossil _____ is a rock cavity in the shape of an organism.

3. A fossil _____ is a model of an organism.

4. _____ means the total amount of time since Earth formed.

5. Earth formed about 4.6 _____ years ago.

6. Scientists do not know for sure why the _____ died out.

7. The _____ is also called the Age of Mammals.

8. _____ occurs when minerals replace organic matter.

9. Insects are sometimes preserved in hardened tree sap called _____.

10. The _____ was an animal that lived millions of years ago.

Concept Review

Number your paper from 1 to 8. Then choose the answer that best completes each sentence. Write the letter of the answer on your paper.

1. The geologic time scale divides Earth's history into four _____.

   a. epochs   b. eras   c. periods

2. Scientists study _____ to learn about the history of life on Earth.

   a. fossils   b. reptiles   c. eras

3. During the _____ Era, dinosaurs and other reptiles were the major form of life on Earth.

   a. Mesozoic   b. Paleozoic   c. Precambrian

4. The _____ Era is known as the Age of Mammals.

   a. Precambrian   b. Cenozoic   c. Mesozoic

5. The _____ Era was a time of great development of ocean life.

   a. Precambrian   b. Mesozoic   c. Paleozoic

6. During the Cenozoic Era, the Great Lakes basins were carved out by _____.

   a. rivers   b. ice   c. wind

7. We live in the _____ Era.

   a. Paleozoic   b. Mesozoic   c. Cenozoic

8. The _____ parts of an organism usually become fossils.

   a. hard   b. soft   c. molded

Critical Thinking

Write the answer to each of the following questions.

1. Bacteria, algae, and jellyfish developed during the Precambrian Era. Why is it so hard to find fossils of these organisms?

2. Examine the drawing. What do you think the large organism on the left is? (Hint: You saw a picture of its fossil in this chapter.) During what era did this organism live?

Chapter

14

Earth's Water

If you were able to ride a drop of water in a mountain stream, you would experience an incredible journey. You might spend parts of the journey tumbling over rocks, plunging down waterfalls, creeping along underground passages, and emerging to rush headlong out to sea. But your journey would not end there. All water keeps moving. In this chapter, you will learn how water moves and changes. You will also learn about different bodies of water, such as rivers, lakes, and oceans.

ORGANIZE YOUR THOUGHTS

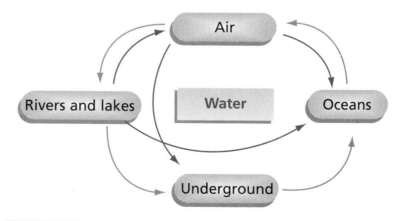

Goals for Learning

▶ To describe the water cycle
▶ To explain how rivers and lakes form
▶ To describe the ocean floor and other ocean features

After reading this lesson, you should be able to

► describe the water cycle.

► explain how groundwater collects and moves.

► describe how a river develops.

Groundwater
Water that sinks into the ground.

Precipitation
Water that falls to Earth from the atmosphere.

Runoff
Water that runs over Earth's surface and flows into streams.

Water cycle
Movement of water between the atmosphere and Earth's surface.

Three-fourths of Earth's surface is covered with water. Water is everywhere. Most of it is in the oceans. It is also in rivers, in lakes, in the air, and even in your own body.

The Water Cycle

Earth's water is in continuous motion. It moves from the atmosphere to Earth's surface and back to the atmosphere. This movement of water is called the **water cycle.** Study the diagram below and notice the different forms that water takes as it goes through a complete cycle.

The sun powers the water cycle. Heat from the sun evaporates surface water, and the water vapor rises into the atmosphere. The rising water vapor cools and condenses into clouds. Water droplets or ice crystals in the clouds grow larger, then fall to Earth as **precipitation**.

What happens after precipitation falls? Some of it sinks into the ground and becomes **groundwater.** Precipitation that does not sink into the ground is called surface water. Some surface water evaporates. But most of it becomes **runoff—** surface water that flows into streams.

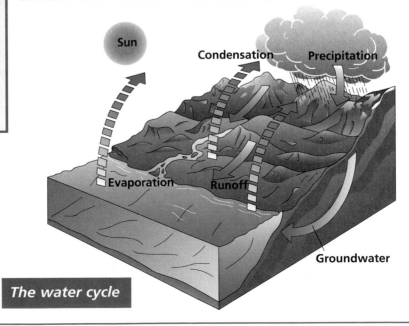

The water cycle

Groundwater

Precipitation and runoff can sink into the ground because most soil is **porous**, or has spaces between its particles. The bedrock below the soil may also be porous. Water trickles around broken rock pieces and through cracks. Eventually, water comes to a solid rock layer. The water collects on top of the rock layer, filling the spaces above it. The top of this wet earth layer is the **water table.**

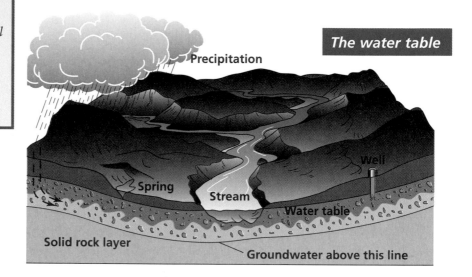

The water table

Precipitation

Well

Spring

Stream

Water table

Solid rock layer

Groundwater above this line

Rivers

Much of the freshwater above ground flows as rivers. Rivers begin as runoff moves over the land, carving small paths in the ground. These paths get wider and deeper as water continues to flow through them. The paths become tiny streams. As the streams flow, they join and become larger rivers. These rivers then join and form even larger rivers. Rivers that join other rivers are called **tributaries.** The land area in which runoff drains into a river and its tributaries is a **drainage basin.**

Lakes

Surface water does not always flow along a path. Some of it collects in depressions, or low areas. Water eventually fills the depressions, forming lakes. Even though some of the water evaporates, lakes continue to be fed by precipitation, runoff, springs, and rivers.

Self-Check

1. How does water move between the atmosphere and the oceans?
2. What is runoff?
3. What is a water table?
4. How can runoff in a mountain end up in the ocean 2,000 kilometers away?
5. What is a tributary?

SCIENCE IN YOUR LIFE

What is your water budget?

A water budget describes the amount of water coming in and going out of an area. By creating your own personal water budget, you can cut down on wasted water. Use the information in the table to find out how much water is used in your household in one week. Think of ways to save water to lower these numbers. Then try to set and keep a weekly limit on water use.

Average water use for one person (gallons)			
Daily		**Weekly**	
Washing hands	0.5	Doing laundry (1 load)	30
Shower	20	Washing car	20
Bath	30	Watering lawn (30 min.)	240
Flushing toilet	1.5		
Brushing teeth	0.5		
Washing dishes	12		

Modeling a Water Table

Materials

✓ clear glass or plastic jar
✓ foam rubber, about 3 cm thick
✓ pen
✓ scissors
✓ gravel
✓ sand
✓ soil
✓ water

Purpose

To model groundwater soaking through different materials

Procedure

1. Put the jar on the foam rubber. Trace around the bottom of the jar with a pen. Cut out the circle. Put the foam rubber circle in the bottom of the jar.

2. On top of the foam rubber, add a layer of gravel about 3 cm deep. Then add a layer of sand about 2 cm deep. On top, put a layer of soil about 2 cm deep.

3. Gently pour some water into the jar. Observe what happens to the water. Keep pouring until the top of the water is about halfway into the gravel layer. Observe the layers of materials.

Questions

1. What did pouring the water represent in your model?

2. What happened to the water after you poured it into the jar?

3. Which layers let water soak through them? Why did the water soak through those layers?

4. Which part of your model represents solid rock?

5. Which place in your model represents the water table?

Objectives

After reading this lesson, you should be able to

▶ identify two properties of ocean water.

▶ explain what causes ocean waves and currents.

▶ describe several features of the ocean floor.

Properties of Ocean Water

The water in the oceans is salt water. The circle graph below shows why. Notice that 96.5 percent of ocean water is pure water. But 3.5 percent is dissolved salts. Most of the salt is sodium chloride—common table salt. Some sodium chloride and other salts come from rocks on the ocean floor. Salts also wash into the ocean from rivers. Not all parts of the ocean are equally salty. The saltiness, or **salinity**, of ocean water varies.

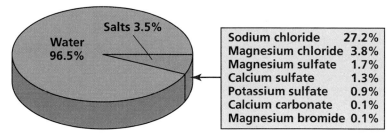

Sodium chloride	27.2%
Magnesium chloride	3.8%
Magnesium sulfate	1.7%
Calcium sulfate	1.3%
Potassium sulfate	0.9%
Calcium carbonate	0.1%
Magnesium bromide	0.1%

Salinity
The saltiness of water.

Thermocline
Layer of the ocean between about 300 and 800 meters, where the temperature drops sharply.

Ocean water is warmest at the surface where the sun heats it. The drawing at right shows how water temperature decreases with depth. The temperature is constant near the surface because winds and waves keep the water well mixed. In the **thermocline**, the temperature drops sharply. Below the thermocline, the temperature drops slowly. The water at the bottom of the ocean is near freezing.

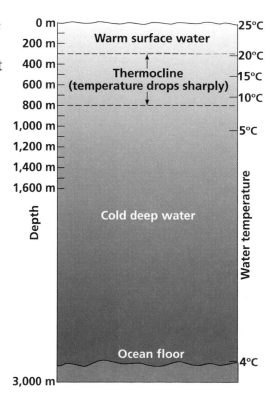

The Ocean Floor

Until the middle of this century, the ocean floor was a great mystery. Today we have new measuring devices and the ability actually to travel to the ocean floor. The drawing shows some of the features of the ocean floor.

Continental shelf

The **continental shelf** is part of the continent that extends underwater. The continental shelf slopes gently. Average water depth is 130 meters. Average width is 75 kilometers.

Continental slope

The **continental slope** dips sharply to the ocean floor.

Plains

About one-half of the ocean floor consists of flat plains, where sediment constantly settles. Average depth is about 4,000 meters.

Mid-ocean ridge

Underwater mountain chains called midoceanic ridges extend for thousands of kilometers along the ocean floor.

Seamount

Seamounts are underwater mountains. Many of these are active or extinct volcanoes. A seamount that rises above sea level forms an island.

Trench

Trenches are long, deep valleys. They are the deepest places on Earth. Some are 10 kilometers deep.

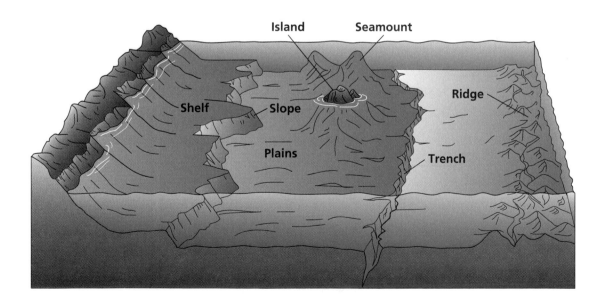

Ocean Waves

A **wave** is the regular up-and-down motion of water caused by energy traveling through the water. A wave gets its energy from wind. When the wind blows, it pushes up the water to start small waves. The waves become larger as the wind blows longer and harder. No matter what the size, all waves have the parts described below.

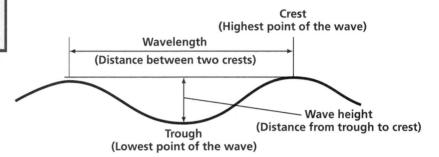

Have you ever seen a leaf bob up and down on passing waves? The waves move forward but the leaf does not. Although it looks like waves constantly push water forward, the water generally stays in the same place. Only the waves move forward.

As a wave approaches the shore and shallow water, the wave rubs against the ocean floor. Friction slows the bottom of the wave, but the crest keeps moving at the same speed. Therefore, the crest moves ahead of the rest of the wave. The wave tilts forward and tumbles over, or breaks. After a wave breaks on shore, the water actually moves. It may be hurled against rocks or pushed up the slope of a beach.

Ocean Currents

Although waves do not move water, **currents** do. Ocean currents are large streams of water that move through the ocean. Currents are caused by the heating of water near the equator. They tend to follow Earth's major wind patterns. Use the map on the next page to compare the trade winds with ocean currents near the equator. Both the winds and the currents flow westward.

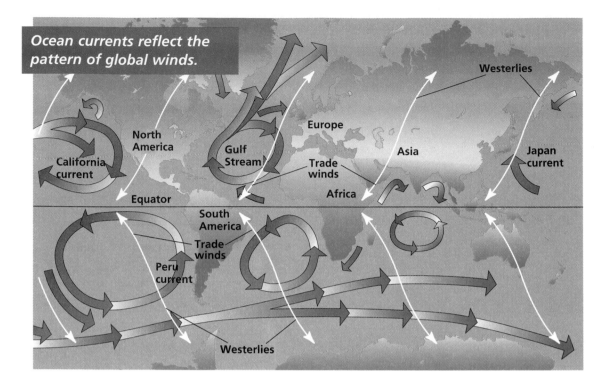

Ocean currents reflect the pattern of global winds.

Currents carry warm water from the equator toward the poles and bring cold water back toward the equator. In so doing, currents affect climates on land by warming or cooling the coasts of continents. Both wind and land absorb heat from warm ocean currents. The Gulf Stream is an ocean current that has a warming effect. Find the Gulf Stream on the map. Notice that it carries warm water from the tropics up along the east coast of North America and then across the Atlantic. The Gulf Stream gives Western Europe mild summers and winters. For example, even though Great Britain is far north, warm winds from the Gulf Stream keep the temperatures mild.

Self-Check

1. Which type of salt is most common in ocean water?
2. What are two sources of salts in ocean water?
3. How does water temperature change as you go deeper in the ocean?
4. What causes most ocean waves and currents?
5. What are three features of the ocean floor?

Chapter 14   SUMMARY

- Water moves between the land, the atmosphere, and the ocean in the water cycle.

- Water that flows over the ground is called runoff.

- Water below Earth's surface is called groundwater.

- Groundwater moves downward in the ground and collects to form a soaked layer. The top of the soaked layer is called the water table.

- Rivers and their tributaries drain runoff from large areas of land called drainage basins.

- Lakes form when water collects in a depression on land.

- Ocean water is salt water because it contains dissolved salts.

- The temperature of ocean water decreases with depth.

- A wave is the up and down motion of water caused by energy from the wind.

- Features of the ocean floor include the continental shelf, the continental slope, midoceanic ridges, trenches, hills, plains, and mountains.

- Currents move ocean water from place to place. The currents are caused by heating of water near the equator. They follow the same general pattern as the global winds.

Science Words		
continental shelf, 238		salinity, 237
continental slope, 238		seamount, 238
current, 239		thermocline, 237
drainage basin, 234		trench, 238
groundwater, 234		tributary, 234
porous, 234		water cycle, 233
precipitation, 233		water table, 234
runoff, 234		wave, 239

WORD BANK

continental shelf

drainage basin

porous

trench

tributary

water table

Vocabulary Review

Number your paper from 1 to 6. Then choose the term from the Word Bank that best completes each sentence. Write the answer on your paper.

1. A river that flows into another river is a _____.

2. The land area in which runoff flows into a river and its tributaries is a _____.

3. Underground water forms a soaked layer, the top of which is the _____.

4. A deep valley on the ocean floor is called a _____.

5. Because soil has spaces between its particles, it is _____.

6. The _____ extends from the shoreline into the ocean.

Concept Review

Number your paper from 1 to 6. Choose the answer that best completes each sentence. Write the letter of the answer on your paper.

1. Water moves from the ocean to the atmosphere by _____.

   a. evaporation   b. condensation   c. precipitation

2. Porous rock contains many _____.

   a. particles   b. salts   c. spaces

3. As you go deeper in ocean water, the temperature _____.

   a. gets warmer   b. gets colder   c. stays the same

4. The top of a wave is the _____.

   a. trough   b. wave height   c. crest

5. Ocean currents are caused by _____.

   a. waves   b. tides   c. winds

6. The water cycle is powered by _____.

    a. the sun   b. ocean currents   c. winds

Number your paper from 7 to 12. Then match each ocean feature below with a letter in the diagram. Write the letter of each answer on your paper.

7. trench

8. continental slope

9. midoceanic ridge

10. island

11. plain

12. continental shelf

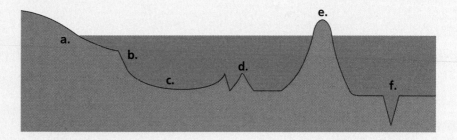

Critical Thinking

Write the answer to each of the following questions.

1. Suppose an area has had a summer with little rain. What do you think has happened to the water table? Why?

2. One way to make salt water safe to drink is to heat it and collect the water vapor. How is this method like the water cycle? Suggest a way to collect the water vapor.

Test Taking Tip   Make sure you have the same number of answers on your paper as there are items on the test.

Earth's Atmosphere

Earth's atmosphere is a thin blanket of air hugging the planet. This blanket provides much of what we need to survive. It keeps Earth warm enough to support life. It provides the oxygen we breathe. It even shields us from the sun's deadly radiation. How does the air do all this and more? You'll find out in this chapter.

ORGANIZE YOUR THOUGHTS

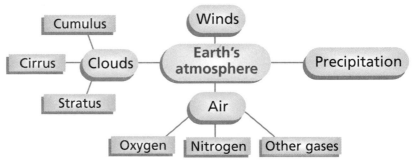

Cumulus

Winds

Cirrus — Clouds — Earth's atmosphere — Precipitation

Stratus

Air

Oxygen   Nitrogen   Other gases

Goals for Learning

► To describe Earth's atmosphere
► To describe the structure of the atmosphere
► To classify clouds
► To explain how precipitation forms
► To describe Earth's wind patterns

Atmosphere
Layer of gases that surrounds a body in space.

What basic things do you need to live? At the top of the list is the air you breathe. When you breathe, you take in gases that your body needs to work. You, in turn, release gases that other living things need.

The Atmosphere's Major Gases

The layer of gases that surrounds Earth is called the **atmosphere.** Most people simply call the atmosphere "air." Earth's atmosphere is relatively thin. Although some other planets have atmospheres, ours is the only one known to support life.

Earth's atmosphere contains many different gases. Some of these gases are elements. Others are compounds. From the circle graph, you can see that oxygen and nitrogen make up most of Earth's atmosphere. What other gases make up the air?

All living things need oxygen and nitrogen. Plants and animals take these gases from the atmosphere, use them, and then return them to the atmosphere. Oxygen and nitrogen go through these natural cycles over and over. You will learn about these cycles in Chapter 21.

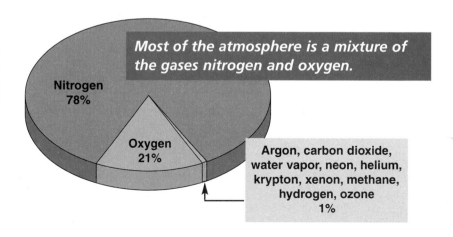

Most of the atmosphere is a mixture of the gases nitrogen and oxygen.

Nitrogen 78%

Oxygen 21%

Argon, carbon dioxide, water vapor, neon, helium, krypton, xenon, methane, hydrogen, ozone 1%

Layers of the Atmosphere

Imagine four glass balls, one inside the other. Now picture Earth at the very center of the glass balls. You've just imagined a model of Earth and its atmosphere.

The atmosphere consists of four layers. Look at the diagram as you read about each one.

You live in the **troposphere**, the bottom layer of the atmosphere. The troposphere extends from Earth's surface upward to about 17 kilometers. It is the thinnest and densest of the four layers. Air molecules are packed more tightly in this layer because of the weight of the air above. The troposphere contains 75 percent of the air molecules in the entire atmosphere.

Air gets colder and thinner as you go higher in the troposphere. That's why mountain climbers often need extra clothing and oxygen tanks when they climb. This layer of air is characterized by up-and-down as well as horizontal air currents. Also, most of the clouds you see in the sky are in the troposphere.

The **stratosphere** is above the troposphere. It extends to about 50 kilometers above Earth's surface. The stratosphere is clear and dry. The ozone layer is near the top of the stratosphere. Temperature increases higher in the stratosphere because the ozone at the top absorbs ultraviolet radiation from the sun.

Layers of the atmosphere

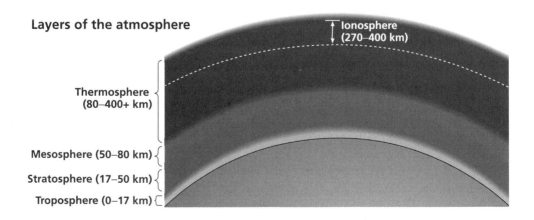

Ionosphere (270–400 km)

Thermosphere (80–400+ km)

Mesosphere (50–80 km)

Stratosphere (17–50 km)

Troposphere (0–17 km)

Ionosphere
Upper thermosphere, where ions form as electrons are stripped away from atoms.

Mesosphere
Third layer of the atmosphere, which is the coldest layer.

Thermosphere
Outermost layer of the atmosphere.

Above the stratosphere is the **mesosphere.** Here, temperature decreases with increasing height. The mesosphere is the coldest layer of the atmosphere. It is located from about 50 to 80 kilometers above Earth's surface.

The outermost layer is called the **thermosphere.** The air is the thinnest. Temperatures increase with height. They reach 2,000°C because the nitrogen and oxygen atoms absorb the sun's energy. The energy strips electrons from these atoms, making them electrically charged particles, or ions. Therefore, the upper thermosphere is also called the **ionosphere.**

If you have ever wondered how you are able to pick up a radio station hundreds of kilometers away, one answer may be the ionosphere. AM radio waves bounce off the ions in the ionosphere and back to Earth. As the diagram shows, this reflection of waves can carry radio messages great distances. This is especially true at night, when the sun's energy does not cause interference.

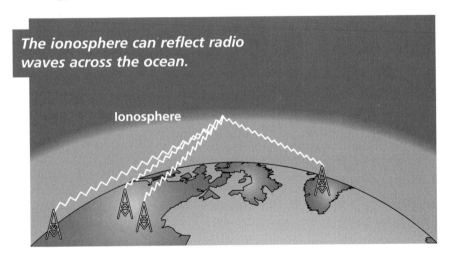

The ionosphere can reflect radio waves across the ocean.

Ionosphere

Self-Check

1. What are the two main gases in the atmosphere?
2. What are the four layers of the atmosphere?
3. In which layer of the atmosphere do you live?
4. Where is the ozone layer?
5. Why is the thermosphere also called the ionosphere?

Ozone—protector and pollutant

Ozone makes up a tiny but important part of the atmosphere. Ozone is a form of oxygen. A thin layer of ozone high in the atmosphere absorbs ultraviolet radiation from the sun, preventing most of it from reaching Earth. This radiation can cause sunburn and skin cancer.

For the last 20 years, scientists have been monitoring a "hole" that has appeared in the ozone layer. Gases called CFCs from spray cans and refrigeration equipment drift high into the atmosphere and break down the ozone. Laws now limit the amount of CFCs that can be produced.

Too little ozone in the upper atmosphere is harmful. But too much of it at Earth's surface is also harmful. Ozone is one of the ingredients of smog. This hazy mixture of gases damages people's lungs and worsens heart disease. The ozone at ground level is made by humans. Factories make ozone to use for cleaning flour, oil, fabrics, and water. Car exhaust also releases ozone.

Objectives

After reading this lesson, you should be able to

▶ explain how clouds and precipitation form.

▶ identify three kinds of clouds.

Condense
Change from a gas to a liquid.

Evaporate
Change from a liquid to a gas.

Water vapor
Water in the form of a gas.

Have you ever "seen your breath" on a cold day? You are seeing a cloud. It forms the same way as a cloud in the sky.

How Clouds Form

Much of Earth's surface is covered with water. The sun's heat causes some of this liquid water to **evaporate**, or change to a gas. This gas, called **water vapor**, becomes part of the air. As the air is heated, it becomes less dense than the surrounding air. Therefore, the heated air rises, taking the water vapor with it. As the air continues to rise, it cools. Then the water vapor **condenses**, or changes back to liquid water. The droplets of water are so tiny that they stay afloat in the air and form a cloud, as shown in Figure A.

Figure B shows that clouds also form when air is forced upward over a mountain. As the air rises, it cools. The water vapor condenses into tiny droplets of water to form clouds.

The droplets of most clouds are small enough to stay in the air, suspended by air currents. But if the droplets grow large enough, they fall to Earth. Moisture that falls from the atmosphere to Earth's surface is called precipitation. Rain, snow, sleet, and hail are forms of precipitation.

Clouds form when warmed air rises or when air is forced to rise over a mountain.

Figure A   **Figure B**

Stratus clouds are flat and low in the sky.

When you think of clouds, you probably picture white, puffy cumulus clouds like these.

Thin, wispy cirrus clouds are made of ice crystals.

Types of Clouds

Clouds are grouped according to their shape and **altitude**, or height above Earth's surface. The table describes the three main cloud types.

Altitude
Height above Earth's surface.

Cirrus cloud
High, wispy cloud made of ice crystals.

Cumulus cloud
Puffy, white cloud occurring at medium altitudes.

Stratus cloud
Low, flat cloud that forms in layers.

Stratus clouds
- Low clouds (surface to 2,000 meters) ■ Form in layers
- These clouds are wider than they are high, often covering the entire sky like a blanket ■ Often can see only their gray bottoms because they block out much of the sunlight ■ Often bring rain ■ Stratus cloud near the ground is fog

Cumulus clouds
- Middle clouds (2,000 to 7,000 meters) ■ Puffy white; look like piles of cotton balls ■ Often can see sides and tops shine brilliant white in sunlight but shaded bottoms are gray ■ Usually a sign of fair weather

Cirrus clouds
- High clouds (7,000 to 13,000 meters) ■ Thin, wispy streaks ■ Made of ice crystals instead of water droplets because the air at that altitude is below freezing ■ Sign of fair weather but may mean rain or snow is on the way

Self-Check

1. What is precipitation?
2. How do clouds form?

INVESTIGATION

15

Making a Model of Rain

Materials

✓ newspaper
✓ flat plastic surface (such as a binder or tray)
✓ books
✓ spray mister
✓ magnifying glass
✓ paper towel

Purpose

To make a model of raindrops forming and observe water droplets combining

Procedure

1. Copy the data table below on your paper.

Spray number	How many running droplets?	Mist description
1		
2		
3		
4		
5		

2. Cover your work surface with newspaper. Set up the materials as shown in the drawing on the next page. The plastic surface should make a slope.

3. Adjust the mister nozzle to produce a fine mist. Hold the mister about 30 cm from the plastic surface. Then gently spray the surface just once with the mister.

4. Using a magnifying glass, look closely at the mist on the surface. Notice the different sizes of water droplets. Notice if any water droplets run down the slope.

5. Record your observations in your data table.

6. Repeat steps 3 and 4 at least four more times. Record your observations each time you spray.

7. Wipe the surface with a paper towel. Dispose of the newspaper as instructed by your teacher.

Questions

1. How many times did you spray before one droplet ran down the surface?

2. How did the size of the mist droplets on the plastic surface change?

3. How is this activity like raindrops forming?

Objectives

After reading this lesson, you should be able to

▶ explain what causes air to move.

▶ recognize how air moves in wind cells.

Wind cell
Continuous cycle of rising warm air and falling cold air.

When you see a flag waving or leaves blowing, you know that moving air is moving these objects. But what do you think starts the air moving?

Wind

Earth's atmosphere is constantly in motion. Moving air is known as wind. The motion of air is caused by unequal heating of Earth's surface by the sun. Air expands when the sun's energy heats it. The warming air's molecules move farther apart, and the warming air becomes lighter, or less dense, than the colder air around it. The lighter air begins to rise. Then more air moves in to take the place of rising air. The new air is then warmed.

Wind Cells

On Earth, some of the warmest air is near the equator. Warm air near the equator rises. It moves toward the North Pole and the South Pole. As the air gets closer to the poles, it becomes colder. The cold air falls back to Earth and moves back toward the equator. Such a continuous cycle of air flow is called a **wind cell**.

Global Wind Patterns

The rotation of Earth breaks large wind cells into smaller cells. These smaller wind cells make up the wind patterns of Earth. For example, at about 30° north and south latitude, some of the air headed for the poles falls back to Earth. As this mass of air hits the surface, it divides into two masses. One half of the air returns to the equator. The other half moves toward the North Pole. Similar divisions of air occur at other places on Earth.

As warm air rises, more air takes its place.

Cold air

Warm air

Prevailing westerlies

Winds north and south of the equator that blow from the west.

Wind belt

Pattern of wind movement around Earth.

Winds move around the globe in patterns called **wind belts**. Most of the United States is affected by the wind belt of the **prevailing westerlies**. These winds blow generally from west to east. The next time you watch a weather forecast, notice that weather moves across the United States from west to east. The weather comes from the west because it is carried by the prevailing westerlies.

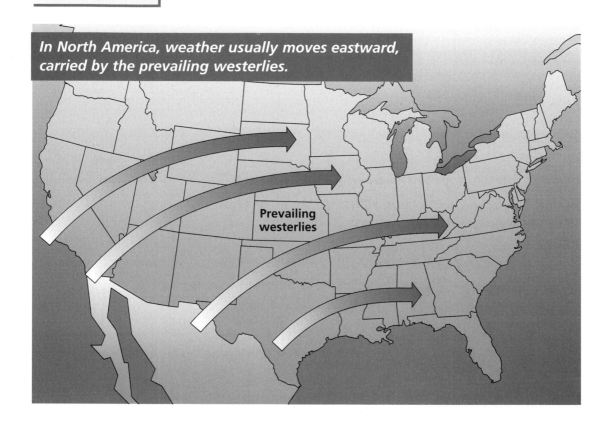

In North America, weather usually moves eastward, carried by the prevailing westerlies.

Prevailing westerlies

Self-Check

1. What causes air to move?
2. Where is Earth's warmest air?
3. Does the weather in the United States usually move to the east or to the west? Why?

- The atmosphere is the layer of gases that surrounds Earth.

- Earth's atmosphere consists mostly of the gases nitrogen and oxygen.

- The four layers of the atmosphere are the troposphere, stratosphere, mesosphere, and thermosphere.

- The upper thermosphere is also called the ionosphere. It contains ions, which are positively charged particles.

- Clouds are masses of water droplets or ice crystals that form in the atmosphere when water vapor is cooled.

- Three main types of clouds are stratus, cumulus, and cirrus.

- Precipitation is moisture that falls to Earth from the atmosphere. It may fall as rain, snow, sleet, or hail.

- The sun's unequal heating of Earth's surface causes wind.

- Continuous cycles of rising warm air and falling cold air occur in the atmosphere and are known as wind cells.

- Winds move around the globe in patterns called wind belts.

Science Words		
altitude, 250	prevailing westerlies, 254
atmosphere, 245	stratosphere, 246
cirrus cloud, 250	stratus cloud, 250
condense, 249	thermosphere, 247
cumulus cloud, 250	troposphere, 246
evaporate, 249	water vapor, 249
ionosphere, 247	wind belt, 254
mesosphere, 247	wind cell, 253

Vocabulary Review

Number your paper from 1 to 12. Match each word in Column A with the correct description in Column B. Write the letter of the description on your paper.

Column A

____ 1. evaporates

____ 2. prevailing westerlies

____ 3. ionosphere

____ 4. mesosphere

____ 5. precipitation

____ 6. stratus

____ 7. wind cell

____ 8. condenses

____ 9. stratosphere

____ 10. thermosphere

____ 11. troposphere

____ 12. wind belt

Column B

a. layer of atmosphere in which you live

b. water that falls from the atmosphere

c. what water vapor does to become cloud droplets

d. what liquid water does to become water vapor

e. outermost layer of the atmosphere

f. the wind belt that affects most of the United States

g. pattern of wind movement around the globe

h. layer above the stratosphere

i. layer of atmosphere where protective ozone occurs

j. the upper layer of the thermosphere

k. low, flat cloud that forms in layers

l. continuous cycle of rising warm air and falling cold air

Concept Review

Number your paper from 1 to 6. Then choose the answer that best completes each sentence. Write the letter of the answer on your paper.

1. The layer of gases surrounding Earth is called the _____.

    a. atmosphere   **b.** wind cell   **c.** wind belts

2. The _____ reflects radio signals.

  a. troposphere   **b.** stratosphere   **c.** ionosphere

3. The _____ is important because it absorbs most of the harmful ultraviolet radiation of the sun.

  a. troposphere   **b.** ozone layer   **c.** mesosphere

4. Fluffy white clouds are called _____.

  a. cumulus clouds   **b.** stratus clouds   **c.** rain clouds

5. Rain forms when _____.

  a. clouds trap solar energy

  b. radio waves reflect from a layer of the atmosphere

  c. water collects as heavy droplets

6. The prevailing westerlies are _____.

  a. winds that affect most of North America

  b. layers of the atmosphere

  c. rain clouds

Critical Thinking

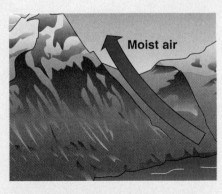

Moist air

Write the answer to each of the following questions.

1. Suppose the moist air shown in the diagram continues to move in the direction of the arrow. How might the weather on this side of the mountains be different from the weather on the other side?

2. Suppose that when you got up this morning, the sky was covered by gray stratus clouds. What kind of weather would you expect?

Test Taking Tip	When you have vocabulary words to learn, make flash cards. Write a word on the front of each card. Write the definition on the back. Use the flash cards to test your vocabulary skills.

Chapter

16

Weather and Climate

I n a fraction of a second, an electric current heats the air to temperatures hotter than the sun. The result is a blinding streak of lightning and a deafening clap of thunder. A thunderstorm is just one of the forces of nature you will learn about in this chapter. You will discover how different weather conditions are measured. You will also learn about different climates throughout the world.

ORGANIZE YOUR THOUGHTS

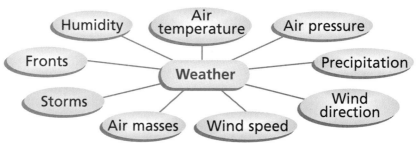

Humidity · Air temperature · Air pressure · Fronts · Weather · Precipitation · Storms · Air masses · Wind speed · Wind direction

Goals for Learning

▶ To explain what weather is
▶ To identify instruments that measure weather conditions
▶ To explain how air masses and fronts affect weather
▶ To read a weather map
▶ To describe various kinds of storms
▶ To describe Earth's major climates

Weather
State of the atmosphere at a given time and place.

The Atmosphere and Weather

Look out the window. Is it a cloudy day? Is it windy? *Cloudy* and *windy* refer to conditions of the atmosphere. **Weather** describes these and other conditions of the atmosphere.

The weather is always changing because conditions in the atmosphere are always changing. A meteorologist studies these conditions, gathers information, and uses these data to predict the weather.

Air Temperature

One of the first weather conditions you hear on a weather report is the temperature of the air. Air temperature is measured with a thermometer. Most thermometers are made of a thin tube filled with colored alcohol. Heat causes a liquid to expand, or take up more space. So when the air gets warmer, the liquid in the thermometer expands and moves up the tube. If the air gets cooler, the liquid contracts, or takes up less space. Then the liquid moves down the tube.

The unit of measurement for temperature is the degree (°). Two scales for measuring temperature are shown in the diagram. People in the United States usually use the Fahrenheit scale. People in most other countries use the Celsius scale. All scientists use the Celsius scale. Compare the common temperatures shown on both scales in the diagram.

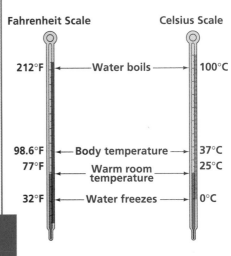

Fahrenheit Scale   Celsius Scale

212°F ◄———Water boils———► 100°C

98.6°F ◄——Body temperature——► 37°C
77°F ◄——Warm room temperature——► 25°C

32°F ◄———Water freezes———► 0°C

At what temperature does water boil on each scale?

Air Pressure

Air pressure
Force of air against a unit of area

Barometer
Instrument used to measure air pressure.

Think about what happens when you blow air into a balloon. The balloon gets bigger because the air molecules push against the inside wall of the balloon. The push of air against an object is called **air pressure**.

Air in the atmosphere exerts pressure too. The air above you and around you constantly pushes against your body. You don't feel this pressure because air in your body pushes out with the same amount of force. But what happens if air pressure suddenly changes? For example, while riding upward in an elevator, you may have felt your ears "pop." Your ears pop because they are adjusting to a drop in air pressure. As you move higher in the atmosphere, there is less air present to push on you, so air pressure drops.

Air pressure is measured with an instrument called a **barometer**. Two kinds of barometers are shown here. In a mercury barometer, air pushes down on a dish of mercury, forcing the mercury to rise in a tube. In an aneroid barometer, air pushes on a flat metal can. A pointer connected to the can shows the amount of air pressure.

Instruments use different scales to measure air pressure. Most weather reports give the air pressure in inches. Air pressure usually ranges from 29–31 inches (74–79 cm), which is the height of mercury in a mercury barometer.

A change in air pressure indicates a change in weather. A rise in air pressure usually means drier weather is on the way. A drop in air pressure often means precipitation is coming.

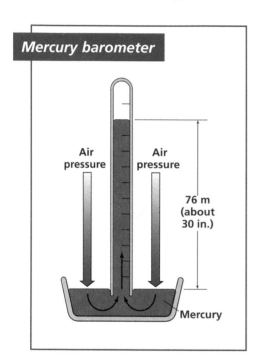

Mercury barometer

Air pressure

Air pressure

76 m (about 30 in.)

Mercury

Aneroid barometer

Anemometer
Instrument used to measure wind speed.

Humidity
Amount of water vapor in the air.

Psychrometer
Instrument used to measure humidity.

Wind vane
Instrument used to find wind direction.

Humidity

Have you ever described a hot day as *sticky* or *muggy*? Such days are uncomfortable because of high **humidity**. Humidity is the amount of water vapor in the air. When the air contains a lot of water vapor, the humidity is high. The amount of water vapor that the air can hold depends on the air temperature. Warmer air can hold more water vapor than colder air can.

A **psychrometer** is used to measure humidity. One of these instruments is made up of two thermometers. The bulb of one thermometer is covered with a damp cloth. As water evaporates from the cloth, it cools. The temperature of this thermometer is lower than the temperature of the dry thermometer. The lower the humidity, the faster the water evaporates and the lower the temperature drops. The humidity is then found by comparing the temperatures of the two thermometers to a special humidity chart.

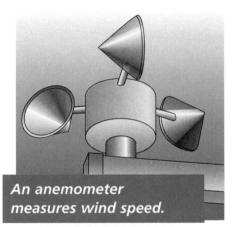

An anemometer measures wind speed.

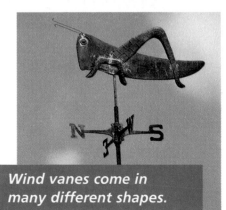

Wind vanes come in many different shapes.

Wind Speed and Direction

The speed of the wind is important to know because it helps meteorologists predict how fast an approaching storm will arrive. Wind speed is measured with an **anemometer**. An anemometer has three or four arms. Notice the cup on the end of each arm in the drawing. These cups catch the wind and cause the arms to rotate. When the wind speed increases, the arms rotate faster. Their spinning rate is indicated on a meter.

A **wind vane** shows the direction from which the wind is blowing. Notice the wind vane in the photo. Wind hits the larger back section of the grasshopper. The grasshopper turns so that it points into the wind. In this picture, the wind is blowing from the north.

Precipitation

If any precipitation falls, a weather report usually tells you how much. A **rain gauge** measures the amount of rainfall. As you can see in the photo at right, a rain gauge is a container that collects rain. A scale along the side shows the amount in millimeters or inches. Snow depth is usually measured simply by inserting a meterstick in a flat area of snow.

A rain gauge measures rainfall.

Self-Check

1. What is weather?

2. What weather condition does each of these instruments measure: barometer, thermometer, rain gauge, anemometer, psychrometer?

3. What does a change in air pressure tell you about the weather?

Air mass
Large section of the atmosphere with the same temperature and humidity throughout.

Cold front
Boundary ahead of a cold air mass that is pushing out and wedging under a warm air mass.

Front
Boundary between two air masses.

Warm front
Boundary ahead of a warm air mass that is pushing out and riding over a cold air mass.

To predict the weather, meteorologists collect data from weather stations, weather balloons, weather satellites, and radar.

Air Masses and Fronts

An **air mass** is a huge body of the lower atmosphere that has similar temperature and humidity throughout. An air mass can be warm or cold. It can have a lot of water vapor or very little. Air masses are so large that two or three of them can cover the United States. As air masses move, they bring their weather to new places.

A **front** is the boundary between two air masses. Two types of fronts are shown in the diagram. A **warm front** occurs where a warm air mass glides up and over a cooler air mass. As the warm air rises, it cools and water condenses. Typically, high cirrus clouds appear. Low stratus clouds follow. The barometer falls continuously, and a period of steady precipitation begins. When the front passes, skies clear and the barometer rises. The temperature rises as warm air replaces the cooler air.

At a **cold front**, a cold air mass pushes beneath a warmer air mass. The warm air mass rises quickly. If the warm air mass has a lot of water vapor, storm clouds form quickly. Heavy precipitation follows, but only for short periods of time. Several hours after the front passes, the weather becomes clear and cool.

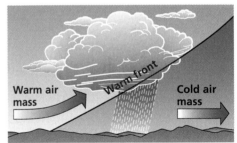

Warm front

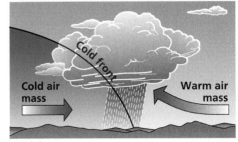

Cold front

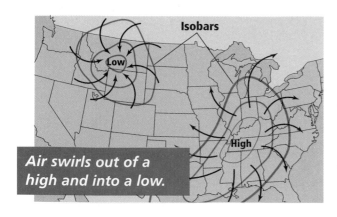
Isobars

Low

High

Air swirls out of a high and into a low.

Isobar
Line on a weather map connecting areas of equal air pressure.

Tornado
Powerful wind storm with a whirling, funnel-shaped cloud and extremely low air pressure.

Highs and Lows

Cold air is denser than warm air. Therefore, cold air exerts more pressure on Earth's surface than warm air does. A cold air mass is usually an area of high pressure, or a high. Highs often have fair weather. Look at the map. You can see that air moves outward from a high in a clockwise rotation. The air moves into an area of low pressure, or a low. Notice that the air coming into a low rotates counterclockwise. Lows often have clouds and precipitation. On a map, lines called **isobars** connect areas of equal pressure. Isobars form a circular pattern around highs and lows.

Because most of the United States is in the area of the prevailing westerly winds, most of our weather moves from west to east. Therefore, a cold front passing through eastern Oklahoma will soon be passing through western Arkansas. The front will likely bring similar weather to both places.

Storms

Storms are violent kinds of weather. They are caused by rapid changes in the movement of air masses. Storms usually include precipitation and high winds.

Perhaps the most familiar kind of storm is the thunderstorm. This kind of storm occurs when warm air is forced upward. Large, dark cumulus clouds form. Such clouds are also called thunderheads. They can produce lightning and thunder.

A **tornado** is a small but powerful wind storm with a whirling, funnel-shaped cloud. Tornadoes sometimes occur in thunderstorms, but their exact cause is unknown. Tornadoes may rotate at speeds up to 400 kilometers per hour. They can uproot trees, toss cars, and destroy buildings.

Hurricanes cover wide areas.

A **hurricane** is a large tropical storm that often covers tens of thousands of square kilometers. Hurricanes may have wind speeds of up to 240 kilometers per hour. At the center of a hurricane is an area of calm air called the eye. Clouds spiral around the eye as shown in the satellite photo.

All hurricanes form over the ocean near the equator. They collect warm, moist air and begin to spin. They grow stronger over the warm tropical water. As hurricanes approach land, their wind pushes the water of the ocean against the shore, and flooding occurs. Hurricanes may drop tremendous amounts of rain as they move inland, causing further damage.

Hurricane
A severe tropical storm with high winds that revolve around an eye.

Weather Maps

A meteorologist must consider a lot of data to develop a weather forecast. These data are organized on a weather map, as shown on the next page. A weather map can look confusing at first. But if you compare each symbol to the key, you can soon read the map easily. Weather maps generally include information about precipitation, cloud cover, air masses, highs, lows, and fronts. Weather maps may also include isobars, temperatures, wind speeds, and wind directions.

Self-Check

1. How is a cold front different from and similar to a warm front?
2. Name three kinds of weather information found on a weather map.
3. What is a tornado?
4. What do hurricanes need in order to form?
5. What is the eye of a hurricane?

16

Using a Weather Map

Materials

✓ outline map of the United States

✓ pencil

Purpose

To make and interpret a weather map

Procedure

1. On your map of the United States, copy the weather information from the weather map below. Be sure to include the key of weather symbols.

2. On your map, show that it is raining across all of Florida.

3. Show that snow is falling in Minnesota behind the cold front.

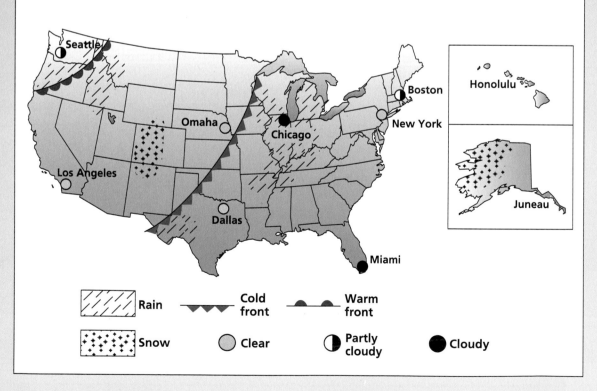

⬛ Rain	⬛ Cold front	⬛ Warm front	
⬛ Snow	⬛ Clear	◖ Partly cloudy	⬤ Cloudy

4. Show that a warm front is heading across Alabama, Georgia, and South Carolina toward Florida.

5. Show that it is cloudy in Honolulu, Hawaii, and partly cloudy in Juneau, Alaska.

Questions

1. Which cities labeled on the map have clear skies?

2. Which kind of front is heading toward Dallas and Chicago? What kind of weather will these cities have after the front passes them?

3. From your map, predict what will happen to temperatures in Florida over the next day. Explain your answer.

Explore Further

1. Suggest two more symbols that could be added to your map. Explain the symbols. How do they make the map more useful?

2. Look in a newspaper. Compare weather maps for two days in a row. How accurate was the first day's forecast? Did the fronts move as expected? Are there any new fronts? From which direction did they arrive?

Objectives

After reading this lesson, you should be able to

▶ compare and contrast the three major climate zones.

▶ identify factors that affect climate.

Climate

Average weather of a region over a long period of time.

What kind of weather do people have on the other side of the world? It may be similar to yours. Scientists have identified global patterns in weather.

Climate Zones

Like weather, **climate** describes conditions of the atmosphere. Weather is the state of the atmosphere at a given time and place. Climate is the average weather of a region over a long period of time. Climate is based largely on average yearly temperature and precipitation. The climates of the world can be divided into three major climate zones, shown on the map below.

Each of the three major climate zones is further divided into climate regions. The table on the next page summarizes the characteristics of each region. Notice the differences in temperature and precipitation between the regions. Also notice the types of plants that grow in different regions.

The world can be divided into three main climate zones.

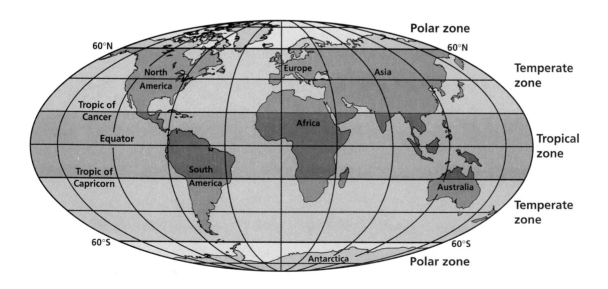

Polar Climates

Ice cap climate

Average yearly temperature below freezing	Precipitation less than 25 centimeters per year	No visible plant life

Tundra climate

Temperature slightly higher than ice cap	Precipitation less than 25 centimeters per year	Mosses and small shrubs

Subarctic climate

Cold winter, short summer	Precipitation 25–30 centimeters per year	Small pines, spruce, and fir

Temperate Climates

Marine west coast climate

Temperatures generally above freezing	Precipitation 50–76 centimeters per year	Thick evergreen forests

Deserts and steppes

Cold winter, warm to hot summer	Precipitation less than 25 centimeters per year	Cactus in deserts, grasses in steppes

Mediterranean climate

Warm summer; mild, wet winter	Average precipitation 25 centimeters per year	Scattered trees, low shrubs

Humid subtropical climate

Warm and humid summer, mild winter	Precipitation 76–165 centimeters per year	Heavy plant growth and forests

Humid continental climate

Warm and humid summer, cold winter	Average precipitation 76 centimeters per year	Hardwood and softwood forests, grass prairies

Tropical Climates

Tropical rain forest

Always hot and humid	Average precipitation 254 centimeters per year	Very thick forests and plant growth

Tropical desert

Dry and relatively hot summer and winter	Precipitation less than 25 centimeters per year	Almost no plant life

Savannah

Humid and warm summer, dry and cooler winter	Precipitation 76–152 centimeters per year	Scattered trees and shrubs, tall grasses

Factors That Affect Climate

Why is one climate different from another? The main factor is the angle at which sunlight hits Earth. Because Earth is a sphere, sunlight hits the tropics more directly than areas toward the poles. The more direct sunlight provides warmer temperatures.

Climate is also affected by how high a place is above sea level. The temperatures in a mountain region are cooler than the temperatures in a nearby valley. In general, higher places tend to be cooler. This is why you can find snow-capped mountains near the equator.

The nearness of large bodies of water also affects climate. In general, areas that are close to an ocean or a large lake get more precipitation than areas farther from water. Water heats up and cools off more slowly than land. As a result, the temperatures of areas near large bodies of water are milder than areas far from water.

Self-Check

1. Where do tropical climates occur?
2. Where do polar climates occur?
3. Which climate zone has hot summers and cold winters?
4. How does height above sea level affect climate?
5. What effect does a large body of water have on climate?

SCIENCE IN YOUR LIFE

How do people affect climate?

Human-made factors can affect climate. For example, cities are like "heat islands." Their average temperatures tend to be one to two degrees Celsius higher than nearby rural areas. One reason cities have higher temperatures is the way materials absorb the sun's heat. Building materials and asphalt pavements absorb more solar energy than plants and soil do. The materials then transfer heat to the surrounding air.

- Weather is the state of the atmosphere at a given time and place.

- To study weather, meteorologists gather information about many conditions of the atmosphere. These include air temperature, air pressure, humidity, wind speed, wind direction, type of precipitation, and amount of precipitation.

- A barometer measures air pressure.

- A psychrometer measures humidity.

- An anemometer measures wind speed. A wind vane measures wind direction.

- Air masses bring with them the weather conditions of the areas in which they formed.

- Fronts are the boundaries between air masses.

- Isobars are lines on a map that connect areas of equal pressure. Isobars form a circular pattern around highs and lows.

- Storms are severe weather conditions and include thunderstorms, tornadoes, and hurricanes.

- Data on weather maps, including information about fronts, air masses, highs, and lows, are used by meteorologists to forecast the weather.

- Climate is the average weather of a region over a long period of time.

- The climates of the world can be divided into three major climate zones: polar, temperate, and tropical.

- Climate is affected by the angle of sunlight, height above sea level, and nearness of large bodies of water.

Science Words

air mass, 263	hurricane, 265
air pressure, 260	isobar, 264
anemometer, 261	psychrometer, 261
barometer, 260	rain gauge, 262
climate, 268	tornado, 264
cold front, 263	warm front, 263
front, 263	weather, 259
humidity, 261	wind vane, 261

Vocabulary Review

Number your paper from 1 to 11. Match each word in Column A with the correct definition in Column B. Write the letter of the definition on your paper.

Column A

_____ 1. anemometer

_____ 2. barometer

_____ 3. climate

_____ 4. humidity

_____ 5. hurricane

_____ 6. air mass

_____ 7. psychrometer

_____ 8. isobar

_____ 9. weather

_____ 10. rain gauge

_____ 11. tornado

Column B

a. large storm that forms over tropical oceans

b. instrument for measuring air pressure

c. state of the atmosphere at a given time and place

d. instrument for measuring precipitation

e. storm with a dangerous funnel cloud

f. instrument for measuring wind speed

g. instrument for measuring humidity

h. average weather over a long period of time

i. line connecting areas of equal air pressure

j. amount of water vapor in the air

k. large section of the atmosphere with the same temperature and humidity throughout

Concept Review

Number your paper from 1 to 7. Then choose the answer that best completes each sentence. Write the letter of the answer on your paper.

1. A thermometer measures _____.

   a. air pressure   b. air temperature   c. humidity

2. The force of the atmosphere against Earth's surface is _____.

   a. air pressure   **b.** air temperature   **c.** precipitation

3. A wind vane measures _____.

   a. wind direction **b.** wind speed   **c.** air pressure

4. Air pressure is measured with a(n) _____.

   a. psychrometer   **b.** anemometer   **c.** barometer

5. The boundary between two air masses is called a(n) _____.

   a. eye   **b.** front   **c.** isobar

6. Hurricanes form over _____.

   a. oceans   **b.** prairies   **c.** forests

7. The _____ climate zone has hot summers and cold winters.

   a. polar   **b.** tropical   **c.** temperate

Critical Thinking

Write the answer to each of the following questions.

1. The picture shows two cities in the temperate climate zone. Describe how you would expect the climates of the cities to be the same and different. Explain your answer.

2. As a high pushes out a low in your area, what weather changes would you expect?

Test Taking Tip Read the test directions twice. Sometimes they will give you a hint. For example, the directions may remind you to look for the *best* answer.

The Solar System

Have you ever seen a picture of a volcano? How about a volcano in outer space? The planet Jupiter has a moon with erupting volcanoes. If you could travel to other planets, how would you find your way to Jupiter? What planets and other objects would you see along the way? In this chapter, you will explore the planets and their moons. What you discover may surprise you.

ORGANIZE YOUR THOUGHTS

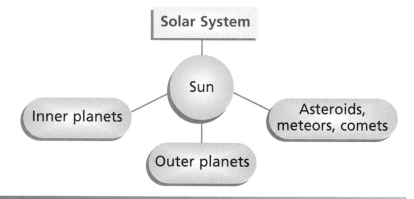

Solar System

Sun

Inner planets

Outer planets

Asteroids, meteors, comets

Goals for Learning

▶ To explain what the solar system is
▶ To identify the four inner planets
▶ To identify the five outer planets
▶ To tell something about each planet
▶ To describe the motions and positions of the planets
▶ To compare comets and asteroids

Planet
A large body in space that orbits a star such as the sun.

Solar system
A star, such as the sun, and all the bodies that revolve around it in space.

Star
A glowing ball of hot gas that makes its own energy and light.

Stars Versus Planets

If you stand outside on a clear night, away from bright lights, you should be able to see hundreds of shining objects in the sky. Most of the objects are **stars**. These glowing balls of hot gas shine because they make their own light. A few of the objects are **planets**. Planets are large bodies in space that orbit the sun. The planets shine because they reflect the light of the sun, our closest star.

The Solar System

Compared to stars, the planets are relatively close to us. The sun and all of the planets and other bodies that revolve around the sun make up the **solar system**. *Solar* refers to the sun. Our solar system has nine planets. Look at the diagram to find out what they are. Some of the planets have satellites, or moons, that revolve around them. You already know at least one planet with a moon—Earth.

The entire solar system holds together because the gravity of the sun, the planets, and other objects attracts these objects to each other. There is a gravitational pull between all the objects in the solar system.

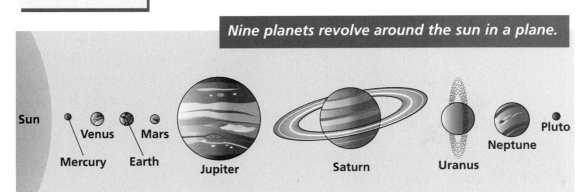

Nine planets revolve around the sun in a plane.

Sun · Venus · Mercury · Mars · Earth · Jupiter · Saturn · Uranus · Neptune · Pluto

The Sun

The largest object in the solar system is the sun. In fact, the sun is larger than all of the planets put together. Its mass is 99 percent of the entire solar system. Mass is the amount of material that an object contains. So 99 percent of the "stuff" in the solar system is in the sun! The diagram compares the size of Earth and the sun.

The sun is made mostly of two gases, hydrogen and helium. The sun also contains very small amounts of the elements found on Earth. Because the sun is mostly gas, it has no solid surface.

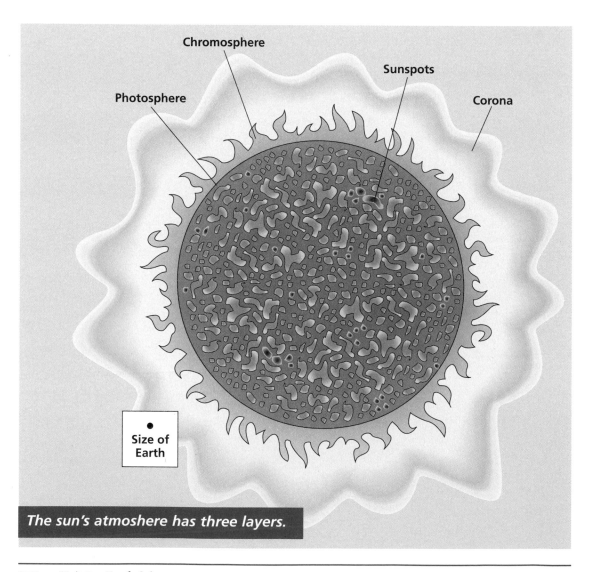

Chromosphere

Sunspots

Photosphere

Corona

Size of Earth

The sun's atmoshere has three layers.

Chromosphere
Middle layer of gas in sun's atmosphere.

Corona
Outer layer of sun's atmosphere.

Photosphere
Layer of sun's atmosphere that gives off light.

Sunspot
Dark area of the sun's surface that gives off less energy than the rest of the sun.

The outer temperature of the sun is about 5,500°C. This high temperature is caused by nuclear reactions inside the sun. In the sun's center, high temperatures of 15,000,000°C cause hydrogen particles to fuse and form helium. These nuclear reactions produce energy that we see as light and feel as heat.

The only part of the sun that can be seen is its atmosphere. The inner layer of the sun's atmosphere is called the **photosphere**. This is the layer of gas that gives off light. Just outside of this layer is another layer of gas called the **chromosphere**. The gas of the chromosphere can sometimes be seen during a total solar eclipse, when the photosphere is blocked. The outer layer of the sun's atmosphere is the **corona**. It is a layer of gas thicker than the chromosphere. The corona also can be seen during a solar eclipse.

Notice that the photosphere contains dark areas called **sunspots**. Sunspots give off less energy and are, therefore, cooler than the rest of the sun. But they are still about 3,500°C.

Did You Know?

Sometimes tremendous explosions, called solar flares, move outward from the sun's surface. Solar flares send electrically charged particles into space. Some of the particles reach Earth 150 million kilometers away and cause static on radios. The particles also change the amount of power in electric lines.

Self-Check

1. Why do planets shine in the night sky?
2. What makes up our solar system?
3. List the features or characteristics of the sun.
4. How would you describe the sun?
5. Which layer of the sun gives off light?

Objectives

After reading this lesson, you should be able to

▶ identify the four inner planets.

▶ describe the four inner planets.

▶ explain what the greenhouse effect is and how it affects Venus.

The Inner Planets

The planets of the solar system are divided into two groups, the inner planets and the outer planets. The inner planets are the ones that are closest to the sun: Mercury, Venus, Earth, and Mars. All of the inner planets are solid and similar in size. But these rocky worlds are also very different from one another.

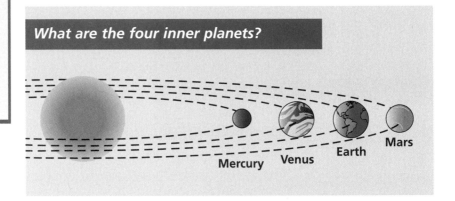

What are the four inner planets?

Mercury Venus Earth Mars

Mercury

The planet closest to the sun is Mercury. Named after the Roman god of speed, Mercury is the fastest-moving planet. Its average speed as it orbits the sun is about 50 kilometers per second. Mercury completes an entire revolution of the sun in 88 Earth days, but it rotates slowly. One day on Mercury lasts about 59 Earth days.

Several spacecraft have taken pictures of Mercury's surface. The pictures show that the surface is like that of Earth's moon. It is covered with craters and flat areas. Mercury has almost no atmosphere.

Mercury's surface looks like the surface of the moon.

Mercury is not easy to see in the sky because it is so close to the sun. When the sun is above the horizon, all the stars and planets seem to fade away. On some nights you can see Mercury in the western sky just after sunset. Mercury also appears in the east sometimes just before sunrise.

Venus

The planet that is next closest to the sun is Venus. It was named after the Roman goddess of love and beauty. Venus is one of the brightest objects in the sky. Like the moon, you can sometimes see Venus during the day. Depending on the time of the year, Venus is known as the "morning star" or the "evening star."

Venus is different from most of the other planets because it rotates in the opposite direction. Earth and the other inner planets rotate from west to east. Venus rotates from east to west. That means the sun rises in the west on Venus. Also, it takes a long time for Venus to rotate. A day on Venus is 243 Earth days.

Venus has a thick atmosphere that is very different from Earth's.

The atmosphere of Venus contains great amounts of the gas carbon dioxide. Carbon dioxide in the atmosphere traps heat energy from the sun. As a result, the atmosphere heats up. This warming is called the **greenhouse effect**. The greenhouse effect occurs on Earth, too. The clouds of Venus's atmosphere are made of tiny drops of sulfuric acid. These clouds trap heat and add to the greenhouse effect. Because of the greenhouse effect, the surface temperature of Venus is very high—about 500°C. The surface of the planet would be much cooler without the greenhouse effect.

Earth

Our own planet, Earth, is the third planet from the sun. Earth has several differences from the other inner planets. For one thing, it is the largest. Earth also has a mild surface temperature, a dense atmosphere, and a great deal of water. Because of these features, Earth can support life. There is no evidence of life on the other planets, although some form of life may have existed on Mars billions of years ago. Earth is also the closest planet to the sun that has a moon.

Earth's land areas and oceans are visible from space.

Mars has a reddish color in the night sky.

Mars

Mars, the fourth planet from the sun, is named for the Roman god of war. Mars has two small moons. Mars rotates once every 24 hours and 38 minutes. It takes Mars 687 Earth days to complete one revolution around the sun.

The atmosphere on Mars is much less dense than Earth's. The atmosphere is mostly carbon dioxide. Mars is colder than Earth because it is farther from the sun and has a thinner atmosphere that does not trap heat.

Facts About the Inner Planets				
	Mercury	**Venus**	**Earth**	**Mars**
Distance from the sun (millions of kilometers)	58	107	149	227
Diameter (kilometers)	4,800	12,000	12,640	6,720
Number of satellites (moons)	0	0	1	2
Length of day (Earth days)	59	243	1	1
Length of year (Earth days)	88	225	365	687

Self-Check

1. What are the names of the inner planets?
2. How would you describe Mercury?
3. What is the greenhouse effect?
4. What features enable Earth to support life?
5. What is the atmosphere of Mars mostly made of?

Objectives

After reading this lesson, you should be able to

▶ identify the five outer planets.

▶ describe the five outer planets.

The outer planets, except for Pluto, are larger than the inner planets and are made up mostly of frozen gases. Over the last 20 years, *Voyager* and *Galileo* spacecraft have collected much information about these planets.

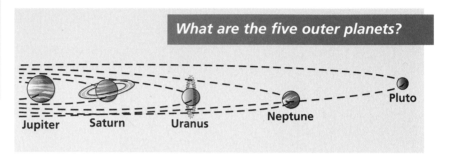

What are the five outer planets?

Jupiter   Saturn   Uranus   Neptune   Pluto

Jupiter

Jupiter is the largest planet in the solar system. It has a mass $2\frac{1}{2}$ times that of all the other planets put together. The diameter of Jupiter is more than ten times larger than Earth's. It's no wonder Jupiter was named for the Roman king of the gods.

Jupiter's colorful bands are made mostly of hydrogen and helium.

Among the most noticeable features of Jupiter are the colorful bands. These bands are clouds of gases where storms are taking place. The bands change shape every few days but generally run in the same direction. Jupiter's fast rotation might cause these bands. It takes Jupiter only ten hours to rotate once.

Find the oval at the lower left in the photo. This area is called the Great Red Spot.

The red spot is more than twice as wide as the entire Earth. It is a storm that has lasted for more than 300 years!

When Voyager spacecraft flew by Jupiter in 1979, astronomers discovered faint rings around the planet. Astronomers also discovered more moons than they had thought existed. At least 16 moons orbit this giant planet.

The largest of Jupiter's moons is Ganymede. It is bigger than the planet Mercury. The smallest moon is named Leda and is only about 20 kilometers in diameter. A moon called Europa is an icy world with a smooth, cracked surface. It has been described as a giant cue ball.

The photograph below shows the moon Io. Like Earth, Io has active volcanoes. The volcanoes erupt constantly, spewing out sulfur that colors the moon yellow, orange, and red. In fact, the photograph of Io shown here might remind you of a pizza!

Io's colorful surface comes from sulfur erupting from volcanoes.

Saturn

You are probably familiar with the rings of Saturn. Saturn, the sixth planet from the sun, was named for the Roman god of agriculture. Saturn is the second largest planet in the solar system.

The rings that orbit Saturn's equator are made up mostly of ice particles and dust. When you look at Saturn through a telescope, you can see the rings only at certain times during Saturn's orbit. That is because the rings are very thin, and Saturn is tilted on its axis. When the edge of the ring system is pointed toward Earth, the rings disappear from view.

Saturn's rings are made of ice particles and dust.

Like Jupiter, Saturn is a giant planet of gases with stormy bands of clouds running along its surface. Winds in these storms reach speeds of 1,800 kilometers per hour. Also like Jupiter, Saturn spins very fast. One day is about ten hours.

Saturn has 18 known moons, the largest of which is Titan. Titan is the only moon in the solar system that is known to have an atmosphere of its own. This atmosphere is mostly nitrogen. Titan may also have active volcanoes.

Uranus

The seventh planet from the sun is Uranus. This planet was named for the Greek god of the sky. One unusual thing about Uranus is the tilt of its axis. Uranus rotates on its side. During some parts of its revolution, one pole of Uranus points directly at the sun.

In 1977, astronomers discovered that Uranus has a ring system. They were using a telescope to observe Uranus as it passed in front of a star. They noticed that the star dimmed briefly many times. Each dimming occurred as another ring passed in front of the star. A Voyager spacecraft has studied the rings and Uranus's 15 moons up close.

Because Uranus is so far out in the solar system, it takes 84 Earth years to complete a single orbit of the sun. Uranus rotates on its axis once every 17 hours.

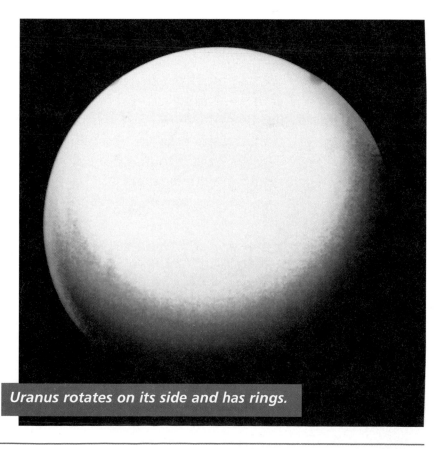

Uranus rotates on its side and has rings.

Neptune

Neptune is the eighth planet from the sun. Named after the Roman god of the sea, Neptune cannot be seen without a telescope. Like Uranus, Neptune appears greenish blue because of methane gas in its atmosphere. Neptune also has a ring system.

Methane gas gives Neptune's atmosphere its color.

It takes Neptune 165 Earth years to complete a revolution around the sun. The planet rotates once on its axis every 16 hours.

Neptune has eight moons. One of them, Triton, is unusual because it rotates in the opposite direction from Neptune's rotation. Triton also has active volcanoes.

Pluto

Pluto is the outermost planet of the solar system, but it is not always the farthest from the sun. Part of its orbit goes inside the orbit of Neptune.

Pluto is much smaller than the other outer planets, and it is the only outer planet without a thick atmosphere. Pluto has one known moon, Charon. At an average distance from the sun of almost six billion kilometers, Pluto takes 248 Earth years to make one revolution. Pluto seems to rotate about once every six days.

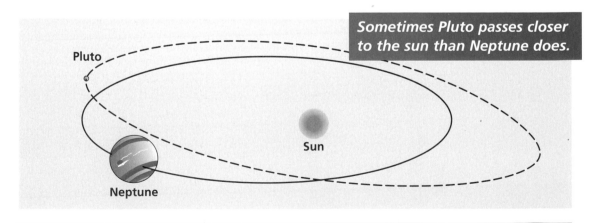

Sometimes Pluto passes closer to the sun than Neptune does.

Pluto

Sun

Neptune

Facts About the Outer Planets

	Jupiter	Saturn	Uranus	Neptune	Pluto
Distance from the sun (millions of kilometers)	774	1,420	2,853	4,470	5,866
Diameter (kilometers)	143,000	120,000	51,520	50,000	2,300
Number of satellites (moons)	16	18	15	8	1
Length of day (Earth hours)	10	10	17	16	6 days
Length of year (Earth years)	12	29	84	165	248

Self-Check

1. What are the five outer planets of the solar system?
2. What kind of matter are the large outer planets made of?
3. Which of the outer planets have rings?
4. Which is the largest planet in the solar system?
5. Which outer planet has the same number of moons as Earth has?

SCIENCE IN YOUR LIFE

How fast is that CD?

The planet Uranus takes 84 years to revolve around the sun. You could also say that Uranus has a period of revolution of 84 years. Mercury's period of revolution is 88 days, more than 300 times greater than that of Uranus. An extremely fast period of revolution is measured in revolutions per minute, or rpm. One rpm is equal to one full turn every minute. A compact disc can turn at 500 revolutions per minute. At that speed, how many times does a CD turn in one second? How many times in one hour? How did you find out? How fast is that CD?

Materials

✓ one 12-m long piece of adding machine paper

✓ meterstick

✓ tape

Distances in the Solar System

Purpose

To use a scale to show the distance between each planet and the sun

Procedure

1. Tape the strip of adding machine paper to the floor. Draw a circle at one end of the paper. The circle represents the sun.

2. The table at the bottom of the page shows the relative distances of the planets from the sun. Use this table and a meter stick to mark the location of each of the planets on the adding machine paper. Label the position of each planet with its name.

3. Each centimeter on the strip of paper represents five million kilometers in space. Next to each planet on the paper, record its distance in kilometers from the sun.

Questions

1. What is the scale of this model?

2. Which four planets are closest together?

3. Which planets have the greatest distance between their orbits?

Explore Further

Make a scale model that shows the diameters of all nine planets.

Planet on model	Distance from sun on model (cm)	Planet on model	Distance from sun on model (cm)
Mercury	12	Saturn	286
Venus	22	Uranus	574
Earth	30	Neptune	900
Mars	46	Pluto	1,180
Jupiter	156		

What Other Objects Make Up the Solar System?

Asteroids

Our solar system has other objects besides the sun and the planets. Some of these objects are **asteroids**. An asteroid is a rocky object smaller than a planet that has its own orbit around the sun. Most asteroids are smaller than one kilometer in diameter, but a few are 1,000 kilometers across.

As the diagram shows, a large number of asteroids lie between the orbits of Mars and Jupiter. This area is known as the **asteroid belt**. As many as a million asteroids make up this belt, orbiting the sun. The belt may have formed as Jupiter's gravity pulled matter toward this region of space.

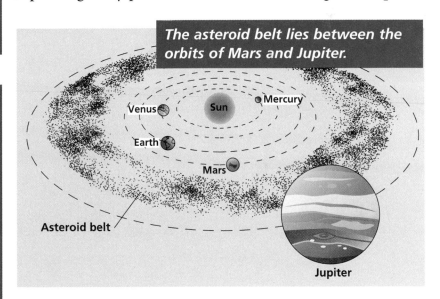

The asteroid belt lies between the orbits of Mars and Jupiter.

Not all of these asteroids stay in their orbits. Sometimes they are pulled out of orbit by the gravity of other planets. Asteroids may also be pulled in toward the sun.

A few asteroids come close to Earth and, at times, are captured by Earth's gravity. If an asteroid enters Earth's atmosphere, it heats up and becomes a ball of glowing gases. It is then called a **meteor**. You probably know meteors as "shooting stars" or "falling stars."

A meteor crater in Arizona is more than a kilometer across.

If a meteor is big enough and does not completely burn up, it may hit Earth. A meteor that strikes Earth is called a meteorite. Large meteorites can leave craters. About 50,000 years ago, a meteorite created Meteor Crater in Arizona, shown in the photograph.

Comets

Comet
A ball of ice, rock, frozen gases, and dust that orbits the sun.

Other objects of the solar system include **comets**. Most of these objects follow large orbits. Most comets are not on the same orbital plane as the planets. A comet's orbit may take it far beyond the orbit of Pluto.

Scientists have found that comets are made of ice, rock, frozen gases, and dust. When a comet approaches the sun, it begins to warm up. Some of the ice turns to gases, and dust is also released. The gases and the dust reflect sunlight, making the comet visible. A stream of particles from the sun, called the solar wind, pushes the gas and dust away from the head of the comet. This gas and dust form a tail that points away from the sun.

Comet Hyakutake made headlines when it appeared in 1996.

Self-Check

1. What is an asteroid?
2. Where is the asteroid belt located?
3. What is a meteor?
4. When does a meteor become a meteorite?
5. What are comets made of?

- Stars shine because they give off their own light. Planets shine because they reflect light from the sun.

- The solar system is made up of the sun, the planets and their moons, and other bodies that revolve around the sun.

- The sun is made mostly of the gases hydrogen and helium. The sun's atmosphere has three layers—the photosphere, the chromosphere, and the corona.

- The inner planets are Mercury, Venus, Earth, and Mars. They are all solid, rocky worlds.

- Mercury has almost no atmosphere and has craters like the moon.

- Venus rotates in the opposite direction from most other planets, has an atmosphere that is mostly carbon dioxide, and is very hot.

- Earth has moderate temperatures, a dense atmosphere, and much water. Earth is the only planet known to have life on it.

- Mars has a thin atmosphere and is colder than Earth. Mars has two moons.

- The outer planets are Jupiter, Saturn, Uranus, Neptune, and Pluto. Pluto is small and solid. The others are large and made up mostly of gases.

- Jupiter is the largest planet, rotates fast, and has 16 moons.

- Saturn has rings and 18 moons.

- Uranus rotates on its side. It has a ring system and 15 moons.

- Neptune has a ring system and two moons.

- Pluto is the outermost planet in the solar system. It has one moon.

- Asteroids are rocky objects that orbit the sun. A large number of asteroids lie between the orbits of Mars and Jupiter.

- A meteor is an asteroid that enters Earth's atmosphere.

- Comets are made of ice, rock, frozen gases, and dust.

Science Words		
asteroid, 289		meteor, 289
asteroid belt, 289		photosphere, 277
chromosphere, 277		planet, 275
comet, 290		solar system, 275
corona, 277		star, 275
greenhouse effect, 280		sunspot, 277

WORD BANK

asteroid belt

comet

greenhouse effect

meteor

photosphere

planets

solar system

star

sunspots

Vocabulary Review

Number your paper from 1 to 9. Then choose a term from the Word Bank that best completes each sentence. Write the answer on your paper.

1. The planets and the sun form our _____.

2. The sun is the _____ that the planets orbit.

3. The inner layer of the sun's atmosphere is the _____.

4. The dark areas that appear on the sun are called _____.

5. Venus has a hot surface temperature because of the _____.

6. Between Mars and Jupiter, there is a zone called the _____.

7. Mars and Neptune are examples of _____.

8. A shooting star is a(n) _____.

9. A(n) _____ is made of ice, frozen gases, and dust.

Concept Review

Number your paper from 1 to 9. Then write the answers to each of the following questions.

1. Identify each member of the solar system shown in the diagram below. Write the name after each letter.

2. The sun is made up mostly of two gases. Name one of them.

3. Name five different kinds of objects that make up the solar system.

4. Four of the outer planets are very similar. Give two features that they share.

5. What holds the solar system together?

6. How does the greenhouse effect keep the surface of Venus hot?

7. Which two planets do not have moons?

8. What is the Great Red Spot?

9. Describe the Jupiter moon Io.

Critical Thinking

Write the answers to each of the following questions.

1. What is the difference between a star and a planet?

2. One of Jupiter's moons is as big as the planet Mercury. If the moon is so big, why is it a moon and not a planet?

Test Taking Tip | If a word looks new to you, take it apart. Try comparing the parts to words you know.

Modeling the Water Cycle

Purpose

To observe stages in the water cycle

Procedure

Materials

- ✓ clear plastic box, such as shoebox or small terrarium
- ✓ dry soil or sand
- ✓ china marker
- ✓ small shallow dish
- ✓ water
- ✓ plastic wrap
- ✓ rubber band
- ✓ ice cubes

1. Copy the data table below on your paper.

When observations were made	Observations
after 10 minutes	
after 20 minutes	
after 30 minutes	
after ice cubes were added	

2. Put a layer of dry soil or sand 3 or 4 cm deep in the box.

3. Mark the side of the dish halfway between the top and the bottom. Fill the dish to the mark with water. Put the dish on the bottom of the box at one end. Push it down into the soil or sand.

4. Cover the top of the box with a piece of plastic wrap. Secure the plastic wrap with a rubber band.

5. Put the box in a sunny place. After 10 minutes, examine the plastic wrap from the top and through the side of the box. Also observe the water level in the dish. Record your observations. Examine again after 20 minutes and 30 minutes.

6. Take the box out of the sun. Put about 10 ice cubes on the plastic wrap at the end of the box opposite the dish. Observe and record your observations.

Questions

1. What did you observe in steps 5 and 6?

2. Which part of your model showed the stage of evaporation in the water cycle? Which part showed condensation? Which part showed precipitation?

- Rotation is the spinning of Earth on its axis. Earth's rotation causes day and night.

- Revolution is Earth's movement in an orbit around the sun.

- Intersecting lines of latitude and longitude make it possible to locate a single point anywhere on Earth's surface.

- A mineral can be identified by its properties, including color, luster, streak, and hardness.

- The three main types of rocks are igneous, sedimentary, and metamorphic. Rocks change from one type to another in the rock cycle.

- Mechanical weathering is the process of breaking up rocks without changing their minerals. Chemical weathering is the process of breaking up rocks by changing the minerals in them.

- Soil is a mixture of weathered rock and the remains of plants and animals.

- Erosion is caused by water, glaciers, wind, and gravity.

- Earth has three main layers: the core, the mantle, and the crust.

- The theory of plate tectonics states that Earth's crust is made up of several large plates that move about over the mantle.

- Rocks contain clues about events that happened in Earth's past.

- The events in Earth's history occurred over geologic time and are outlined on the geologic time scale.

- Water moves between the land, the atmosphere, and the ocean in the water cycle.

- Features of the ocean floor include the continental shelf, the continental slope, mid-ocean ridges, trenches, hills, plains, and mountains.

- The atmosphere is the layer of gases that surrounds Earth.

- Precipitation is moisture that falls to Earth from the atmosphere as rain, snow, sleet, or hail.

- The sun's unequal heating of Earth's surface causes wind.

- Weather is the state of the atmosphere at a given time and place.

- Climate is the average weather of a region over a long period of time.

- The solar system is made of the sun, the planets and their moons, and other bodies that revolve around the sun.

WORD BANK

atmosphere

axis

fossil

humidity

mantle

oxidation

precipitation

rock cycle

water table

Vocabulary Review

Number your paper from 1 to 9. Then choose the term from the Word Bank that best completes each sentence. Write the answer on your paper.

1. The imaginary line through Earth around which it rotates is called the _____.

2. Rocks change from one type to another as they go through the _____.

3. An example of chemical weathering is _____.

4. The layer of Earth between the core and the crust is the _____.

5. A(n) _____ is a trace or remains of an organism preserved in Earth's crust.

6. Underground water forms a soaked layer, the top of which is the _____.

7. Solid or liquid water that falls from the atmosphere is _____.

8. The amount of water vapor in the air is called _____.

9. The gases around a planet make up its _____.

Concept Review

Number your paper from 1 to 8. Choose the answer that best completes each sentence. Write the letter of the answer on your paper.

1. Earth rotates from _____.

   a. east to west   b. north to south   c. west to east

2. Rocks that have been changed by heat, pressure, and chemical reactions form _____ rocks.

   a. metamorphic   b. igneous   c. sedimentary

3. The main process that creates a beach is _____.

   a. erosion   b. deposition   c. weathering

4. Earth's surface is part of the _____.

   a. core   b. mantle   c. crust

5. The _____ Era is known as the Age of Mammals.

   a. Cenozoic   b. Paleozoic   c. Mesozoic

6. Fluffy white clouds are called _____ clouds.

   a. stratus   b. cumulus   c. cirrus

7. The boundary between two air masses is called a(n) _____.

   a. eye   b. front   c. isobar

8. Between Mars and Jupiter is a zone called the _____.

   a. atmosphere   b. greenhouse effect   c. asteroid belt

Number your paper from 9 to 14. Then match each ocean feature below with a letter in the diagram. Write the letter of each answer on your paper.

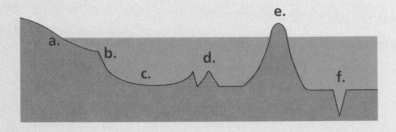

9. mid-ocean ridge

10. continental shelf

11. island

12. plain

13. continental slope

14. trench

Critical Thinking

Write the answer to each of the following questions.

1. One way to make salt water safe to drink is to heat it, collect the water vapor, and condense it. How is this method like the water cycle? Suggest a way to collect the water vapor.

2. Suppose you are going to a picnic today. Fluffy white clouds are floating across the sky. Do you think it will rain at the picnic? Explain.

"To me nature is . . . spiders and bugs, and big fish eating little fish, and plants eating plants, and animals eating. . . . It's like an enormous restaurant, that's the way I see it."

Woody Allen in the film *Love and Death*

Life Science

This unit is about living things, including animals, plants, and ecology. You will learn how living things are alike and how they develop and change.

Every object in the world around you is either a living thing or a nonliving thing. Wolves, earthworms, bacteria, clams, and pine trees are examples of living things. Nonliving things include water, air, and rocks. You learned about nonliving things in Units 1 and 2. In this unit you will learn about animals, plants, ecology and how living things develop and change. In Unit 4, you will learn about the human body.

Chapters in Unit 3

Chapter 18: How Living Things Are Alike . . .302

Chapter 19: Animals 318

Chapter 20: Plants 342

Chapter 21: Ecology 366

Chapter 22: Heredity and Evolution 390

What Is Life Science?

The Study of Living Things

The study of living things is called **life science**. Another word for life science is *biology*. Scientists who study living things are called *biologists*. Many biologists specialize in one field of life science. The table below lists just a few of those fields.

Some of the fields in the table can be broken down into even more specialized branches. For example, zoology, the study of animals, has many branches. Ornithology, the study of birds, is one branch. Another branch is herpetology, the study of amphibians and reptiles. Entomology is the study of insects.

Field of Life Science	What Is Studied
Zoology	Animals
Botany	Plants
Anatomy	The structure of living things—what body parts they are made of
Physiology	The functioning of living things—how their body parts work
Cytology	Cells and how they work
Microbiology	Tiny living things that can be seen only with a microscope
Ecology	The interactions among different kinds of living things and their environment
Genetics	How characteristics are passed from parents to offspring
Taxonomy	How living things can be classified into groups

How Biologists Work

When you hear the word *biologist*, do you think of someone wearing a white coat and working in a laboratory? Many biologists do work in a laboratory, at least part of the time. A biologist who studies genetics, for example, might do lab experiments with fruit flies or other living things that reproduce quickly. A microbiologist studying bacteria or a cytologist studying cancer cells would need to work with powerful microscopes in a lab. A zoologist studying how animals learn might do lab experiments with monkeys or pigs.

This cytologist is studying blood cells in a laboratory.

In contrast, other biologists work mostly outdoors. They observe living things in their natural environments and collect information to be analyzed later. For example, a zoologist might study the family life of wolves, elephants, or chimpanzees. An ecologist might analyze how cutting down a forest to create farmland affects different kinds of animals living in the area. Biologists sometimes do experiments outdoors, too.

You can see that biologists study many different things and work in different ways. But all biologists are similar in one major way: they study living things.

Biologists often study living things in nature.

Chapter

18

How Living Things Are Alike

All living things are alike in several ways. They all are made of the same basic unit. Living things all contain the same basic chemicals. They all carry out similar basic life activities such as using food, moving, growing, and reproducing. But living things are very different from one another too. Living things are organized into groups based on their similarities and differences.

ORGANIZE YOUR THOUGHTS

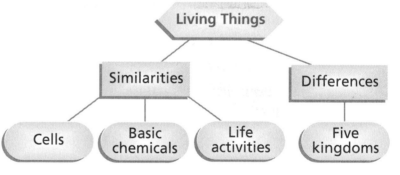

Living Things

Similarities — Differences

Cells | Basic chemicals | Life activities | Five kingdoms

Goals for Learning

▶ To explain what a cell is and describe the organization of cells in living things

▶ To identify chemicals that are important for life and explain how living things use these chemicals

▶ To describe some basic life activities

▶ To describe the similarities and differences between living things in the five kingdoms

Cell
The basic unit of life.

Microscope
An instrument used to magnify things.

Organelle
A tiny structure inside a cell.

Organism
A living thing.

A living thing is called an **organism**. All organisms are made of **cells**. A cell is the basic unit of life. It is the smallest thing that can be called "alive." Some organisms, such as bacteria, are made of only one cell. That one cell performs all of the necessary life functions. Most organisms that you have seen are made of many cells. Depending on their size, plants and animals are made of thousands, millions, billions, or even trillions of cells. Cells are found in all parts of an animal: in blood, bones, skin, nerves, and muscles. Cells also are found in all parts of a plant: in roots, stems, leaves, and flowers.

Cells carry out many functions. Some of the functions of the cells in your body are listed below.

■ Skin cells: cover and protect

■ Muscle cells: allow for movement

■ Bone cells: support and protect

■ Nerve cells: send and receive messages

■ Blood cells: transport materials and fight diseases

Observing Cells

Most cells are so small that they are invisible to the naked eye. They can be seen only with a **microscope**. A microscope is an instrument that scientists use to magnify small things, or make them appear larger.

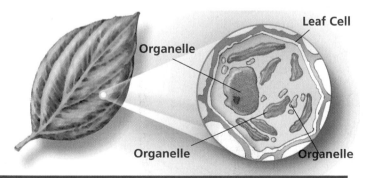

Leaf Cell

Organelle

Organelle

Organelle

Plants are made of cells that contain organelles.

When a cell is viewed with a powerful microscope, tiny structures inside the cell can be seen. These tiny structures are called **organelles**. They perform specific functions in the cell. The picture shows organelles in a plant cell.

Tissues

Groups of cells that are similar and act together to do a certain job are called a **tissue**. For example, muscle cells are joined together to make muscle tissues. These tissues include leg muscles, arm muscles, stomach muscles, and heart muscles. The cells in muscle tissues work together to make the body move. Other examples of tissues in animals are nerve tissue, bone tissue, and skin tissue.

Plants also have different kinds of cells, such as root cells, stem cells, and leaf cells. Similar cells are organized together into tissues. Different tissues carry out different functions necessary for plant growth. These functions include covering the plant and moving water and other substances in the plant.

Organs

Different kinds of tissues join together to form an **organ**. Organs are the main working parts of animals and plants. Organs do special jobs. Your heart is an organ. It pumps blood through your body. Your lungs are organs. They allow you to breathe. Other organs in your body include your stomach, liver, kidneys, and eyes.

The main organs of plants are roots, leaves, and stems. Roots take in water from the soil. Leaves make food for the plant. Stems support the plant and carry water and food to different parts of the plant.

Self-Check

1. What are cells?
2. What are three functions of cells?
3. What are tissues made of?
4. What are organs made of?
5. Name four kinds of organs.

18

Comparing Cells

Purpose

To observe differences and similarities among different types of cells

Materials

✓ prepared slides of animal, plant, and bacterial cells

✓ microscope

✓ pencil

✓ paper

Procedure

1. *Safety Alert: Handle glass microscope slides with care. Dispose of broken glass properly.* Choose one of the prepared slides. On a sheet of paper, record the type of cells you selected. Look at the slide without using the microscope. What can you see?

2. Place the slide on the stage of the microscope. Refer to the instructions for the microscope you are using. Focus and adjust the microscope so that you can see the cells on the slide clearly. Look at the slide under different levels of magnification. How does what you see now differ from what you saw without the microscope?

3. Observe one of the cells on the slide. What is its shape? Do you see any organelles inside the cell? If so, what do they look like? Make a drawing of the cell on your paper.

4. Repeat the procedure, observing at least one type of animal cell, one type of plant cell, and one type of bacterial cell.

Questions

1. What were some similarities between the plant cells and the animal cells? What were some differences?

2. How did the plant cells and animal cells differ from the bacterial cells?

Solution
A mixture in which one substance is dissolved in another.

Did You Know?

Humans can survive up to several weeks with no food. However, they can survive only a few days without water.

Besides having cells, organisms are alike because they use similar chemicals. They need these chemicals to stay alive. Water is one of the chemicals all living things use.

Importance of Water

Life cannot exist without water. It is the most plentiful chemical in organisms. Water is found in each of the approximately 100 trillion cells in the adult human body.

Water is a useful chemical. Have you ever put sugar in a cup of tea? When you put sugar in tea, you stir the liquid until the sugar disappears. The sugar dissolves in the liquid. As the sugar dissolves, it breaks apart into tiny pieces that you can no longer see. The water in the tea is the chemical that does the dissolving. Special properties of water allow it to break things apart into tiny particles. When the water, sugar, and tea particles become equally mixed, they form a **solution**.

The ability to dissolve other chemicals is one of the most important properties of water for life. Cells are so small that the materials that go in and out of them must be very tiny. When a material dissolves into tiny pieces, it can move more easily from cell to cell.

Have you ever accidentally bitten your tongue so hard that it bled? Blood tastes salty. Your body fluids and the liquid in your cells are not pure water. They are a solution of many things, including salts. One example of a salt is sodium chloride. Another name for sodium chloride is table salt. The liquid found in living things is a solution of salts, water, and other chemicals.

Other important chemicals found in organisms are carbohydrates, fats, and proteins. Each of these common chemicals has a job to do in an organism's body.

Carbohydrates

Carbohydrates are sugars and starches. Cane sugar is a carbohydrate that is used to sweeten drinks and cakes. Many fruits and vegetables, such as oranges and tomatoes, contain sugar too. Starches are found in foods such as bread, cereal, pasta, rice, and potatoes. Plants use the energy from sunlight to make carbohydrates from carbon dioxide and water. Carbon dioxide is a gas found in air. Animals get energy from the carbohydrates that plants make.

Energy is needed to carry on life activities. Energy comes from fuel. You can think of carbohydrates as fuel chemicals. Carbohydrates in your body work like gasoline in a car. Gasoline from the fuel tank gets to the engine, where it is broken down and energy is released. This released energy runs the engine. When carbohydrates are broken down in your body, energy is released. This energy powers your body. The same thing happens in other animals. Plants and other organisms use carbohydrates for energy too.

Fats

Fats also can be thought of as fuel chemicals. Fats store large amounts of energy that are released when they are broken down. Of all the chemicals important for life, fats contain the most energy. They are found in foods such as beef, butter, cheese, and peanut butter. Fats are related to oils. Fats are solid at room temperature. Oils, such as corn oil used for frying foods, are liquid at room temperature.

Foods contain water, carbohydrates, fats, and other chemicals important for life.

Proteins

Proteins are another kind of chemical important for life. Meats and fish contain large amounts of proteins. Beans, nuts, eggs, and cheese also contain large amounts of proteins.

Like carbohydrates and fats, proteins provide energy for organisms. But they have other important functions too. Proteins help repair damaged cells and build new ones. Hair, muscles, and skin are made mostly of proteins. Proteins also help control body activities such as heart rate and the breaking down of food in the body.

Importance of Nutrients

Keeping your body working properly is not a simple job. You must get a regular supply of carbohydrates, proteins, and fats from the foods you eat. Each kind of food provides different chemicals your body needs. Therefore, it is important to eat a variety of foods every day.

In addition to water, carbohydrates, proteins, and fats, your body also needs **minerals** and **vitamins**. Your body needs these chemicals in small amounts only. Different foods contain different kinds of minerals and vitamins. The chemicals that are needed for life and that come from foods are called **nutrients**. To be healthy, organisms need to take in the right amounts of nutrients every day.

Self-Check

1. What is one of the most important properties of water for life?
2. How does your body use carbohydrates and fats?
3. What do proteins do in your body?
4. What are vitamins and minerals?
5. How can you get all the nutrients you need?

Cellular respiration
The process in which cells break down food to release energy.

Digestion
The process by which organisms break down food.

Excretion
The process by which organisms get rid of wastes.

Most organisms carry on the same kinds of activities. These activities allow organisms to stay alive. Some examples of basic life activities are described below.

Getting Food

A familiar example of a life activity is getting food. Animals get food by eating plants or other animals. Plants make their own food. They use the energy from sunlight to make carbohydrates from carbon dioxide and water.

Using Food and Removing Wastes

Digestion is a life activity that breaks down food into chemicals that cells can use. Respiration inside cells is another basic life activity. During **cellular respiration**, cells release the energy that is stored in the chemicals. Respiration also produces wastes. **Excretion** is the process that removes wastes from an organism's body.

Movement

Movement is another life activity. Most animals move freely from place to place. Plants do not move from one place to another, but their parts move. For example, stems and leaves bend toward sunlight.

Besides outward movement, there is constant movement inside organisms. Liquids are flowing, food is being digested, and materials are moving into and out of cells.

The movements of most animals are obvious.

Sensing and Responding

Organisms sense and respond. Animals and plants have tissues and organs that pick up, or sense, signals from their surroundings. These signals include light, sound, chemicals, and touch. Plants and animals change something, or respond, based on the kinds of signals they pick up.

Growth and Development

Growing is part of being alive. You were once a baby, but you have grown into a larger person. You are still growing. You will continue to grow until you reach your adult size. Most organisms go through a similar pattern of growth.

Many organisms develop as they grow. **Development** means becoming different, or changing, over time. For example, when a tadpole hatches from an egg, it looks like a fish. As the tadpole develops, its legs form and its tail is absorbed into its body.

Reproduction

Organisms produce offspring through the basic life activity of **reproduction**. Some organisms reproduce by themselves. For example, bacteria reproduce by dividing in two. For other organisms, such as humans, reproduction requires two parents. The offspring of all organisms resemble their parent or parents.

Self-Check

1. List three basic life activities.
2. How do animals and plants get food?
3. What happens during cellular respiration?
4. What is the difference between growth and development?
5. What does "sensing and responding" mean?

Kingdom
One of the five groups into which organisms are classified.

Scientists divide the world of living things into five groups, or **kingdoms**. Organisms are grouped, or classified, according to how they are alike and how they are different. Most of the organisms you know are in either the plant kingdom or the animal kingdom. There are three other kingdoms that you may not know very well.

The Plant Kingdom

Most plants are easy to recognize. Examples of plants are trees, grasses, ferns, and mosses. Plants don't move from place to place like animals. Plants make their own food using light and substances around them. All plants have many cells. These cells are organized into tissues. Many plants also have organs.

The Animal Kingdom

Animals have many different sizes and shapes. You probably recognize dogs, turtles, and fish as animals. Corals, sponges, and insects are animals too.

Animals cannot make their own food. They get their food from other organisms. They eat plants, or they eat other animals that eat plants. Most animals move around to capture or gather their food. Moving also helps them to find shelter, escape danger, and find mates. All animals have many cells. These cells form tissues in all animals except sponges. In most animals, the tissues form organs.

Animals get their food by eating plants or by eating other animals that eat plants.

The Protist Kingdom

At one time, biologists divided the living world into only two kingdoms, plants and animals. When the microscope was invented, biologists discovered tiny organisms that did not fit into either the plant or animal kingdom. Biologists placed these organisms in a separate kingdom. They called the organisms **protists**.

Most protists have only one cell. A few have many cells. Some protists make their own food. Others absorb food from other sources. **Algae** are plant-like protists. **Protozoans** are animal-like protists. Some protozoans are like both plants and animals. All protists can carry out the basic life activities.

Algae live in lakes, streams, rivers, ponds, and oceans. The green scum on a pond is thousands of tiny algae. Seaweeds are also algae. Like plants, algae make their own food. Algae are food for other organisms. Algae also produce oxygen that other organisms use.

Protozoans live in water, soil, and the bodies of animals. Protozoans behave like animals by getting food and moving. Different kinds of protozoans have different ways of moving. Amoebas push out a part of their cell. This part, called a **pseudopod**, pulls the amoeba along. Some protozoans have tails, or **flagella**, that move them. Others, such as paramecium, use **cilia** to move. Cilia are tiny hair-like structures that beat like paddles.

Euglenas are protozoans that behave like both plants and animals. Like plants, they make their own food when sunlight is present. Like animals, they can absorb food from the environment. They absorb food when sunlight is not present.

Algae

Protists that make their own food and usually live in water.

Cilia

Hair-like structures that help some one-celled organisms move.

Flagella

Whip-like tails that help some one-celled organisms move. Singular is flagellum.

Protist

An organism that usually is one-celled and has plant-like or animal-like properties.

Protozoan

A protist that has animal-like qualities.

Pseudopod

Part of some one-celled organisms that sticks out like a foot to move the cell along.

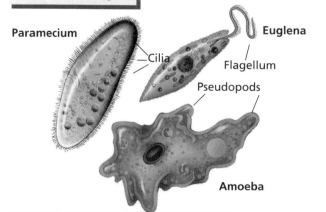

Paramecium · Cilia · Euglena · Flagellum · Pseudopods · Amoeba

Protozoans can use flagella, cilia, or pseudopods to move.

Decompose
To break down or decay matter into simpler substances.

Fungus
An organism that usually has many cells and decomposes material for its food.

Moneran
An organism that is one-celled and does not have organelles.

Parasite
An organism that absorbs food from another organism and harms it.

Fungi decompose dead plant and animal material.

The Fungi Kingdom

Mushrooms and the mold that grows on bread are **fungi** (plural of *fungus*). Most fungi have many cells. Like plants, fungi do not move around by themselves. But unlike plants, fungi do not make their own food. They absorb food from other organisms.

Fungi release chemicals on dead plant and animal matter. The chemicals break down, or **decompose**, the matter. The fungi then absorb the decomposed matter. Some of the decomposed matter also gets into the soil. Other organisms, such as plants, can then use it. Some fungi are **parasites**. They absorb food from a living organism and harm it.

The Monera Kingdom

Monerans are one-celled organisms. The kingdom has only one kind of organism, bacteria. The cells of bacteria are different from the cells of all other organisms. Bacteria cells do not have organelles. Like animals, some bacteria can move and get food. Like plants, some stay put and make their own food. Like fungi, bacteria help decompose the remains of plants and animals.

Did You Know?

Athlete's foot is a disease caused by a fungus.

Self-Check

1. Name the five kingdoms of living things.
2. List two differences between plants and animals.
3. How are protists similar to plants and animals?
4. What is an important function of fungi?
5. Why are bacteria placed in a kingdom by themselves?

Bacteria: Helpful and harmful

Bacteria live everywhere. They are in the ocean, on top of mountains, in polar ice, on your hands, and even inside you. You cannot go anywhere without coming in contact with bacteria.

Most bacteria are helpful. Bacteria in soil break down plant and animal material and release nutrients. They also take in gases from the air, such as nitrogen. They change nitrogen into a form that plants and animals can use. Bacteria in your intestines make vitamin K. This vitamin helps your blood clot when you are cut.

Bacteria can also be harmful. Many bacteria cause diseases in people. Bacteria cause diseases such as tuberculosis, tetanus, and cholera. Food that is contaminated by certain kinds of bacteria can cause illness.

Microbiologists are scientists who work with bacteria and other microorganisms. Some microbiologists help to identify bacteria that cause disease. They grow the bacteria on special plates. Each cell multiplies until it forms millions of bacteria cells, called a colony. It is impossible to see a single bacterium without a microscope. But it is easy to see colonies of bacteria.

There are ways to get rid of most harmful bacteria. Antibiotics are drugs that kill bacteria in people and animals. Pasteurization, or rapid heating, kills harmful bacteria in milk. Drinking water is purified to remove bacteria and other microorganisms. Sewage is treated so that it will not pollute water supplies. Sometimes bacteria help to clean up sewage. Helpful bacteria break down material in the sewage so that it does not harm people.

- Organisms are made of cells. Cells carry out many different functions.

- Cells are organized into tissues. Tissues are organized into organs.

- Water is one of the chemicals necessary for life. An important property of water is its ability to dissolve other substances.

- Cells use carbohydrates, fats, and proteins for energy.

- Water, carbohydrates, proteins, fats, minerals, and vitamins are nutrients that are needed for life.

- All organisms carry on basic life activities. These include getting and using food, removing wastes, moving, sensing and responding, growing, developing, and reproducing.

- Organisms are classified into five kingdoms: plants, animals, protists, fungi, and monerans.

- Plants make their own food, do not move from place to place, and have many cells that are organized into tissues and sometimes organs.

- Animals eat other organisms for food, can move around to get food, and have many cells that are organized into tissues and organs.

- Protists are one-celled organisms that are like both animals and plants. Some make their own food. Others absorb their food. Some do both.

- Fungi obtain food by decomposing the remains of other organisms.

- Monerans are bacteria. They are one-celled organisms that do not have organelles. Some make their own food, and others absorb it. Bacteria help decompose plant and animal remains.

Science Words

algae, 312	fat, 307	organism, 303
carbohydrate, 307	flagella, 312	parasite, 313
cell, 303	fungus, 313	protein, 308
cellular respiration, 309	kingdom, 311	protist, 312
cilia, 312	microscope, 303	protozoan, 312
decompose, 313	mineral, 308	pseudopod, 312
development, 310	moneran, 313	reproduction, 310
digestion, 309	nutrient, 308	solution, 306
excretion, 309	organ, 304	tissue, 304
	organelle, 303	vitamin, 308

WORD BANK

algae

cells

decompose

digestion

excretion

fats

fungi

moneran

nutrients

organelles

organism

organs

protozoan

reproduction

tissues

Vocabulary Review

Number your paper from 1 to 15. Then choose the word from the Word Bank that best completes each sentence. Write the answer on your paper.

1. Organisms get rid of wastes by the process of _____.

2. Large amounts of energy are stored in _____.

3. The process of _____ produces offspring.

4. During _____, food is broken down into chemicals that cells can use.

5. Groups of different kinds of tissues form _____.

6. Tiny structures found inside cells are called _____.

7. _____ are made of groups of similar cells that work together to do a certain job.

8. Water, carbohydrates, proteins, fats, vitamins, and minerals are _____.

9. _____ are the basic unit of life.

10. Mushrooms are in the _____ kingdom.

11. Another word for a living thing is _____.

12. Fungi release chemicals that _____ matter.

13. _____ are protists that make their own food and usually live in water.

14. A _____ is an animal-like protist.

15. An organism that has only one cell and does not have organelles is a _____.

Concept Review

Number your paper from 1 to 4. Then choose the answer that best completes each sentence. Write the letter of the answer on your paper.

1. All living things are made of _____.

   a. only one cell   b. one or more cells   c. many cells

2. The most plentiful chemical in living things is _____.

   a. water   b. fat   c. minerals

3. Plants make _____ using carbon dioxide, water, and energy from the sun.

   a. minerals   b. vitamins   c. carbohydrates

4. Bacteria are organisms in the _____ kingdom.

   a. monera   b. fungi   c. protist

Critical Thinking

Write the answer to the following question.

What basic life activities are described in the following paragraph?

A kitten sees a ball of yarn and pounces on it. It was just a few weeks ago that the kitten was not even able to walk. When it was born, the kitten was tiny. Its eyes were continually closed, and it could barely crawl. Now, suddenly, the kitten stops and sniffs the air. Its mother has returned from hunting for food. The kitten walks over to its mother and begins to nurse, drinking milk.

Test Taking Tip | When looking for information in a paragraph, read through the entire paragraph first. Then study it one sentence at a time.

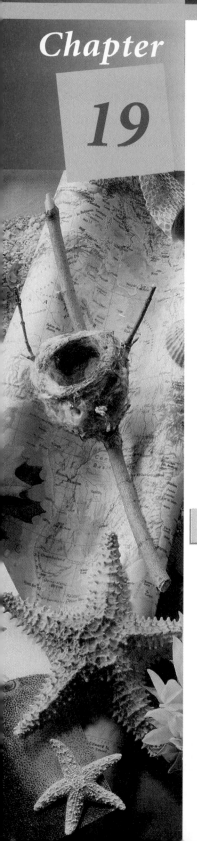

Chapter

19

Animals

In the previous chapter, you learned that biologists use similarities and differences to classify organisms into five kingdoms. The organisms in each kingdom are further classified into smaller groups. In this chapter you will learn how animals are classified into groups and how they are given scientific names. You will also learn about some basic life activities of animals.

ORGANIZE YOUR THOUGHTS

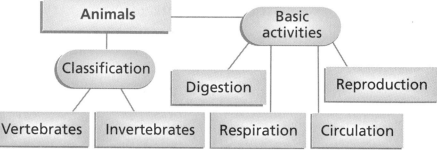

Animals — Basic activities

Classification

Vertebrates | Invertebrates | Digestion | Respiration | Circulation | Reproduction

Goals for Learning

▶ To learn how biologists classify and name animals
▶ To identify the features of different groups of vertebrates
▶ To identify the features of different groups of invertebrates
▶ To understand how animals obtain and digest food
▶ To explore respiration and circulation in animals
▶ To learn how animals reproduce

Biologists classify all organisms based on their similar features. The science of classifying organisms according to their similarities is called **taxonomy**.

The Seven Levels of Classification

The diagram below shows that there are seven levels in the classification system of organisms: kingdom, **phylum**, class, order, family, genus, and species.

Kingdoms represent the highest level in the classification system. You learned that biologists classify all organisms into five kingdoms. The animal kingdom is one of the five kingdoms. Each kingdom is divided into groups called phyla (plural of *phylum*). The phyla represent the second-highest level of classification. More organisms are included in a kingdom than in any one of its phyla. Each phylum is divided into classes, each class is divided into orders, and so on.

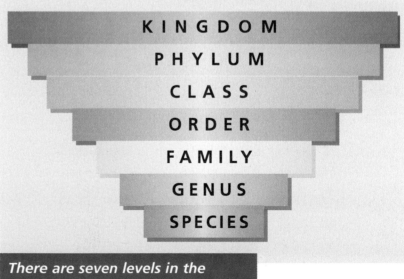

K I N G D O M

P H Y L U M

C L A S S

O R D E R

F A M I L Y

G E N U S

S P E C I E S

There are seven levels in the classification system of organisms.

The lowest level in the classification system is the **species**. Each species represents a single type of organism. Members of the same species can breed and produce offspring like themselves.

Classification of Animals

Every organism that has been identified has its own place in the classification system. The diagram on this page shows how biologists classify four particular species of animals. Notice that the African elephant, the red tree mouse, and the heather mouse belong to the same phylum. The boll weevil belongs to a different phylum. This means that the first three animals are more similar to each other than they are to the boll weevil. Also notice that the two species of mice belong to the same order. The elephant belongs to a different order. This means that the red tree mouse and the heather mouse are more similar to each other than they are to the elephant. Organisms that are very similar belong to the same genus. Which animals in the diagram belong to the same genus?

Some classification groups contain a large number of species. For example, the order Coleoptera contains about 500,000 species, including the boll weevil. Other orders may have just a few species. For example, the African elephant and the Asian elephant are the only two species in the order Proboscidea.

Did You Know?

The Greek philosopher Aristotle was the first person to classify organisms. More than 2,000 years ago, he divided all living things into the two groups of plants and animals.

Kingdom		Animalia		
Phylum	Arthropoda	Chordata		
Class	Insecta	Mammalia		
Order	Coleoptera	Proboscidea	Rodentia	
Family	Curculionidae	Elephantidae	Cricetidae	
Genus	*Anthonomus*	*Loxodonta*	*Phenacomys*	
Species	*grandis*	*africana*	*longicaudus*	*intermedius*
	Boll weevil	African elephant	Red tree mouse	Heather mouse

Scientific Names

Most people call animals by their common names, such as mockingbird and mountain lion. However, using common names can be confusing. The mountain lion in the picture has at least four other common names—puma, cougar, catamount, and American panther. All five names refer to the same species. People who use one of these names may not know that the other names refer to the same species. The opposite problem occurs with the common name "June bug." At least a dozen different beetle species have that name. When someone says "June bug," you have no way of knowing which species that is. The same animal may have different names in different languages, too. For example, an owl is called *gufo* in Italian, *hibou* in French, and *búho* in Spanish.

To overcome these problems, biologists give each species a **scientific name**. An organism's scientific name consists of two words. The first word is the organism's genus, and the second word is its species label. For example, the scientific name of the mountain lion is *Felis concolor*. Thus, the mountain lion belongs to the genus *Felis* and the species *concolor*. Look again at the diagram on page 320. What is the scientific name of the African elephant?

The mountain lion has several common names but only one scientific name: Felis concolor.

The scientific name given to each species is unique. This means that different species have different scientific names, even if they have the same common name. Scientific names are in Latin, so they are recognized by biologists around the world. For example, *Felis concolor* means the same thing in France, the United States, and Mexico. As you may have noticed, scientific names are always printed in *italics* or are underlined. The first word in the name is capitalized, but the second word is not.

Has everything been classified?

You may think that every kind of organism on Earth has already been studied, classified, and named. In fact, biologists continue to discover species that no one has identified before. Many of the newly found species are insects. Some biologists think there could be millions of insect species that still have not been identified.

Some new species may be useful in finding new medicines. Others may help control pests that damage crops. To learn how a new species might be useful, biologists must study the organism closely. They must learn how it carries out its life activities. Then they can classify the organism.

Self-Check

1. On what do biologists base their classification of organisms?
2. List the seven levels of classification of organisms, from highest to lowest.
3. What is a species?
4. The banana slug and the cuttlefish belong to the same phylum. The clownfish belongs to a different phylum. Is the banana slug or the clownfish more similar to the cuttlefish?
5. The barn owl belongs to the genus *Tyta* and the species *alba*. What is the barn owl's scientific name?

Classifying Objects

Materials

✓ assortment of classroom objects

Purpose

To make a classification system for objects found in the classroom

Procedure

1. Form a team with two or three other students. On a sheet of paper, make a list of objects in your classroom. Include objects that may be on shelves or in drawers in cabinets.

2. Divide the objects on your list into groups based on their similarities. Name each group.

3. Make up a classification system for the objects on your list. Your system should have several levels. Each level should include all of the groups in the next-lower level.

4. Write your classification system on a sheet of paper. List the objects that belong in each group. Show how the different levels are related to each other.

5. Compare your classification system with the systems made up by other student teams.

Questions

1. What were the names of the groups your team came up with?

2. How many levels did your classification system have?

3. How did your classification system differ from the systems of other student teams?

4. How does this investigation show the value of having a single system for classifying organisms?

Cartilage
A soft material found in vertebrate skeletons.

Vertebra
One of the bones or blocks of cartilage that make up a backbone.

Vertebrate
An animal with a backbone.

The animals that are probably most familiar to you are animals with backbones. These animals are called **vertebrates**. Vertebrates include tiny hummingbirds and enormous blue whales. Humans also are vertebrates. Altogether, there are nearly 50,000 species of vertebrates.

Features of Vertebrates

Vertebrates have three features that set them apart from other animals. First, all vertebrates have an internal skeleton, which is inside their body. The skeleton of vertebrates is made of bone or a softer material called **cartilage**. Some other animals also have an internal skeleton, but it is made of different materials.

The second feature of vertebrates is their backbone. A backbone is made up of many small bones or blocks of cartilage. For example, the human backbone contains 26 bones. Each bone or block of cartilage in the backbone is called a **vertebra.** That is why animals with backbones are known as vertebrates.

The third feature of vertebrates is the skull. The skull surrounds and protects the brain. Find the backbone and skull in this drawing of a cow's skeleton.

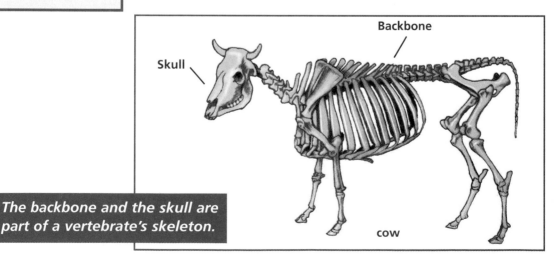

Backbone

Skull

cow

The backbone and the skull are part of a vertebrate's skeleton.

A bony fish is covered with scales.

Vertebrates are divided into seven classes. Three of the classes consist of different types of fishes. The other four classes are amphibians, reptiles, birds, and mammals.

Fishes

Biologists have identified about 24,000 species of fishes. There are more species of fishes than of any other kind of vertebrate. All fishes live in water and breathe with structures called **gills**.

Amphibian
A vertebrate that lives at first in water and then on land.

Gill
A structure used by some animals to breathe in water.

Metamorphosis
A major change in form that occurs as some animals develop into adults.

Swim bladder
A gas-filled organ that allows a bony fish to move up and down in the water.

Most fishes have a skeleton made of bone and are called bony fishes. They include bass, trout, salmon, and many others. You can see in the photo that the body of a bony fish is covered with scales that overlap like roof shingles. The scales protect the fish and give it a smooth surface. Many bony fishes have an organ called a **swim bladder** that is filled with gas. By changing the amount of gas in its swim bladder, the fish can move up or down in the water.

Sharks, rays, and skates have a skeleton made of cartilage instead of bone. Many of these fishes have powerful jaws and rows of sharp teeth. Their tiny, toothlike scales make their skin feel like sandpaper. Lampreys and hagfishes also have a skeleton made of cartilage, but they have no jaws or scales.

Amphibians

Amphibians include about 4,000 species of frogs, toads, and salamanders. The word *amphibian* comes from two Greek words meaning "double life." This refers to the fact that many amphibians spend part of their life in water and part on land. Frogs begin their life as tadpoles that live in water. Over time, a tadpole grows legs, loses its gills and tail, and develops into an adult frog. This change is called **metamorphosis**. The frog may spend much of its life on land.

Adult amphibians breathe with lungs or through their skin. The skin is thin and moist. To keep from drying out, amphibians must stay near water or in damp places. Since amphibian eggs do not have shells, they must be laid in water or where the ground is wet.

Reptiles

Snakes, lizards, turtles, alligators, and crocodiles are **reptiles**. There are about 7,000 species of reptiles. Some reptiles, such as sea turtles, live mostly in water. Others, such as tortoises, live on land. The skin of reptiles is scaly and watertight, so reptiles can live in dry places without drying out. Some tortoises, for example, live in deserts where water is scarce. Most reptiles lay eggs on land. The eggs have a soft shell that keeps the young inside from drying out. All reptiles breathe with lungs. Reptiles that live in water must come to the surface to breathe. They also must come up on land to lay their eggs. A few species of snakes give birth to live young.

Vertebrates (Animals With Backbones)

Group	Description	Examples
Chordate *Phylum*	Internal skeleton of bone or cartilage; skull; sexual reproduction; bilateral symmetry	
Jawless Fish *Class*	Skeleton of cartilage; no scales or jaw; unpaired fins; breathe with gills; live in water; cold blooded	lamprey, hagfish
Cartilage Fish *Class*	Skeleton of cartilage; toothlike scales; jaw; paired fins; breathe with gills; live in water; cold blooded	shark, ray
Bony Fish *Class*	Skeleton of bone; bony scales; jaw; paired fins; breathe with gills; live in water; swim bladder in most; cold blooded	trout, salmon, swordfish, goldfish
Amphibian *Class*	Skeleton of bone; moist, smooth skin; young breathe with gills, adults breathe with lungs, eggs lack shells; cold blooded	newt, frog, toad
Reptile *Class*	Skeleton of bone; dry, scaly skin; claws; breathe with lungs all stages; four legs except snakes; eggs have shell; cold blooded	turtle, snake alligator, lizard,
Bird *Class*	Skeleton of bone; feathers; wings; beaks; claws; breathe with lungs all stages; eggs have shell; warm blooded	hawk, robin, penguin
Mammal *Class*	Skeleton of bone; hair; mammary glands; breathe with lungs all stages; young develop within mother; warm blooded	bat, dog, whale human

Birds

There are more than 9,000 species of birds, and almost all of them can fly. Feathers make flight possible by providing lift and streamlining the body. Birds also have hollow bones, which keep their skeleton light. Flying requires a lot of energy, so birds cannot go long without eating. Feathers act like a warm coat that keeps heat inside the bird's body. All birds breathe with lungs and have a horny beak. Birds lay eggs that are covered by a hard shell.

Mammals

Mammals are named for their **mammary glands**, which are milk-producing structures on the chest or abdomen. As shown in the photo, female mammals nurse their young with milk from these glands. Mammals also have hair covering most of their body. Hair helps keep in body heat. Most mammals live on land, but some, such as whales and porpoises, live in water. All mammals have lungs.

Most of the 4,400 species of mammals have young that develop inside the mother. These mammals include bears, elephants, mice, and humans. About 300 species of mammals, including opossums and kangaroos, have young that develop in a pouch on the mother. The duck-billed platypus and the spiny anteater are the only mammals that lay eggs.

Mammals feed their young with milk produced by mammary glands.

Self-Check

1. What three features do all vertebrates have?
2. How does a trout's skeleton differ from a shark's skeleton?
3. What happens during metamorphosis in a frog?
4. Why are a reptile's eggs able to survive in dry places?
5. What two features do mammals have that other vertebrates do not have?

Bilateral symmetry
A body plan that consists of left and right halves that look the same.

Invertebrate
An animal that does not have a backbone

Radial symmetry
An arrangement of body parts that resembles the arrangement of spokes on a wheel.

Tentacle
An armlike body part in invertebrates that is used for capturing prey.

An animal that does not have a backbone is called an **invertebrate**. Invertebrates belong to more than 30 phyla. You will learn about eight of those phyla in this lesson.

Sponges

Sponges are the simplest animals. Their bodies consist of two layers of cells without any tissues or organs. All sponges live in water. Sponges strain food particles out of the water as it moves through their bodies.

Cnidarians

Cnidarians include animals such as jellyfish, sea anemones, corals, and hydras. All cnidarians live in water. They have a type of body plan called **radial symmetry**. Their body parts are arranged like spokes on a wheel. Cnidarians have armlike **tentacles** with stinging cells. The tentacles capture small prey and push them into the body to be digested.

Flatworms

As their name suggests, flatworms are flat and thin. Their bodies have a left half and a right half that look the same. This type of body plan is called **bilateral symmetry**. Most flatworms are parasites that live on or inside other animals.

The tentacles of this sea anemone show radial symmetry.

Did You Know?

Doctors sometimes use leeches to remove blood from the wounds of patients who have had surgery.

Tube foot
A small structure used by echinoderms for movement.

Roundworms

Roundworms have long, round bodies that come to a point at the ends. Roundworms may live in soil or water. Some soil-dwelling roundworms help plants by eating insect pests. Other roundworms are parasites.

Segmented Worms

Segmented worms have a body that is divided into many sections, or segments. These worms may live in the soil, in fresh water, or in the ocean. Earthworms are segmented worms. Earthworms tunnel through the soil, eating small food particles. Their tunnels loosen the soil and allow air to enter it, which helps plants grow. Leeches are another kind of segmented worm.

Mollusks

Some mollusks live on land, while others live in fresh water or in the ocean. Snails and slugs make up the largest group of mollusks. Snails have a coiled shell, but slugs have no shell at all. Another group of mollusks includes clams, scallops, and oysters. Their shell is made of two hinged pieces that can open and close. Squids and octopuses have no outer shells. These mollusks can move quickly as they hunt and catch prey with their tentacles.

A squid uses its tentacles to capture prey.

Echinoderms

Echinoderms include sea stars, sea urchins, sand dollars, and sea cucumbers. All echinoderms live in the ocean. Like cnidarians, echinoderms have radial symmetry as adults. Echinoderms also have **tube feet** that work like suction cups. Echinoderms use their tube feet to move and to pry open clams.

Invertebrates (Animals Without Backbones)

Group	Description	Examples
Porifera *Phylum*	Body wall of two cell layers; pores and canals; no tissues or organs; no symmetry; live in water; strain food from water	sponge
Cnidarian *Phylum*	Baglike body of two cell layers; one opening leading into a hollow body; tissues; usually mouth surrounded by tentacles; stinging cells; radial symmetry; live in water	jellyfish, coral, hydra
Flatworm *Phylum*	Ribbonlike body; three cell layers; organs; flat, unsegmented body; digestive system with one opening; nervous system; bilateral symmetry; most are parasitic	tapeworm, planarian, fluke
Nematode *Phylum*	Round, slender body; unsegmented body; digestive system with two openings; nervous system; bilateral symmetry; some are parasitic	hookworm, pinworm, vinegar eel
Mollusk *Phylum*	Soft body covered by a fleshy mantle; move with muscular foot; some have shells; all organ systems; bilateral symmetry	
Gastropod *Class*	One shell (slugs have no shell); head, eyes, and tentacles	snail, slug
Bivalve *Class*	Two shells; no head, eyes, or tentacles	clam, oyster, scallop
Cephalopod *Class*	No shell; head; eyes; foot divided into tentacles	squid, octopus, nautilus
Annelid *Phylum*	Round, segmented body; digestive system, nervous system, circulatory system; bilateral symmetry; most are not parasitic	earthworm, leech
Arthropod *Phylum*	Segmented body; jointed legs; most have antennae; all organ systems; external skeleton	
Arachnid *Class*	Two body segments; four pairs of legs; no antennae	spider, scorpion, tick, mite
Crustacean *Class*	Two body segments; usually five pairs of legs; two pairs of antennae; breathe with gills	crayfish, lobster, crab, shrimp, sowbug, barnacle
Chilopod *Class*	usually 15–170 body segments; one pair of legs on each segment; poison claws; flattened body	centipede
Diplopod *Class*	usually 25–100 body segments; two pairs of legs on each segment; body often rounded	millipede
Insect *Class*	Three body segments; three pairs of legs; one pair of antennae; most have two pairs of wings	fly, beetle, grasshopper, earwig, silverfish, water strider, butterfly, bee, ant
Echinoderm *Phylum*	Covered with spines; body has five parts; radial symmetry in adults stages; live in ocean	sea star, sea urchin, sand dollar

Arthropods

Arthropods have segmented bodies and jointed legs. Most arthropods also have antennae that they use to feel, taste, or smell. The major groups of arthropods are crustaceans, arachnids, centipedes, millipedes, and insects. Crabs, lobsters, and crayfish are crustaceans. Spiders, scorpions, mites, and ticks are arachnids.

All arthropods have an external skeleton that supports the body and protects the organs inside. However, an external skeleton cannot grow as an internal skeleton does. For that reason, an arthropod must shed its skeleton to grow in size. The shedding process is called **molting**.

Insects

Insects live almost everywhere except in the deep ocean. Insects have three pairs of legs. Most have one or two pairs of wings. Insects are the only invertebrates that can fly. Like frogs, most insects go through metamorphosis. The metamorphosis of a butterfly is shown in the diagram.

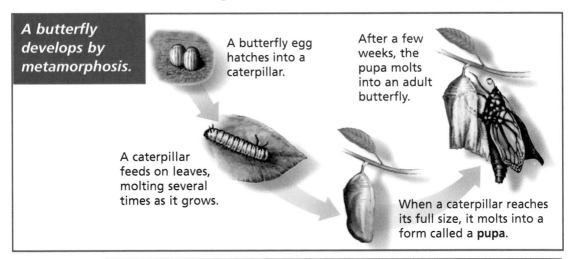

A butterfly develops by metamorphosis.

A butterfly egg hatches into a caterpillar.

After a few weeks, the pupa molts into an adult butterfly.

A caterpillar feeds on leaves, molting several times as it grows.

When a caterpillar reaches its full size, it molts into a form called a **pupa**.

Self-Check

1. How do sponges get food?
2. What is the difference between radial symmetry and bilateral symmetry?
3. How do squids and octopuses get food?
4. How do echinoderms move?
5. Explain why arthropods molt.

Objectives

After reading this lesson, you should be able to

▶ describe three main ways that animals get food.

▶ explain the difference between a gastrovascular cavity and a digestive tract.

Filter feeding
Getting food by straining it out of the water.

Did You Know?

The Komodo monitor lizard can weigh 75 kilograms and hunt deer and water buffalo.

Unlike plants, animals cannot make their own food. They must get food from other organisms. Different animals have different ways of getting food.

Filter Feeding

Many animals that live in water get food by filtering, or straining, it. This way of getting food is called **filter feeding**. Filter feeding lets animals gather food while they stay in one place. Sponges and clams are filter feeders. Some filter feeders do move. Many whales catch millions of tiny animals by swimming with their mouths open.

Feeding on Fluids

Some animals get food from the fluids of plants or other animals. The fluids are rich in nutrients. Aphids and cicadas are insects that have piercing mouthparts. They suck sap from plant roots and stems. Spiders capture insects and suck the fluid from their bodies.

Eating Large Pieces of Food

Most animals eat large pieces of solid food. Sometimes they eat entire organisms. Such animals use different kinds of body structures to capture and eat their food. In the previous lesson, you read about some animals that catch food with tentacles. Many insects have mouthparts for cutting and chewing. The mouthparts break the food into pieces that are small enough to swallow.

Vertebrates are the only animals that have teeth. Mammals have teeth of different shapes and sizes. Each kind of tooth does a certain job. Chisel-like teeth at the front of the mouth cut food into pieces. Long, pointed teeth grip and pierce food. Teeth that have a flat surface grind and crush food. A mammal's teeth tell what kind of food it eats. Meat eaters have sharp, pointed teeth that tear flesh. Plant eaters have large flat teeth for grinding.

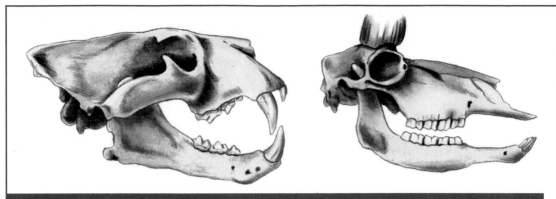

Look at the teeth in these skulls. What kind of food did each animal eat?

Digesting Food

Cnidarians and flatworms digest food in a hollow space called a **gastrovascular cavity**. This space has only one opening, the mouth. Food enters through the mouth. In the cavity chemicals break the food into small particles. The cells can then absorb the particles. Material that is not digested leaves through the mouth.

Animals that are more developed have a **digestive tract**. This is a tubelike digestive space with an opening at each end. Food enters the digestive tract through the mouth and moves in one direction. Material that is not digested leaves the digestive tract through the opening at the other end. The main functions of a digestive tract are storing food, digesting food, and absorbing nutrients.

Self-Check

1. What is filter feeding?
2. How do spiders obtain food?
3. Name and describe the type of digestive space found in a cnidarian.
4. What kinds of teeth do mammals have, and what is the function of each kind of tooth?
5. What major functions does a digestive tract perform?

All animals must take oxygen into their bodies and eliminate carbon dioxide. This process of gas exchange is called **respiration**. Animals respire in different ways.

Gas Exchange

The body wall of sponges and other simple animals is very thin. The animal's cells take in oxygen and get rid of carbon dioxide by **diffusion**. Diffusion is the movement of a material from an area of high concentration to an area of low concentration. The concentration of oxygen is higher in the surrounding water than in the animal's cells. Therefore, oxygen diffuses from the water into the cells. The concentration of carbon dioxide is higher in the animal's cells than in the water. Therefore, carbon dioxide diffuses from the cells into the water.

Most animals have a special organ for gas exchange. Animals that live in water usually have gills. Oxygen diffuses from the water into the gills. Carbon dioxide diffuses from the gills into the water.

Diffusion
The movement of materials from an area of high concentration to an area of low concentration.

Respiration
The process of gas exchange in which animals take in oxygen and release carbon dioxide.

The gills on this brown trout provide a large surface area for exchanging gases.

Circulatory system
The system that moves blood throughout the body.

Land animals exchange gases with the air around them. Insects have a system of tubes to carry air into the body. The tubes have very fine branches that reach almost all of the animal's cells.

Most other land animals, including humans, have lungs for gas exchange. When you inhale, or breathe in, you draw air into your lungs. When you exhale, or breathe out, you force the air back out.

Circulatory Systems

The **circulatory system** moves blood throughout an animal's body. In the gills or lungs, oxygen enters the blood. As the blood circulates, it delivers oxygen to cells and picks up carbon dioxide. When the blood returns to the gills or lungs, it releases the carbon dioxide.

All circulatory systems have a set of tubes and one or more pumps. The tubes are called blood vessels. The pumps are called hearts. When a heart contracts, or squeezes together, it pushes blood through the blood vessels.

Arthropods have an open circulatory system. The blood leaves one set of vessels, flows through spaces, and then enters another set of vessels and returns to the heart.

Earthworms and vertebrates have a closed circulatory system. The blood stays inside one set of vessels. The smallest vessels have very thin walls. Oxygen and carbon dioxide diffuse into or out of the blood across these walls.

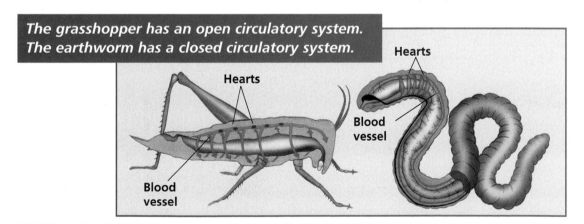

The grasshopper has an open circulatory system. The earthworm has a closed circulatory system.

Hearts

Blood vessel

Hearts

Blood vessel

Vertebrate Circulatory Systems

Atrium

A heart chamber that receives blood returning to the heart. Plural is atria.

Ventricle

A heart chamber that pumps blood out of the heart.

The circulatory system of a vertebrate includes a single heart. The heart is divided into enclosed spaces called chambers. The **atria** are chambers that receive blood returning to the heart. The **ventricles** are chambers that pump blood out of the heart. Fish have one atrium and one ventricle. Amphibians and most reptiles have two atria and one ventricle. Birds, mammals, and some reptiles have two atria and two ventricles.

The diagram shows how blood circulates through the body of a mammal or bird. The left atrium receives blood from the lungs. This blood has a lot of oxygen that was picked up in the lungs. The blood has little carbon dioxide. The left atrium sends the blood to the left ventricle. The left ventricle pumps it to the rest of the body. The blood delivers oxygen to body tissues. It picks up carbon dioxide that has formed as waste. The blood returns to the right atrium. The blood has little oxygen and a lot of carbon dioxide. The right atrium pumps the blood to the right ventricle. The right ventricle pumps the blood to the lungs. In the lungs, oxygen enters the blood. Carbon dioxide leaves the blood. The carbon dioxide is exhaled as waste. The blood returns to the left atrium, and the cycle repeats.

The heart of a bird or mammal pumps blood along two separate paths.

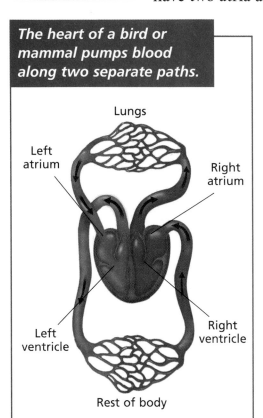

Lungs

Left atrium

Right atrium

Left ventricle

Right ventricle

Rest of body

Self-Check

1. How are gases exchanged in a sponge?
2. How does air reach an insect's cells?
3. What is the difference between an open and a closed circulatory system?
4. What is the difference between atria and ventricles?
5. In a bird's heart, where does blood go when it is pumped from the right ventricle?

After reading this lesson, you should be able to

▶ compare asexual reproduction and sexual reproduction.

▶ recognize the advantages and disadvantages of each type of reproduction.

Asexual reproduction
Reproduction that involves one parent and no egg or sperm.

Egg cell
A female sex cell.

Ovary
The female sex organ that produces egg cells.

Sexual reproduction
Reproduction that involves an egg from a female and sperm from a male.

Sperm cell
A male sex cell.

Testes
Male sex organs that produce sperm cells.

Some animals need only one parent to reproduce. Other animals reproduce with two parents. In this lesson, you will learn about these two types of reproduction.

Asexual Reproduction

Some simple animals reproduce by asexual reproduction. This form of reproduction involves only one parent. The new organisms are identical to the parent organism. For example, a piece of a parent sponge can fall off and grow into a new sponge. If a sea star is broken into pieces, new sea stars can grow from the larger pieces. A sea anemone can split apart to form two or more sea anemones.

One advantage of **asexual reproduction** is that an organism can reproduce alone. It does not have to find a mate. A disadvantage of asexual reproduction is that the offspring are exact copies of the parent. They are likely to respond to changes in the environment in the same way. If a change kills one of the offspring, it will probably kill them all. Thus, asexual reproduction is favorable in environments that do not change much.

Sexual Reproduction

Most animals reproduce by **sexual reproduction**. During sexual reproduction, a cell from one parent joins with a cell from the other parent.

Sexual reproduction involves both a female parent and a male parent. The female produces **egg cells**. The male produces **sperm cells**. Sperm cells and egg cells are called sex cells. In many animals, **testes** are the male sex organs that produce sperm cells. **Ovaries** are the female sex organs that produce egg cells. An egg cell contains food for the early stage of the developing offspring.

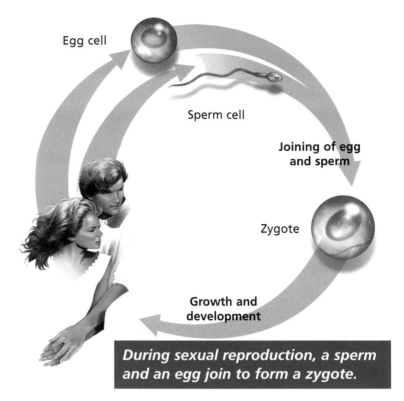

Egg cell

Sperm cell

Joining of egg and sperm

Zygote

Growth and development

During sexual reproduction, a sperm and an egg join to form a zygote.

Fertilization
The joining of an egg cell and a sperm cell.

A sperm cell usually has a tail that allows it to move toward an egg. When a sperm reaches an egg, the nucleus of the sperm cell and the nucleus of the egg cell join. **Fertilization** is the process by which a sperm cell and an egg cell join to form one cell. The cell, called a zygote, begins to develop into a new organism.

A disadvantage of sexual reproduction is that an organism must find a mate to reproduce. However, a big advantage of sexual reproduction is that each offspring is unique. Its combination of traits is different from the combination of traits in either parent.

Self-Check

1. What is an advantage and a disadvantage of asexual reproduction?
2. Name some animals that reproduce by asexual reproduction.
3. What is the main advantage of sexual reproduction?
4. What method of reproduction is used by most animals?
5. Describe the process of fertilization.

- Organisms are classified based on their similar features.

- The classification system used by biologists has seven levels: kingdom, phylum, class, order, family, genus, and species.

- Every species has a two-word scientific name consisting of its genus and its species label.

- Vertebrates are animals that have a backbone.

- Invertebrates are animals without a backbone.

- Animals feed by filtering food from water, sucking fluids, or consuming large pieces of food.

- Simple animals digest food in a gastrovascular cavity with only one opening. More developed animals have a digestive tract with an opening at each end.

- Animals take in oxygen and release carbon dioxide in the process called respiration.

- Most animals that live in water have gills to exchange oxygen and carbon dioxide. Land animals have lungs or tubes.

- The circulatory system moves blood throughout an animal's body.

- Asexual reproduction involves one parent and no egg or sperm. It produces offspring that are identical to the parent.

- Sexual reproduction involves an egg from a female parent and a sperm from a male parent. It produces offspring that are unique.

- In fertilization, a sperm cell and an egg cell unite to form a zygote. The zygote develops into a new organism.

Science Words

amphibian, 325	gastrovascular cavity, 333	scientific name, 321
asexual reproduction, 337	gill, 325	sexual reproduction, 337
atrium, 336	invertebrate, 328	species, 320
bilateral symmetry, 328	mammary gland, 327	sperm cell, 337
cartilage, 324	metamorphosis, 325	swim bladder, 325
circulatory system, 335	molting, 331	taxonomy, 319
diffusion, 334	ovary, 337	tentacle, 328
digestive tract, 333	phylum, 319	testes 337
egg cell, 337	pupa, 331	tube foot, 329
fertilization, 338	radial symmetry, 328	ventricle, 336
filter feeding, 332	reptile, 326	vertebra, 324
	respiration, 334	vertebrate, 324

WORD BANK

bilateral symmetry

digestive tract

gastrovascular cavity

invertebrates

mammary glands

metamorphosis

scientific name

swim bladder

taxonomy

vertebrates

Vocabulary Review

Number your paper from 1 to 11. Then choose the term from the Word Bank that best completes each sentence. Write the answer on your paper.

1. Animals that have a backbone are called _____.

2. A tubelike digestive space with an opening at each end is called a _____.

3. A fish uses its _____ to move up or down in the water.

4. Animals with _____ have bodies with a left half and right half that look the same.

5. An animal's _____ consists of its genus and its species label.

6. The science of classifying organisms according to their similarities is called _____.

7. Female bears produce milk from their _____.

8. A _____ is a digestive space with a single opening.

9. The change of a tadpole into a frog is an example of _____.

10. Sponges, cnidarians, and mollusks are all _____.

Concept Review

Number your paper from 1 to 8. Then choose the answer that best completes each sentence. Write the letter of the answer on your paper.

1. In the classification system of organisms, the highest level is _____ .

   a. kingdom   b. phylum   c. species

2. The genus of the western rattlesnake, *Crotalus viridis*, is _____.

   a. *viridis*   b. *Crotalus*   c. western

3. Squids capture prey with their _____.

   a. tentacles   **b.** tube feet   **c.** shells

4. Insects use a system of _____ to carry air into the body.

   a. gills   **b.** lungs   **c.** tubes

5. _____ allows crustaceans to grow larger in size.

   a. Bilateral symmetry   **b.** Molting   **c.** Metamorphosis

6. The bodies of _____ are made of segments.

   a. arthropods   **b.** flatworms   **c.** cnidarians

7. Reproduction that involves only one parent is _____.

   a. sexual reproduction   **c.** fertilization
   b. asexual reproduction

8. All vertebrates have a(n) _____ skeleton.

   a. internal   **b.** external   **c.** bony

Critical Thinking

Write the answer to each of the following questions.

1. A biologist is studying vertebrates in the desert. Would she be more likely to find amphibians or reptiles during her studies? Explain your answer.

2. What method of feeding is used by the animals shown in the photo? Explain your reasoning.

Test Taking Tip If you have to choose the correct beginning to a sentence, combine the last part of the sentence with each available choice. Then choose the beginning that best fits the sentence.

Plants

P lants come in all shapes and sizes. They include tiny moss smaller than your fingernail and giant redwood trees 30 stories tall! These plants are very different from one another. However, they are alike in some ways. In this chapter, you will learn how plants are classified. You will also learn how plants make food and reproduce.

ORGANIZE YOUR THOUGHTS

Plants

Classification

Basic activities

Vascular plants

Nonvascular plants

Making food

Reproduction

Seed plants

Seedless plants

Goals for Learning

▶ To explain the difference between vascular and nonvascular plants

▶ To explain the differences and similarities between seed plants and seedless plants

▶ To identify the main parts of a plant

▶ To explain how plants make food, transport food and water, and produce oxygen

▶ To describe how plants reproduce

Scientists have discovered over 300,000 kinds of plants. That sounds like a lot. However, scientists think even more kinds have yet to be discovered.

Classification of Plants

In Chapter 19 you learned that biologists classify organisms based on their similarities. The classification system has seven levels: kingdom, phylum, class, order, family, genus, and species. You also learned that every species has a two-word scientific name consisting of its genus and its species label. Chapter 19 also explained how animals are classified and named.

The same classification system is used to classify and name plants. For example, maple trees belong to the genus *Acer*. Each kind of maple tree has its own species name. The scientific name of the sugar maple tree is *Acer saccharum*. The scientific name of the red maple is *Acer rubrum*.

Scientists classify plants based on whether they have body parts such as seeds, transport tubes, roots, stems, and leaves. The three main groups of plants are seed plants, ferns and mosses. For plants, scientists use the word *Division* instead of *Phylum*.

Seed Plants

Group	Description	Examples
Palmlike *Division*	Naked seeds in cones; gymnosperm (nonflowering seed plant); male and female cones on different trees; palm-shaped leaves	cycad, sago palm
Ginkgo *Division*	Naked seeds in conelike structures; gymnosperm; male and female cones on different trees; fan-shaped leaves; only one known species	ginkgo
Conifer *Division*	Naked seeds in cones; gymnosperm; male and female cones; most are evergreen; needlelike or scalelike leaves	pine, fir, spruce, yew
Angiosperm *Division*	Produce flowers; seeds protected by ovary that ripens into a fruit; organs of both sexes often in same flower	
Monocot Class	One seed leaf; parallel veins; flower parts in multiples of three	grass, palm, corn
Dicot Class	Two seed leaves; crisscross veins; flower parts in multiples of 4 or 5	cactus, maple, rose

Vascular plant
A plant that has tubelike tissue.

Vascular tissue
A group of plant cells that form tubes through which food and water move.

Vascular and Nonvascular Plants

Seed plants and ferns are **vascular plants**. *Vascular* means "vessel" or "tube." Vascular plants have specialized cells that form tubelike tissue. The tissue is called **vascular tissue**. The tubes transport food, water, and nutrients throughout the plant. Vascular plants have well-developed leaves, stems, and roots.

Vascular tissue is important in two ways. First, it allows food and water to be transported over a distance. Plants can grow in places where water is deep under the ground. Second, vascular tissue is thick and provides support for a plant. This also allows plants to grow tall.

The veins of a leaf are vascular tissue.

Did You Know?

The tallest living thing in the world is one of California's redwood trees. It is 112 meters (368 ft.) tall. The oldest living thing in the world is a 4,060-year-old bristlecone pine tree in California.

Mosses are **nonvascular plants**. Nonvascular plants do not have tubelike tissue to transport water or to support them. These plants are short and must have constant contact with moisture. These small plants usually grow in damp, shady places on the ground and on the sides of trees and rocks. Unlike vascular plants, nonvascular plants do not have true leaves, stems, or roots.

Seedless Plants

Group	Description	Examples
Bryophyte *Division*	Nonvascular (no tubes for carrying materials in plant); live in moist places	liverwort, hornwort, moss
Club Moss *Division*	Spores in cones at end of stems; simple leaves	club moss
Horsetail *Division*	Spores in cones at end of stems; hollow, jointed stem	horsetail
Fern *Division*	Spores in sori; fronds	fern

Self-Check

1. What are the three main groups of plants?
2. What do scientists use as the basis for classifying plants?
3. How are vascular and nonvascular plants different?
4. What are two ways that vascular tissue is important?
5. Why are mosses short plants?

Objectives

After reading this lesson, you should be able to

▶ explain how seed plants are different from the other plant groups.

▶ explain the differences between angiosperms and gymnosperms.

Angiosperm
A flowering plant.

Embryo
A beginning plant or animal.

Seed
A plant part that contains a beginning plant and stored food.

Recall that scientists classify plants into three main groups: seed plants, ferns, and mosses. Seed plants are different from the other plant groups because they use seeds to reproduce. A **seed** is a plant part that contains a beginning plant and stored food. The beginning plant is called an **embryo**. A seed has a seed coat that holds in moisture. When conditions are right, the embryo grows into a full-sized plant.

Seed plants have the most advanced vascular tissue of all plants. They have well-developed leaves, stems, and roots.

Seed plants have many sizes and shapes. The duckweed plant that floats on water may be just one millimeter long. Giant redwood trees are the largest plants in the world. A pine tree has long, thin needles. A rose has soft petals. The different sizes and shapes of seed plants help them to live in many different places. Grass, trees, garden flowers, bushes, vines, and cacti are all seed plants.

Seed plants are the largest group of plants. They are divided into two subgroups. These are flowering plants and nonflowering plants.

Angiosperms

Most species of plants are **angiosperms**, or flowering plants. The word *angiosperm* is made from the Greek words *angeion*, "capsule," and *sperma*, "seed." A capsule, or fruit, protects the seeds of angiosperms. The fruit develops from part of the flower.

The flowers of some plants are colorful and showy.

Gymnosperms

Nonflowering seed plants are called **gymnosperms**. They do not produce flowers. The word *gymnosperm* means "naked seed." The seeds of gymnosperms are not surrounded by a fruit. The seeds are produced inside cones. For example, the seeds of pine trees form on the scales of cones.

Conifers and Other Gymnosperms

There are about 700 species of gymnosperms. The major group of gymnosperms is conifers. **Conifers** are cone-bearing gymnosperms. There are about 600 species of conifers. All conifers are woody shrubs or trees. They make up most of the forests around the world. Pines, spruces, and firs are conifers. Plants such as junipers, yews, and spruces decorate the landscape of many homes. Conifers are a major source of lumber. For example, people make the wood frame of many houses out of pine. Conifers are the main source of paper and other wood products.

Most conifers have green leaves all year. Therefore, they are called evergreens. They lose only some of their leaves at any time. The leaves of conifers are shaped like needles. They do not lose water as easily as the broad leaves on other trees do. This enables conifers to live in dry places where trees must store water for a long time.

Conifers have cones and needle-shaped leaves.

Conifers grow in places where other plants cannot grow, such as shallow, rocky soil and along seashores.

Besides conifers, there are other gymnosperms. The ginkgo tree is one of the most familiar. Gingko trees have peculiar fan-shaped leaves. These trees are planted along many city streets because they are able to survive pollution better than other trees. Gingko trees also are more resistant to disease than other trees. Other types of gymnosperms are tropical trees that look like palm trees or ferns.

The leaves of the gingko tree are shaped like fans.

Self-Check	1. What are other names for flowering plants and nonflowering seed plants?
	2. What is contained inside a seed?
	3. What part of a seed plant develops into the fruit?
	4. Why are the seeds of gymnosperms called "naked seeds"?
	5. Why are conifers able to live where other plants cannot?

Objectives

After reading this lesson, you should be able to

▶ describe similarities and differences between ferns and seed plants.

▶ describe mosses and how they reproduce.

Fern
A seedless vascular plant.

Frond
A large feathery leaf of a fern.

Spore
The reproductive cell of ferns and some other organisms.

There are two main groups of seedless plants. The largest group includes ferns and related plants. Like seed plants, ferns are vascular plants. Unlike seed plants, they do not have seeds. The second group of seedless plants is mosses and related plants. They are different from ferns because they are nonvascular plants.

Ferns

Ferns are seedless vascular plants. Like other vascular plants, ferns have well-developed leaves, stems, and roots. The leaves, or **fronds**, usually are large, flat, and feathery. Each frond is divided into small sections, or leaflets, that spread out from a center rib.

On the underside of fronds are small dots called sori. Sori contain the reproductive cells of ferns. These cells are called **spores**. When the spores are ripe, the sori burst open and release the spores into the air.

After they are released, spores must land in a moist place. If they do not, they will dry up because they do not have a seed coat to hold in moisture. Spores that land in a moist place produce a tiny plant. The plant must have constant moisture to grow. Seeds, on the other hand, carry moisture and food inside their seed coats. Seeds usually survive longer than spores when conditions are dry. This is one reason why there are more seed plants than seedless plants.

Frond

Young leaf

Rhizome

Roots

Young fern fronds uncoil as they grow.

Mosses

Moss
A seedless nonvascular plant that has simple parts.

Rhizoid
A tiny root-like thread of a moss plant.

Mosses are seedless nonvascular plants that have simple leaflike and stemlike parts. They do not have well-developed leaves, stems, and roots. Mosses do not have vascular tissue to transport water, so they must live in moist, shady places. Mosses grow best where the air is humid and the soil is wet. They get water through rootlike threads called **rhizoids**.

Like ferns, mosses reproduce by means of spores. Millions of tiny spores form inside spore cases on special stalks. The spore case breaks open when it is ripe. It shoots the spores into the air. The spores produce new plants when they fall on moist soil.

SCIENCE IN YOUR LIFE

Energy from ferns and mosses

Ferns that lived millions of years ago are important to your life today. About 300 million years ago, forests and swamps contained many ferns, some the size of trees. Over time, these ferns died, and layers of dead ferns and other plants built up. Pressure and heat on the deep layers of plant material changed the material to coal. Coal is burned to produce steam in power plants, which produce electricity.

Self-Check

1. How are ferns and seed plants similar? How are they different?
2. What are sori?
3. Why do spores need to land in a moist place?
4. Where do mosses need to live, and why?
5. What are the two major differences between mosses and seed plants?

Objectives

After reading this lesson, you should be able to

▶ identify the main parts of a plant.

▶ describe the structure and functions of roots.

▶ describe the structure and functions of stems.

▶ describe the structure and functions of leaves.

To make food and survive, plant roots take water and minerals from the soil. Plant leaves collect light from the sun and carbon dioxide from the air. A vascular system of tiny tubes runs through the roots, leaves, and stems of most plants. It connects all parts of the plant. Without this system, the parts of the plant could not do their jobs.

What Roots Do

Have you ever tried to pull a weed out of the ground? You were probably surprised by how hard you had to pull. You discovered an important function of roots. They hold plants firmly in the ground. Roots also have three other functions. First, they absorb water and minerals from the soil. Roots push their way through the soil to reach the water and minerals they need. Second, roots store water and minerals. They can also store food that is made in leaves. Third, the roots' vascular system carries water and minerals to other parts of the plant.

Roots hold a plant in the ground, absorb water and minerals, and store food.

The Parts of a Root

The tip of a root is always growing. As it grows, it pushes its way through the soil.

Millions of tiny root hairs cover the tip of each root. It is the root hairs that absorb water and minerals from the soil. Roots can store the water and minerals until needed. Water and minerals can also move to the stems and leaves through the root's vascular tissue. **Xylem** vascular tissue forms tubes that carry water and minerals from roots to stems and leaves. The leaves use the water and minerals to make food. **Phloem** vascular tissue forms tubes that carry food from leaves to stems and roots.

What Stems Do

Stems are the parts of plants that connect the leaves with the roots. Most stems are above the ground. Stems have three functions. First, stems support the leaves. They hold the leaves up so that they can receive sunlight. Second, stems transport food, water, and minerals through the plant. Third, stems can store food.

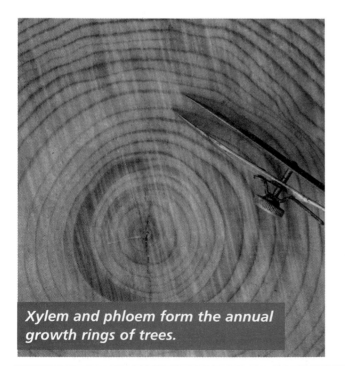

Xylem and phloem form the annual growth rings of trees.

The Parts of a Stem

Like roots, stems contain xylem and phloem. They also contain a special layer of growth tissue. It produces new layers of xylem and phloem cells. These layers build up in some plants, so stems become thicker as they get taller. In trees, these layers become wood. In a tree trunk, one layer forms a new ring each year. You can count these rings, called annual growth rings, to tell the tree's age.

What Leaves Do

Leaves are the parts of the plant that trap sunlight. Leaves have four functions. First, they make food. Second, they store food. Third, they transport food to stems. Fourth, they allow gases to enter and leave the plant.

The Parts of a Leaf

Leaves have three main parts: the **petiole**, the blade, and the veins. The petiole, or stalk, attaches the leaf to a stem or a branch. The blade is the main part of the leaf. It collects light from the sun to make food. Many leaves are thin and have flat surfaces. A tree full of leaves can gather large amounts of energy from the sun.

The veins are part of the plant's vascular system. They are thin tubes that are arranged in a pattern. Veins run throughout the blade. They also run through the petiole to the stem. The veins of leaves transport food and water between the stem and the leaf.

The underside of each leaf has many small openings called stomata. Each opening is called a **stoma**. Stomata allow gases such as carbon dioxide and oxygen to enter and leave the leaf. Water vapor also leaves through stomata.

The parts of a leaf are the petiole, the blade, and the veins.

Self-Check

1. What are the functions of roots?
2. What is the difference between xylem and phloem tissue?
3. How are annual growth rings made?
4. What are the main parts of a leaf?
5. What do stomata do?

Objectives

After reading this lesson, you should be able to

▶ describe how plants make food.

▶ explain the chemical equation for photosynthesis.

▶ describe the carbon dioxide–oxygen cycle.

Photosynthesis
The process in which a plant makes food.

All plants make food in a process called **photosynthesis**. Why is this important to you? To live, people need the food that plants make. Much of the food you eat comes directly from plants. The rest comes from animals that eat plants or that feed on plant-eating animals.

The Process of Photosynthesis

During photosynthesis, plants use the energy of sunlight to turn carbon dioxide and water into simple sugars (food) and oxygen. How do plants get the energy, carbon dioxide, and water they need for photosynthesis? Carbon dioxide comes from the air. It enters the leaves through the stomata. Water comes up from the roots through the xylem. The minerals that the roots absorb also help the plant make food.

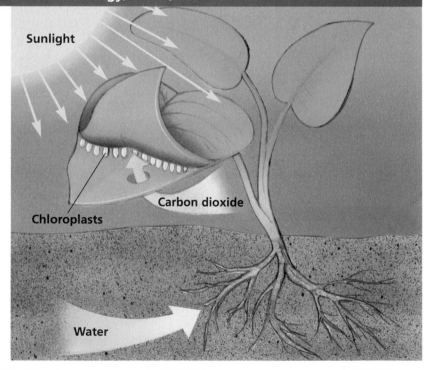

Plants use energy, water, and carbon dioxide to make food.

Sunlight

Chloroplasts

Carbon dioxide

Water

Chlorophyll
The green pigment in plants that captures light energy for photosynthesis.

Pigment
A chemical that absorbs certain types of light.

Plants get the energy they need when light shines on their chloroplasts. Chloroplasts are the organelles in plant cells where photosynthesis takes place. Chloroplasts contain a green **pigment** called **chlorophyll**. A pigment is a chemical that absorbs certain types of light. The cells of the green parts of plants, such as leaves, contain many chloroplasts. When sunlight hits chloroplasts in the leaves, the chlorophyll absorbs light. The sunlight then supplies the energy for photosynthesis.

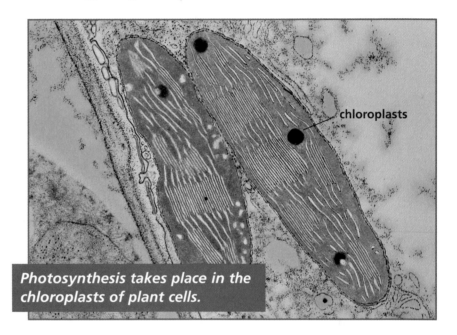

chloroplasts

Photosynthesis takes place in the chloroplasts of plant cells.

Plants use the energy to split water molecules apart into hydrogen atoms and oxygen atoms. The oxygen leaves the plant through the stomata and goes into the air. The hydrogen combines with the carbon dioxide to make a simple sugar called glucose. Plants store the energy of sunlight in the glucose as chemical energy.

Did You Know?

Leaves contain several other pigments besides chlorophyll. During the summer, leaves contain a lot of chlorophyll, so you cannot see the other pigments. In autumn the pigments in leaves break down. Chlorophyll breaks down first. Then you can see the red, yellow, and orange colors of the other pigments.

The Chemical Equation for Photosynthesis

You can write a chemical equation that shows how photosynthesis works. In an equation, the left side and the right side are balanced. Each side of this equation has the same number of oxygen, hydrogen, and carbon atoms. The chemical equation for photosynthesis looks like this:

$$6CO_2 + 6H_2O + \text{light energy} \longrightarrow C_6H_{12}O_6 + 6O_2$$

6 molecules of carbon dioxide	+	6 molecules of water	+	light energy	yields	1 molecule of glucose	+	6 molecules of oxygen

The substances to the left of the arrow are the reactants needed for photosynthesis: carbon dioxide (CO_2), water (H_2O), and light from the sun. The substances to the right of the arrow are the products of photosynthesis: glucose ($C_6H_{12}O_6$) and oxygen (O_2).

Photosynthesis and Cellular Respiration

Two of the most important gases in the air that you breathe are carbon dioxide and oxygen. Oxygen is important to most organisms. They use oxygen to break down food and release the chemical energy stored in it. As you learned in Chapter 18, this process is called cellular respiration.

Photosynthesis happens only in plants. Cellular respiration happens in both plants and animals. Cellular respiration is a special low-temperature kind of burning that breaks down the glucose made by plants during photosynthesis. Glucose is your body's main source of energy. You get that energy when your cells burn sugars and starches that come from plants you eat. Your body cells use oxygen to break apart the sugar molecules. During cellular respiration, oxygen combines with hydrogen to make water. Carbon dioxide is released as a waste product. Does this sound familiar? It is the opposite of photosynthesis.

Photosynthesis and respiration are part of the carbon dioxide–oxygen cycle. During photosynthesis plants take in carbon dioxide and water and give off oxygen. During respiration, animals take in oxygen and give off carbon dioxide. This cycle is necessary for life on Earth.

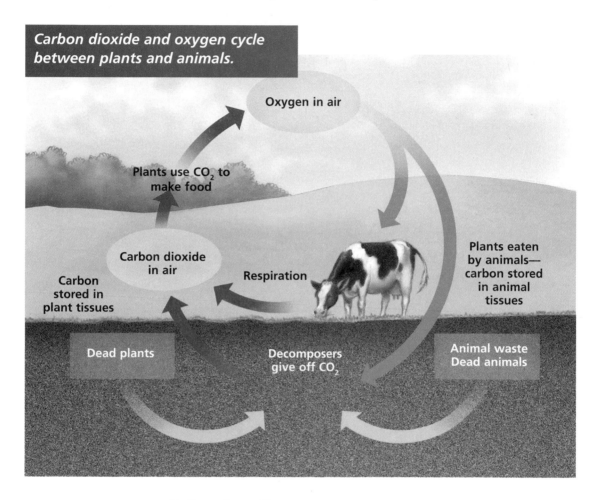

Carbon dioxide and oxygen cycle between plants and animals.

Oxygen in air

Plants use CO$_2$ to make food

Carbon dioxide in air

Carbon stored in plant tissues

Respiration

Plants eaten by animals— carbon stored in animal tissues

Dead plants

Decomposers give off CO$_2$

Animal waste Dead animals

Releasing Oxygen

The oxygen that plants produce comes from water. Recall that photosynthesis splits water molecules into hydrogen atoms and oxygen atoms. The hydrogen combines with the carbon dioxide to produce glucose and more water. The oxygen becomes oxygen gas. The plant uses some of the oxygen for cellular respiration. However, a plant produces more oxygen than it needs. The rest of the oxygen leaves the plant and goes into the air.

Guard cell
A cell that opens and closes stomata.

The oxygen that goes out of the plant into the air leaves through the stomata. Remember that stomata are small openings on a leaf. Each stoma has two special cells called **guard cells**. The size and shape of the guard cells change as they take up and release water. When the guard cells take up water and swell, the stomata open. Oxygen, carbon dioxide, and water vapor can move in and out of the leaf through the openings. When the guard cells lose water, the stomata close.

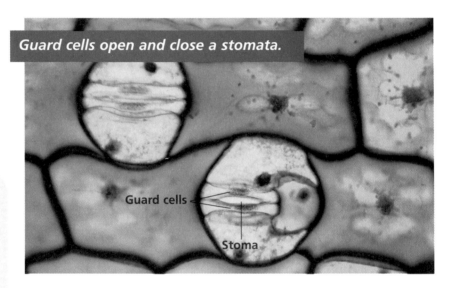

Guard cells open and close a stomata.

Guard cells

Stoma

Did You Know?

Most of the oxygen that we breathe comes from plants and algae.

The amount of light affects the opening and closing of stomata. The stomata of most plants close at night. They open during the day when photosynthesis takes place. The amount of water also affects the opening and closing of stomata. When the soil and air are dry, stomata close, even during the day. This prevents the plant from losing water during short dry periods.

Self-Check

1. What is photosynthesis and where does it occur?
2. What is the chemical equation for photosynthesis?
3. How is respiration the opposite of photosynthesis?
4. What happens to water during photosynthesis?
5. What do guard cells do?

Pistil

The female part of a flower.

Pollen

The tiny structures of seed plants that contain sperm.

Stamen

The male part of a flower.

Plants can reproduce by sexual reproduction or asexual reproduction. As you learned in Chapter 19, sexual reproduction involves two parents. A sperm cell and an egg cell join to start a new organism. Asexual reproduction involves only one parent and no egg or sperm.

Reproduction in Plants

Mosses and ferns reproduce both asexually and sexually. Asexual reproduction happens when a small piece of the parent plant breaks off. That piece forms a new plant. Seedless plants also reproduce sexually from spores.

Seed plants can reproduce asexually when a new plant grows from a piece of a plant. However, seed plants usually reproduce sexually.

Sexual Reproduction in Angiosperms

The flower is the part of an angiosperm that contains eggs and sperm. In a flower, the **stamens** are the male organs of reproduction. They produce the **pollen**, which contain sperm. The **pistil** is the female organ of reproduction. The lower part of the pistil is the ovary, which contains eggs.

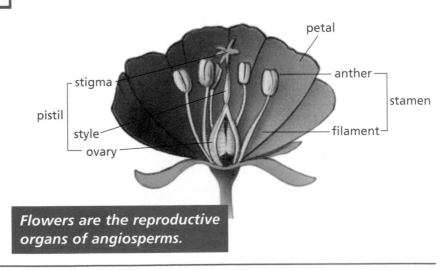

Flowers are the reproductive organs of angiosperms.

For reproduction to take place, the sperm in pollen must fertilize the egg. When insects and birds drink nectar in the flower, pollen sticks to their bodies. They carry the pollen to the pistil of another flower or the same flower. Wind also spreads pollen. The transfer of pollen from the stamen to the pistil is called **pollination**.

After pollination, the pollen grain grows a tube. The tube reaches down through the pistil to the eggs in the ovary. When the pollen meets an egg, fertilization takes place. The ovary develops into a fruit with seeds inside. If the temperature and amount of water are just right, the seed **germinates**, or starts to grow into a new plant.

Sexual Reproduction in Gymnosperms

How are male and female cones different?

The reproductive organs of gymnosperms are in cones, not flowers. Some cones are male. Some are female. During reproduction, male cones release millions of pollen grains into the air. Some of the pollen reaches female cones. As in flowering plants, the pollen grain grows a tube that reaches eggs in the ovary. When the pollen and egg meet, fertilization takes place. But unlike angiosperms, a fruit does not cover gymnosperm seeds. The uncovered seeds are under the scales of the cones.

Self-Check

1. What is the difference between sexual reproduction and asexual reproduction?
2. Which types of plants use spores to reproduce?
3. Describe the process of fertilization in angiosperms.
4. What happens when a seed germinates?
5. Describe the process of reproduction in a conifer.

Growing an African Violet From a Leaf

Materials

✓ African violet plant
✓ water
✓ 2 paper cups
✓ aluminum foil
✓ pencil
✓ potting soil

Purpose

To grow a plant, using asexual reproduction

Procedure

1. Have your teacher cut a leaf with a long stem from the African violet plant.

2. Fill a cup with water, then cover it with aluminum foil. With a pencil, poke a hole in the center of the foil.

3. Insert the leaf into the hole. The end of the stem should be in the water.

4. Place the leaf and cup in a window where the leaf will get sunlight.

5. Change the water in the cup every few days. As you do, observe the end of the stem. Observe and record any changes.

6. When roots appear and begin to grow, plant your leaf in a cup of potting soil. Bury the roots and part of the stem in the soil. Water the soil.

7. Place the potted leaf on a windowsill. Keep the soil moist. What eventually happens?

Questions

1. What was the first change that you observed in the leaf? Describe your observation.

2. Why do you think the plant produced this type of new growth?

3. How does the plant change after the leaf is planted in soil?

4. What type of reproduction occurred in this investigation? Explain your answer.

Explore Further

Many plants will grow from leaf or stem cuttings. Try to grow some other plants this way. You may want to use a book on houseplants as a reference.

Chapter 20 SUMMARY

- Plants are classified according to whether they have body parts such as seeds, transport tubes, roots, stems, and leaves.

- The three main groups of plants are seed plants, ferns, and mosses.

- Vascular plants have vascular tissue that forms tubes for transporting food, nutrients, and water.

- Flowering plants are called angiosperms. Their seeds are surrounded by a fruit.

- Gymnosperms are nonflowering plants that have seeds. Their seeds are not surrounded by a fruit.

- Ferns and mosses are seedless plants that reproduce by spores. Ferns are vascular plants. Mosses are nonvascular plants.

- Roots hold plants in the ground, absorb water and minerals, and store food.

- Stems support the leaves, store food, and transport food, water, and minerals through the plant.

- Leaves make and store food, transport food to stems, and let gases enter and leave the plant.

- Plants make food in their green parts. The cells in those parts contain chloroplasts, where photosynthesis takes place.

- Plants use carbon dioxide, water, and sunlight to produce glucose and oxygen.

- Animals take in the oxygen that plants produce and give off carbon dioxide.

- Plants can reproduce by sexual reproduction, which involves two parents, or by asexual reproduction, which involves only one parent.

Science Words

angiosperm, 346	moss, 350	rhizoid, 350
chlorophyll, 355	nonvascular plant, 345	seed, 346
conifer, 347	petiole, 353	spore, 349
embryo, 346	phloem, 352	stamen, 359
fern, 349	photosynthesis, 354	stoma, 353
frond, 349	pigment, 355	vascular plant, 344
germinate, 360	pistil, 359	vascular tissue, 344
guard cell, 358	pollen, 359	xylem, 352
gymnosperm, 347	pollination, 360	

WORD BANK

asexual
  reproduction

chlorophyll

fern

frond

germinate

moss

photosynthesis

pollen

pollination

seed

sexual
  reproduction

spore

stomata

vascular plant

Vocabulary Review

Number your paper from 1 to 14. Then choose the term from the Word Bank that best completes each sentence. Write the answer on your paper.

1. A(n)_____ is a seedless nonvascular plant.

2. _____ happens when a small piece of a plant breaks off and forms a new plant.

3. Gases move in and out of a leaf through openings called _____.

4. The large feathery leaf of a fern is called a(n) _____.

5. A(n) _____ is a seedless vascular plant.

6. Plants make simple sugars during _____.

7. Pollen is transferred from the stamen to the pistil in the process of _____.

8. The sperm of seed plants is contained in _____.

9. A(n) _____ is the reproductive cell of ferns and mosses.

10. Seed plants usually reproduce by _____.

11. A plant that has tubelike tissue is called a(n) _____.

12. A green pigment called _____ captures light energy for photosynthesis.

13. A(n) _____ contains a plant embryo and stored food.

14. When conditions are right, a seed will _____, or start growing into a new plant.

Concept Review

Number your paper from 1 to 4. Then choose the answer that best completes each sentence. Write the letter of the answer on your paper.

1. The main parts of a vascular plant are roots, stems, and _____.

   a. leaves   **b.** stomata   **c.** pollen

2. All angiosperms have _____.

   a. fronds   **b.** rhizoids   **c.** flowers

3. Water vapor, carbon dioxide, and oxygen enter and leave a plant through the _____.

   a. roots   **b.** flowers   **c.** stomata

4. _____ are plants that must live in moist, shady places.

   a. Angiosperms   **b.** Mosses   **c.** Conifers

Critical Thinking

Write the answer to each of the following questions.

1. Suppose a plant does not have seeds. Can you tell if the plant is vascular or nonvascular? Explain your answer.

2. The chemical formula for glucose is $C_6H_{12}O_6$. What atoms are in glucose? How many of each kind of atom are in one molecule of glucose?

Test Taking Tip | When choosing answers from a word bank, answer all of the questions you know first. Then, study the remaining words to choose the answers for the questions you are not sure about.

Ecology

Living things depend on one another and on the non-living things in the world around them. Animals depend on plants for food. They also use air, water, soil, and energy from the sun to help them meet their needs. In this chapter, you will learn how organisms depend on one another as they live together in groups. You will also learn how organisms use the nonliving things in their environment to help them survive.

ORGANIZE YOUR THOUGHTS

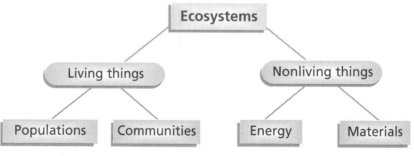

Ecosystems

Living things   Nonliving things

Populations   Communities   Energy   Materials

Goals for Learning

▶ To identify ways in which living things interact with one another and with nonliving things

▶ To describe feeding relationships among the organisms in a community

▶ To explain how energy flows through ecosystems

▶ To identify materials that cycle through ecosystems

After reading this lesson, you should be able to

► explain the relationships among organisms, populations, communities, and ecosystems.

► describe the process of succession.

► describe how pollution affects ecosystems.

► identify what a biome is.

Ecology
The study of the interactions among living things and the nonliving things in their environment.

Interact
To act upon or influence something.

Organisms act upon, or **interact** with, one another and with nonliving things in their environment. For example, you interact with the air when you inhale oxygen and exhale carbon dioxide. You interact with plants when you eat fruits and vegetables. **Ecology** is the study of the interactions among living things and the nonliving things in their environment.

Levels of Organization

Organisms interact at different levels. For example, organisms of the same species interact with one another. Organisms of different species also interact. The diagram shows the organization of living things into different levels. The higher the level, the more interactions there are.

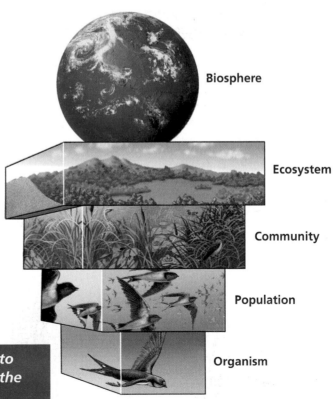

Biosphere

Ecosystem

Community

Population

Organism

Life on Earth is organized into levels. The higher the level, the more interactions there are.

Notice that the lowest level of organization is the individual organism. The place where an organism lives is its **habitat**. Each organism is adapted to live in its habitat. For example, tuna use their fins to swim through the ocean. A spider monkey uses its long tail to hang from trees.

Populations

The next level of organization is a **population**. A group of organisms of the same species that live in the same area form a population. The grizzly bears in Yellowstone National Park make up a population. The members of a population interact with one another when they mate or compete for food, water, and space.

Communities

A **community** is the third level of organization of living things. Populations of different species that live in the same area make up a community. Bears, rabbits, pine trees, and grass are different populations of organisms, but they all may live together in the same forest community.

The populations in a community interact with one another in many ways. For example, trees provide shelter and food for animals such as squirrels. Some of the nuts that squirrels bury grow to become new trees. A hawk may eat squirrels and build a nest in the tree.

A pond community changes into a forest community by the process of succession.

Climax community
A community that changes little over time.

Ecosystem
The interactions among the populations of a community and the nonliving things in their environment.

Succession
The process by which a community changes over time.

Ecosystems

All the interactions among the populations of a community and the nonliving things in their environment make up an **ecosystem**. Organisms interact with nonliving things when they breathe air, drink water, or grow from the soil. Ecosystems occur on land and in water.

Changes in Ecosystems

As the community of organisms and the nonliving things of an ecosystem interact, they may cause changes. These changes may result in the community changing into a different type of community. The changes that occur in a community over time are called **succession**. The illustration shows the succession of a pond community into a forest community.

Eventually, a community reaches a point at which it changes little over time. A community that is stable is called a **climax community**. A climax community, such as an oak–hickory forest, may stay nearly the same for hundreds of years. A climax community usually has a great diversity of organisms. However, a volcano, forest fire, or earthquake can destroy large parts of a climax community within a short time. When that happens, the community goes through succession once again.

Acid rain
Rain that is caused by pollution and is harmful to organisms because it is acidic.

Biome
An ecosystem found over a large geographic area.

Pollution
Anything added to the environment that is harmful to living things.

Effects of Pollution on Ecosystems

People produce a variety of wastes and poisons that affect ecosystems. **Pollution** is anything added to the environment that is harmful to living organisms. Pollution is most often caused by human activities. For example, the burning of coal, oil, or gasoline releases a colorless, poisonous gas called sulfur dioxide. This gas poisons organisms that breathe it. Sulfur dioxide in the air also makes rainwater more acidic. This **acid rain** decreases the growth of plants and harms their leaves. Acid rain that falls into lakes and streams can harm or kill organisms living in the water.

Other types of pollution affect lakes and other bodies of water as well. Topsoil that is washed off the land because of construction and bad farming practices fills up streams and lakes. Fertilizer that washes off the land into bodies of water pollutes the water with chemicals. Chemicals that factories dump into lakes and streams kill plants and animals in the water. This affects birds and other animals that depend on the water animals and plants for food.

Biomes

Some ecosystems are found over large geographic areas. These ecosystems are called **biomes**. Some biomes, such as deserts, pine forests, and grasslands, are on land. Water biomes include oceans, lakes, and rivers.

Different biomes are found in different climates. Temperature, sunlight, and rainfall are all part of a biome's climate. For example, tropical rain forests get plenty of rainfall and are hot. Tundras are found in areas that are dry and cold. A desert is the driest of all biomes. Some deserts get as little as 2 centimeters of rain in a year.

Tundra

Biosphere
The part of Earth where living things can exist.

Resource
A thing that an organism uses to live.

The types of organisms found in a particular biome depend on the **resources** available to the organisms. Resources are things that organisms use to live. Resources include water, air, sunlight, and soil. Fish are not found in a desert biome because a desert has little water. Most cactuses do not grow in a tropical rain forest because the soil in the forest is too wet.

The Biosphere

Look back at the diagram on page 367. Notice that the highest level of organization of life is the **biosphere**. The desert biome, the ocean biome, and all the other biomes on Earth together form the biosphere. The biosphere is the part of Earth where life can exist.

Think of Earth as an orange or an onion. The biosphere is like the peel of the orange or the skin of the onion. It is the thin layer on a large sphere. The biosphere includes the organisms living on Earth's surface, in water, underground, and in the air. The biosphere also includes nonliving things, such as water, minerals, and air, that interact with organisms.

The biosphere is a tiny part of Earth. This thin surface layer can easily be damaged. Thus, humans need to be aware of how they can protect the biosphere. One way is to avoid polluting it. The survival of living things depends on the conditions of the nonliving parts of the biosphere.

Self-Check

1. What is the difference between a population and a community?
2. What kinds of interactions make up an ecosystem?
3. When a pond community changes into a forest community, what is the process called?
4. How does acid rain affect plants and animals?
5. Define biome and list three or more examples of biomes.

INVESTIGATION

21

Testing the pH of Rain

Purpose
To find out if the rain in your area is acid rain

Materials

✓ 3 small trash cans
✓ 3 new plastic trash bags
✓ pH paper
✓ pH scale
✓ distilled water

Procedure

1. Copy the data table below on a sheet of paper.

Date	pH of sample 1	pH of sample 2	pH of sample 3	Average pH of samples
pH of distilled water:				

2. On a rainy day, place open plastic bags inside the trash cans.

3. If there is no thunder and lightning, place the containers outside in the rain. Make sure that the containers collect rainwater that has not touched anything on the way down, such as a roof or the leaves of a tree.

4. When a small amount of rainwater has been collected, touch the edge of the pH paper to the rainwater in one of the containers.

5. Notice the change in color of the pH paper. Compare the color of the pH paper to the colors on the pH scale. The matching color on the scale indicates the pH of the sample of rainwater. In your data table under sample 1, record the pH value of the rainwater.

6. Repeat steps 4 and 5 for the other two samples of rainwater. Record the pH of the samples in the correct columns.

7. If the pH values that you recorded for the three samples are not the same, compute the average pH of the samples. To do this, add all of the pH values and divide by 3. Record this number in the last column in your table.

8. Use the pH paper to determine the pH of distilled water. Record the pH in your data table.

9. Repeat this Investigation on one or two more rainy days. Record in your data table the dates on which you collected the rainwater.

Questions

1. How does the pH of distilled water compare with the pH of the rainwater you tested?

2. When water has a pH lower than 7, it is acidic. Normal rain is always slightly acidic and has a pH between 4.9 and 6.5. When rain has a pH of less than 4.9, it is called acid rain. Were any of the samples of rainwater you tested acid rain?

3. Recall from Lesson 1 how acid rain forms. Is acid rain more likely to fall in cities or in rural areas? Explain.

4. Was the pH of the rainwater the same every day you collected samples? What are some reasons the pH of rainwater could vary from day to day?

Explore Further

Test the pH of the water in a local pond, lake, or stream. *Safety Alert: Wear protective gloves when you collect the water samples.* Is the pH of the body of water the same as that of rainwater? Why might the values be different?

A water plant captures the energy from sunlight. It uses the energy to make sugars and other molecules. A small fish eats the plant. A bigger fish eats the small fish. A bird eats the big fish. This feeding order is called a **food chain**. Almost all food chains begin with plants or other organisms that capture the energy of the sun.

Producers

Plants, some protists, and some bacteria make their own food. Organisms that make, or produce, their own food are called **producers**. Every food chain begins with a producer. Most producers use the energy of sunlight to make food by the process of photosynthesis.

Consumers

Organisms that cannot make their own food must get food from outside their bodies. These organisms get their food from other organisms. **Consumers** are organisms that feed on, or consume, other organisms. All animals and fungi and some protists and bacteria are consumers.

Consumer
An organism that feeds on other organisms.

Food chain
The feeding order of organisms in an ecosystem.

Producer
An organism that makes its own food.

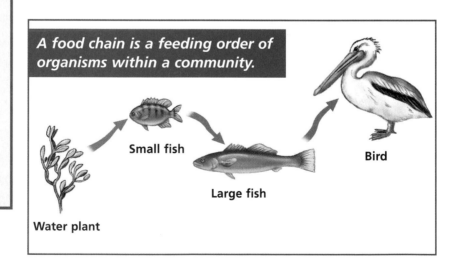

A food chain is a feeding order of organisms within a community.

Water plant

Small fish

Large fish

Bird

Carnivore
A consumer that eats only animals.

Herbivore
A consumer that eats only plants.

Omnivore
A consumer that eats both plants and animals.

Pyramid of numbers
A diagram that compares the sizes of populations at different levels of a food chain.

Consumers may eat plants or other consumers. Consumers that eat only plants are called **herbivores**, and those that eat only animals are called **carnivores**. Consumers that eat both plants and animals are called **omnivores**.

The consumers in a food chain are classified into different feeding levels, called orders, depending on what they consume. First-order consumers eat plants. Rabbits are first-order consumers. Second-order consumers eat animals that eat plants. A snake that eats the rabbit is a second-order consumer. A hawk that eats the snake is a third-order consumer.

Numbers of Producers and Consumers

The African plains are covered with billions of grass plants. Herds of antelope feed on the grasses. However, the number of antelope is far less than the number of grass plants. In the same area, there may be only a few dozen lions. Lions need many antelope and other prey animals to survive.

You might think of a food chain as a pyramid with the highest-level consumers at the top. Notice in the **pyramid of numbers** that a food chain begins with a large number of producers. There are more producers in a community than there are first-order consumers feeding on the producers. The size of the population decreases at each higher level of a food chain.

The pyramid of numbers compares population sizes at different levels of a food chain.

Food Webs

Few consumers eat only one kind of food. The American crow is an example of a bird that eats a wide range of foods. It eats grains, seeds, berries, insects, dead animals, and the eggs of other birds. Eating a variety of foods helps to ensure that the consumer has a sufficient food supply.

The frogs in a pond eat a variety of foods, including insects and worms. The frogs in turn may be eaten by snakes or birds. Thus, frogs are part of more than one food chain. The diagram shows some food chains in a pond community. Trace the different food chains. Notice that the food chains are linked to one another at certain points. Together, the food chains form a **food web**.

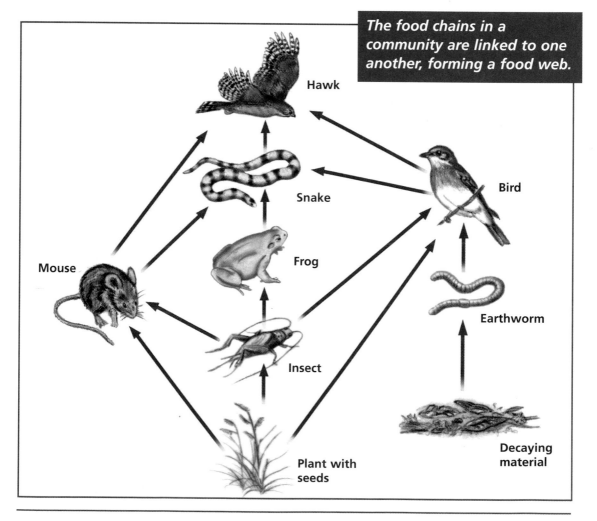

The food chains in a community are linked to one another, forming a food web.

Hawk

Snake

Bird

Frog

Mouse

Earthworm

Insect

Plant with seeds

Decaying material

Decomposers

If a first-order consumer, such as a rabbit, dies but is not eaten by another animal, does the food chain stop there? No, because decomposers continue the food chain by feeding on the dead animal. Recall that decomposers are certain bacteria, fungi, and protists that feed on dead organisms. Decomposers feed on both producers and consumers.

Decomposers get food by breaking down complex chemicals in dead organisms into simple chemicals. The simple chemicals become part of the soil. Plants take in these chemicals through their roots and use them to grow.

Self-Check

1. What is the difference between a producer and a consumer?
2. Define the terms *herbivore*, *carnivore*, and *omnivore*.
3. Diagram a food chain that includes three levels of consumers. Which level of consumers has the smallest population size?
4. What is the relationship between food chains and food webs?
5. What is the role of decomposers in an ecosystem?

SCIENCE IN YOUR LIFE

What kind of consumer are you?

Like all consumers, you cannot make your own food. You must eat, or consume, food. Are you a first-order, second-order, or third-order consumer? When you eat plants or parts of plants, you are a first-order consumer. For example, if you eat an apple or a peanut, you are a first-order consumer.

When you eat the meat or products of animals that feed on plants, you are a second-order consumer. For example, if you eat a hamburger or drink milk, you are a second-order consumer. Milk and hamburger come from cows, which feed on plants. When you eat the meat or products of animals that feed on other animals, you are a third-order consumer. If you eat swordfish or lobster for dinner, you are a third-order consumer.

Objectives

After reading this lesson, you should be able to

▶ explain why organisms need energy.

▶ describe how energy flows through a food chain.

▶ compare the amounts of energy available at different levels of a food chain.

▶ explain how the amount of available energy affects the size of a population.

Plants use energy from the sun to make food. You get energy from the food you eat. In Chapter 4, you learned that energy is the ability to do work—to move things or change things. Energy comes in many forms. For example, light and heat from the sun are energy. Electricity also is energy. Batteries store chemical energy. A moving bicycle has mechanical energy.

You and all organisms need energy to live. Your muscles use energy to contract. Your heart uses a lot of energy to pump blood. Your brain uses energy when you think. Your cells use energy when they make new molecules.

You probably get tired when you work hard. You might even say that you have "run out of energy" to describe how you feel. You take a break and eat some lunch to "get your energy back." Food contains energy.

Food gives us the energy we need to do work.

Energy in Food

Recall from Chapter 20 that plants absorb energy from the sun. A plant's chlorophyll and other pigments absorb some of the light energy. By the process of photosynthesis, the plant uses the absorbed energy to make sugar molecules. Photosynthesis is a series of chemical reactions. During these reactions, light energy is changed into chemical energy. The chemical energy is stored in the sugar molecules.

Plants use the sugar to make other food molecules, such as starches, fats, and proteins. All these nutrients store chemical energy. When plants need energy, they release the energy stored in the nutrients. Plants need energy to grow, reproduce, make new molecules, and perform other life processes. To use the energy stored in nutrients, plant cells break down the molecules into simpler molecules. As the molecules are broken down, they release the stored energy.

Plants also use the nutrients they make to produce tissues in their leaves, roots, and stems. The nutrients' chemical energy is stored in the tissues. When you eat potatoes, asparagus, or other plant parts, you are taking in the plants' stored chemical energy.

Flow of Energy Through Food Chains

Animals and other consumers are unable to make their own food. They must eat plants or other organisms for food. As organisms feed on one another, the energy stored in the organisms moves from one level of the food chain to the next.

The flow of energy in a food chain begins with the producers, such as plants. As you know, plants absorb the sun's energy to make food. They use some of the energy in the food for life processes. As plants use this energy, some is changed to heat. The heat becomes part of the environment. The rest of the energy is stored as chemical energy in the plants' tissues.

The energy stored in plants is passed on to the organisms that eat the plants. These first-order consumers use some of the food energy and lose some energy as heat. The rest of the energy is stored as chemical energy in the nutrients in their body.

The energy stored in the first-order consumers is passed on to the second-order consumers. Then, energy stored in the second-order consumers is passed on to the third-order consumers. At each level of the food chain, some energy is used for life processes, some is lost as heat, and the rest is stored in the organisms.

Energy Pyramid

The **energy pyramid** below compares the amounts of energy available to the populations at different levels of a food chain. The most energy is available to the producers. They get energy directly from the sun. Less energy is available to the insects, the first-order consumers that feed on the producers. That is because the producers have used some of the sun's energy for their own needs. Also, some of the energy was lost as heat. Only the energy that is stored in the producers is passed on to the insects.

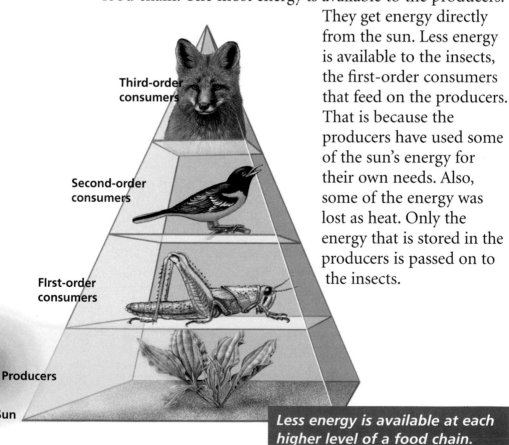

Third-order consumers

Second-order consumers

First-order consumers

Producers

Sun

Less energy is available at each higher level of a food chain.

The insects use some of the energy they take in for their own needs. Again, some energy is lost as heat. Thus, the amount of energy available to the birds, the second-order consumers, is less than the amount of energy available to the insects. Notice that the amount of available energy decreases at each higher level of a food chain. The foxes have the least amount of energy available. They are at the highest level of the food chain.

The amounts of energy available to the different populations of a food chain affect the sizes of the populations. Look back at the pyramid of numbers shown on page 375. Recall that the size of the population decreases at each higher level of a food chain. That is because less energy is available to the population at each higher level.

Importance of the Sun

Without the sun, there would be no life on Earth. All plants and animals and most other organisms depend on energy from the sun. Energy flows from the sun to producers and then to consumers. The amount of energy that can be stored is reduced as energy flows through food chains. The sun continuously replaces the energy that was used for life processes and lost as heat.

Self-Check

1. Why do organisms need energy?
2. Which organisms in a community get energy directly from the sun?
3. How does energy flow through a food chain?
4. Explain why less energy is available at each higher level of a food chain.
5. How does the amount of energy available to a population affect the size of the population?

How Do Materials Cycle Through Ecosystems?

Objectives

After reading this lesson, you should be able to

▶ describe how water cycles through ecosystems.

▶ explain the roles of photosynthesis and cellular respiration in the water, carbon, and oxygen cycles.

▶ describe how nitrogen cycles through ecosystems.

▶ explain how cycles in ecosystems are linked to one another.

Materials continuously cycle between organisms and the nonliving parts of Earth. Some materials important for life are water, carbon, oxygen, and nitrogen.

The Water Cycle

You learned about the water cycle in Chapter 14. The diagram below shows how water cycles between the living and nonliving parts of an ecosystem.

Organisms produce water during cellular respiration. Plants release water vapor through their leaves. Animals release water vapor with their breath. They also release liquid water with their wastes.

Organisms need water for life processes. Plants need water to make food during photosynthesis. Plants take in water from the soil through their roots. Animals drink water and get water in foods they eat.

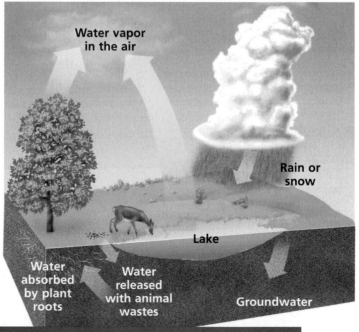

Water vapor in the air

Rain or snow

Lake

Water absorbed by plant roots

Water released with animal wastes

Groundwater

Water continuously cycles through ecosystems.

The Carbon Cycle

All living things are made of chemicals that include carbon. Carbohydrates, fats, and proteins contain carbon. Carbon is also found in the nonliving parts of the environment.

The diagram below shows how carbon cycles through an ecosystem. Plants and other organisms that undergo photosynthesis take in carbon dioxide and use it to make food. Animals take in carbon-containing chemicals when they eat plants or other animals.

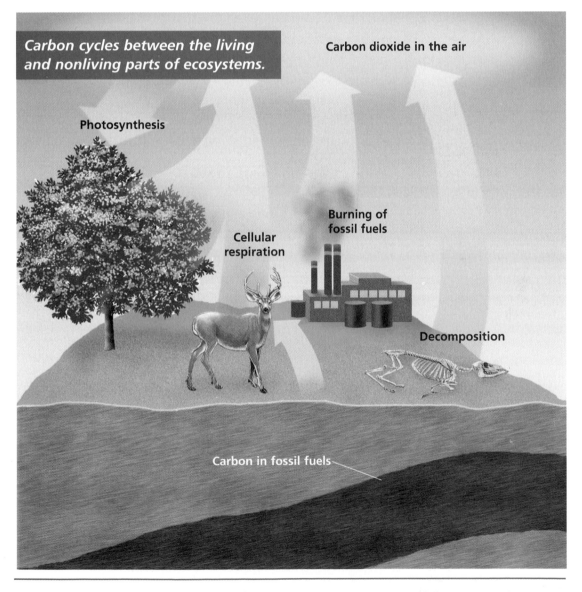

Carbon cycles between the living and nonliving parts of ecosystems.

Carbon dioxide in the air

Photosynthesis

Cellular respiration

Burning of fossil fuels

Decomposition

Carbon in fossil fuels

During cellular respiration, plants, animals, and other organisms produce carbon dioxide. Plants release carbon dioxide through their leaves and other plant parts. Animals release carbon dioxide when they exhale. Decomposers release carbon dioxide as they break down dead organisms. The carbon dioxide that is released by organisms may become part of the air or a body of water. People also produce carbon dioxide when they burn fossil fuels. In these ways, carbon continues to cycle through ecosystems.

The Oxygen Cycle

Oxygen is essential to almost every form of life. Most of the oxygen that organisms use comes from producers, such as plants. Producers use oxygen for cellular respiration. They release oxygen as a waste product during photosynthesis. Consumers take in some of the oxygen and use it themselves. Thus, oxygen continuously cycles between producers and consumers in an ecosystem.

The Nitrogen Cycle

Nitrogen is a gas that makes up about 78 percent of the air. Many materials that are important to living things contain nitrogen. However, the nitrogen in the air is not in a form that organisms can use. Certain bacteria are able to change nitrogen gas into ammonia, which plants can use. These bacteria live in the soil and in the roots of some plants. The process by which the bacteria change nitrogen gas into ammonia is called **nitrogen fixation**.

The diagram of the nitrogen cycle on the next page shows that plants take in the ammonia through their roots. Some of the ammonia, however, is changed by bacteria into chemicals called nitrates. Plants use both ammonia and nitrates to make proteins and other chemicals they need.

Not all of the nitrates are used by plants. Notice in the diagram that bacteria change some of the nitrates back into nitrogen gas. The return of nitrogen gas to the air allows the nitrogen cycle to continue.

Animals get the nitrogen they need by feeding on plants or on animals that eat plants. When organisms die, decomposers change the nitrogen-containing chemicals in the organisms into ammonia. The ammonia may then be used by plants or may be changed into nitrates by bacteria.

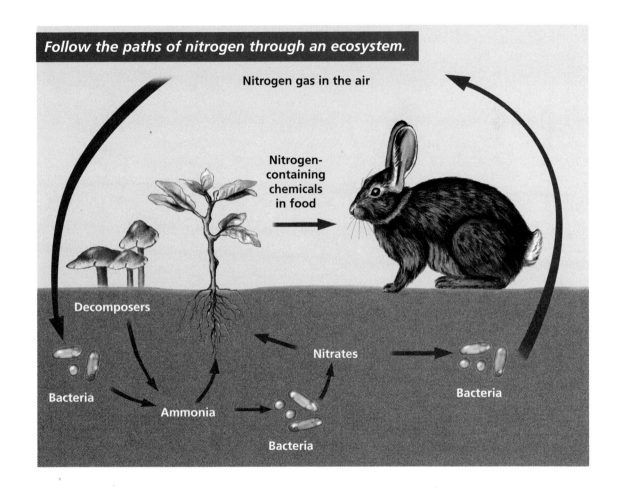

Follow the paths of nitrogen through an ecosystem.

Nitrogen gas in the air

Nitrogen-containing chemicals in food

Decomposers

Bacteria

Ammonia

Bacteria

Nitrates

Bacteria

System of Cycles

The different cycles in an ecosystem are linked to one another. For example, the carbon cycle, oxygen cycle, and water cycle are linked by photosynthesis and cellular respiration. Plants take in carbon dioxide and water for photosynthesis, and release oxygen. Animals, plants, and other organisms use the oxygen for cellular respiration and release carbon dioxide and water.

When plants make nitrogen-containing chemicals from ammonia and nitrates, they use carbon and oxygen. Many other materials cycle through ecosystems. Iron, calcium, phosphorus, and other chemicals used by living organisms are cycled.

Scientists may study one cycle at a time to make it easier to understand the cycle. However, each cycle is only a small part of a system of cycles that interact with one another.

Self-Check

1. Describe how water may move from a plant to a cloud and back to a plant.
2. Why is carbon important to living things?
3. How are photosynthesis and cellular respiration part of the carbon cycle?
4. How are photosynthesis and cellular respiration part of the oxygen cycle?
5. How is nitrogen gas from the air changed into a form that plants can use?

■ A population is a group of organisms of the same species that live in the same area.

■ A community is a group of different populations that live in the same area.

■ Communities may change over time by a process called succession.

■ All the interactions among the populations of a community and the nonliving things in their environment make up an ecosystem. Ecology is the study of these interactions.

■ The feeding order of organisms in an ecosystem is called a food chain. Every food chain begins with producers.

■ All the food chains in an ecosystem that are linked to one another make up a food web.

■ Energy flows through food chains. The amount of available energy decreases at each higher level of a food chain.

■ Materials such as water, carbon, oxygen, and nitrogen cycle through ecosystems.

■ During photosynthesis, organisms take in carbon dioxide and water and release oxygen. During cellular respiration, organisms take in oxygen and release carbon dioxide and water.

■ In the nitrogen cycle, certain bacteria in the soil change nitrogen gas into nitrogen-containing chemicals that plants can use. Other bacteria change nitrogen-containing chemicals back to nitrogen gas.

Science Words		
acid rain, 370	ecosystem, 369	omnivore, 375
biome, 370	energy pyramid, 380	pollution, 370
biosphere, 371	food chain, 374	population, 368
carnivore, 375	food web, 376	producer, 374
climax community, 369	habitat, 368	pyramid of numbers, 375
community, 368	herbivore, 375	resource, 371
consumer, 374	interact, 367	succession, 369
ecology, 367	nitrogen fixation, 384	

Chapter 21 REVIEW

WORD BANK

biomes

biosphere

consumers

ecology

ecosystem

food chains

habitat

herbivores

nitrogen fixation

omnivores

pollution

population

producers

succession

Vocabulary Review

Number your paper from 1 to 14. Then choose the term from the Word Bank that best completes each sentence. Write your answer on your paper.

1. _____ absorb the energy of the sun.

2. The study of how living things interact with one another and with nonliving things in their environment is _____.

3. Consumers that eat both plants and animals are _____.

4. Deserts, grasslands, and oceans are all examples of _____.

5. Anything added to the environment that is harmful to living things is _____.

6. The place where an organism lives is its _____.

7. All the biomes on Earth together form the _____.

8. _____ feed on other organisms.

9. All the _____ in a community that are linked to one another make up a food web.

10. A(n) _____ consists of all the interactions among populations and the nonliving things in their environment.

11. The process by which a community changes over time is called _____.

12. Consumers that eat only plants are _____.

13. All the deer of the same species living in a forest make up a(n) _____.

14. Certain bacteria change nitrogen gas from the air into ammonia by the process of _____.

Concept Review

Number your paper from 1 to 4. Then choose the answer that best completes each sentence. Write the letter of the answer on your paper.

1. More energy is available to second-order consumers in food chains than is available to _____.

   a. first-order consumers   **c.** third-order consumers
   b. producers

2. Photosynthesis and cellular respiration help to cycle _____ through ecosystems.

   a. carbon, oxygen, and water   **c.** nitrogen
   b. only carbon

3. Decomposers feed on _____.

   a. only consumers   **c.** both producers and consumers
   b. only producers

4. Plants store _____ energy in their tissues.

   a. chemical   **b.** heat   **c.** light

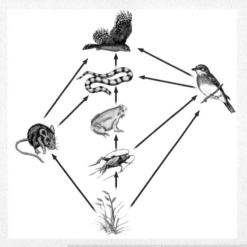

Critical Thinking

Write the answer to each of the following questions.

1. What would Earth be like if there were no decomposers?

2. Identify the producer(s) and the first-order, second-order, and third-order consumers in the food web shown here. Remember that organisms may be part of more than one food chain.

Test Taking Tip When taking a test, first answer all the questions that have short answers. Then divide the remaining time among the questions that require longer answers.

Chapter

22

Heredity and Evolution

Are birds and dinosaurs related? Many scientists believe that the ancient ancestors of today's birds evolved from certain types of dinosaurs. How does evolution happen? Why do new kinds of organisms develop over time? How are characteristics passed from one generation to the next? You will find the answers to those questions in this chapter.

ORGANIZE YOUR THOUGHTS

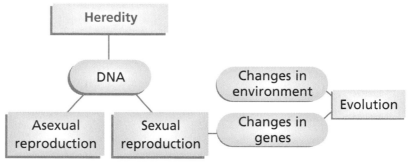

Goals for Learning

▶ To describe the role of DNA in heredity

▶ To compare mitosis and meiosis

▶ To recognize how populations change over time

▶ To explain the theory of natural selection

▶ To give examples of evidence that supports evolution

Chromosome
A rod-shaped structure that contains DNA and is found in the nucleus of a cell.

Gene
The information about a trait that a parent passes to its offspring.

Genetics
The study of heredity.

Heredity
The passing of traits from parents to offspring.

Mutation
A change in a gene.

All organisms pass characteristics, or traits, to their offspring. The passing of traits from parents to offspring is called **heredity**. **Genetics** is the study of heredity.

The nucleus of a cell contains rod-shaped bodies called **chromosomes**. Chromosomes are made of proteins and a chemical called DNA. Sections of DNA make up an organism's **genes**. Genes determine all the traits of an organism. A chromosome may contain hundreds of genes.

Heredity and Environment

You are born with certain genes. That is your heredity. Your genes determine your skin color, eye color, body shape, and other traits. Your family, the air you breathe, and everything else in your surroundings make up your environment. To find out how environment affects a person's characteristics, scientists study identical twins who have been separated since birth. Both twins have the same genes, but they grew up in different environments. Scientists look for differences in the characteristics of the twins. If they find any different characteristics, they know the environment caused those differences.

Food, sunlight, air, and other parts of the environment can affect a person's traits. For example, a person who doesn't have good nutrition may not grow tall, even though he has a gene for tallness. A person who avoids sunlight may not form freckles, even though she has a gene for freckles.

The environment can directly affect a person's genes. For example, X rays and some types of chemicals cause changes in genes. These changes are called **mutations**. Mutations can be harmful to organisms. How do mutations occur? Before you can understand mutations, you need to know more about DNA.

DNA

Recall that DNA in chromosomes is the material that contains an organism's genes. DNA passes the genes from one cell to another during cell division. All the information needed to carry out life activities is in DNA. All the information that makes a duck a duck is in the duck's DNA. All the information that makes you a human is in your DNA.

DNA is a large molecule shaped like a twisted ladder. The rungs of the ladder are made of four different kinds of molecules called **bases**. The order of the bases in a DNA molecule provides a code for all the information that the cell needs to live.

The DNA molecules of different organisms have different orders of bases. The greater the difference between the organisms, the greater the difference in the order of their bases. Thus, the order of bases in a frog's DNA is very different from the order of bases in your DNA. The difference between the order of bases in your DNA and the order in another person's DNA is not as great.

Recall that a gene is a section of a DNA molecule. A gene is made up of a certain order of bases. Different genes have different orders of bases. This difference allows genes to provide different kinds of information. For example, the order of bases in a gene for hair color determines whether the hair will be black, red, or blonde.

An important feature of DNA is that it can **replicate**, or make copies of itself. Every time a cell divides, the new cells receive copies of the DNA molecules. In this way, genetic information is passed on from cell to cell.

A DNA molecule has a twisted-ladder shape.

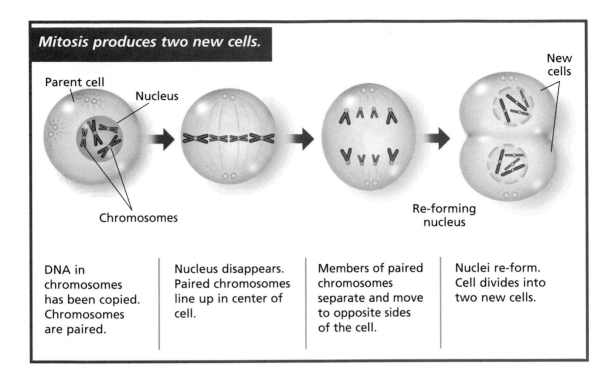

Mitosis produces two new cells.

Parent cell

Nucleus

Chromosomes

Re-forming nucleus

New cells

| DNA in chromosomes has been copied. Chromosomes are paired. | Nucleus disappears. Paired chromosomes line up in center of cell. | Members of paired chromosomes separate and move to opposite sides of the cell. | Nuclei re-form. Cell divides into two new cells. |

Mitosis

The process that results in two cells identical to the parent cell.

Mitosis

In cells that have a nucleus, asexual reproduction occurs in the form of **mitosis**. Before a cell undergoes mitosis, it makes a copy of its DNA. When the DNA is copied, the chromosomes form pairs.

The diagram on this page shows the main steps of mitosis. During mitosis, the nucleus disappears. The pairs of chromosomes line up in the center of the cell. Then, the members of each pair separate and move to opposite ends of the cell. Next, the cell membrane pinches in between the two sets of chromosomes. A nucleus forms around each set. Two identical cells are formed. Each new cell has an exact copy of the chromosomes that were in the parent cell.

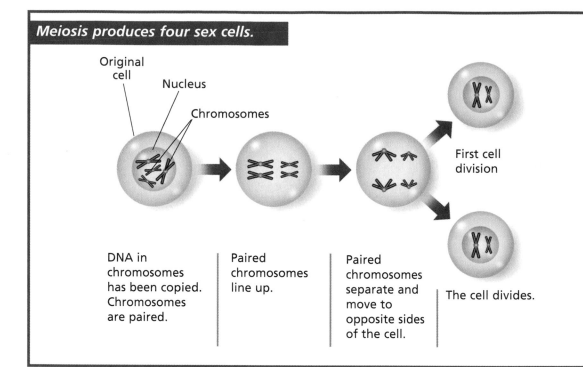

Meiosis produces four sex cells.

Original cell
Nucleus
Chromosomes

First cell division

DNA in chromosomes has been copied. Chromosomes are paired.

Paired chromosomes line up.

Paired chromosomes separate and move to opposite sides of the cell.

The cell divides.

Meiosis

Meiosis
The process that results in sex cells.

Sex cells form by **meiosis**. The diagram on these two pages shows the steps in meiosis. As in mitosis, meiosis begins after the cell's chromosomes have been copied. During meiosis, the nucleus disappears. The pairs of chromosomes line up in the center of the cell and then separate. A nucleus forms around each set of chromosomes. Next, the cell divides into two new cells. Unlike mitosis, each new cell then divides once again. In this way, one original cell produces four sex cells. Each sex cell contains half the number of chromosomes of the original cell. When a male and a female sex cell join in fertilization, the new cell has the full number of chromosomes.

Self-Check

1. What are chromosomes?
2. What is a gene?
3. How is a frog's DNA different from a snake's DNA?
4. What happens during mitosis?
5. What happens during meiosis?

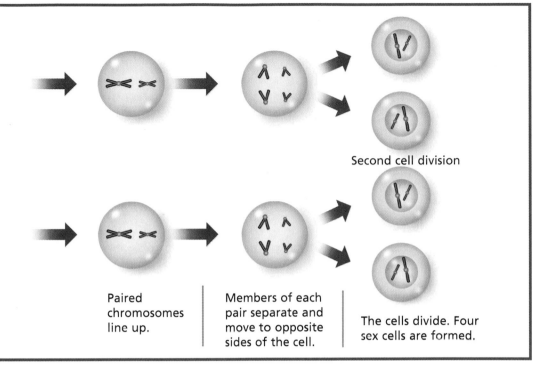

Second cell division

Paired chromosomes line up.

Members of each pair separate and move to opposite sides of the cell.

The cells divide. Four sex cells are formed.

What is genetic engineering?

In the 1970s, scientists began introducing new genes into organisms. This process is called genetic engineering. At first, scientists transferred genes from one species of bacterium to another species of bacterium. Today, scientists are able to transfer genes between entirely different organisms. For example, scientists have transferred human genes into bacteria. The human genes function in the bacteria as they do in human cells. When scientists transferred the gene for human insulin into bacteria, the bacteria produced human insulin. The insulin has been used to treat people with diabetes.

Genetic engineering has also been used to improve crop plants. For example, scientists have transferred bacterial genes into plants to make them resistant to plant diseases and insect pests. Tomatoes have been genetically engineered to ripen more slowly so they stay fresh longer.

Objectives

After reading this lesson, you should be able to

▶ relate genes and mutations to the process of evolution.

▶ describe how a new species can form.

▶ give two types of evidence that support the theory of evolution.

Evolution
The changes in a population over time.

The great variety of organisms today and in the past is the result of a process called **evolution**, or change over time.

Changes in Population

An organism changes as it grows and develops. However, these changes are not evolution. Individual organisms do not evolve. Evolution occurs in a population of organisms over time. As you learned in Chapter 21, a population is made up of individuals of the same species that live in the same place. The process of evolution takes place over many generations in a population.

Changes in Genes

Evolution involves changes in a population's gene pool. As you learned in Lesson 1, X rays and chemicals in the environment can cause genes to change. Genes also change if DNA molecules are copied incorrectly when cells divide.

Not all mutations are passed on to offspring. Only mutations found in sex cells can be passed on to offspring that are produced sexually.

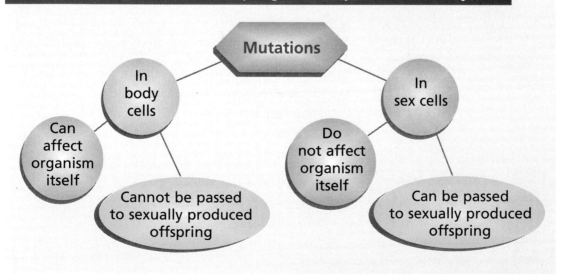

Adaptation
A trait that enables an organism to live in a certain environment.

Recall that a change in a gene is called a mutation. Notice in the diagram that mutations may occur in two different kinds of cells. Some mutations occur in an organism's body cells. These mutations can cause cancers and other changes in the organism. In organisms that reproduce sexually, body-cell mutations are not passed on to the offspring.

Mutations can also occur in an organism's sex cells. If the genes in an organism's sex cells change, these mutations usually do not affect the organism itself. However, the mutations are passed on to the organism's offspring. The mutations can affect the traits of the offspring and of future generations.

Effects of Mutations Over Time

Often, mutations cause harmful changes in traits. Organisms that inherit a harmful mutation usually do not live long enough to reproduce. As a result, the mutation is not passed on to offspring.

Sometimes a mutation results in a trait that improves an organism's chances for survival. An organism that survives is more likely to reproduce. The favorable mutation is then passed on to the offspring. As the mutation is passed on to future generations, it becomes more and more common within the population. Over time, all of the members of the population may have the mutation.

Changes in a Population's Environment

If a population's environment changes, members of the population that have certain traits may be more likely to survive. Traits that enable organisms to survive in certain environments are called **adaptations**.

Organisms that survive and reproduce pass their genes to following generations of the population. In this way, traits that help organisms survive in the environment become more common within the population. Over time, changes in the population's gene pool can produce a new species.

The Theory of Natural Selection

In the mid-1800s, naturalist Charles Darwin developed the theory of natural selection to explain how evolution occurs. The following four points summarize Darwin's theory.

1. Organisms tend to produce more offspring than can survive. For example, fish lay thousands of eggs, but only a few live to be adult fish.

2. Individuals in a population have slight variations. For example, fish in a population may differ slightly in color, length, fin size, or speed.

3. Individuals struggle to survive. Individuals that have variations best suited to the environment are more likely to survive.

4. Survivors pass on their genes to their offspring. Gradually, the population changes.

Evidence of Evolution

If populations really do change over time, then there should be evidence of the change. The fossil record shows recent species that are slightly different from earlier species. This is one type of evidence that supports the theory of evolution.

Other evidence is that the embryos of some kinds of organisms go through similar stages of development. For example, an early human embryo has a tail and gill pouches, just as an early fish embryo has. Similarities in the development of vertebrate embryos are an indication that all vertebrates descended from a common ancestor.

Vestigial structures are another indication that certain organisms are related to one another. A vestigial structure is a body part that appears to be useless to an organism. For example, in humans, there is no known function for the tailbone at the tip of the spine. The tailbone in humans is a vestigial structure. It is thought to be a "leftover" structure that once had an important function in pre-human ancestors who had tails.

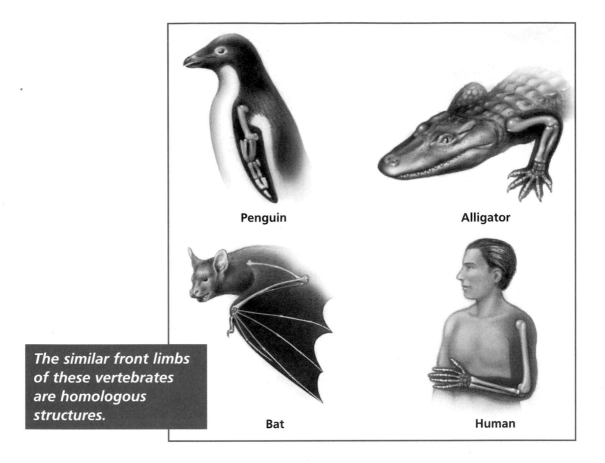

Penguin

Alligator

Bat

Human

The similar front limbs of these vertebrates are homologous structures.

Homologous structures
Body parts that are similar in related organisms.

Look at the front limbs of the vertebrates in the picture. Notice how similar they are. The limbs are **homologous structures**. Homologous structures are body parts that are similar in related organisms. Homologous structures are thought to have first appeared in an ancestor that is common to all the organisms that have the homologous structures. Thus, vertebrates probably share a common ancestor that had front limbs like those you see above.

Self-Check

1. Do individual organisms evolve? Explain your answer.
2. In organisms that reproduce sexually, through what type of cells are mutations passed to offspring?
3. What causes changes in genes?
4. Explain the process of natural selection.
5. Give two types of evidence other than fossils that support the theory of evolution.

Observing a Plant Adaptation

Purpose

To observe an adaptation of plants

Procedure

1. Moisten paper towels so they are damp but not wet.
2. Fill the jar with the damp paper towels.
3. Insert bean seeds between the towels and the side of the jar, as shown in the illustration. Screw the lid on the jar.
4. Put the jar in a warm place out of sunlight. Check the jar every day to see if the seeds have germinated. When they do, draw what you see.
5. Let the plants' stems and roots grow until they are at least 2 cm long. Then turn the jar upside down.
6. Examine the seeds each day for three days. Draw what you see.
7. Turn the jar rightside up again. Repeat step 6.

Questions

1. When the seeds germinated in step 4, how did their stems and roots grow?
2. What did the stems and roots do when you turned the jar upside down?
3. What did the stems and roots do when you turned the jar rightside up again?
4. How does this adaptation help plants survive?

Materials

✓ clear jar with lid
✓ paper towels
✓ water
✓ 3 bean seeds

- Heredity is the passing of traits from parents to their offspring.

- Genes determine all the physical traits of an organism. Genes are located on chromosomes in a cell's nucleus.

- Genes are made of DNA. When organisms reproduce, they pass copies of their DNA to their offspring.

- In cells that have a nucleus, asexual reproduction occurs by mitosis and cell division. Mitosis produces two new cells. Each new cell receives an exact copy of the parent cell's DNA.

- Sexual reproduction occurs by meiosis and cell division. Meiosis produces four sex cells. Each sex cell contains half the number of chromosomes in the parent cell.

- Evolution is change in a population over time.

- Mutations and changes in a population's environment can cause changes in the population's gene pool. Genetic changes may produce new species.

- Darwin's theory of natural selection explains how evolution occurs.

- Scientific evidence of evolution includes fossils, homologous structures, and vestigial structures.

Science Words		
adaptation, 397	homologous structures, 399
base, 392	meiosis, 394
chromosome, 391	mitosis, 393
evolution, 396	mutation, 391
gene, 391	replicate, 392
genetics, 391	vestigial structure, 398
heredity, 391	

WORD BANK

adaptations

chromosomes

evolution

gene

heredity

homologous
    structures

meiosis

mitosis

mutations

vestigial
    structures

Vocabulary Review

Number your paper from 1 to 10. Then choose the term from the Word Bank that best completes each sentence. Write the answer on your paper.

1. The process of _____ produces four sex cells.

2. The passing of traits from parents to offspring is _____.

3. _____ are body parts that appear to be useless to organisms but were probably useful to their ancestors.

4. _____ is changes in a population over time.

5. Traits that enable an organism to survive in a certain environment are _____.

6. A(n) _____ is a section of a DNA molecule.

7. Changes in an organism's DNA are _____.

8. DNA is found in structures called _____.

9. Body parts that are similar in related organisms are called _____.

10. The process of _____ produces two new cells exactly like the parent cell.

Concept Review

Number your paper from 1 to 8. Then choose the answer that best completes each sentence. Write the letter of the answer on your paper.

1. Darwin's theory of _____ explains how evolution occurs.

   a. heredity   b. genetics   c. natural selection

2. After _____, each new cell has the same number of chromosomes as the parent cell.

   a. meiosis   b. mitosis   c. reproduction

3. Offspring resemble their parents because they have copies of their parents' _____.

   a. DNA   b. sex cells   c. body cells

4. _____ can cause either harmful or helpful changes in traits.

   a. genetics   b. adaptations   c. mutations

5. Evolution occurs in the gene pool of a(n) _____.

   a. individual   b. population   c. cell

6. The similar front limbs of vertebrates is an example of _____.

   a. homologous structures   c. a scientific theory

   b. vestigial structures

7. The rod-shaped structures in a cell's nucleus that contain DNA are called _____.

   a. genes   b. chromosomes   c. mutations

8. A _____ is a large molecule shaped like a twisted ladder.

   a. gene   b. chromosome   c. DNA molecule

Critical Thinking

Write the answer to each of the following questions.

1. What is the name of the process shown in the diagram? What happens during this process?

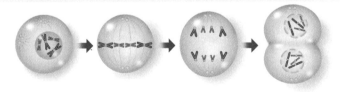

2. Suppose a mouse loses its tail in a mousetrap. Will the mouse's offspring be born without tails? Explain your answer.

Test Taking Tip | Answer all questions you are sure of first. Then go back and answer the others.

Observing the Function of Stomata

Purpose

To observe one function of stomata on a plant's leaves

Procedure

1. Copy the data table below on a sheet of paper. Add rows as needed for recording your observations.

Time	Observation

2. Put a clear plastic bag over the entire plant. Do *not* cover the plant's pot.

3. Tape the bag closed around the bottom of the plant's stem, just above the soil.

4. Water the plant so the soil is damp but not wet.

5. Put the plant in a sunny place.

6. Examine the plastic bag every half hour. Record your observations in the data table.

Questions

1. What material did you see when you examined the plastic bag in step 6?

2. How did that material get into the bag?

Explore Further

Repeat, coating the top of one leaf with petroleum jelly. Coat the bottom of another leaf with petroleum jelly. Cover each leaf with a small plastic bag. Tape the bag closed around the leaf's petiole—the part of the leaf that attaches it to a stem. What happens?

Materials

✓ plant with large, flat leaves

✓ clear plastic bag large enough to cover the plant

✓ tape

- All organisms are made of cells. Cells are organized into tissues. Tissues are organized into organs.

- Organisms need certain chemicals to survive and carry on their basic life functions.

- Biologists classify organisms into five kingdoms: plants, animals, protists, fungi, and monerans. Within each kingdom, organisms are classified by phylum, class, order, family, genus, and species. Every organism has a scientific name consisting of its genus and its species label.

- Vertebrates are animals with a backbone. Invertebrates are animals without a backbone.

- Animals take in oxygen and release carbon dioxide during respiration. Plants take in carbon dioxide and release oxygen during photosynthesis.

- Plants are classified according to whether they have body parts such as seeds, vascular tissue, roots, stems, and leaves.

- Both animals and plants can reproduce by sexual reproduction, which involves two parents, sperm, and an egg. Many plants and some simple animals can also reproduce by asexual reproduction, which involves only one parent.

- The feeding order of organisms in an ecosystem is called a food chain. Every food chain starts with producers. All the food chains in an ecosystem together form a food web.

- Energy flows through food chains. The amount of available energy decreases at each higher level of a food chain.

- Materials such as water, carbon, oxygen, and nitrogen cycle through ecosystems.

- Heredity is the passing of traits from parents to their offspring. When organisms reproduce, they pass copies of their DNA to their offspring.

- Evolution is change in a population over time.

- Mutations and changes in a population's environment can cause changes in the population's gene pool. Genetic changes may produce new species.

Vocabulary Review

Number your paper from 1 to 8. Match each word in Column A with the correct definition in Column B. Write the letter of the definition on your paper.

Column A

_____ 1. tissue

_____ 2. mutation

_____ 3. kingdom

_____ 4. population

_____ 5. photosynthesis

_____ 6. reproduction

_____ 7. consumer

_____ 8. invertebrate

Column B

a. the process by which organisms produce offspring

b. one of five major groups for classifying organisms

c. an animal without a backbone

d. the process in which plants make their own food

e. a group of similar cells that work together

f. an organism that feeds on other organisms

g. a change in an organism's DNA

h. a group of organisms of the same species that live in the same area

Concept Review

Complete the diagram below to show how organisms are organized into levels. Write the answers on your paper.

Organism → 1. ___ → 2. ___ → 3. ___ → Biosphere

Number your paper from 4 to 10. Then choose the answer that best completes each sentence. Write the letter of your answer on your paper.

4. Plants use carbon dioxide, water, and energy from the sun to make _____.

    a. vitamins   b. minerals   c. carbohydrates

5. The genus of the gray wolf, *Canis lupus*, is _____.

    a. gray   b. *Canis*   c. *lupus*

6. Water vapor, carbon dioxide, and oxygen enter and leave a plant through the _____.

    a. vascular tissue b. stomata   c. rhizoids

7. After _____, each new cell has half the number of chromosomes as the parent cell.

    a. meiosis   b. mitosis   c. metamorphosis

8. Snakes, reptiles, and alligators are examples of _____.

    a. protists   b. amphibians   c. reptiles

9. Reproduction that involves only one parent is _____.

    a. asexual reproduction   c. fertilization

    b. sexual reproduction

10. The process by which a community changes over time is called _____.

    a.   evolution   b. succession   c. mutation

Critical Thinking

Write the answer to each of the following questions.

1. Suppose a biologist discovers a new vertebrate animal. It has gills when it is young and lungs when it is an adult. In which class of vertebrates should the animal be classified? Where does the animal live when it is young? Where does it live when it is an adult? How can you tell?

2. What type of molecule is shown in the diagram to the left? Explain how this molecule passes traits from parents to offspring.

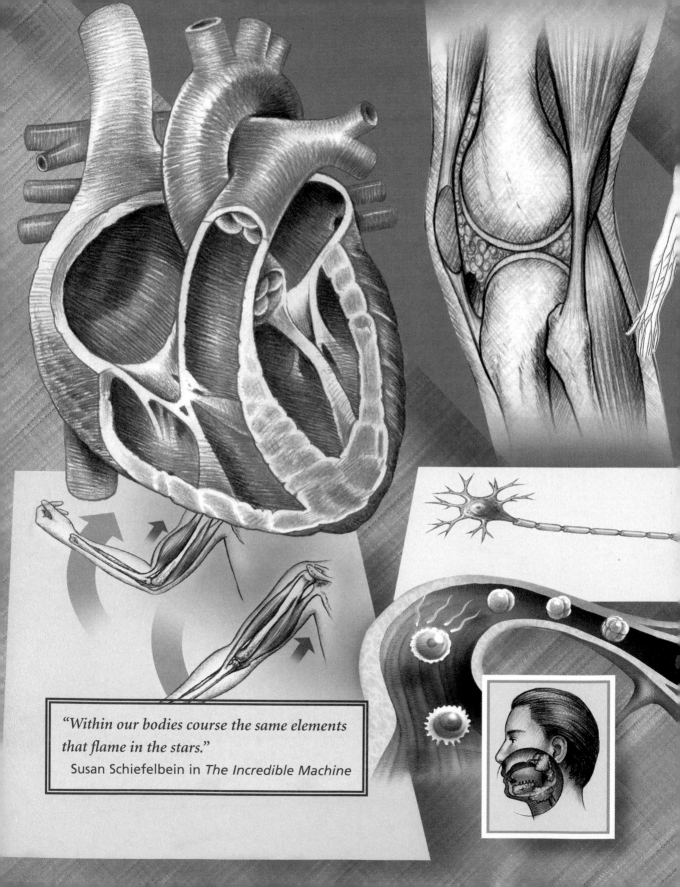

"Within our bodies course the same elements that flame in the stars."

Susan Schiefelbein in *The Incredible Machine*

The Human Body

Unit 4

*I*f someone asked you to name the most amazing machine, what would your answer be? Suppose you got some hints. This machine has a strong, yet light, frame. It can move from place to place. If it gets a scratch, it fixes itself in a day or two. The machine carries food to its working parts. It lasts an average of 75 years. It produces more machines like itself. It has many systems that work together. You have probably figured out already that the most amazing "machine" is the human body—you.

Chapters in Unit 4

Chapter 23: Meeting the Body's Basic Needs . . .410

Chapter 24: The Body's Control Systems 440

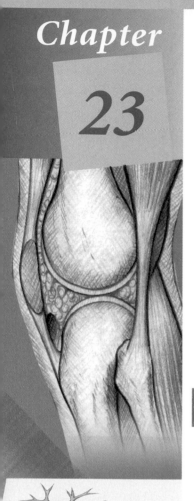

Meeting the Body's Basic Needs

All of your body systems work together to maintain your good health. In this chapter, you will learn about the body systems that carry out basic life activities. First, you will learn about the skeletal and muscular systems, the digestive system, and the circulatory system. Then you will learn how the respiratory system works, and how the body gets rid of wastes and how human reproductive systems work.

ORGANIZE YOUR THOUGHTS

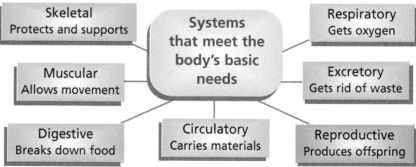

Skeletal
Protects and supports

Muscular
Allows movement

Digestive
Breaks down food

Systems that meet the body's basic needs

Circulatory
Carries materials

Respiratory
Gets oxygen

Excretory
Gets rid of waste

Reproductive
Produces offspring

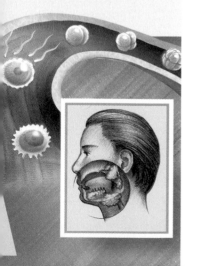

Goals for Learning

▶ To identify the seven body systems that carry out basic life activities

▶ To describe the structure and function of each body system

▶ To recognize that body systems work together to carry out basic life activities

Objectives

After reading this lesson, you should be able to

▶ identify five functions of bones.

▶ explain how bones and muscles work together to produce movement.

▶ describe the three different kinds of muscles.

Red marrow
The spongy material in bones that makes blood cells.

The Skeletal System

The 206 bones of the human body make up the skeletal system. Bones have several functions. First, bones support the body. They give the body a shape. Bones form a framework that supports the softer tissues of the body. Second, bones protect organs. For example, the rib cage protects the heart and lungs. Vertebrae protect the spinal cord. Vertebrae are the 33 bones that make up the backbone, or spinal column. The pelvis protects reproductive organs. Find these bones in the drawing on the next page.

A third function of bones is to produce movement. Muscles attach to bones and move them. The body has long bones, short bones, flat bones, and bones that have irregular shapes. The variety of bones helps a person move in different ways. Fourth, bones are the place where blood cells are formed. Some bones contain spongy material called **red marrow**. Red marrow has special cells that make blood cells. Finally, bones store minerals such as calcium, phosphorous, and magnesium.

Most bones start as cartilage. Cartilage is not as hard as bone but is more flexible. Before birth, the entire skeleton is cartilage. Most of the cartilage is gradually replaced with bone. A newborn baby has more than 300 bones. Over time, some of the bones join, so an adult has only 206 bones. Some parts of the body continue to have cartilage. Feel the end of your nose. It is made of cartilage. Your outer ear also contains cartilage.

How Bones Change

Bones are living organs that are made of tissue. Your bones are built up and broken down throughout your life. For example, when the body needs calcium, chemicals break down bone tissue. The calcium is released into the bloodstream.

The Skeletal System

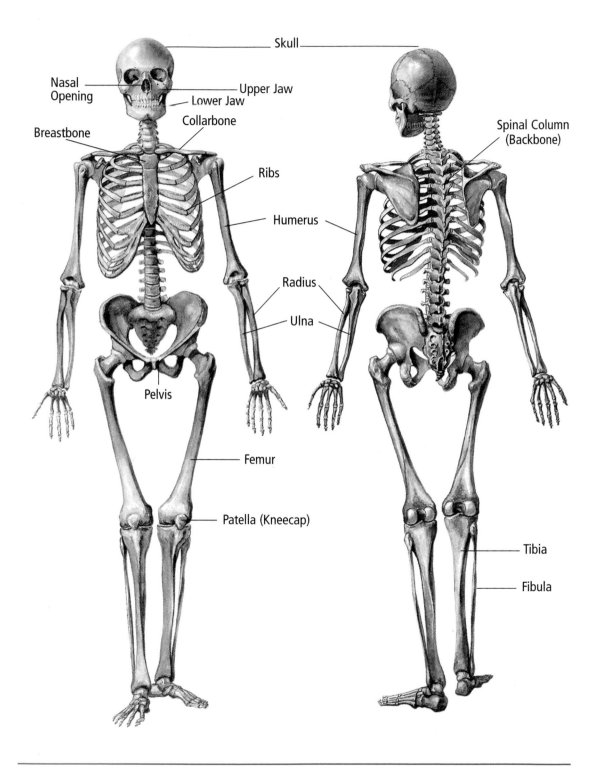

Skull

Nasal Opening

Upper Jaw

Lower Jaw

Collarbone

Breastbone

Ribs

Humerus

Radius

Ulna

Pelvis

Femur

Patella (Kneecap)

Spinal Column (Backbone)

Tibia

Fibula

Joints

Bones come together at joints. Cartilage covers the ends of the bones at a joint. This cartilage acts like a cushion. It protects the bones from rubbing against each other. At a movable joint, such as the knee or shoulder, strips of strong tissue called **ligaments** connect the bones to each other.

There are several kinds of joints. A ball-and-socket joint allows the greatest range of motion. This type of joint is located at the hips and shoulders. It allows you to move your arms and legs forward, backward, side to side, and in a circular motion. Some joints, such as your rib and spine joints, can move only a little. A few joints, such as those in your skull, do not move at all.

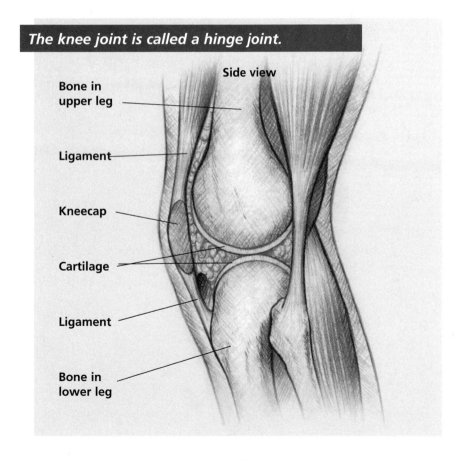

The knee joint is called a hinge joint.

Side view

Bone in upper leg

Ligament

Kneecap

Cartilage

Ligament

Bone in lower leg

Tendon

*A tough strip of
tissue that connects a
muscle to a bone.*

The Muscular System

The muscular system consists of more than 600 muscles. Some of those muscles are shown on the next page. The skeletal and muscular systems work together to produce movement. Tough strips of tissue called **tendons** attach muscles to bones.

Most muscles work in pairs. When a muscle contracts, or shortens, it pulls on the tendon. The tendon pulls on the attached bone, and the bone moves. A muscle cannot push. Therefore, a different muscle on the opposite side of the bone contracts to return the bone to its starting position. The drawing below shows an example of muscles working in pairs to bend and straighten your arm.

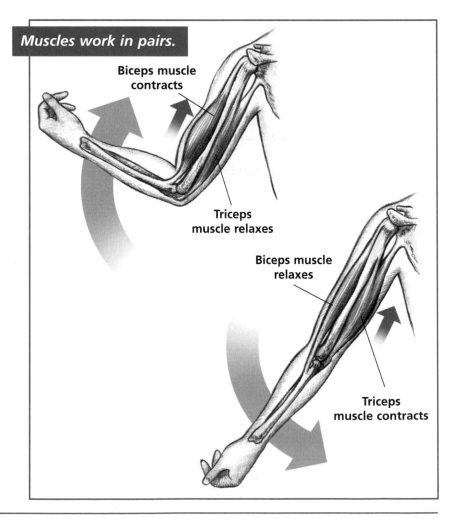

Muscles work in pairs.

Biceps muscle
contracts

Triceps
muscle relaxes

Biceps muscle
relaxes

Triceps
muscle contracts

The Muscular System

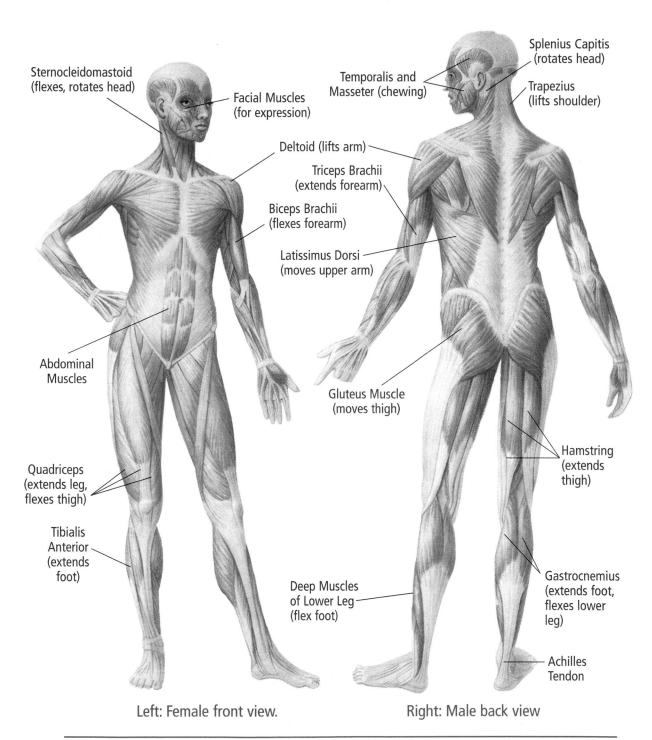

Sternocleidomastoid
(flexes, rotates head)

Facial Muscles
(for expression)

Deltoid (lifts arm)

Biceps Brachii
(flexes forearm)

Abdominal
Muscles

Quadriceps
(extends leg,
flexes thigh)

Tibialis
Anterior
(extends
foot)

Deep Muscles
of Lower Leg
(flex foot)

Temporalis and
Masseter (chewing)

Splenius Capitis
(rotates head)

Trapezius
(lifts shoulder)

Triceps Brachii
(extends forearm)

Latissimus Dorsi
(moves upper arm)

Gluteus Muscle
(moves thigh)

Hamstring
(extends
thigh)

Gastrocnemius
(extends foot,
flexes lower
leg)

Achilles
Tendon

Left: Female front view.

Right: Male back view

Kinds of Muscle Tissue

The body has three kinds of muscle tissue—skeletal muscle, smooth muscle, and cardiac muscle. Skeletal muscles are attached to bones. Skeletal muscles are **voluntary muscles**. That is, you can choose when to use them. The muscles in your arms, legs, and face are voluntary.

The second kind of muscle tissue is smooth muscle. These muscles form layers lining the walls of organs. Smooth muscles are found in the stomach and intestines. These muscles contract in wavelike actions to move food through the digestive system. The walls of the blood vessels also are lined with smooth muscles. These muscles contract and relax to maintain blood pressure. Smooth muscles are **involuntary muscles**. You cannot choose when to use them. They react to changes in the body.

The third kind of muscle tissue is cardiac muscle. These muscles make up the heart. They contract regularly to pump blood throughout your body. Cardiac muscles are also involuntary muscles.

Self-Check

1. What are five functions of bones?
2. How does bone change during a person's lifetime?
3. What is the difference between a ligament and a tendon?
4. How do muscles make bones move?
5. What are the three kinds of muscle tissue?

How Do Body Cells Get Energy From Food?

The Digestive System

Your digestive system breaks down food for your body to use. Food contains energy for your body's cells. However, food particles are too large to enter cells. The food must be broken down into molecules. Digestion breaks down carbohydrates, proteins, and fats into a form that your cells can use for energy. As you read about digestion, refer to the drawing of the digestive system below.

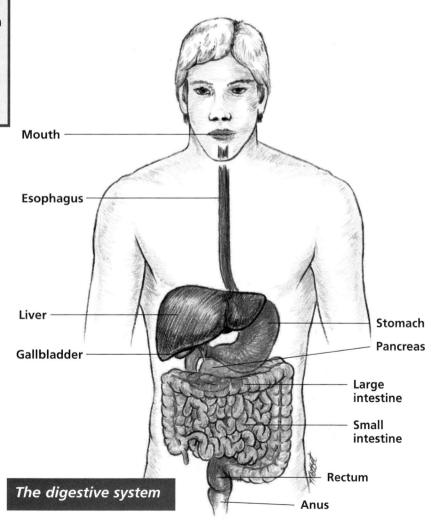

Mouth

Esophagus

Liver

Gallbladder

Stomach

Pancreas

Large intestine

Small intestine

Rectum

Anus

The digestive system

Digestion Begins in the Mouth

Your teeth and jaws chew and crush food while your tongue turns it over. This mechanical action makes pieces of food smaller. As you chew, salivary glands secrete saliva, a fluid that has a digestive **enzyme**. An enzyme is a protein that speeds up chemical changes. Digestive enzymes help break down food. Each part of the digestive system has its own special digestive enzymes. In the mouth, the enzyme in saliva changes carbohydrates into sugars as you chew.

The Esophagus

When you swallow, food moves into your **esophagus**. This long tube connects the mouth to the stomach. Smooth muscles in the esophagus contract to push food toward the stomach. This action is called **peristalsis**.

The Stomach

Digestion continues in the stomach. Strong muscles of the stomach walls contract. This action churns and mixes the food. The stomach walls secrete digestive juices. These juices are hydrochloric acid and digestive enzymes. The acid and enzymes break down large molecules of food. Solid food becomes a thick liquid called chyme. A mucous lining protects the stomach from being eaten away by the acid.

The Small Intestine

Peristalsis moves chyme from the stomach into the small intestine. The small intestine is a coiled tube about 4 to 7 meters long. This is where most digestion takes place.

The liver, the gallbladder, and the pancreas aid digestion. The liver makes a fluid called bile. Bile breaks apart fat molecules. The gallbladder stores the bile. The bile enters the small intestine through a tube called a bile duct. The pancreas produces enzymes that complete the digestion of carbohydrates, proteins, and fats.

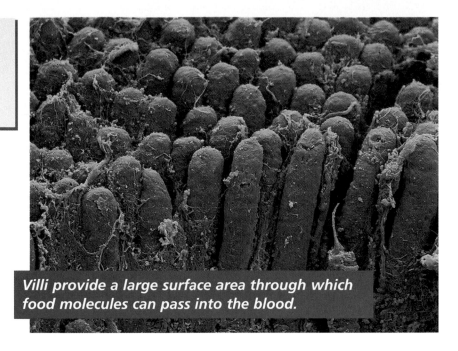

Villi provide a large surface area through which food molecules can pass into the blood.

Food molecules are absorbed into the bloodstream through tiny, fingerlike structures called **villi**. Thousands of villi line the small intestine. The blood carries the food molecules to cells throughout the body.

The Large Intestine

Undigested material moves into the large intestine. The main function of the large intestine is to remove water from undigested material. The water is returned to the body. The undigested material, called feces, is stored in the rectum for a short time and then leaves the body through an opening called the anus.

Self-Check

1. What does the digestive system do?
2. Where and how does digestion begin?
3. Describe the path of food through the digestive system.
4. What does the pancreas do?
5. What is the main function of the large intestine?

23 INVESTIGATION

Reading Food Labels

Materials

- ✓ paper and pencil
- ✓ 8 food labels

Purpose

To determine the kinds and amounts of nutrients in different packaged foods

Procedure

1. Collect food labels from eight different packaged foods. You might choose different kinds of the same food, such as different brands of cereal. That way, you can compare different brands.
2. Copy the table below on your paper.

Food	Serving size	Carbohydrates (in grams)	Proteins (in grams)	Fats (in grams)	Vitamins and minerals (percentage)
1.					
2.					
3.					
4.					
5.					
6.					
7.					
8.					

3. Choose a food label. Write the name of the packaged food in your table.

4. Look for the size of one serving of that food. Write this information in your table.

5. Look for the kinds and amounts of carbohydrates, proteins, and fats in one serving. Notice that the amounts are given in grams and in percentages. In your table, write the number of grams of each nutrient found in one serving.

6. Are any vitamins or minerals in the food? Add to your table the names and percentages of any vitamins and minerals listed on the food label.

7. Repeat steps 3–6 for each food label you collected.

Questions

1. Compare the data in your table. Which food has the most carbohydrates?

2. Which food has the most proteins?

3. Which food has the most fats?

4. Which food has the most vitamins and minerals?

5. Compare the serving sizes of the foods. Which food has the smallest serving size? Which has the largest serving size?

Explore Further

1. Look at all the data you collected. Which food do you think is the healthiest? Give reasons for your choice.

2. Does the information in your table change your ideas about eating certain foods? Why or why not?

How Do Materials Move to and From Cells?

Objectives

After reading this lesson, you should be able to

▶ identify organs in the circulatory system and describe their functions.

▶ tell how arteries and veins are alike and different.

▶ trace the flow of blood through the heart.

▶ identify the parts of blood and describe their functions.

The Circulatory System

Body cells must have a way to get oxygen and nutrients. They must get rid of wastes. The circulatory system performs these functions. As you can see from the pictures on the next page, the circulatory system consists of the heart and blood vessels. The heart pumps blood throughout the body through blood vessels. Blood carries food and oxygen to all the body cells. Blood also carries away wastes from the body cells.

The Heart

The main organ of the circulatory system is the heart. In an adult, the heart is about the size of a human fist. The heart is made mostly of cardiac muscle. The heart contracts and relaxes in a regular rhythm known as the heartbeat.

The heart beats about 70 times a minute in adults who are sitting or standing quietly. The heart beats faster in children and teenagers. The heart beats even faster when a person runs, swims, or does other physical activities. Each time the heart contracts, it pushes a wave of blood out of itself and into blood vessels. You can feel these waves at your wrist and on the side of your neck as the pulse.

Hold two or three fingers of one hand on the thumb-side of your other wrist. You can count the number of times your heart beats each minute.

How Blood Circulates

Look at the picture of the heart below. Notice that it has two sides, left and right. Each side has an upper chamber called the atrium and a lower chamber called the ventricle. Use your finger to trace over the picture as you read how blood moves through the heart.

The right atrium receives blood from the rest of the body. The blood is low in oxygen and high in carbon dioxide. The right atrium pumps the blood into the right ventricle. The right ventricle pumps the blood to the lungs. In the lungs, the blood absorbs oxygen and releases carbon dioxide. From the lungs, blood that is high in oxygen goes back to the heart. It enters the left atrium and is pumped to the left ventricle. The left ventricle is a thick, powerful muscle. It sends the blood surging out through a large vessel called the aorta. From there, the blood then travels to the rest of the body.

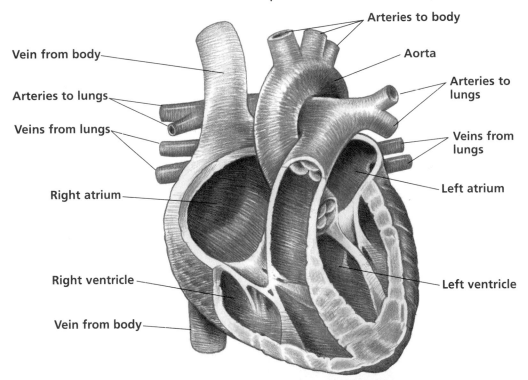

The heart moves blood between the heart and the lungs and between the heart and the rest of the body.

The Circulatory System

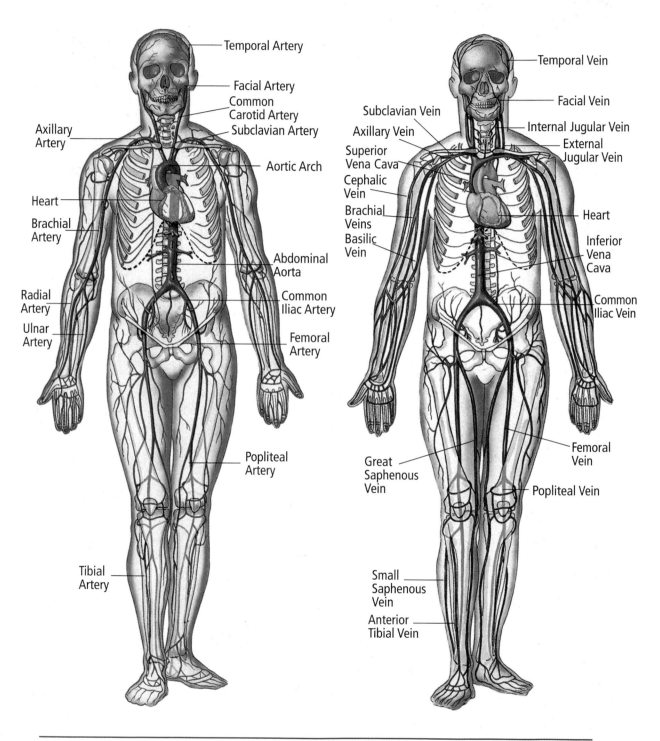

Temporal Artery

Facial Artery

Common Carotid Artery

Subclavian Artery

Axillary Artery

Aortic Arch

Heart

Brachial Artery

Abdominal Aorta

Radial Artery

Common Iliac Artery

Ulnar Artery

Femoral Artery

Popliteal Artery

Tibial Artery

Subclavian Vein

Axillary Vein

Superior Vena Cava

Cephalic Vein

Brachial Veins

Basilic Vein

Temporal Vein

Facial Vein

Internal Jugular Vein

External Jugular Vein

Heart

Inferior Vena Cava

Common Iliac Vein

Femoral Vein

Great Saphenous Vein

Popliteal Vein

Small Saphenous Vein

Anterior Tibial Vein

Blood Vessels

Blood circulates in two loops. In one loop, blood travels from the heart to the lungs and then back to the heart. In the other loop, blood travels from the heart to cells throughout the body and then back to the heart.

Blood vessels that carry blood away from the heart are called **arteries**. Arteries become smaller and smaller farther away from the heart. The smallest arteries branch into tiny blood vessels called **capillaries**. The walls of the capillaries are only one cell thick. Oxygen and food molecules pass easily through the capillary walls and into cells. Carbon dioxide and other wastes move from the cells into the capillaries.

Capillaries join to form small veins. **Veins** are blood vessels that carry blood to the heart. Veins become larger and larger closer to the heart. They have one-way valves that keep the blood from flowing backward.

Did You Know?

If all of your blood vessels could be lined up end to end, they would measure about 96,000 km. That is more than twice around the world!

Blood Pressure

Blood pressure is the push of blood against the walls of blood vessels. When your heart beats, blood is pushed into the arteries. This forces the artery walls to bulge for a moment. Blood pressure is highest in arteries and much lower in veins. If blood vessels become clogged, blood pressure rises. If blood pressure is too high, the heart can be damaged.

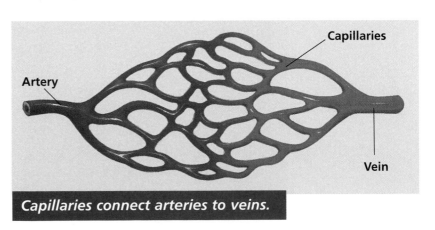

Artery

Capillaries

Vein

Capillaries connect arteries to veins.

Blood and Its Parts

Antibody
A protein in plasma that fights disease.

Hemoglobin
A substance in red blood cells that carries oxygen.

Plasma
The liquid part of blood.

Blood consists of a liquid part and three kinds of cells. The liquid part of blood is called **plasma**. Plasma is mostly water. It contains dissolved substances, including carbon dioxide, food molecules, minerals, and vitamins. Plasma also contains proteins called **antibodies**. Antibodies fight harmful viruses, bacteria, and other microorganisms.

Red blood cells make up almost half of the blood. These cells are filled with **hemoglobin**, which carries oxygen. Oxygen plus hemoglobin gives blood its bright red color.

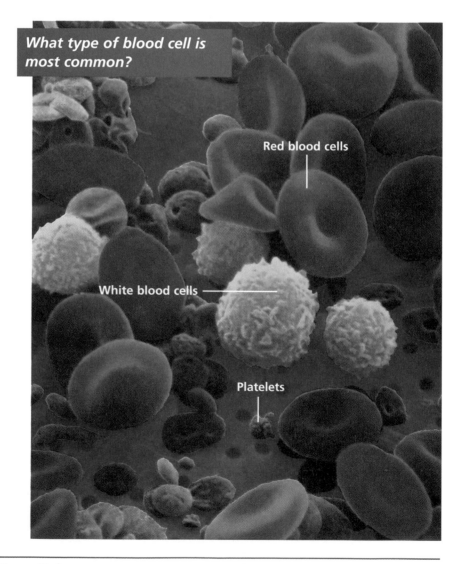

What type of blood cell is most common?

Red blood cells

White blood cells

Platelets

White blood cells are larger than red blood cells. However, they are fewer. There is only about one white blood cell for every 700 red blood cells. Like antibodies, white blood cells protect the body against foreign substances. White blood cells move through the walls of capillaries to where they are needed. Some wrap themselves around invaders and trap them. Others make chemicals that kill harmful bacteria and viruses. Some white blood cells work with antibodies to destroy invaders. One kind of white blood cell makes antibodies.

Platelets are tiny cells that help blood clot to stop bleeding. Platelets do not have a regular shape. Platelets collect at the place where a blood vessel is cut. They stick to each other and to the broken blood vessel. Red blood cells stick to the platelets. This mass of platelets and red blood cells forms a clot that stops the bleeding.

Blood Types

People have one of four blood types. These are type A, type B, type AB, and type O. Different blood types are caused by different proteins in the red blood cells. Sometimes people who are injured or who have certain illnesses need blood. They may receive a blood transfusion to replace lost blood. Before a transfusion, health care workers must identify the patient's blood type. If the wrong blood type is given, the person's blood clumps. This blocks the tiny capillaries. Oxygen does not get to cells. Without oxygen, cells die.

Self-Check

1. What are the two main parts of the circulatory system?
2. What is the difference between arteries and veins?
3. What does blood do?
4. What are the functions of red blood cells, white blood cells, and platelets?
5. Why is it important to know your blood type?

How Does the Body Exchange Oxygen and Carbon Dioxide?

Objectives

After reading this lesson, you should be able to

▶ identify the organs in the respiratory system and describe their functions.

▶ describe the process of gas exchange in the lungs.

▶ explain how the diaphragm moves when a person breathes.

Alveolus
A tiny air sac where gas exchange occurs. Plural is alveoli.

Bronchus
A tube that connects the trachea and lungs. Plural is bronchi.

Trachea
The tube that carries air to the bronchi.

The Respiratory System

The function of the respiratory system is to bring oxygen into the body and get rid of carbon dioxide. Your lungs expose your body to the outside air. The circulatory system then carries the oxygen from your lungs to the rest of your body. You have two lungs. One is in the right side of your chest, and one is in the left side.

How Air Moves into the Lungs

Look at the picture on the next page. Air comes into your body through your nose and mouth. It travels through the pharynx. Air and food share this passageway. From the pharynx, the air moves through the larynx, or voice box. A flap of tissue covers the larynx when you swallow. This flap prevents food from going into your airways. From the larynx, air moves into a large tube called the **trachea**, or windpipe. The trachea branches into two smaller tubes called **bronchi**. One bronchus goes to each lung. In the lungs, each bronchus branches into smaller and smaller tubes. The smallest tubes are called bronchioles.

Gas Exchange in the Lungs

At the end of each bronchiole are tiny air sacs called **alveoli**. They are so small that you need a microscope to see them. The walls of alveoli are only one cell thick. Tiny capillaries wrap around the alveoli.

Recall that blood returning to the heart from the rest of the body is full of carbon dioxide. The right ventricle pumps this blood through an artery to the lungs. There, carbon dioxide passes out of the capillaries and into the alveoli. The carbon dioxide leaves the body when you exhale, or breathe out.

When you inhale, or breathe in, oxygen comes into the lungs and enters the alveoli. The oxygen moves through the walls of the alveoli and into the capillaries. Veins carry oxygen-rich blood to the heart to be pumped to the rest of your body.

Breathing

When you are at rest, you usually breathe about 12 times a minute. With each breath, the lungs stretch and you take in about half a liter of air. A strong muscle below your lungs helps you breathe. This muscle is called the **diaphragm**. It separates the lung cavity from the abdominal cavity.

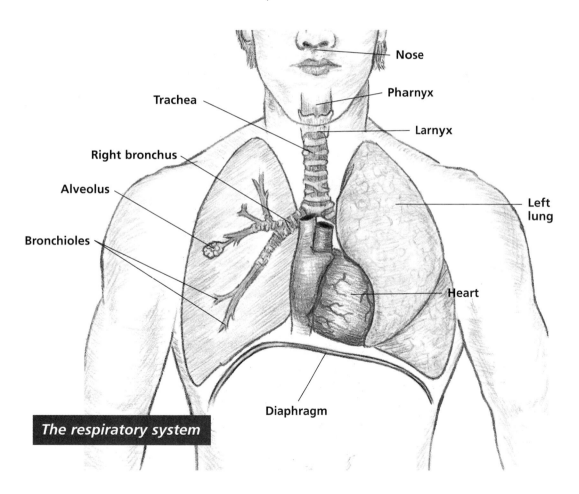

Nose

Pharnyx

Trachea

Larnyx

Right bronchus

Alveolus

Left lung

Bronchioles

Heart

Diaphragm

The respiratory system

Breathing happens because the pressure inside the chest cavity changes. When the diaphragm contracts it moves down. At the same time, the ribs move upward. These movements increase the volume of the chest cavity. Air is inhaled to fill this larger volume. When the diaphragm relaxes, it moves up. The ribs move downward. These movements reduce the volume of the chest cavity. Air is forced out of the lungs.

Self-Check

1. What is the function of the respiratory system?
2. Describe the path of air from the nose to the alveoli.
3. Why doesn't food enter your larynx when you swallow?
4. Where and how does gas exchange take place?
5. How does the diaphragm help you breathe?

SCIENCE IN YOUR LIFE

Cardiopulmonary resuscitation (CPR)

Every day in the United States, about 700 people experience cardiac arrest. This means that the heart stops beating and there is no pulse. Cardiac arrest may occur because of heart disease, electrical shock, poisoning, a drug overdose, drowning, or choking. The circulatory system stops working. Without oxygen, organs begin to shut down. The respiratory system begins to fail. A person can die within minutes if these systems are not working.

A procedure called cardiopulmonary resuscitation (CPR) can fill in temporarily for the heart and lungs. A person performing CPR provides oxygen to the victim until emergency help arrives. In CPR, a person uses rescue breathing and chest compressions.

CPR saves thousands of lives each year in the United States. However, CPR should be performed only by a person who is trained to use it. Find out where you can get CPR training in your community. Call the American Heart Association, the American Red Cross, a fire department, a hospital, a park district, or a library.

Objectives

After reading this lesson, you should be able to

► explain how perspiration gets rid of body wastes.

► describe the function of kidneys.

► explain how urine leaves the body.

Perspiration
Liquid waste released through the skin.

Did You Know?

Perspiration by itself does not have an odor. Body odor occurs when bacteria living on the skin break down the wastes in perspiration.

You know that when you exhale, you get rid of carbon dioxide. Carbon dioxide is one of the wastes that cells produce when they use oxygen to release energy from food. Other body wastes include water, salts, and nitrogen. Some of the extra water is released as water vapor in your breath when you exhale.

The Skin

Many wastes leave your body through its largest organ, the skin. Your blood carries water and salts to sweat glands in your skin. These wastes form a salty liquid called **perspiration**. Thousands of sweat glands in the skin release perspiration through pores onto the skin's surface. Perspiration cools your body as the water evaporates from the skin.

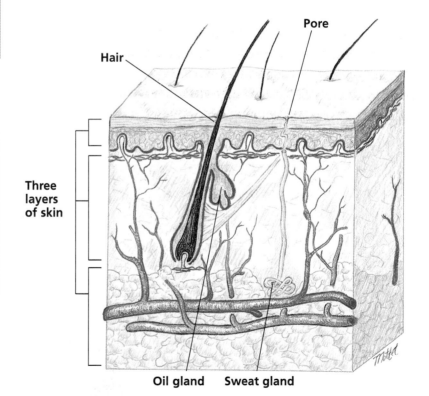

Hair · Pore · Three layers of skin · Oil gland · Sweat gland

One function of the skin is to release wastes.

Kidney
The organ in the excretory system where urine forms.

Ureter
A tube that carries urine from a kidney to the urinary bladder.

Urethra
The tube that carries urine out of the body.

The Excretory System

Your cells produce nitrogen wastes, which are poisonous. The excretory system gets rid of these wastes. The **kidneys** are the main organs of the excretory system. The body has two kidneys, located in the lower back. Kidneys filter nitrogen wastes out of the blood. The kidneys also remove some extra water and salts from the blood.

The filtered wastes form a liquid called urine. Tubes called **ureters** carry urine from the kidneys. The urine collects in the urinary bladder. This muscular bag stretches as it fills. When the urinary bladder is almost full, you feel the need to urinate. When you do, the urinary bladder squeezes urine out of your body through a tube called the **urethra**. Follow the path of urine through the excretory system in the drawing.

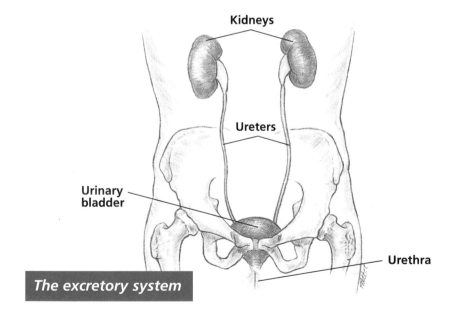

The excretory system

Self-Check

1. List three wastes that your cells produce.
2. What is perspiration?
3. What is the function of kidneys?
4. What is urine made of?
5. Describe how urine travels through the excretory system.

How Do Humans Reproduce?

Objectives

After reading this lesson, you should be able to

- identify the organs in the male and female reproductive systems and describe their functions.
- describe how fertilization occurs and how an embryo develops.

Like other mammals, humans reproduce sexually. A male parent and a female parent together produce a fertilized egg that develops inside the female's body.

The Male Reproductive System

The diagram below shows the main reproductive organs of a human male. The **testes** produce sperm cells. The testes lie outside the body in a sac called the **scrotum**. Because the scrotum is outside the body, it is about 2°C cooler than the rest of the body. Sperm cells are sensitive to heat. The lower temperature of the scrotum helps the sperm survive.

The organs of the male reproductive system

Urinary bladder
Prostate gland
Penis
Urethra
Testis
Scrotum
Anus
Rectum

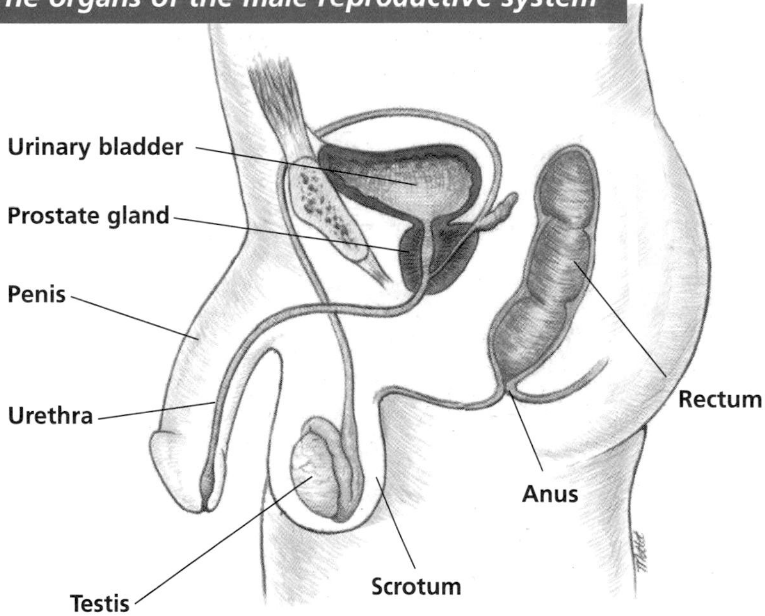

The external male organ, called the **penis**, delivers sperm to the female's body. Before this happens, blood flows into the tissues of the penis. The blood causes the penis to lengthen and become rigid, or erect. The erect penis is inserted into a tubelike canal called a **vagina** in the female's body.

Penis
The male organ that delivers sperm to the female's body.

Scrotum
The exterior sac that holds the testes.

Testis
The male reproductive organ that produces sperm cells. Plural is testes.

Vagina
The tubelike canal in the female body through which sperm enter the body.

Fallopian tube
A tube through which eggs pass from an ovary to the uterus.

Ovulation
The release of an egg from an ovary.

Semen
A mixture of fluid and sperm cells.

Uterus
The female reproductive organ that holds and protects a developing baby.

Sperm cells leave the male body through the urethra. The prostate gland produces fluid that mixes with the sperm cells. The mixture of sperm and fluid is called **semen**. The semen flows through the urethra to the outside of the body. As you learned in Lesson 5, urine also leaves the body through the urethra. However, urine and semen do not flow through the urethra at the same time.

The Female Reproductive System

You can see the main female reproductive organs in the diagram below. Females are born with about 400,000 immature egg cells that are stored in the ovaries. About every 28 days, an egg matures and is released from one of the ovaries. The release of an egg is called **ovulation**.

After its release, the egg travels through one of the **fallopian tubes**. If sperm are present, a sperm cell may fertilize the egg cell. The fertilized egg develops into an embryo, which travels to the **uterus**. The uterus holds and protects a developing baby. If the egg is not fertilized, it passes out of the female's body.

The organs of the female reproductive system

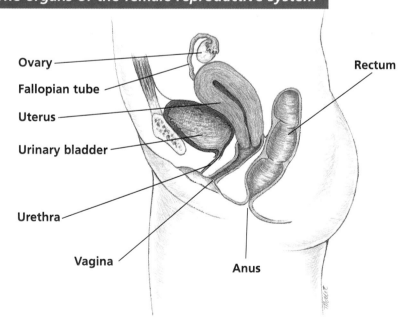

Ovary
Fallopian tube
Uterus
Urinary bladder
Urethra
Vagina
Rectum
Anus

Menstruation

Each month, a female's uterus prepares to receive a fertilized egg. The lining of the uterus thickens to form a blood-rich cushion. The lining will hold and nourish the developing embryo. Recall from Chapter 20 that an embryo is a beginning plant or animal. If the egg is not fertilized and no embryo forms, the lining of the uterus breaks down. The unfertilized egg, blood, and pieces of the lining pass out of the female's body through the vagina. This process is called **menstruation**.

Pregnancy

When the male's penis releases semen into the female's vagina, the sperm cells swim through the uterus and into the fallopian tubes. If a sperm cell fertilizes an egg cell in a fallopian tube, the female begins a period of **pregnancy**. During pregnancy, the fertilized egg develops into a baby.

In the fallopian tube, the fertilized egg divides and becomes an embryo. When the embryo reaches the uterus, it attaches to the lining. There, the embryo forms a **placenta**. The embryo is connected to the placenta by the **umbilical cord**, which contains blood vessels.

The embryo's blood flows through blood vessels in the placenta. The mother's blood flows through blood vessels in the lining of the uterus. The two blood supplies do not mix. However, they are so close together that food and oxygen can pass from the mother's blood to the embryo's blood. Waste products pass from the embryo's blood to the mother's blood. The embryo's wastes pass out of the mother's body along with her own wastes.

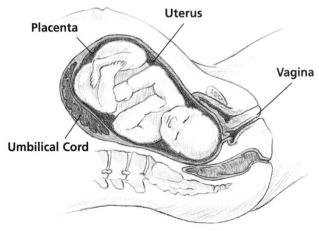

Uterus

Placenta

Vagina

Umbilical Cord

The umbilical cord connects the developing baby to the placenta.

Inside the uterus, the embryo develops rapidly, using the food and oxygen provided by the mother. At eight weeks, the embryo is called a **fetus**. It takes about nine months for an embryo to become a fully developed baby.

Birth of a Baby

When the fetus reaches full size, the uterus begins to contract. At first, the contractions are far apart. Gradually, they become stronger and more frequent.

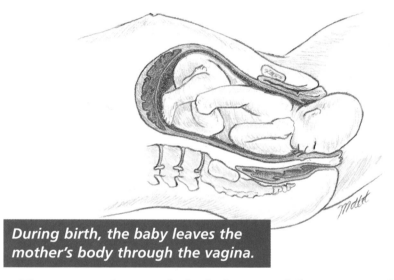

During birth, the baby leaves the mother's body through the vagina.

The contractions push the baby out of the uterus and through the vagina. Soon after the baby is born, more contractions push the placenta out of the mother's body.

The doctor clamps and cuts the umbilical cord. The part of the umbilical cord that remains attached to the baby eventually falls off. A person's "belly button," or navel, is where the umbilical cord was once attached.

Self-Check

1. Describe the path followed by sperm from the testes to the site of fertilization.
2. What happens during ovulation?
3. What is menstruation?
4. How does an embryo get nutrients during pregnancy?
5. What happens during the birth of a baby?

- Bones support and protect the body's soft tissues. Blood cells are made inside some bones. Bones also store minerals.

- Skeletal muscles work in pairs to pull on bones.

- Digestion changes food into a form that can enter cells.

- The circulatory system moves materials to and from cells.

- The main parts of the circulatory system are the heart and blood vessels. Arteries carry blood away from the heart. Veins carry blood to the heart.

- Red blood cells carry oxygen in hemoglobin. White blood cells protect the body from disease. Platelets help blood clot.

- The respiratory system brings oxygen into the lungs and releases carbon dioxide.

- The skin releases wastes in perspiration.

- The kidneys filter blood to remove wastes.

- A male produces sperm cells. A female produces egg cells. When a sperm cell and an egg cell unite in fertilization, pregnancy occurs.

Science Words

alveolus, 428
antibody, 426
artery, 425
blood pressure, 425
bronchus, 428
capillary, 425
diaphragm, 429
enzyme, 418
esophagus, 418
fallopian tube, 434
fetus, 436
hemoglobin, 426

involuntary muscle, 416
kidney, 432
ligament, 413
menstruation, 435
ovulation, 434
penis, 433
peristalsis, 418
perspiration, 431
placenta, 435
plasma, 426
platelet, 427
pregnancy, 435
red marrow, 411

scrotum, 433
semen, 434
tendon, 414
testis, 433
trachea, 428
umbilical cord, 435
ureter, 432
urethra, 432
uterus, 434
vagina, 433
vein, 425
villi, 419
voluntary muscle, 416

Chapter 23   REVIEW

Number your paper from 1 to 10. Then choose the word from the Word Bank that best completes each sentence. Write the answer on your paper.

1. _____ help blood clot to stop bleeding.

2. Sperm cells are produced in the _____.

3. A(n) _____ connects a muscle to a bone.

4. _____ filter nitrogen wastes out of the blood.

5. Oxygen from outside the body enters tiny air sacs in the lungs called _____.

6. The ends of the bones at a joint are covered with _____.

7. The _____ connects the mouth to the stomach.

8. The _____ is a muscle below the lungs that controls breathing.

9. The _____ holds and protects a developing baby in the mother's body.

10. _____ carries oxygen in the blood.

Concept Review

Number your paper from 1 to 8. Choose the answer that best completes each sentence. Write the letter of the answer on your paper.

1. A pregnant woman provides _____ to the developing fetus.

   a. blood   b. nitrogen   c. food and oxygen

2. The heart is made of _____ muscle.

   a. smooth   b. cardiac   c. skeletal

3. Foreign substances that enter the body are attacked by
_____.

    a. platelets   **c.** white blood cells
    b. red blood cells

4. Skeletal muscles work by _____.

    a. pulling   **b.** pushing   **c.** peristalsis

5. Perspiration leaves the body through the _____.

    a. kidneys   **b.** lungs   **c.** skin

6. You get oxygen into your lungs when you _____.

    a. inhale   **b.** respire   **c.** exhale

7. Most digestion takes place in the _____.

    a. esophagus   **b.** stomach   **c.** small intestine

8. The _____ of the heart pumps blood to the rest of
the body.

    a. right ventricle   **b.** left ventricle   **c.** left atrium

Critical Thinking

Write the answer to each of the following questions.

1. The statement, "All arteries carry blood that is high in
oxygen" is incorrect. Why? Write a statement that
describes all arteries.

2. How do the respiratory system, the digestive system,
and the circulatory system work together?

Test Taking Tip | As you read, try to link a new word to something
familiar. This can help remind you of a word's meaning
when you see the word on a test.

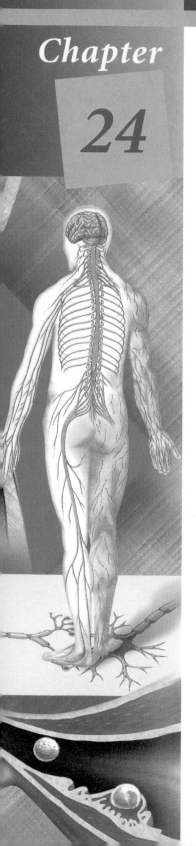

Chapter

24

The Body's Control Systems

Your body systems are always in action. Your body breaks down food molecules for energy. It exchanges oxygen and carbon dioxide with the air around you, circulates materials, and gets rid of wastes. How does your body do all these things at the same time? In this chapter, you will learn about the two systems that control and coordinate all your basic life activities.

ORGANIZE YOUR THOUGHTS

> Systems that control the body's activities

> **Nervous**
> Coordinates all body parts

> **Endocrine**
> Secretes hormones that change cell functions

Goals for Learning

► To identify the structures in the nervous system and describe how they coordinate all other body systems

► To explain how sense organs function

► To explain what hormones are and what they do

► To describe the changes that occur during puberty

Central nervous system
The part of the nervous system that consists of the brain and spinal cord.

Peripheral nervous system
The part of the nervous system that consists of nerves outside of the brain and spinal cord.

Your body systems constantly work together to keep you healthy and functioning. For your systems to work, however, they have to be coordinated. All the different parts have to know what to do and when to do it. Your body has to respond to changes in the environment. For example, if you run, your heart has to pump faster. Your nervous system coordinates all of your body parts. It is your body's communication network.

The Nervous System

The nervous system is divided into two main parts. The **central nervous system** consists of the brain and the spinal cord. This system controls the activities of the body. The **peripheral nervous system** consists of nerves outside the central nervous system. This system carries messages between the central nervous system and other parts of the body.

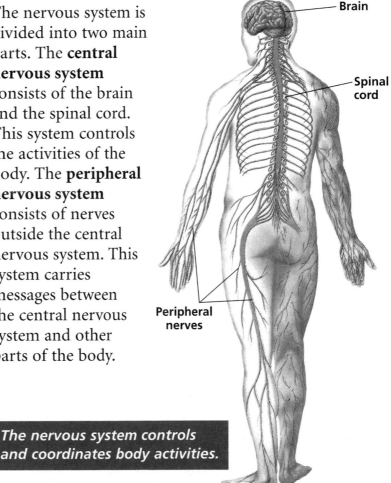

Brain

Spinal cord

Peripheral nerves

The nervous system controls and coordinates body activities.

The Brain

The brain has three major parts—the cerebrum, the cerebellum, and the brain stem. The largest part is the cerebrum, as the drawing shows. The cerebrum controls the way you think, learn, remember, and feel. It controls muscles that let you move body parts, such as your arms and legs. It interprets messages from the sense organs, such as the eyes and ears. The cerebrum is divided into two halves. The left half controls activities on the right side of the body. The right half controls activities on the left side of the body.

The cerebellum lies beneath the cerebrum. The cerebellum controls balance. It helps muscles work together so that you walk and write smoothly.

Under the cerebellum is the brain stem. It connects the brain and the spinal cord. The brain stem controls the automatic activities of your body. This includes heart rate, digestion, respiration, and circulation. The brain stem coordinates movements of muscles that work without your thinking about them, such as your stomach muscles.

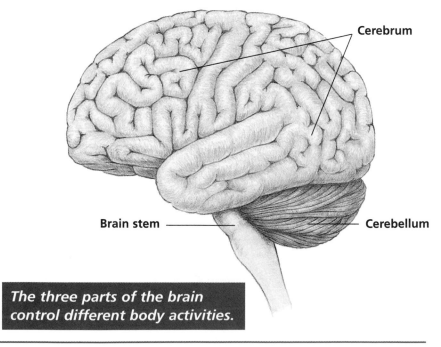

Cerebrum

Brain stem

Cerebellum

The three parts of the brain control different body activities.

The Spinal Cord

The spinal cord is a thick bunch of nerves that start at the brain stem and go down the back. The spinal cord is protected by the vertebrae in the spinal column. The brain sends and receives information through the spinal cord. Thirty-one pairs of spinal nerves branch off from this cord. The spinal nerves send nerve messages all over the body. The spinal cord and the brain are the central controls of the sense organs and body systems.

Impulse
A message that travels from neuron to neuron.

Neuron
A nerve cell.

Synapse
A tiny gap between neurons.

Neurons

Nerve cells are called **neurons**. They send messages in the form of electrical signals all through the body. These messages are called **impulses**. An impulse carries information from one nerve cell to the next.

Neurons do not touch each other. Impulses must cross a small gap, or **synapse**, between neurons. How does this happen? An impulse travels from one end of a neuron to the other end. When the impulse reaches the end of the neuron, a chemical is released. The chemical moves out into the synapse and touches the next neuron. This starts another impulse. Information moves through your body by traveling along many neurons.

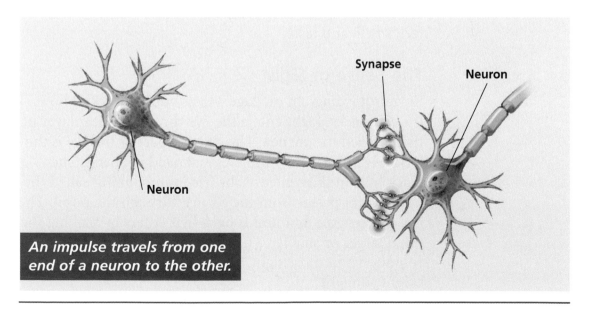

Synapse

Neuron

Neuron

An impulse travels from one end of a neuron to the other.

There are three kinds of neurons in your nervous system. Sensory neurons carry impulses from sense organs to the spinal cord or the brain. Motor neurons carry impulses from the brain and spinal cord to muscles and to organs in the endocrine system. Associative neurons carry impulses from sensory neurons to motor neurons.

Reflex Actions

Sneezing, coughing, and blinking are reflex actions. They happen automatically. What happens if you touch a hot frying pan? Sensory neurons send the "It is hot!" message to the spinal cord. Inside the spinal cord, associative neurons receive the impulses and send them to motor neurons. All of this happens in an instant, and you pull your hand away quickly. Many other reflex actions protect the body from injury. For example, if an object comes flying toward your eyes, you blink without thinking.

Sense Organs

The body connects with the outside world through sense organs. The five main sense organs are the eyes, ears, skin, nose, and tongue. **Receptor cells** in these organs receive information about the outside world. Receptor cells send impulses to your brain through sensory neurons. Your brain makes sense of the impulses. Then you see, hear, feel, smell, and taste.

The Sense of Sight

Review the diagram on page 445 as you read about how the eye works. Light enters the eye through a clear layer of tissue called the **cornea**. The colored part of the eye is the **iris**. It is made of tiny muscles arranged in a ring. The black hole in the center of the iris is an opening called the pupil. Light passes from the cornea through the pupil. The iris controls the amount of light that enters by making the pupil larger or smaller. The pupil opens wide in a dark room to let in more light. The pupil becomes smaller in bright sunlight.

Optic nerve
The nerve that carries impulses from the eye to the brain.

Behind the pupil is a lens. As you learned in Chapter 7, a lens is a curved piece of clear material that refracts, or bends, light waves. The lens in your eye focuses light rays onto the retina at the back of the eye. Receptor cells on the retina send impulses to the **optic nerve**. Nerve impulses travel along the optic nerve to the brain. The brain translates the impulses into images you can see. All of this happens faster than you can blink.

The retina has two kinds of receptor cells. Cells called rods are very sensitive to light, but they cannot detect colors. Rods let you see in dim light. Cells called cones detect colors, but they are not very sensitive to light. When the light is dim, you cannot see colors well.

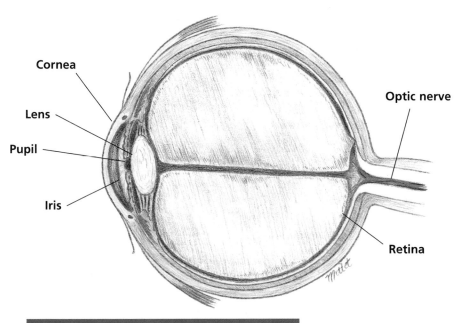

Cornea

Lens

Pupil

Iris

Optic nerve

Retina

The brain interprets impulses from the optic nerve as shapes and colors.

Auditory nerve
The nerves that carries impulses from the ear to the brain.

Cochlea
The organ in the inner ear that sends impulses to the auditory nerve.

Eardrum
A thin tissue in the middle ear that vibrates when sound waves strike it.

The Sense of Hearing

Just as your eyes collect light, your ears collect sound. Review the drawing below as you read about how the ears work. The outer ear acts like a funnel to collect sound waves. The waves travel through the ear canal to the middle ear. The middle ear is made of the **eardrum** and three small bones. The eardrum is a thin tissue that vibrates when sound waves strike it. The vibrations then travel through each of the three bones and to the inner ear. There, the vibrations cause fluid in the **cochlea** to vibrate. The cochlea is a hollow coiled tube that contains fluid and thousands of receptor cells. These cells move when vibrations strike them. The cells send impulses to the **auditory nerve**, which carries the impulse to the brain. The brain translates the impulses into sounds you can hear.

The Sense of Touch

The skin receives messages about heat, cold, pressure, and pain. Receptor cells in the skin send nerve impulses to the brain. Then you can tell if something is cold, hot, smooth, or rough. Your fingertips and lips are most sensitive to touch because they have the most receptor cells.

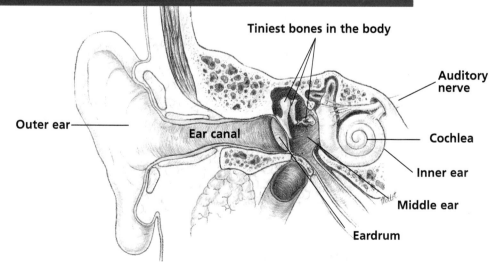

The brain interprets impulses from the auditory nerve as sounds.

Tiniest bones in the body

Auditory nerve

Outer ear

Ear canal

Cochlea

Inner ear

Middle ear

Eardrum

The Senses of Taste and Smell

Taste buds are tiny receptor cells on the tongue that distinguish four basic kinds of tastes. The four tastes are sweet, sour, bitter, and salty. Notice in the drawing that certain parts of the tongue are sensitive to each taste. The taste buds send impulses to the brain. The brain interprets the impulses as tastes.

Much of the sense of taste depends on the sense of smell. Receptor cells in the nose sense smells. If you hold your nose while you chew, much of your sense of taste goes away. Why does this happen? As you chew and swallow, air carrying the smell of the food reaches your nose. When you hold your nose, the air cannot flow freely. The smells never reach the receptor cells.

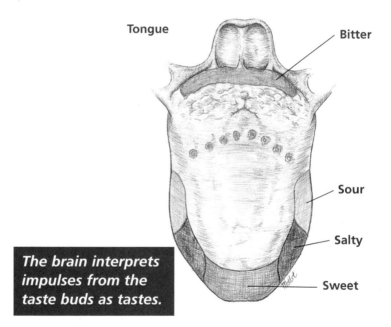

Tongue

Bitter

Sour

Salty

Sweet

The brain interprets impulses from the taste buds as tastes.

Self-Check

1. How is the central nervous system different from the peripheral nervous system?
2. Name the activities that each part of the brain controls.
3. How do impulses travel between neurons?
4. What happens to light after it reaches the retina?
5. Describe the path of sound waves moving through the ear.

INVESTIGATION

Modeling the Human Eye

Materials

- ✓ large index card
- ✓ pencil
- ✓ scissors
- ✓ round, clear glass bowl
- ✓ white tissue paper
- ✓ tape
- ✓ large, round magnifying glass
- ✓ clay
- ✓ flashlight

Purpose

To show how parts of the eye work to focus an image

Procedure

1. Do this investigation with a partner.

2. Fold the index card in half lengthwise. On the fold, draw half of a shape that has a definite top and bottom—for example, a valentine heart or a triangular pine tree. Cut out the shape and unfold the card.

3. Tape a sheet of white tissue paper to one side of the bowl.

4. Set up the magnifying glass near the other side of the bowl. Use clay to hold the magnifying glass up straight on the table.

5. Set up the opened card on the same side of the bowl as the magnifying glass but farther away from the bowl. Use clay to stand the card up straight. Your finished setup should look like the picture on the next page.

6. Darken the room as much as possible. Then shine the flashlight at the card so the light passes through the shape you cut out, the magnifying glass, and the bowl.

7. Look closely at the white paper. Move the bowl back and forth until the image is clear. What do you see?

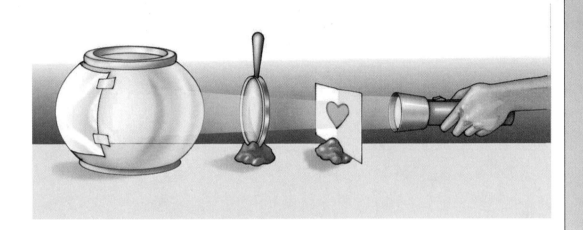

Questions

1. What do you see on the white paper? How is the image different from the shape on the card?

2. In your model, what does the bowl represent?

3. What does the white paper represent?

4. What does the magnifying glass represent?

Explore Further

Move the bowl closer and farther from the lens. What happens to the image?

How do eyeglasses work?

The lens in the human eye is a convex lens. It focuses an image on the retina. Figure 1 shows a normal eye. You can see that the image on the retina is upside down. Your brain interprets the image as right-side up.

Figure 2 shows the eye of a nearsighted person. People who are nearsighted can see close objects clearly but not distant objects. Notice that the image is focused in front of the retina instead of on it. Concave lenses are used in eyeglasses for nearsighted people. Figure 3 shows how a concave lens bends light rays before they enter the eye. This focuses the image on the retina.

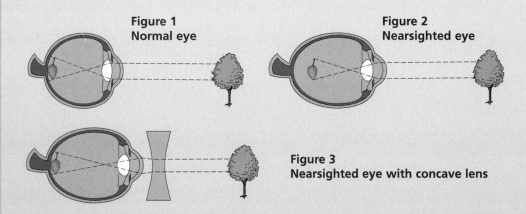

Figure 1
Normal eye

Figure 2
Nearsighted eye

Figure 3
Nearsighted eye with concave lens

Figure 4 shows the eye of a farsighted person. People who are farsighted can see distant objects clearly but not close objects. Notice that the image is focused behind the retina. Convex lenses are used in eyeglasses for farsighted people. Figure 5 shows how a convex lens bends light rays to focus the image on the retina.

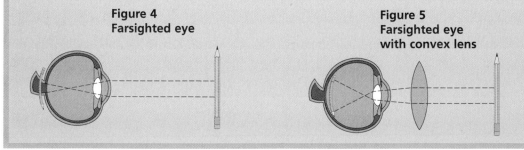

Figure 4
Farsighted eye

Figure 5
Farsighted eye with convex lens

How Does the Endocrine System Control the Body?

Objectives

After reading this lesson, you should be able to

▶ explain what hormones are and what they do.

▶ explain how a feedback loop works.

▶ describe the stress response.

▶ describe the changes that occur during puberty.

Gland
An organ that produces hormones.

Hormone
A chemical messenger secreted by glands that controls certain body functions.

The Endocrine Glands

The endocrine system works closely with the nervous system to control certain body activities. The endocrine system is made of **glands**. These glands secrete substances called **hormones**. Hormones are chemical messengers. Glands release hormones into the bloodstream. The hormones then travel all through the body.

What Hormones Do

There are more than 20 different hormones. They affect everything from kidney function to growth and development. Hormones work by attaching to certain cells. They change the function of the cells. Some examples of hormones are aldosterone, insulin, and growth hormone. The adrenal glands secrete aldosterone. This hormone directs the kidney to release sodium and water into the bloodstream. This may happen when a person has lost fluids. The pancreas secretes insulin. This hormone changes cells so that glucose can enter them. The pituitary gland secretes growth hormone. This hormone causes bones and muscles to grow.

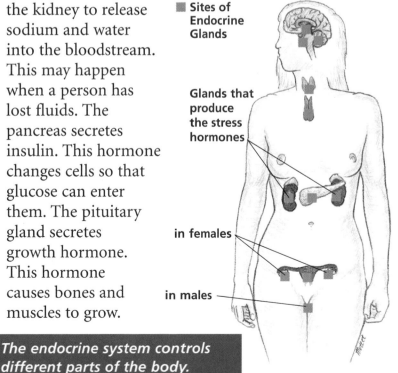

■ Sites of Endocrine Glands

Glands that produce the stress hormones

in females

in males

The endocrine system controls different parts of the body.

Adolescence
The teenage years of a human.

Puberty
The period of rapid growth and physical changes that occurs in males and females during early adolescence.

The Feedback Loop

Glands must secrete the correct amounts of hormones for the body to work properly. After hormones reach the cells, the cells send a chemical signal back to the gland. That signal tells the gland to continue or to stop secreting the hormone. This process is called a *feedback loop*.

Hormones and Stress

When a person feels scared or excited, the adrenal glands secrete a hormone called adrenaline. Adrenaline causes changes in the body. The palms sweat, the heart rate goes up, and the person breathes faster. These are signs of the stress response. The stress response can be harmful if it continues for a long time. But it can also be helpful. Suppose you are running a race. Adrenaline causes changes that increase the amount of glucose and oxygen delivered to your muscles.

Hormones and Puberty

The teenage years are called **adolescence**. At the beginning of adolescence, hormones cause rapid growth and physical changes. This period of growth and change is called **puberty**.

During puberty in males, a boy's voice changes to a low pitch. Hair begins to grow on the face, under the arms, and in the area around the external sex organs. The sex organs become more fully developed. During puberty in females, hair also begins to grow under the arms and around the external sex organs. The breasts enlarge. Ovulation and menstruation begin.

Did You Know?

Scientists have changed some bacteria so that they produce a growth hormone. This hormone is used to treat children whose bodies do not produce enough of it.

Self-Check

1. What is the function of the endocrine system?
2. What are hormones?
3. Name three hormones and how they affect the body.
4. How does the feedback loop work?
5. What changes occur in males and females during puberty?

Chapter 24 SUMMARY

- The nervous system controls and coordinates all body activities.

- The nervous system has two main parts. They are the central nervous system and the peripheral nervous system.

- The brain and the spinal cord make up the central nervous system.

- The brain has three major parts—the cerebrum, the cerebellum, and the brain stem. The three parts control different body activities.

- Impulses carry information from one nerve cell to the next.

- The five main sense organs are the eyes, ears, skin, nose, and tongue.

- Special cells in each of the sense organs receive information from the environment and send impulses to the brain.

- The glands of the endocrine system release hormones into the bloodstream.

- Hormones help control certain body activities. Hormones also cause the rapid growth and physical changes that occur during puberty.

Science Words

adolescence, 452

auditory nerve, 446

central nervous system, 441

cochlea, 446

cornea, 444

eardrum, 446

gland, 451

hormone, 451

impulse, 443

iris, 444

neuron, 443

optic nerve, 445

peripheral nervous system, 441

puberty, 452

receptor cell, 444

synapse, 443

Vocabulary Review

Number your paper from 1 to 9. Match each term in Column A with the correct definition in Column B. Write the letter of the definition on your paper.

Column A

_____ 1. adolescence

_____ 2. central nervous system

_____ 3. cornea

_____ 4. impulse

_____ 5. iris

_____ 6. neuron

_____ 7. peripheral nervous system

_____ 8. puberty

_____ 9. synapse

Column B

a. a nerve cell

b. period of rapid growth and physical changes during the early teenage years

c. consists of the brain and spinal cord

d. tiny gap between neurons

e. the teenage years of a human

f. controls the amount of light entering the eye

g. consists of nerves outside of the brain and spinal cord

h. message that travels from one nerve cell to another

i. clear layer of tissue covering the front of the eye

Concept Review

Number your paper from 1 to 9. Choose the answer that best completes each sentence. Write the letter of the answer on your paper.

1. The retina sends impulses to the _____ nerve.

   a. optic   b. auditory   c. motor

2. The _____ controls automatic activities such as digestion and circulation.

   a. cerebrum   b. cerebellum   c. brain stem

3. Neurons send messages in the form of _____ signals.

   a. visual   **b.** electrical   **c.** chemical

4. Insulin and adrenaline are examples of _____.

   a. hormones   **b.** glands   **c.** receptor cells

5. The lens in the human eye focuses images on the _____.

   a. pupil   **b.** retina   **c.** cornea

6. The _____ vibrates when sound waves strike it.

   a. auditory nerve   **b.** outer ear   **c.** eardrum

7. Increased heart rate and breathing rate are signs of _____.

   a. reflex actions   **c.** associative neurons
   b. the stress response

8. _____ in the retina are very sensitive to light but cannot detect colors.

   a. rods   **b.** cones   **c.** glands

9. _____ protect the body from injury.

   a. synapses   **b.** reflex actions   **c.** hormones

Critical Thinking

Write the answer to each of the following questions.

1. How are the "messengers" of the endocrine system different from those of the nervous system?

2. Why is it important for your brain to control many functions automatically?

Test Taking Tip | Make a labeled drawing to help you remember the names of the parts in a structure.

INVESTIGATION

How Does Exercise Affect Your Heart and Breathing?

Materials

✓ watch or clock with a second hand

✓ paper and pencil

Purpose

To observe how different amounts of activity affect your heart rate and breathing rate

Procedure

1. Copy the table below on a sheet of paper.

Activity	Rate per minute	
	Heartbeat	**Breathing**
Sitting (resting rate)		
After walking		
After running in place		

2. Do this investigation with a partner.

3. Sit quietly for three minutes. Then find your pulse as shown in the photograph on page 422. Count your heartbeats for 15 seconds.

4. While you take your pulse, have your partner watch you and count the number of breaths you take in 15 seconds.

5. Multiply the counts for 15 seconds by 4 to calculate your heart rate and breathing rate per minute. Record these numbers in your chart.

6. Repeat steps 4 and 5 after walking across the room and then after running in place for 200 steps.

7. Switch places and repeat steps 4 through 7.

Questions

1. How does the amount of activity affect your heart rate and breathing rate? Why do the rates change?

- Bones help move the body, support and protect the body's soft tissues and organs, make blood cells, and store minerals.

- The digestive system breaks food down into molecules that can enter cells.

- The circulatory system moves gases, nutrients, and wastes to and from cells.

- The respiratory system brings oxygen into the lungs and releases carbon dioxide.

- The skin and the kidneys release wastes from the body.

- The reproductive system produces sex cells that unite to produce an embryo and begin pregnancy.

- The nervous system controls and coordinates all body activities.

- The endocrine system produces hormones that help control body activities, including the changes that occur during puberty.

WORD BANK

alveoli

cochlea

diaphragm

hemoglobin

impulse

ligament

placenta

synapse

Vocabulary Review

Number your paper from 1 to 8. Then choose the word from the Word Bank that best completes each sentence. Write the answer on your paper.

1. A(n) _____ is a message that travels from one nerve cell to another.

2. The organ in the inner ear that sends impulses to the auditory nerve is the _____.

3. The _____ is a blood-rich tissue that grows into the lining of the uterus during pregnancy.

4. Oxygen from outside the body enters tiny air sacs in the lungs called _____.

5. A bone is held to another bone by a(n) _____.

6. A(n) _____ is a tiny gap between neurons.

7. The substance in blood that carries oxygen is _____.

8. The _____ is a muscle below the lungs that controls breathing.

Concept Review

Number your paper from 1 to 5. Name each part of the eye shown in the diagram. Tell what each part does.

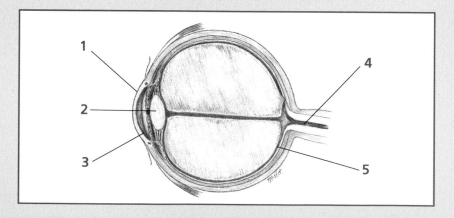

Number your paper from 6 to 10. Choose the answer that best completes each sentence. Write the letter of the answer on your paper.

6. The _____ nervous system consists of the brain and spinal cord.

   a. peripheral   b. central   c. neuron

7. Neurons send messages in the form of _____ impulses.

   a. chemical   b. auditory   c. electrical

8. Foreign substances that enter the body are attacked by _____.

   a. red blood cells   b. platelets   c. white blood cells

9. The _____ of the heart pumps blood to the lungs.

   a. right ventricle   b. left ventricle   c. left atrium

10. Most digestion takes place in the _____.

   a. small intestine   b. large intestine c. esophagus

Critical Thinking

Write the answer to each of the following questions.

1. How do the respiratory system, the digestive system, and the circulatory system work together?

2. Why is it important for your brain to control many functions automatically?

Glossary

A

Acid rain (as´ id rān) rain that is caused by pollution and is harmful to organisms because it is acidic (p. 370)

Adaptation (ad ap tā´ shƏn) a trait that enables an organism to live in a certain environment (p. 397)

Adolescence (ad l es´ ns) the teenage years of a human (p. 452)

Air mass (âr mas) a large section of the atmosphere with the same temperature and humidity throughout (p. 263)

Air pressure (âr presh´ Ər) the force of air against a unit of area (p. 260)

Algae (al´ jē) protists that make their own food and usually live in water (p. 312)

Alluvial fan (Ə lü´ vē Əl fan) a fan-shaped area of land deposited where a mountain stream moves onto flat land (p. 193)

Altitude (al´ tƏ tüd) height above Earth's surface (p. 250)

Alveolus (al vē´ Ə lƏs) a tiny air sac where gas exchange occurs; plural *alveoli* (p. 428)

Ampere (am´ pir) the unit used to describe how much electric current flows through a wire (p. 126)

Amphibian (am fib´ ē Ən) a vertebrate that lives at first in water and then on land (p. 325)

Anemometer (an Ə mom´ Ə tƏr) an instrument used to measure wind speed (p. 261)

Angiosperm (an´ jē Ə spėrm) a flowering plant (p. 346)

Antibody (an´ ti bod ē) a protein in plasma that fights disease (p. 426)

Area (âr´ ē Ə) the amount of space the surface of an object takes up (p. 10)

Artery (âr´ tƏr ē) a blood vessel that carries blood away from the heart (p. 425)

Asexual reproduction (ā sek´ shü ēl rē prƏ duk´ shƏn) reproduction that involves one parent and no egg or sperm (p. 337)

Asteroid (as´ tƏ roid) a rocky object smaller than a planet that orbits a star (p. 289)

Asteroid belt (as´ tƏ roid belt) the region between Mars and Jupiter where most asteroids orbit the sun (p. 289)

Atmosphere (at´ mƏ sfir) the layer of gases that surrounds Earth and other bodies in space (p. 245)

Atom (at´ Əm) the building block of matter (p. 28)

Atrium (ā´ trē Əm) a heart chamber that receives blood returning to the heart; plural is *atria* (p. 336)

Attract (Ə trakt´) to pull together (p. 137)

Auditory nerve (ö´ dƏ tôr ē nėrv) the nerve that carries impulses from the ear to the brain (p. 446)

Axis (ak´ sis) an imaginary line through Earth, connecting the north and south poles (p. 158)

B

Balance (bal´ Əns) 1. *(noun)* an instrument used to measure mass (p. 18); 2. *(verb)* to keep the number of atoms the same on both sides of an equation (p. 56)

Barometer (bƏ rom´ Ə tƏr) an instrument used to measure air pressure (p. 260)

Bilateral symmetry (bī lat´ Ər Əl sim´ Ə trē) a body plan that consists of left and right halves that look the same (p. 328)

Bile (bīl) a substance made in the liver that breaks down fats (p. 418)

Biome (bī´ ōm) an ecosystem found over a large geographic area (p. 370)

Biosphere (bī´ Ə sfir) the part of Earth where living things can exist (p. 371)

Blood pressure (blud presh´ Ər) the push of blood against the walls of blood vessels (p. 425)

Boiling point (boil´ ing point) the temperature at which a liquid changes to a gas (p. 100)

Bronchus (brong´ kƏs) a tube that connects the trachea and lungs; plural *bronchi* (p. 428)

C

Capillary (kap´ Ə ler ē) a blood vessel that exchanges gases, nutrients, and wastes with body cells (p. 425)

Carbohydrate (kär bō hī´ drāt) a sugar or starch which organisms use for energy (p. 307)

Carnivore (kär´ nƏ vôr) a consumer that eats only animals (p. 375)

Cartilage (kär´ tl ij) a soft material found in vertebrate skeletons (p. 324)

Cast (kast) a fossil that forms when minerals fill a cavity, creating a model of an organism (p. 223)

Cell (sel) the basic unit of life (p. 303)

Cellular respiration (sel´ yə lər res pə rā´ shən) the process in which cells break down food to release energy (p. 309)

Celsius scale (sel´ sē əs skāl) the temperature scale used by scientists and by people in most countries, in which water freezes at 0° and boils at 100° (p. 99)

Cenozoic Era (sen ə zō´ ik ir´ə) the era of Earth's history described as the Age of Mammals, beginning about 65 million years ago and continuing today (p. 228)

Central nervous system (sen´ tral nėr´ vəs sis´ təm) the part of the nervous system that consists of the brain and spinal cord (p. 441)

Chemical change (kem´ ə kəl chānj) a change that produces one or more substances that differ from the original substance (p. 47)

Chemical equation (kem´ ə kəl i kwā´ zhən) a statement that uses symbols, formulas, and numbers to stand for a chemical reaction (p. 55)

Chemical formula (kem´ ə kəl fôr´ myə lə) a way to write the kinds and numbers of atoms in a compound (p. 51)

Chemical reaction (kem´ ə kəl rē ak´ shən) a chemical change in which elements are combined or rearranged (p. 53)

Chemical weathering (kem´ ə kəl weᴛH´ ər ing) the breaking apart of rocks caused by a change in their chemical makeup (p. 188)

Chemistry (kem´ ə strē) the study of matter and how it changes (p. 3)

Chlorophyll (klôr´ ə fil) the green pigment in plants that captures light energy for photosynthesis (p. 355)

Chromosome (krō´ mə sōm) a rod-shaped structure that contains DNA and is found in the nucleus of a cell (p. 391)

Chyme (kīm) liquid food in the digestive tract that is partly digested (p. 418)

Cilia (sil´ ē ə) hair-like structures that help some one-celled organisms move (p. 312)

Cinder cone (sin´ dər kōn) a small volcano with steep sides and explosive eruptions of ash and rocks (p. 208)

Circuit (sėr´ kit) a path for electric current (p. 126)

Circulatory system (sėr´ kyə lə tôr ē sis´ təm) the system that moves blood throughout the body (p. 335)

Cirrus cloud (sir´ əs kloud) a high, wispy cloud made of ice crystals (p. 250)

Climate (klī´ mit) the average weather of a region over a long period of time (p. 268)

Climax community (klī´ maks kə myü´ nə tē) a community that changes little over time (p. 369)

Closed circuit (klōzd´ sėr´ kit) a complete, unbroken path for electric current (p. 126)

Cochlea (kok´ lē ə) the organ in the inner ear that sends impulses to the auditory nerve (p. 446)

Coefficient (kō ə fish´ ənt) a number placed before a formula in a chemical equation (p. 56)

Cold front (kōld frunt) the boundary ahead of a cold air mass that is pushing out and wedging under a warm air mass (p. 263)

Comet (kom´ it) a ball of ice, rock, frozen gases, and dust that orbits the sun (p. 290)

Community (kə myü´ nə tē) a group of different populations that live in the same area (p. 368)

Composite volcano (kəm poz´ it vol kā´ nō) a tall volcano formed from eruptions of ash and rock followed by quiet lava flows (p. 208)

Compound (kom´ pound) a substance formed when atoms of two or more elements join together (p. 41)

Concave lens (kon´ kāv lenz) a lens that is thin in the middle and thick at the edges (p. 120)

Concave mirror (kon´ kāv mir´ ər) a mirror that curves in at the middle (p. 119)

Condense (kən dens´) to change from a gas to a liquid (p. 249)

Conduction (kən kuk´ shən) the movement of heat energy from one molecule to the next (p. 104)

a	hat	e	let	ī	ice	ô	order	ù	put	sh	she		ə	a	in about
ā	age	ē	equal	o	hot	oi	oil	ü	rule	th	thin			e	in taken
ä	far	ėr	term	ō	open	ou	out	ch	child	ᴛH	then			i	in pencil
â	care	i	it	ȯ	saw	u	cup	ng	long	zh	measure			o	in lemon
														u	in circus

Conductor (kən duk´ tər) a material through which heat travels easily (p. 104)

Conifer (kon´ ə fər) a cone-bearing gymnosperm (p. 347)

Consumer (kən sü´ mər) an organism that feeds on other organisms (p. 374)

Continent (kon´ tə nənt) one of the seven major land areas of Earth (p. 156)

Continental drift (kon tə nən´ tl drift) the theory that Earth's major landmasses move (p. 204)

Continental shelf (kon tə nən´ tl shelf) the part of a continent that extends from the shoreline out into the ocean (p. 238)

Continental slope (kon tə nən´ tl slōp) the steep slope between the continental shelf and the deep ocean floor (p. 238)

Convection (kən vek´ shən) the flow of energy that occurs when a warm liquid or gas rises (p. 105)

Convection current (kən vek´ shən kėr´ ənt) the circular motion of gas or liquid as it heats (p. 206)

Convex lens (kon veks´ lenz) a lens that is thick in the middle and thin at the edges (p. 120)

Convex mirror (kon veks´ mir´ ər) a mirror that curves outward at the middle (p. 119)

Core (kôr) the solid and molten layer at the center of Earth (p. 203)

Cornea (kôr´ nē ə) the clear layer of tissue that covers the front of the eye (p. 444)

Crust (krust) the top layer of Earth (p. 203)

Cumulus cloud (kyü´ myə ləs kloud) a puffy, white cloud occurring at medium altitudes (p. 250)

Current (kėr´ ənt) a large stream of water flowing in the ocean, in rivers, and in some large lakes (p. 239)

D

Decompose (dē kəm pōz´) to break down or decay matter into simpler substances (p. 313)

Degree (di grē´) a unit of measurement on a temperature scale (p. 99)

Delta (del´ tə) a fan-shaped area of land formed when sediment is deposited where a river empties into a lake or an ocean (p. 193)

Density (den´ sə tē) the amount of matter per unit volume (p. 28)

Deposition (dep ə zish´ ən) the dropping of eroded sediment (p. 193)

Development (di vel´ əp mənt) the changes that occur as an organism grows (p. 310)

Diaphragm (dī´ ə fram) the muscle below the lungs that controls breathing (p. 429)

Diffusion (di fyü´ zhən) the movement of materials from an area of high concentration to an area of low concentration (p. 334)

Digestion (də jes´ chən) the process by which organisms break down food (p. 309)

Digestive tract (də jes´ tiv trakt) a tubelike digestive space with an opening at each end p. 333)

Displacement of water (dis plās´ mənt uv wó´ tər) a method of measuring the volume of irregularly shaped objects (p. 17)

Dissolve (di zolv´) to break apart (p. 54)

Distance (dis´ təns) the length of the path between two points (p. 68)

Drainage basin (drā´ nij bā´ sn) the land area that is drained by a river and its tributaries (p. 234)

E

Eardrum (ir´ drum) a thin tissue in the middle ear that vibrates when sound waves strike it (p. 446)

Earthquake (ėrth´ kwāk) a shaking of Earth's crust (p. 212)

Earth science (ėrth sī´ əns) the study of Earth's land, water, and air and outer space (p. 152)

Ecology (ē kol´ ə jē) the study of the interactions among living things and the nonliving things in their environment (p. 367)

Ecosystem (ē´ kō sis təm) the interactions among the populations of a community and the nonliving things in their environment (p. 369)

Effort force (ef´ ərt fôrs) the force applied to a machine by the user (p. 79)

Egg cell (eg sel) a female sex cell (p. 337)

Elapsed time (i lapst´ tīm) the length of time that passes from one event to another (p. 67)

Electric current (i lek´ trik kėr´ ənt) movement of electric charge from one place to another (p. 126)

Electricity (i lek tris´ ə tē) a flow of electrons (p. 125)

Electron (i lek´ tron) a tiny, negatively charged particle of an atom that moves around the nucleus (p. 31)

Element (el´ ə mənt) matter that has only one kind of atom (p. 33)

Embryo (em´ brē ō) a beginning plant or animal (p. 346)

Energy (en´ ər jē) the ability to do work (p. 63)

Energy pyramid (en´ ər jē pir´ ə mid) a diagram that compares the amounts of energy available to the populations at different levels of a food chain (p. 380)

English system (ing´ glish sis´ təm) the system of measurement that uses inches, feet, and yards (p. 6)

Enzyme (en´ zīm) a protein that speeds up chemical changes (p. 418)

Epicenter (ep´ ə sen tər) the point on Earth's surface directly over the focus of an earthquake (p. 214)

Equator (i kwā´ tər) the line of latitude halfway between the poles (p. 164)

Erosion (i rō´ zhən) the wearing away and moving of weathered rock and soil (p. 192)

Esophagus (i sof´ ə gəs) the tube that connects the mouth to the stomach (p. 418)

Evaporate (i vap´ ə rāt) to change from a liquid to a gas (pp. 95, 249)

Evolution (ev ə lü´ shən) the changes in a population over time (p. 396)

Excretion (ek skrē´ shən) the process by which organisms get rid of wastes (p. 309)

Excretory system (ek´ skrə tôr ē sis´ təm) a series of organs that gets rid of cell wastes in the form of urine (p. 432)

Expand (ek spand´) to become larger in size (p. 96)

F

Fahrenheit scale (far´ ən hīt skāl) the temperature scale commonly used in the United States, in which water freezes at 32° and boils at 212° (p. 99)

Fallopian tube (fə lō´ pē an tüb) a tube through which eggs pass from an ovary to the uterus (p. 434)

Fat (fat) a chemical that stores large amounts of energy (p. 307)

Fault (fôlt) a break in Earth's crust along which movement occurs (p. 210)

Feces (fē´ sēz) solid waste material remaining in the large intestine after digestion (p. 419)

Fern (fėrn) a seedless vascular plant (p. 349)

Fertilization (fėr tl ə zā´ shən) the joining of an egg cell and a sperm cell (p. 338)

Fetus (fē´ təs) an embryo after eight weeks of development in the uterus (p. 436)

Filter feeding (fil´ tər fēd´ ing) getting food by straining it out of the water (p. 332)

Flagella (flə jel´ ə) whip-like tails that help some one-celled organisms move; singular *flagellum* (p. 312)

Focus (fō´ kəs) the point inside Earth where rock first moves, starting an earthquake (p. 214)

Folding (fōld´ ing) the bending of rock layers that are squeezed together (p. 209)

Food chain (füd chān) the feeding order of organisms in an ecosystem (p. 374)

Food web (füd web) all the food chains in an ecosystem that are linked to one another (p. 376)

Fossil (fos´ əl) a trace or remains of an organism preserved in Earth's crust (p. 222)

Freezing point (frēz´ ing point) the temperature at which a liquid changes to a solid (p. 100)

Frond (frond) a large feathery leaf of a fern (p. 349)

Front (frunt) the boundary line between two air masses (p. 263)

Fulcrum (ful´ krəm) the fixed point around which a lever rotates (p. 79)

Fungus (fung´ gəs) an organism that usually has many cells and decomposes material for its food (p. 313)

G

Gallbladder (gôl´ blad´ ər) the digestive organ attached to the liver that stores bile (p. 418)

Gas (gas) a form of matter that has no definite shape or volume (p. 29)

Gastrovascular cavity (gas trō vas´ kyə lər kav´ ə tē) a digestive space with a single opening (p. 333)

Gene (jēn) the information about a trait that a parent passes to its offspring (p. 391)

Generator (jen´ ə rā tər) a device used to convert mechanical energy to electrical energy (p. 65)

a	hat	e	let	ī	ice	ȯ	order	u̇	put	sh	she	ə	a	in about
ā	age	ē	equal	o	hot	oi	oil	ü	rule	th	thin		e	in taken
ä	far	ėr	term	ō	open	ou	out	ch	child	ᵺ	then		i	in pencil
â	care	i	it	ȯ	saw	u	cup	ng	long	zh	measure		o	in lemon
													u	in circus

Genetics (jə net´ iks) the study of heredity (p. 391)

Geologic time (jē ə loj´ ə kəl tīm) all the time that has passed since Earth formed (p. 221)

Geologic time scale (jē ə loj´ ə kəl tīm skāl) an outline of major events in Earth's history (p. 225)

Germinate (jėr´ mə nāt) to start to grow into a new plant; to sprout (p. 360)

Gill (gil) a structure used by some animals to breathe in water (p. 325)

Glacier (glā´ shər) a huge moving body of ice on land (p. 195)

Gland (gland) an organ that produces hormones (p. 451)

Graduated cylinder (graj´ ü āt əd sil´ ən dər) a round glass or plastic cylinder used to measure the volume of liquids (p. 16)

Gram (gram) the basic unit of mass in the metric system (p. 18)

Gravity (grav´ ə tē) the force of attraction between any two objects that have mass (p. 71)

Greenhouse effect (grēn´ hous ə fekt´) the warming of the atmosphere because of trapped heat energy from the sun (p. 280)

Groundwater (ground´ wȯ tər) water that sinks into the ground (p. 234)

Guard cell (gärd sel) a cell that opens and closes stomata (p. 358)

Gymnosperm (jim´ nə spėrm) a non-flowering seed plant (p. 347)

H

Habitat (hab´ ə tat) the place where an organism lives (p. 368)

Hardness (härd´ nəs) the ability of a mineral to resist being scratched (p. 175)

Heat (hēt) a form of energy resulting from the motion of particles in matter (p. 93)

Heat source (hēt sȯrs) a place from which heat energy comes (p. 93)

Hemisphere (hem´ ə sfir) section of Earth north or south of the equator or east or west of the prime meridian (p. 167)

Hemoglobin (hē´ mə hlō bən) a substance in red blood cells that carries oxygen (p. 426)

Herbivore (hėr´ bə vȯr) a consumer that eats only plants (p. 375)

Heredity (hə red´ ə tē) the passing of traits from parent to offspring (p. 391)

Homologous structures (hō mä´ lə gəs struk´ chərs) body parts that are similar in related organisms (p. 399)

Hormone (hȯr´ mōn) a chemical messenger secreted by glands that controls certain body functions (p. 451)

Humidity (hyü mid´ ə tē) the amount of water vapor in the air (p. 261)

Hurricane (hėr´ ə kān) a severe tropical storm with high winds that revolve around an eye (p. 265)

I

Igneous rock (ig´ nē əs rok) rock formed from melted minerals that have cooled and hardened (p. 181)

Image (im´ ij) a copy or likeness (p. 118)

Impulse (im´ puls) a message that travels from neuron to neuron (p. 443)

Inclined plane (in klīnd´ plān) a simple machine made up of a ramp, used to lift an object (p. 84)

Insulator (in´ sə lā tər) a material that does not conduct heat well (p. 104)

Interact (in tər akt´) to act upon or influence something (p. 367)

Invertebrate (in vėr´ tə brāt) an animal that does not have a backbone (p. 328)

Involuntary muscle (in vol´ ən ter ē mus´ əl) a muscle that a person cannot control (p. 416)

Ionosphere (ī on´ ə sfir) the upper thermosphere, where ions form as electrons are stripped away from atoms (p. 247)

Iris (ī´ ris) the part of the eye that controls the amount of light that enters (p. 444)

Isobar (ī´ sə bär) a line on a weather map connecting areas of equal air pressure (p. 264)

J

Joule (jül) the metric unit of work (p. 77)

K

Kidney (kid´ nē) the organ in the excretory system where urine forms (p. 432)

Kinetic energy (ki net´ ik en´ ər jē) the energy of motion (p. 63)

Kingdom (king´ dəm) one of the five groups into which organisms are classified (p. 311)

Latitude (lat´ ə tüd) the distance north or south of the equator (p. 164)

Law of conservation of energy (lȯ uv kon sər vā´ shən uv en´ ər jē) Energy cannot be created or destroyed. (p. 66)

Law of conservation of matter (lȯ uv kon sər vā´ shən uv mat´ ər) Matter cannot be created or destroyed in any chemical change. (p. 56)

Law of universal gravitation (lȯ uv yü nə vėr´ səl grav ə tā shən) Gravitational force depends on the mass of the two objects involved and on the distance between them. (p. 71)

Lens (lenz) a curved piece of clear material that refracts light waves (p. 120)

Lever (lev´ ər) a simple machine containing a bar that can turn around a fixed point (p. 79)

Life science (līf sī´ əns) the study of living things (p. 300)

Ligament (lig´ ə mənt) a tissue that connects bone to bone (p. 413)

Light (līt) a form of energy that can be seen (p. 114)

Lines of force (līnz uv fôrs) lines that show a magnetic field (p. 138)

Liter (lē´ lər) the basic unit of volume in the metric system (p. 15)

Liquid (lik´ wid) a form of matter that has a definite volume but no definite shape (p. 29)

Longitude (lon´ jə tüd) the distance east or west of the prime meridian (p. 166)

Luster (lust´ tər) the way a mineral reflects light (p. 174)

Magnet (mag´ nit) an object that attracts certain kinds of metals, such as iron (p. 136)

Magnetic field (mag net´ ik fēld) the area around a magnet in which magnetic forces can act (p. 138)

Magnetic poles (mag net´ ik pōlz) the opposite points or ends of a magnet, where magnetic forces are greatest (p. 137)

Mammary gland (mam´ ər ē gland) a milk-producing structure on the chest or abdomen of a mammal (p. 327)

Mantle (man´ tl) the layer of Earth that surrounds the core (p. 203)

Mass (mas) the amount of material an object has (pp. 18, 276)

Matter (mat´ ər) anything that has mass and takes up space (p. 28)

Mechanical advantage (mə kan´ ə kəl ad van´ tij) the factor by which a machine multiplies the effort force (p. 82)

Mechanical weathering (mə kan´ ə kəl weᴛH´ ər ing) the breaking apart of rocks without changing their mineral composition (p. 187)

Meiosis (mē ō´ sis) the process that produces sex cells (p. 394)

Melting point (melt´ ing point) the temperature at which a solid changes to a liquid (p. 100)

Meniscus (mə nis´ kəs) the curved surface of a liquid (p. 16)

Menstruation (men strü ā´ shən) the process during which an unfertilized egg, blood, and pieces of the lining of the uterus exit the female's body (p. 435)

Meridian (mə rid´ ē ən) a line of longitude (p. 166)

Mesosphere (mes´ ə sfir) the third layer of the atmosphere, which is the coldest layer (p. 247)

Mesozoic Era (mes ə zō´ ik ir´ə) the era of Earth's history characterized by dinosaurs, beginning about 230 million years ago and ending about 65 million years ago (p. 227)

Metamorphic rock (met ə mōr´ fik rok) rock that has been changed by intense heat, pressure, and chemical reactions (p. 181)

Metamorphosis (met ə môr´ fə sis) a major change in form that occurs as some animals develop into adults (p. 325)

Meteor (mē´ tē ər) an asteroid that enters Earth's atmosphere (p. 289)

Meteorologist (mē tē ə rol´ ə jist) a scientist who studies the air and weather (p. 153)

Meter (mē´ tər) the basic unit of length in the metric system, equal to about 39 inches (p. 7)

Meterstick (mē´ tər stik) a common tool for measuring length in the metric system (p. 8)

Metric system (met´ rik sis´ təm) the system of measurement used by scientists (p. 6)

a	hat	e	let	ī	ice	ȯ	order	u̇	put	sh	she	ə	a	in about
ā	age	ē	equal	o	hot	oi	oil	ü	rule	th	thin		e	in taken
ä	far	ėr	term	ō	open	ou	out	ch	child	ᴛH	then		i	in pencil
â	care	i	it	ȯ	saw	u	cup	ng	long	zh	measure		o	in lemon
													u	in circus

Microscope (mī´ krə skōp) an instrument used to magnify things (p. 303)

Midocean ridge (mid´ ō shən rij) the mountain chain on the ocean floor (p. 238)

Mineral (min´ ər əl) an element or compound found in Earth's crust (p. 173); a natural substance needed for fluid balance, digestion, and other bodily functions that organisms need in small amounts (p. 308)

Mitosis (mī tō´ sis) the process that results in two cells identical to the parent cell (p. 393)

Mixture (miks´ chər) a combination of substances in which no reaction takes place (p. 53)

Model (mod´ l) a picture, an idea, or an object that is built to explain how something else looks or works (p. 30)

Mold (mōld) a fossil that is an impression left in a rock by an organism (p. 223)

Molecule (mol´ ə kyül) the smallest particle of a substance that has the same properties as the substance (p. 27)

Molting (mōlt´ ing) the process by which an arthropod sheds its external skeleton (p. 331)

Moneran (mə nir´ ən) an organism that is one-celled and does not have organelles (p. 313)

Moraine (mə rān´) a ridge of sediment deposited by a glacier (p. 196)

Moss (mos) a seedless nonvascular plant that has simple parts (p. 350)

Motion (mō´ shən) a change in position (p. 67)

Mutation (myü tā´ shən) a change in a gene (p. 391)

N

Natural element (nach´ ər əl el´ ə mənt) an element that is found in nature (p. 33)

Neuron (nur´ on) a nerve cell (p. 443)

Neutron (nü´ tron) a tiny uncharged particle in the nucleus of an atom that is similar in size to a proton (p. 31)

Nitrogen fixation (ni´ trə jən fik sā´ shən) the process by which certain bacteria change nitrogen gas from the air into ammonia (p. 384)

Nonvascular plant (non vas´ kyə lər plant) a plant that does not have tubelike tissue (p. 345)

Normal fault (nôr´ məl fôlt) a break in the crust in which the overhanging block of rock has slid down (p. 210)

North pole (nôrth pōl) the point farthest north on Earth (p. 158)

Nucleus (nü´ klē əs) the central part of an atom (p. 31)

Nutrient (nü´ trē ənt) any chemical found in foods that is needed by organisms (p. 308)

O

Omnivore (om´ nə vôr) a consumer that eats both plants and animals (p. 375)

Open circuit (ō´ pən sėr´ kit) an incomplete or broken path for electric current (p. 127)

Optic nerve (op´ tik nėrv) the nerve that carries impulses from the eye to the brain (p. 445)

Organ (ôr´ gən) a group of different tissues that work together (p. 304)

Organelle (ôr gə nel´) a tiny structure inside a cell (p. 303)

Organism (ôr´ gə niz əm) a living thing (p. 303)

Ovary (ō´ vər ē) the female sex organ that produces egg cells (p. 337)

Ovulation (ov yə lā´ schən) the release of an egg from an ovary (p. 434)

Oxidation (ok sə dā´ schən) the process in which minerals combine with oxygen to form new substances (p. 188)

P

Paleozoic Era (pā lē ə zō´ ik ir´ ə) the era of Earth's history marked by great development in sea life, beginning about 570 million years ago and ending about 230 million years ago (p. 225)

Pangaea (pan jē´ ə) the single landmass from which the continents separated (p. 204)

Parallel (par´ ə lel) a line of latitude (p. 164)

Parallel circuit (par´ ə lel sir´ kut) a circuit in which there is more than one path for current (p. 133)

Parasite (par´ ə sīt) an organism that absorbs food from another living organism and harms it (p. 313)

Penis (pē´ nis) the male organ that delivers sperm to the female's body (p. 433)

Peripheral nervous system (pə rif´ ər əl nėr´ vəs sis´ təm) the part of the nervous system that consists of nerves outside of the brain and spinal cord (p. 441)

Peristalsis (per ə stal´ sis) the movement of digestive organs that pushes food through the digestive tract (p. 418)

Perspiration (pėr spə rā´ shən) liquid waste released through the skin (p. 431)

Petrification (pe trə fə kā´ shən) the replacement of organic matter with minerals (p. 222)

Phloem (flō′ əm) the vascular tissue in plants that carries food from leaves to other parts of the plant (p. 352)

Photons (fō′ tonz) small bundles of energy that make up light (p. 114)

Photosynthesis (fō tō sin′ thə sis) the process in which a plant makes food (p. 354)

Phylum (fī′ ləm) a subdivision of a kingdom (p. 319)

Physical change (fiz′ ə kəl chanj) a change in which the appearance of a substance changes but the properties stay the same (p. 48)

Physical science (fiz′ ə kəl sī′ əns) the study of matter and energy (p. 2)

Physics (fiz′ iks) the study of how energy acts with matter (p. 2)

Pigment (pig′ mənt) a chemical that absorbs certain types of light (p. 355)

Placenta (plə sen′ tə) a blood-rich tissue that grows into the lining of the uterus during pregnancy (p. 435)

Plane mirror (plān mir′ ər) a flat, smooth mirror (p. 118)

Planet (plan′ it) a large body in space that orbits a star such as the sun (p. 275)

Plasma (plaz′ mə) the liquid part of blood (p. 426)

Plate (plāt) a large section of Earth's crust that moves (p. 205)

Platelet (plāt′ lit) a blood cell that helps form clots (p. 427)

Plate tectonics (plāt tik ton′ iks) the theory that Earth's crust is made up of large sections that move (p. 205)

Pollen (pol′ ən) the tiny structures of seed plants that contain sperm (p. 359)

Pollination (pol li nā′ shən) the process by which pollen is transferred from the stamen to the pistil (p. 360)

Pollution (pə lü′ shən) anything added to the environment that is harmful to living things (p. 370)

Population (pop yə lā′ shən) a group of organisms of the same species that live in the same area (p. 368)

Porous (pôr′ əs) containing many spaces through which air and water can move (p. 234)

Potential energy (pə ten′ shəl en′ ər jē) stored energy (p. 63)

Precambrian Era (prē kam′ brē ən ir′ ə) the oldest and longest era of Earth's history, beginning about 4.6 billion years ago and ending about 570 million years ago (p. 225)

Precipitation (pri sip ə tā′ shən) moisture that falls to Earth from the atmosphere (p. 249)

Pregnancy (preg′ nən sē) the period during which a fertilized egg develops into a baby inside a female's body (p. 435)

Prevailing westerlies (pri vā′ ling wes′ tər lēs) winds north and south of the equator that blow from the west (p. 254)

Prime meridian (prīm mə rid′ ē ən) the line of 0° longitude (p. 166)

Prism (priz′ əm) a clear piece of glass or plastic that is shaped like a triangle and can be used to separate white light (p. 116)

Producer (pr′ dü′ sər) an organism that makes its own food (p. 374)

Product (prod′ əkt) a substance that is formed in a chemical reaction (p. 55)

Property (prop′ ər tē) a characteristic that helps identify an object (p. 25)

Protein (prō′ tēn) a chemical used by organisms to build and repair body parts and regulate body activities (p. 308)

Protist (prō′ tist) an organism that usually is one-celled and has plant-like or animal-like properties (p. 312)

Proton (prō′ ton) a tiny positively charged particle in the nucleus of an atom (p. 31)

Protozoan (prō tə zō ′ ən) a protist that has animal-like qualities (p. 312)

Pseudopod (sü′ də pod) a part of some one-celled organisms that sticks out like a foot to move the cell along (p. 312)

Psychrometer (sī krä′ mə tər) an instrument used to measure humidity (p. 261)

Puberty (pyü′ bər tē) the period of rapid growth and physical changes that occurs in males and females during early adolescence (p. 452)

a	hat	e	let	ī	ice	ò	order	ù	put	sh	she		a	in about
ā	age	ē	equal	o	hot	oi	oil	ü	rule	th	thin		e	in taken
ä	far	ėr	term	ō	open	ou	out	ch	child	ᴙᴙ	then	ə	i	in pencil
â	care	i	it	ò	saw	u	cup	ng	long	zh	measure		o	in lemon
													u	in circus

Pulley (pùl´ lē) a simple machine made up of a rope, chain, or belt wrapped around a wheel p. 83)

Pupa (pyü´ pə) a stage in the development of some insects that leads to the adult stage (p. 331)

Pyramid of numbers (pir´ ə mid uv num´ bərz) a diagram that compares the sizes of populations at different levels of a food chain (p. 375)

R

Radial symmetry (rā´ dē əl sim´ ə trē) an arrangement of body parts that resembles the arrangement of spokes on a wheel (p. 328)

Radiation (rā dē ā´ shən) the movement of energy through a vacuum (p. 103)

Rain gauge (rān gāj) an instrument used to measure the amount of rainfall (p. 262)

Reactant (rē ak´ tənt) a substance that is changed to form a product in a chemical reaction (p. 55)

Receptor cell (ri sep´ tər sel) a cell that receives information about the environment and starts nerve impulses to send that information to the brain (p. 444)

Rectum (rek´ təm) lower part of the large intestine where feces are stored (p. 419)

Red marrow (red mar´ ō) the spongy material in bones that makes blood cells (p. 411)

Reflection (ri flek´ shən) the bouncing back of a light wave (p. 118)

Refraction (ri frak´ shən) the bending of a wave as it moves from one material to another (p. 119)

Repel (ri pel´) to push apart (p. 137)

Reproduction (rē prə duk´ shən) the process by which organisms produce offspring (p. 310)

Reptile (rep´ tīl) a vertebrate that breathes with lungs and lays soft-shelled eggs on land (p. 326)

Resistance force (ri zis´ təns fôrs) the force applied to a machine by the object to be moved (p. 80)

Resource (rē´ sôrs) a thing that an organism uses to live (p. 371)

Respiration (res pə rā´ shən) the process of gas exchange in which animals take in oxygen and release carbon dioxide (p. 334)

Reverse fault (re vèrs´ fôlt) a break in the crust in which the overhanging block of rock has been raised (p. 210)

Revolution (rev ə lü´ shən) the movement of one object in its orbit around another object in space (p. 162)

Rhizoid (rī´ zoid) a tiny root-like thread of a moss plant (p. 350)

Richter scale (rik´ tər skāl) a scale used to measure the strength of an earthquake (p. 214)

Rock (rok) a natural solid material made of one or more minerals (p. 180)

Rock cycle (rok sī´ kəl) the series of changes through which one kind of rock becomes another kind of rock (p. 182)

Rotation (rō tā´ shən) the spinning of Earth (p. 158)

Runoff (run´ òf) water that runs over Earth's surface and flows into streams (p. 234)

S

Salinity (sə lin´ ə tē) the saltiness of water (p. 237)

Schematic diagram (ski mat´ ik dī´ ə gram) a diagram that uses symbols to show the parts of a circuit (p. 128)

Scientific name (sī ən tif´ ik nām) the name given to each species, consisting of its genus and its species label (p. 321)

Screw (skrü) a simple machine made up of an inclined plane wrapped around a straight piece of metal (p. 85)

Scrotum (skrō´ təm) the exterior sac that holds the testes (p. 433)

Sea-floor spreading (sē´ flôr spred´ ing) the theory that the ocean floor spreads apart as new crust is formed at the mid-oceanic ridge (p. 205)

Seamount (sē´ mount) an underwater mountain that is usually a volcano (p. 238)

Sedimentary rock (sed ə men´ tər ē rok) rock formed from pieces of other rock and organic matter that was pressed and cemented together (p. 181)

Seed (sēd) a plant part that contains a beginning plant and stored food (p. 346)

Seismograph (sīz´ mə graf) an instrument that detects and records earthquake waves (p. 213)

Semen (sē´ mən) a mixture of fluid and sperm cells (p. 434)

Series circuit (sir´ ēz sèr´ kit) a circuit in which all current flows through a single path (p. 129)

Sexual reproduction (sek´ shü əl rē prə duk´ shən) reproduction that involves an egg from a female parent and sperm from a male parent (p. 337)

Shield volcano (shēld vol kā´ nō) a volcano with wide crater, developing from layers of lava (p. 208)

Simple machine (sim´ pəl mə shēn´) a tool with few parts that makes it easier or possible to do work (p. 79)

Soil (soil) a mixture of tiny pieces of weathered rock and the remains of plants and animals (p. 189)

Solar system (sō´ lər sis´ təm) a star, such as the sun, and all the bodies that revolve around it in space (p. 275)

Solid (sol´ id) a form of matter that has a definite shape and volume (p. 28)

Solute (sol´ yüt) the substance that is dissolved in a solution (p. 54)

Solution (sə lü´ shən) a mixture in which one substance is dissolved in another (pp. 54, 306)

Solvent (sol´ vənt) the substance in which the dissolving occurs in a solution (p. 54)

Sound wave (sound wāv) a wave produced by vibrations (p. 112)

South pole (south pōl) the point farthest south on Earth (p. 158)

Species (spē´ shēz) a group of organisms that can breed with each other to produce offspring like themselves (p. 320)

Speed (spēd) the rate at which the position of an object changes (p. 68)

Sperm cell (spėrm sel) a male sex cell (p. 337)

Spore (spôr) the reproductive cell of ferns and some other organisms (p. 349)

Standard mass (stan´ dərd mas) a small object that is used with a balance to determine mass (p. 18)

Standard time zone (stan´ dərd tīm zōn) an area that has the same clock time (p. 159)

Star (stär) a glowing ball of hot gas that makes its own energy and light (p. 275)

State of matter (stāt uv mat´ ər) the form that matter has—solid, liquid, or gas (p. 29)

Static electricity (stat´ ik i lek tris´ ə tē) a buildup of electrical charges (p. 125)

Stoma (stō´ mə) a small opening in a leaf that allows gases to enter and leave; plural *stomata* (p. 353)

Stratosphere (strat´ ə sfir) the second layer of the atmosphere, which includes the ozone layer (p. 247)

Stratus cloud (strat´ əs kloud) a low, flat cloud that forms in layers (p. 250)

Streak (strēk) the color of the mark a mineral makes on a white tile (p. 175)

Strike-slip fault (strīk slip fȯlt) a break in the crust in which the blocks of rock move horizontally past each other (p. 210)

Subscript (sub´ skript) a number in a formula that tells the number of atoms of an element in a compound (p. 52)

Subsoil (sub´ soil) the layer of soil directly below the topsoil (p. 190)

Succession (sək sesh´ ən) the process by which a community changes over time (p. 369)

Sunspot (sun´ spot) a dark area of the sun's surface that gives off less energy than the rest of the sun (p. 277)

Swim bladder (swim blad´ ər) a gas-filled organ that allows a bony fish to move up and down in the water (p. 325)

Symbol (sim´ bəl) one or two letters that represent the name of an element (p. 39)

Synapse (sin´ aps) a tiny gap between neurons (p. 443)

T

Taxonomy (tak son´ ə mē) the science of classifying organisms based on the features they share (p. 319)

Temperature (tem´ pər ə chər) a measure of how fast an object's particles are moving (p. 97)

Tendon (ten´ dən) a tough strip of tissue that connects a muscle to a bone (p. 414)

Tentacle (ten´ tə kəl) an armlike body part in invertebrates that is used for capturing prey (p. 328)

Testis (tes´ tis) the male reproductive organ that produces sperm cells; plural *testes* (p. 433)

a hat	e let	ī ice	ȯ order	ů put	sh she
ā age	ē equal	o hot	oi oil	ü rule	th thin
ä far	ėr term	ō open	ou out	ch child	ŦH then
â care	i it	ȯ saw	u cup	ng long	zh measure

ə { a in about / e in taken / i in pencil / o in lemon / u in circus }

Thermocline (thėr′ mō klīn) the layer of the ocean between about 300 and 800 meters, where the temperature drops sharply (p. 237)

Thermometer (thər mom′ ə tər) a device that measures temperature (p. 98)

Thermosphere (thėr′ mə sfir) the outermost layer of the atmosphere (p. 247)

Tissue (tish′ ü) a group of cells that are similar and work together (p. 304)

Topsoil (top′ soil′) the top layer of soil, rich with remains of plants and animals (p. 190)

Tornado (tôr nā′ dō) a powerful wind storm with a whirling, funnel-shaped cloud and extremely low air pressure (p. 264)

Trachea (trā′ kē ə) the tube that carries air to the bronchi (p. 428)

Trench (trench) a deep valley on the ocean floor (p. 238)

Tributary (trib′ yə ter ē) a river that joins another river of equal or greater size (p. 234)

Troposphere (trop′ ə sfir) the bottom layer of the atmosphere, extending from ground level up to about 17 kilometers (p. 246)

Tsunami ((t)sü nä′ mē) a large sea wave caused by an earthquake on the ocean floor (p. 215)

Tube foot (tüb fût) a small structure used by echinoderms for movement (p. 329)

U

Umbilical cord (um bil′ ə kəl kôrd) the cord that connects an embryo with the placenta (p. 435)

Unit (yü′ nit) a known amount used for measuring (p. 5)

Ureter (yû rē′ tər) a tube that carries urine from the kidney to the urinary bladder (p. 432)

Urethra (yû rē′ thrə) the tube that carries urine out of the body (p. 432)

Urine (yûr′ ən) liquid waste formed in the kidneys (p. 432)

Uterus (yü′ tər əs) the female reproductive organ that holds and protects a developing baby (p. 434)

V

Vacuum (vak′ yüm) space that contains no matter (p. 103)

Vagina (və jī′ nə) the tubelike canal in the female body through which sperm enter the body (p. 433)

Vascular plant (vas′ kyə lər plant) a plant that has tubelike tissue (p. 343)

Vascular tissue (vas′ kyə lər tish′ ü) a group of plant cells that form tubes through which food and water move (p. 343)

Vein (vān) a blood vessel that carries blood to the heart (p. 425)

Vent (vent) an opening through which magma reaches Earth's surface (p. 207)

Ventricle (ven′ trə kəl) a heart chamber that pumps blood out of the heart (p. 336)

Vertebra (vėr′ tə brə) one of the bones or blocks of cartilage that make up a backbone (p. 324)

Vertebrate (vėr′ tə brāt) an animal with a backbone (p. 325)

Vestigial structure (ve stij′ ē əl struk′ chər) a body part that appears to be useless to an organism but was probably useful to the organism's ancestors (p. 398)

Vibrate (vī′ brāt) to move rapidly back and forth (p. 111)

Villi (vil′ ī) structures in the small intestine through which food molecules enter the bloodstream (p. 419)

Visible spectrum (viz′ ə bəl spek′ trəm) the band of colors that make up white light (p. 116)

Vitamin (vī′ tə mən) a chemical needed in small amounts for growth and activity (p. 308)

Volcano (vol kā′ nō) a mountain that develops where magma erupts onto Earth's surface (p. 207)

Volt (vōlt) the metric unit used to measure electromotive force (p. 126)

Voltage (vōl′ tij) the energy that a power source gives to electrons in a circuit (p. 126)

Volume (vol′ yəm) the amount of space an object takes up (p. 14)

Voluntary muscle (vol′ ən ter ē mus′ əl) a muscle that a person can control (p. 416)

W

Warm front (wôrm frunt) the boundary ahead of a warm air mass that is pushing out and riding over a cold air mass (p. 263)

Water cycle (wȯ′tər sī′ kəl) the movement of water between the atmosphere and Earth's surface (p. 233)

Water table (wȯ′tər tā′ bəl) the top of the groundwater layer (p. 234)

Water vapor (wȯ′tər vā′ pər) water in the form of a gas (p. 249)

Wave (wāv) an up and down motion of water caused by energy moving through the water (p. 239)

Weather (weт͟н′ ər) the state of the atmosphere at a given time and place (p. 259)

Weathering (weт͟н′ ər ing) the breaking down of rocks on Earth's surface (p. 187)

Wedge (wej) a simple machine made up of an inclined plane or pair of inclined planes that are moved (p. 86)

Weight (wāt) the measure of gravitational pull on an object (p. 19)

Wheel and axle (wēl and ak′ sel) a simple machine made up of a wheel attached to a shaft (p. 86)

Wind belt (wind belt) a pattern of wind movement around Earth (p. 254)

Wind cell (wind sel) a continuous cycle of rising warm air and falling cold air (p. 253)

Wind vane (wind vān) an instrument used to find wind direction (p. 261)

Work (wėrk) what happens when something changes its motion in the direction of the force being applied (p. 77)

X

Xylem (zī′ lem) the vascular tissue in plants that carries water and minerals from roots to stems and leaves (p. 352)

a	hat	e	let	ī	ice	ȯ	order	u̇	put	sh	she	
ā	age	ē	equal	o	hot	oi	oil	ü	rule	th	thin	
ä	far	ėr	term	ō	open	ou	out	ch	child	т͟н	then	
â	care	i	it	ȯ	saw	u	cup	ng	long	zh	measure	

ə { a in about / e in taken / i in pencil / o in lemon / u in circus }

Index

A

Acceleration, 72
Acid rain, 370
  testing pH of, 372-373
Adaptations, 397
Adolescence, 452
Africa, 156
Air masses, 263
Air pressure, 260
  in highs and lows, 264
Air resistance, 63, 72
Air temperature, 259
Alchemists, 53
Algae, 312, 358
Alluvial fan, 193
Altitude, 250
Alveoli, 428–429
Ampere, 126
Amphibians
  circulatory system of,
    336
  features of, 325–326
Anatomy, 300
Anemometer, 261
Angiosperms
  features of, 346
  sexual reproduction
    in, 359–360
Animal kingdom, 311
Annual growth rings, 352
Antarctica, 156
Antibodies, 426, 427
Anus, 419
Aorta, 423
Arctic Ocean, 156, 157
Area, 10–11
Arteries, 425
Arthropods
  circulatory system of,
    335
  features of, 331
Asexual reproduction
  advantages and
    disadvantages of, 337
  and mitosis, 393
  of plants, 359
  of simple animals, 337
Asia, 156
Associative neurons, 444
Asteroid, 289

Asteroid belt, 289
Astronomy, 152
Atlantic Ocean, 156, 157
Atmosphere, 245
  gases in, 245
  layers of, 246–247
  of sun, 277
Atoms, 28
  bonds between, 64
  in compounds, 41, 51
  in elements, 33
  models of, 30–32
  and nuclear energy, 94
  in reactions, 55–56
Atria, 336, 423
Australia, 156
Axis, 158
  Earth's, 162
  other planets', 284,
    285, 286

B

Bacteria
  as consumers, 374
  as decomposers, 377
  in genetic engineering,
    395
  helpful and harmful,
    314
  in monera kingdom,
    313
  in nitrogen cycle, 314,
    384–385
Balance, 18
Balancing equations,
  56–57
Barometer, 260
Basic life activities,
  309–310
Batteries, 131, 134
Bilateral symmetry, 328
Bile, 418
Biologist, 300, 301
Biology, 300
Biomes, 370–371
Biosphere, 367, 371
Birds
  circulatory system of,
    336
  features of 327
Birth, human, 436

Blood, 426–427
Blood pressure, 425
Blood vessels, 335, 425
Boiling point, 100
Bones, functions of, 411
Botany, 300
Brain, human, 441, 442
Brain stem, 442
Breathing, 429–430
Bronchi, 428
Bronchioles, 428

C

Capillaries, 425
Carbohydrates, 307, 308
  digestion of, 418
Carbon cycle, 383–384
Carbon dioxide-oxygen
  cycle, 357
Cardiac arrest, 430
Cardiac muscle, 416, 422
Cardiopulmonary resus-
  citation (CPR), 430
Carnivores, 375
Cartilage, 325
  in fish, 326
  in human skeleton, 411
Cast, 223
Cells
  as basic unit of life,
    303–304
  in blood, 426
  division of, 393,
    394–395
Cellular respiration
  as basic life activity, 309
  in carbon cycle,
    383–384
  relationship to photo
    synthesis, 356
Celsius scale, 99–100, 259
Cenozoic Era, 228
Central nervous system,
  441
Cerebellum, 442
Cerebrum, 442
Charon, 286
Chemical change, 47
  of minerals in rock,
    188–189
Chemical energy, 65

Chemical equations,
  55–57
  for photosynthesis, 356
Chemical formulas, 51–52
Chemical reactions, 53
  in photosynthesis, 379
Chemical weathering,
  188–189
Chemistry, 3
Chlorophyll, 355, 379
Chloroplasts, 355
Chromosomes, 391
  in asexual
    reproduction, 393
  in meiosis, 394
  in mitosis, 393
  in sexual reproduction,
    394–395
Chromosphere, 276, 277
Chyme, 418
Cilia, 312
Cinder cone volcano, 208
Circuit, 126
  closed, 126
  open, 127
  parallel, 133–134
  series, 129–132
  schematic diagram of,
    128
Circuit breaker, 132, 134
Circulatory system
  in animals, 335–336
  in humans, 422–425
  open and closed, 335
  in vertebrates, 336
Cirrus clouds, 250
Classes
  grouping organisms
    into, 319
  of vertebrates, 324–327
Classification
  of animals, 319–322
  of invertebrates,
    328–331
  of organisms, 311, 319
  of plants, 343–345
  scientific system of, 319
  of vertebrates, 324–327
Climate, 268
  of biomes, 370

factors that affect, 270
Climate zones, 268
   chart of, 269
Climax community, 369
Closed circuit, 126
Closed circulatory system, 335
Clouds, 249–250
Cnidarians, 328, 333
   symmetry in, 329
Coefficient, 56–57
Cold front, 263
Colors
   detection of by human eye, 445
   of minerals, 174, 175
   in white light, 116
Comets, 290
Communities, 367, 368
   succession in, 368–369
Compass, 139
Composite volcano, 208
Compounds, 41–42
   characteristics of, 48
   formulas for, 51–52
   in minerals, 173
   water as, 41, 47
Concave lens, 120
Concave mirror, 119
Condensation, 233, 249
Conduction, 104
Conductor, 104
Cones
   in human eye, 445
   seeds produced in, 347
Conifers, 347–348
Conodonts, 228
Conservation
   of energy, 66
   of matter, 55–56
Consumers
   in food chain, 374
   levels of, 375, 377, 380
Continental drift, 204
Continental shelf, 238
Continental slope, 238
Continents, 156, 204
Convection, 105
   currents, 206
Convex lens, 120
Convex mirror, 119
Core, 203
Cornea, 444
Corona, 276, 277

CPR (Cardiopulmonary resuscitation), 430
Crust, 203
   formation of new, 205
   movement of, 205–206
Cumulus clouds, 250
Currents, ocean, 239–240
Cytology, 300

D

Darwin, Charles, 398
Day and night, cause of, 159
Daylight Savings Time, 160
Decomposers
   bacteria as, 313, 314, 377
   in carbon cycle, 383–384
   fungi as, 313, 377
Delta, 193
Deposition, 193
   by glaciers, 196
   by rivers, 193
   by waves, 194
   by wind, 197
Diaphragm, role of in breathing, 429–430
Diffusion, 334
Digestion
   as basic life activity, 309
   in animals, 332–333
   in humans, 417–419
Digestive enzymes, 418
Digestive system, human, 417–419
Digestive tract, 333
   organs in, 417
Displacement of water, 17
Dissolving, 54
Distance, 68
   in calculating speed, 68–69
   in calculating work, 77–78
   effect on gravity, 71
DNA, 391, 392
   copying, 392, 393, 394, 396
Drainage basin, 234
Dry cell battery, 130

E

Eardrum, 446

Earth, 280, 281
   axis of, 158
   continents of, 156
   distance around, 155
   land area of, 156
   layers of, 203
   oceans of, 157
   poles of, 158
   revolution of, 162–163
   rotation of, 158–159, 162
   shape of, 155
   water area of, 156
Earthquakes, 212
   causes of, 206, 212
   detecting, 213
   effects of, 215
   locating, 214
   predicting, 215
   strength of, 214
Earthquake waves, 213
Earth science, 152–153
Eastern hemisphere, 167
Echinoderms, 329
Ecology, 300, 367
Ecosystems, 367, 369
   as biomes, 370
   changes in, 369
   cycles of materials in, 382–386
   effect of pollution on, 370
   energy flow in, 378–381
   food chains in, 374–375
   food webs in, 376
Effort force, 79
Egg cells, 337, 338
   in flower, 360
   and ovulation, 434
Elapsed time, 67
Electrical energy, 65
Electric current, 126
Electricity, 125
   as form of energy, 65, 94
   as heat source, 94
   as movement of electrons, 125–126
   production of with generator, 65
   static, 125
   See also Batteries,

Circuit, Electric current, Voltage
Electromagnet, 142
Electron, 31, 65
   movement of, 125–126, 130, 133
Elements, 33
   in compounds, 47, 53
   in healthy diet, 35
   in minerals, 173
   natural, 33
   Periodic Table, 36–37
   symbols for, 39–40, 51
   in water, 34
Embryo
   human, 434, 435, 436
   in seed, 346
   similarities as evidence of evolution, 398
Endocrine glands, 451
Endocrine system, human, 451–452
Energy, 2, 63
   chemical, 64, 94
   in earthquakes, 212
   electrical, 65, 66, 94
   flow of in ecosystems, 378–381
   in food, 379, 431
   forms of, 64–66, 378
   heat, 64, 93, 379
   kinetic, 63, 66
   law of conservation of, 66
   light, 114
   mechanical, 64, 93
   nuclear, 64, 94
   potential, 63, 66
   radiant, 65
   stored, 63, 379, 381
   use of in photo synthesis, 379
Energy pyramid, 380–381
English system, 6
Environment
   effect of on traits, 391
   and evolution, 397
Enzymes, 418
Epicenter, 214
Equations, chemical, 55
   balancing, 56–57
Equator, 164
Erosion, 192
   by glaciers, 195

by gravity, 198
human actions and, 194
by rivers, 192
by waves, 194
by wind, 197
Esophagus, 418
Europa, 283
Europe, 156
Evaporation
heat as cause of, 95
of perspiration, 431
in water cycle, 233, 249
Evolution, 396
Darwin's theory, 398
evidence of, 398
as result of changes in environment, 397
as result of mutations, 396–397
theory of natural selection, 398–399
Excretion, as basic life activity, 309
Excretory system, human, 432
Expand, 96
Eyeglasses, lenses in, 450

F

Fahrenheit scale, 99–100, 259
Fallopian tubes, 434
Families, grouping organisms into, 319
Fats, 307, 308, 379
digestion of, 418
Faults, 210
movement along, 212
types of, 210
Feces, 419
Feedback loop, 452
Female reproductive system, 434
Ferns
energy from, 350
reproduction of, 349
as vascular plants, 343
Fertilization, in sexual reproduction, 338, 434
Fetus, 436
Film, photographic, 58
Filter feeding, 332
Fish, 326, 336

Fixed pulley, 83
Flagella, 312
Flatworms, 328, 333
Flower, parts of, 359
Flowering plants See Angiosperms
Focus, 214
Folding, 209
Food chains, 374–375
in food web, 376
Food webs, 376
Force, 77–78
effort, 79, 82
resistance, 80, 82
Formula, chemical, 51–52
Fossils, 222–223
conodonts, 228
on continents, 204
mold and cast, 223
Freezing point, 100
Friction, 63, 93
along faults, 212
Fronds, 349
Front, 263
Fruit, of angiosperms, 346, 360
Fulcrum, 79
Fungi
as consumers, 374
as decomposers, 313, 377
kingdom, 313
Fuse, 132, 134

G

Gallbladder, 418
Ganymede, 283
Gas exchange, 334–335
in human lungs, 428–429
Gases, 29
changing from liquid to, 95, 100
in Earth's atmosphere, 245
expansion and contraction of, 96
in solutions, 54
in sun, 276
Gastrovascular cavity, 333
Generator, 65
Genes, 391
and DNA, 391, 392
and evolution, 396–397

Genetic engineering, 395
Genetics, 300, 391
Genus
grouping organisms into, 319
in scientific name, 322
Geologic time, 221
Geologic time scale, 225
chart of, 226
Geology, 152
Germination, 360
Gills, 326, 334
Glaciers, 195–196
Glands, 451–452
Glucose
as energy source for organisms, 356
production of by plants, 355, 357
Graduated cylinder, 16–17
Gram, 18
Gravity, 71
and acceleration, 72
Earth's, 20, 71
erosion by, 198
on other planets, 20
in solar system, 275
Great Red Spot, 282–283
Greenhouse effect, 280
Groundwater, 233–234
Growth, as basic life activity, 310
Guard cells, 358
Gymnosperms
features of, 347–348
sexual reproduction in, 360

H

Habitat, 368
Hardness
of minerals, 175
quick test for, 175–176
Hearing, sense of, 446
Heart
in circulatory system, 335
of humans, 422, 423
role in circulation, 423
of vertebrates, 336
Heartbeat, 422
Heat, 64, 93
detection of by skin, 446

effect of on matter, 95–96
and mass, 101
measurement of, 97
release of by organisms, 379, 380–381
sources of, 93–94
and temperature, 101
travel of, 103–105
Heating systems, 106
Hemispheres, 167
Hemoglobin, 426
Herbivores, 375
Heredity, 391
Highs, 264
Homologous structures, 399
Hormones, 451–452
Humidity, 261
Hurricane, 265

I

Igneous rock, 181
in rock cycle, 182
Image, 118
Impulse, nerve, 443
Inclined plane, 84–85
Indian Ocean, 156, 157
Inner planets, 278–281
diagram of, 278
facts about, 281
Insects
features of, 331
gas exchange in, 335
mouth parts of, 332
Insulators, 104
Interact, 367
Invertebrates, 328–331
Involuntary muscle, 416
Io, 283
Ionosphere, 247
Ions, 247
Iris, in human eye, 444
Isobar, 264

J

Joints, 413
Joule, 77
Jupiter, 282–283, 287

K

Kidneys, 432, 451
Kinetic energy, 63
Kingdoms, 311, 319

Animal, 311
Fungi, 313
Monera, 313
Plant, 311
Protist, 312

L

Lakes, formation of, 235
Large intestine, 419
Larynx, 428
Lasers, uses of, 117
Latitude, 164
    estimating, 165
    lines of, 164
    locating points by, 167
Law of conservation of
    energy, 66
Law of conservation of
    matter, 55–56
Law of universal
    gravitation, 71
Laws of motion, 71
Leaves
    of conifers, 347
    of ferns, 349
    functions and parts of,
    353
    role of in photo-
    synthesis, 354–355
    of seed plants, 346
    of vascular plants, 343,
    353
Leda, 283
Length
    measuring, 7–9
    metric equivalents, 9
Lenses
    in eyeglasses, 450
    in human eye, 445
    types of, 120
Lever, 79
    classes of, 80–81
    mechanical advantage
    of, 82
Life science, 300–301
Ligaments, 413
Light, 114
    detection of by human
    eye, 445
    reflection of, 118
    refraction of, 119–120
    speed of, 115
    as waves, 115
Lightning, 125

Lines of force, 138
Liquid, 29, 54
    changing state, 95, 100
    expansion and
    contraction of, 96
    measuring mass of, 19
    measuring volume of,
    15–16
Liter, 15
Liver, function of, 418
Lodestone as magnet, 136
Longitude, 166
    estimating, 166
    locating points by, 167
Lows, 264
Lungs,
    for gas exchange, 335
    in human respiration,
    428–430
Luster, 174

M

Machines See Simple
    machines
Magma, 181
    on ocean floor, 205
    in rock cycle, 182
    in volcano, 207
Magnet, 136
    Earth as, 139
Magnetic field, 138, 142
Magnetic poles, 137
Male reproductive
    system, 433
Mammals
    circulatory system of,
    336
    features of, 327
    teeth of, 332
Mammary glands, 327
Mantle, 203, 206
Mars, 281
Mass, 2
    effect of on gravity, 71
    of Jupiter, 282
    measuring, 19–20
    metric equivalents, 18
    of sun, 276
    and temperature, 101
    and weight, 20
Matter, 28
    effect of heat on, 95–96
    law of conservation of,
    55–56

states of, 28–29
Measurement, 5–6
    of area, 10–11
    of length, 7–9
    of mass, 18–20
    systems of, 6
    of temperature,
    98–100
    of volume, 14–17
Mechanical advantage
    (MA), 82
    of inclined plane, 85
    of lever, 82
    of pulley, 83–84
    of screw, 85
    of wedge, 86
    of wheel and axle, 86
Mechanical energy, 64
Mechanical weathering,
    187–188
Meiosis, 394
Melting point, 100
Meniscus, 16
Menstruation, 435, 452
Mercury, 278, 281
Meridians, 166 See also
    Longitude
Mesosphere, 247
Mesozoic Era, 227
Metamorphic rock, 181
    in rock cycle, 182
Metamorphosis, 326
    of frog, 326
    of insects, 331
Meteorites, 290
Meteorologist, 153, 259
Meteorology, 152
Meteors, 289–290
Meter, 7
Meterstick, 8
Metric system, 6
    to measure area, 10–11
    to measure length, 7–9
    to measure mass,
    18–20
    to measure tempera-
    ture, 99
    to measure volume,
    14–17
    prefixes in, 9
Microbiology, 300
Microscope, 303
Midocean ridge, 204,
    205, 238

Minerals, 173, 308
    chemical weathering
    of, 188–189
    color of, 174, 175
    features of, 173
    in fossils, 222
    hardness of, 175–176
    importance of, for life,
    308
    luster of, 174
    in rocks, 180
    streak of, 175
    uses of, 177
Mirrors, 118–119
Mitosis, 393
Mixture, 53
Model, 30
    of atoms, 30–31
Mohs scale of hardness,
    175
Mold, of fossil, 223
Molecules, 27
    in gas, 29
    and heat, 104
    in liquid, 29
    in mixtures, 54
    movement of, 28–29,
    97
    in solid, 28
    of water, 27–28, 34, 41
Mollusks, 329
Molting, of arthropods,
    331
Monera kingdom, 313
Monerans, 313
Moons
    of inner planets, 281
    of Jupiter, 283, 287
    of Neptune, 286, 287
    of outer planets, 287
    of Pluto, 286, 287
    of Saturn, 284, 287
    of Uranus, 285, 287
Moraine, 196
Mosses
    energy from, 350
    as nonvascular plant,
    345
    reproduction of, 350
    as seedless plant, 349
Motion, 67–69, 71
Motor neurons, 444
Mountains, formation of,
    209–210

Mouth, role of in digestion, 418
Movable pulley, 83
Movement
    as basic life activity, 309
    by muscles and bones, 413
Muscular system, human, 414–416
Mutations, 391
    causes of, 391, 396
    effects of, 397
    and evolution, 396–397

N

Natural elements, 33
Natural selection, theory of, 398–399
Neptune, 286, 287
Nervous system, human
    brain in, 442
    parts of, 441
    sense organs in, 444–447
    spinal cord in, 443
Neurons, 443–444
Neutron, 31
Newton, Sir Isaac, 71
Nitrogen cycle, 384–385
    and bacteria, 314
Nitrogen fixation, 384
Nonvascular plants, 345
Normal fault, 210
North America, 156
Northern hemisphere, 167
    seasons in, 163
North Pole, 158
    latitude of, 164
Nuclear energy, 64
Nucleus, 31, 64
Nutrients, 308, 379

O

Ocean currents, 239–240
Ocean floor, 238
Oceanography, 152
Oceans, major, 157
Ocean water, properties of, 237
Ocean waves, 239
Omnivores, 375
Open circuit, 127
Open circulatory system, 335

Optic nerve, 445
Order, grouping organisms into, 319
Organelles, 303
    and bacteria, 313
    chloroplasts as, 355
Organisms, 303, 367–368
Organs, 304
    bones as, 411
    in circulatory system, 335–336, 422–423
    in digestive system, 333, 417
    in endocrine system, 451
    in excretory system, 432
    in nervous system, 441
    in reproductive system, 337, 433–434
    in respiratory system, 334–335, 429
    sense, 444–447
    skin as, 431
Outer planets, 282–287
    diagram of, 282
    facts about, 287
Ovaries, 337
    in flowers, 360
    in humans, 434
Ovulation, 434, 452
Oxidation of rock, 188
Oxygen cycle, 384
Ozone layer, 248

P

Pacific Ocean, 156, 157
Paleozoic Era, 225
Pancreas, 418, 451
Pangaea, 204
Parallel circuit, 133–134
Parallels, 164 See also Latitude
Parasites, 313
Penis, 433, 435
Periodic Table, 36–37
Peripheral nervous system, 441
Peristalsis, 418
Perspiration, 431
Petiole, 353
Petrification, 222
Pharynx, 428
Phloem, 352
Photons, 114

Photosphere, 276, 277
Photosynthesis
    chemical equation for, 356
    description of, 354–355
    in food chain, 374
    role in carbon dioxide-oxygen cycle, 356–357
Phylum
    grouping organisms into, 319
    of invertebrates, 329–331
Physical change, 48
Physical science, 2–3
Physics, 3
Physiology, 300
Pigment, 355
Pistil, 359, 360
Placenta, 435, 436
Plane mirror, 118
Planets, 275
    distances from sun, 281
    Earth, 280, 281
    inner, 278–281
    Jupiter, 282–283, 287
    Mars, 281
    Mercury, 278, 281
    Neptune, 286, 287
    outer, 282–287
    Pluto, 286, 287
    Saturn, 284, 287
    Uranus, 285, 287
    Venus, 279–280, 281
Plant kingdom, 311
Plasma, in blood, 426
Platelets, 427
Plates, 205
    and formation of mountains, 209
    movement of, 206
Plate tectonics, 205
Pluto, 286, 287
Polar climates, 269
Pollen, 359–360
Pollination, 360
Pollution, 370
Populations, 367–368
    in energy pyramid, 380
    and evolution, 396
Porous, 234
Potential energy, 63

Precambrian Era, 225
Precipitation
    in different climate zones, 268–270
    forms of, 249
    measuring, 262
    in water cycle, 233
Pregnancy, in humans, 435–436
Prevailing westerlies, 254, 264
Prime meridian, 166
Prism, 116
Producers
    in food chains, 374–375, 379–381
    as source of oxygen, 384
Products of chemical reactions, 55
Properties
    in chemical changes, 47
    of minerals, 174–176
    of objects, 25–26
    of ocean water, 237
    in physical changes, 48
Prostate gland, 434
Proteins, 308, 379
    digestion of, 418
Protist kingdom, 312
Protists, 312
    as consumers, 374
    as decomposers, 377
Proton, 31
Protozoans, 312
Pseudopods, 312
Psychrometer, 261
Puberty, 452
Pulley, 83–84
Pulse, 422
Pupa, 331
Pupil, in human eye, 444–445
Pyramid of numbers, 375

R

Radial symmetry, 328, 329
Radiant energy, 65
Radiation
    of heat, 103
    ultraviolet, 248
Rain gauge, 262
Ramp See Inclined plane
Reactants, 55

Reactions, 53, 55–57
Receptor cells, 444, 445, 446
Rectum, 419
Red blood cells, 426
Red marrow, 411
Reflection of light, 118
Reflex actions, 444
Refraction of light, 119
Repel, 137
Replicate, 392
Reproduction
 of animals, 337–338
 asexual, 337, 359, 393
 as basic life activity, 310
 of humans, 433–436
 of seedless plants, 359
 of seed plants, 359–360
 sexual, 337–338, 359, 394–395
Reproductive system, human, 433–436
Reptiles, 326, 336
Resistance force, 80
Resources in biomes, 371
Respiration
 in animals, 334–335
 in humans, 428–430
 See also Cellular respiration
Respiratory system, human, 428–430
Responding, as basic life activity, 310
Retina, 445
Reverse fault, 210
Revolution
 of Earth, 162
 of Mars, 281
 of Mercury, 278
 of Neptune, 286
 of Pluto, 286
 of Uranus, 285
Rhizoids, 350
Richter scale, 214
Rift, 204
Rivers
 deposition by, 193
 erosion by, 192
 formation of, 234
Rock cycle, 182
Rocks, 180
 igneous, 181, 182

metamorphic, 181, 182
 minerals in, 180
 sedimentary, 181, 182
 types of, 181
 weathering of, 187
Rods, in human eye, 445
Roots
 functions of, 351
 parts of, 352
 role in photosynthesis, 354–355
 of seed plants, 346
 in vascular plants, 343, 351–352
Rotation
 of Earth, 158–159
 of Jupiter, 282
 of Mars, 281
 of Mercury, 278, 287
 of Neptune, 286
 of Pluto, 286
 of Saturn, 284
 of Uranus, 285, 287
 of Venus, 279
Roundworms, 329
Runoff, 233–234

S

Salinity, 237
Salivary glands, 418
Sand dune, formation of, 197
Saturn, 284, 287
Schematic diagrams, 128
Scientific names, 321–322
Screw, 85
Scrotum, 433
Sea-floor spreading, 204–205
Seamount, 238
Seasons, 162–163
Sedimentary rocks, 181
 in rock cycle, 182
Seedless plants
 features of, 349–350
 reproduction in, 359
Seed plants
 features of, 346–348
 reproduction in, 359–360
Seeds, 346, 360
Segmented worms, 329
Seismograph, 213, 214

Semen, 434
Sense organs, 444
 ears, 446
 eyes, 444–445
 nose, 447
 skin, 431, 446
 tongue, 447
Sensing, as basic life activity, 310
Sensory neurons, 444
Series circuit, 129–132
Sexual reproduction
 advantages and disadvantages of, 337–338
 in angiosperms, 359
 in animals, 337–338
 in gymnosperms, 360
 in humans, 433–436
 in mammals, 337–338
 in plants, 359–360
Shield volcano, 208
Sight, sense of, 444–445
Simple machines, 79
 at home, 87
 inclined plane, 84–85
 lever, 79–82
 pulley, 83–84
 screw, 85
 wedge, 86
 wheel and axle, 86
Skeletal muscle, 416
Skeletal system, human, 411–412
Skeleton
 external, 331
 of humans, 412
 of vertebrates, 325
Skin
 of amphibians and reptiles, 327
 of humans, 431, 446
Small intestine, 418
Smell, sense of, 447
Smog, 248
Smooth muscle, 416
Soil
 erosion of, 192
 layers of, 189–190
 materials in, 189
Solar flares, 277
Solar system, 275
Solid, 28, 54

changing state, 95, 100
 expansion and contraction of, 96
 measuring mass of, 19
 measuring volume of, 14, 17
Solute, 54
Solutions, 54, 306
Solvent, 54
Sori, 349
Sound, 111–112
 detection of by human ear, 446
 speed of, 115
 waves, 112
South America, 156
Southern hemisphere, 167
 seasons in, 163
South Pole, 158
 latitude of, 164
Species, 320
 grouping organisms into, 319
 in scientific name, 322–323
Speed, 68
 calculating, 68–69
 of wind, 261
Sperm cells, 337, 338
 in flower, 360
 of humans, 433, 434
Spinal cord, 441, 443
Sponges
 features of, 328
 filter feeding of, 332
 gas exchange in, 334
Spores
 of ferns, 349
 of mosses, 350
 in seedless plant reproduction, 359
Stamen, 359, 360
Standard mass, 18
Standard time zones, 159
Stars, 275
States of matter, 28–29
 changing, 95
Static electricity, 125
Stems
 functions and parts of, 352
 of seed plants, 346
 in vascular plants, 343, 352

Stomach, 418
Stomata, 353, 354, 358
Storms, 264–265
  on other planets, 283,
    284
Stratosphere, 246–247
Stratus clouds, 250
Streak, 175
Stress response, 452
Strike-slip fault, 210
Subscript, 52
Subsoil, 190
Succession, 368–369
Sun
  characteristics of,
    276–277
  as energy source in
    food chains, 381
Sunspots, 276, 277
Sweat glands, 431
Swim bladder, 326
Switch, 127
Symbols
  in chemical equations,
    55–57
  for elements, 39–40, 51
  in schematic diagrams,
    128
  on weather maps, 266
Synapse, 443

T

Taste, sense of, 447
Taxonomy, 300, 319
Teeth
  role of in digestion, 418
  types of, 332
Temperate climates, 269
Temperature, 97
  °C °F conversion
    table, 100
  in different climate
    zones, 268–270
  scales, 99
Tendons, 414
Tentacles, 328, 329
Testes, 337, 433
Theory of natural
  selection, 398–399
Thermocline, 237
Thermometer, 98, 259
Thermosphere, 247
Time zones, 159
Tissue, 304

Titan, 284
Topsoil, 190
Tornado, 153, 264
Touch, sense of, 446
Trachea, 428
Trench, 238
Tributary, 234
Triton, 286
Tropical climates, 269
Troposphere, 246
Tsunami, 215
Tube feet, 329

U

Ultraviolet radiation, 248
Umbilical cord, 435, 436
Units of measurement,
  5–6
  for area, 10
  for length, 7–8
  for mass, 18–19
  metric equivalents, 9,
    15, 18
  prefixes for in metric
    system, 9
  for volume, 14–15
Universal gravitation, law
  of, 71
Uranus, 285, 287
Ureters, 432
Urethra, 432, 434
Urine, 432
Uterus, 434, 435, 436

V

Vacuum, 103
Vagina, 433, 435, 436
Vascular plants
  characteristics of, 344,
    349
  parts of, 351–353
Vascular tissue, 344
  functions of, 345, 352
  in seed plants, 346
Veins
  in circulatory system,
    425
  in leaf, 345
Vent, 207
Ventricles, 336, 423
Venus, 279–280, 281
Vertebra, 324
  in humans, 411
Vertebrates

circulatory system of,
  335–336
  features of 324, 332
Vestigial structures, 398
Vibrate, 111
Villi, 419
Visible spectrum, 116
Vitamins, 308
Volcanoes, 207
  causes of, 206, 207
  cinder cone, 208
  composite, 208
  on moons in solar
    system, 283, 284, 286
  shield, 208
  types of 207–208
Voltage, 126
  and electromagnet, 142
  in parallel circuit, 134
  in series circuit, 130
Volts, 126
Volume, 14
  measuring for liquids,
    15–16
  measuring for solids,
    14, 17
  measuring with grad-
    uated cylinder, 16
  metric equivalents, 15
Voluntary muscles, 416

W

Warm front, 263
Water
  chemical formula for,
    52
  as chemical needed for
    life, 306
  deposition by, 193, 194
  elements in, 34
  erosion by, 192
  molecule of, 27–28,
    34, 41
Water budget, 235
Water cycle, 233, 382
Water table, 234
Water vapor, 249
Waves
  earthquake, 213
  erosion and deposition
    by, 194
  ocean, 239
  sound, 112
Weather, 259, 268

maps, 265
  predicting, 263–265
  See also Weather
    conditions, Weather
    instruments
Weather conditions
  air pressure, 260
  air temperature, 259
  humidity, 261
  precipitation, 262
  wind speed and
    direction, 261
Weathering, 187
  chemical, 188–189
  mechanical, 187–188
  of rock, 187
  and soil formation, 189
Weather instruments
  anemometer, 261
  barometer, 260
  psychrometer, 261
  rain gauge, 262
  thermometer, 259
  wind vane, 261
Weather maps, 265
Wedge, 86
Wegener, Alfred, 204
Weight, 19
Western hemisphere, 167
Wheel and axle, 86
White blood cells, 427
White light, colors in, 116
Wind
  cause of, 253
  erosion and deposition
    by, 197
  patterns of, 253
  speed and direction of,
    261
Wind belts, 254
Wind cells, 253
Wind vane, 261
Work, 77–78

X, Y, Z

Xylem, 352, 354
Zoology, 300
Zygote, 338